ZAPPA GEAR

ZAPPA GEAR

THE UNIQUE GUITARS, AMPLIFIERS, EFFECTS UNITS, KEYBOARDS, AND STUDIO EQUIPMENT OF FRANK ZAPPA

MICK EKERS

FOREWORD BY DWEEZIL ZAPPA

Backbeat Books

Guilford, Connecticut

Published by Backbeat Books
An imprint of The Rowman & Littlefield Publishing Group, Inc.
4501 Forbes Blvd., Ste. 200, Lanham, MD 20706
www.rowman.com

Distributed by NATIONAL BOOK NETWORK

Copyright © 2019 by Mick Ekers and the Zappa Family Trust 2018

Editing: Richard Ekers
Technical consultancy: Christopher G. Ekers
Interview transcription and translations: Steven Ekers
Access: Gail Zappa

Any trademarks, service marks, product names, or named features are assumed to be the property of their respective owners, and are used only for reference.

"Frank Zappa", "Zappa", and "FZ" are registered trademarks owned by the Zappa Family Trust and used by permission. All quoted statements, comments, and lyrics by Frank Zappa are his intellectual property.

All rights reserved. No part of this book may be reproduced in any form or by any electronic or mechanical means, including information storage and retrieval systems, without written permission from the publisher, except by a reviewer who may quote passages in a review.

Library of Congress Cataloging-in-Publication Data available

ISBN 978-1-5400-1202-9 (hardback)

♾️™ The paper used in this publication meets the minimum requirements of American National Standard for Information Sciences—Permanence of Paper for Printed Library Materials, ANSI/NISO Z39.48-1992

Printed in the United States of America

This book is dedicated to the memory of my father, William Anthony Ekers, known as Bill to everyone, including his children.

A great optimist and positive thinker, he told me that if you genuinely believe you can achieve something, then you most probably will.

And here we are!

CONTENTS

Foreword by Dweezil Zappa   ix

Introduction   xi

Chapter One: Guitars   1

Chapter Two: Amplifiers   81

Chapter Three: Effects Units   107

Chapter Four: Keyboards and Synthesizers   137

Chapter Five: Studio and Recording   175

Chapter Six: Percussion and Other Gear   199

Acknowledgments   213

Notes   215

Glossary   225

Selective Bibliography   229

Selective Videography   231

About the Author   233

FOREWORD

If you are reading this, then it is conceivable that you have an overwhelming edacity for highly specialized information regarding my father's musical instruments and his modus operandi. The author of this book, Mr. Mick Ekers, suffers from this affliction and as part of his therapy, he has prepared this exceptionally detailed manuscript. Well actually it was not part of his therapy, but the book nevertheless is exceptionally detailed, and I for one am grateful that he did all of this research.

It is truly fascinating to see the tools my father used to shape the audio world he created, compiled in one location. It is important to understand that behind every decision made about which instrument to play or which effect to use to enhance the audio listening experience, my father was guided by his own curiosity and experience.

He was wise to focus on the universal human element of music. Great musicians playing great music recorded with great equipment is the simplified recipe for his aural achievements. By surrounding himself with talented and forward-thinking audio engineers, he was able to capture his music with superb detail in a way that defies decades, even leaving us with a moment to ponder if it has arrived from the future.

We must all keep in mind that during the 1960s and 1970s many sounds we now take for granted had not yet been invented, or were so new that they had not been fully explored. Even something as ubiquitously exploited as the wah-wah pedal was brand new cutting-edge technology when my father was in the early stages of his career. He would go on to use that pedal in expressive ways that were quite different from his contemporaries and the circuit itself would prove to be an integral component aboard some of his instruments.

He sought to improve all elements of the recording process in the studio and on stage. He was also instrumental in improving the sound reinforcement designs for live concerts as well. He went to great lengths to captivate audiences around the world with his music and with the way he treated the sound. He maintained this integrity throughout his career and we are all fortunate to have so many audiophile-quality releases to enjoy.

My father was very knowledgeable about the science of sound and he was not tethered by traditional theories of operation. He was as unique in his approach to writing music as he was with arranging and recording it. He used the recording process as an instrument that could heighten each of his compositions. Whether using tape machines to transpose or create new

instruments or using effects to add character to instruments, there was no area within the production process that was left unexamined for extra "tweezing" opportunities.

When it comes to guitars, I can tell you from my own experience that the playability of my father's guitars was set for ease and speed. Comfortable necks and low action with tone-shaping tools at his fingertips are what he liked. For him his guitars were tactile tools of expression. He did not revere them as works of art or covet them as many collectors might. They were made for playing and were intended to improve his connection to his sound source and have unsurpassed control over the frequency range.

As you read through this book you will discover his innovations, and like me you may marvel at how he was able to continually break new ground sonically and musically. I hope you enjoy this book and continue to enjoy the music my father made with all of the gear you will discover in these pages.

Dweezil Zappa
Los Angeles, California
July 8, 2013

INTRODUCTION

"Frank would take about any piece of gear that you can imagine, and squeeze it and churn it and pull it, like a pit bull with a steak! Frank dug really deep into every parameter, and when he squeezed it as hard as he could, he'd call the company and tell them what they needed to do to make it better."

—Steve Vai[1]

Frank Zappa was an unremitting innovator and experimenter, and was forever looking at ways to exploit the latest advances in musical instruments, amplification, effects units, and sound recording. His working life coincided with the explosion in the development of music technology that started in the 1960s and continued throughout the following three decades. Consequently, he ended up using a unique and fascinating range of guitars and other musical equipment during his career. Without such inventions as the Marshall amplifier, the Gibson SG, the wah-wah pedal, and the Synclavier, FZ's "air sculptures," as his music has been described, would have had a significantly different shape and texture. Furthermore, many of his guitars and musical appliances were specially modified and customized (or "tweezed," as he put it), and often used in ways for which they had never been designed.

Although numerous excellent books have been produced on the history of electric guitars and amplifiers, much of the gear that FZ used has received scant coverage. As a musician, self-confessed equipment geek, and lifelong Zappa fan, these were things I wanted to know more about. In the end, the only solution was to write the book myself. Of course I wildly underestimated the amount of work involved, but even more wildly underestimated the amount of fun I'd have in the process. As a direct result of this project I have made so many great new friends that, for me at any rate, writing has turned out to be far from a lonely craft. Whenever I needed motivation during a long late-night writing session, I could always imagine FZ looking over my shoulder, frowning, drinking coffee, and smoking a lot of cigarettes (to paraphrase his endnote in *The Frank Zappa Guitar Book*).

This book may particularly appeal to electric guitarists, but other musicians, and general fans and students of FZ's work, should also find some interest here. As well as looking at the equipment itself, it also introduces some of the pioneering inventors, engineers, and entrepreneurs without whom the products would not exist. I have steered clear of topics such as "how to play guitar like Frank Zappa," "which Zappa band was the best," or "the real meaning behind the lyrics of 'Billy the Mountain.'" If you have not already formed your own opinions on these and similar subjects, there are more than enough books and other sources that cover such matters. I have not attempted to dissect or analyze the music itself, but wherever possible I have indicated recordings that feature the specific instrument or item under discussion. I have included a glossary of technical terms for those readers who might need it.

Zappa's Gear is about music hardware, how it was made, and how it was used by one of the most innovative and creative musician and composer that the twentieth century ever produced. It is a book for those of you who, like me, find this kind of stuff interesting.

Mick Ekers
Leigh-on-Sea, Essex, England
July 2018

ZAPPA GEAR

FZ's custom Tobacco Sunburst Strat at the UMRK in 2012
(Mick Ekers)

CHAPTER ONE
GUITARS

"If there's ever an obscene noise to be made on an instrument, it's gonna come out of a guitar! On a sax you can play sleaze, on a bass you can play balls, but on a guitar you can be truly obscene! Let's be realistic about this, the guitar can be the single most blasphemous device on the earth. The guitar makes a stink noise. That's why I like it!"

—FZ[2]

Early Guitars
The First Telecaster
Fender Jazzmaster
Gibson ES-5 Switchmaster
Hagström Viking Deluxe
Gibson Les Paul Goldtop
The Bath Festival Gibson SG Special
Gibson ES-355TD-SV
The Rainbow Theatre Telecaster
Jacobacci Studio 3
Fender Stratocasters
The Roxy Gibson SG
Acoustic Control Corporation Black Widow
The Hendrix Strat
Rex Bogue Semi-Acoustic
Vox Wah-Wah Guitar
Baby Snakes SG
Les Paul Custom
Bouzouki

D'Mini Guitars
Coral Electric Sitar
Rickenbacker 360 12-string
Fender Electric XII
Performance Blonde Stratocaster
The Fretless Stratocaster
Custom Stratocasters
Custom Telecasters
Ovation Acoustics
Gibson Super Jumbo J-200N
Guild "Aragon" F-30R-NT Acoustic
Martin D18S
Gibson J-160E
Candelas Flamenco Guitar
Höfner 500/8 BZ Bass
Fender Jazz Bass
Picks
Strings
Floyd Rose Vibrato

ZAPPA GEAR

Early Guitars

"It was an archtop, f-hole, ugly motherfucker with the strings about a half-inch off the fingerboard. I liked it because it was so tinny-sounding."
— FZ[3]

FZ did not start playing guitar until 1958, when he was seventeen years old; before then he had concentrated on playing drums. His father had an old acoustic guitar that he kept in a closet, which he would bring out and play on rare occasions. FZ remembered looking at it as a child wondering how you got different notes out of it, not understanding what the frets were for.

FZ started playing on a guitar that had been bought by his younger brother Bobby for $1.50 at a yard sale. After Bobby brought it home, he attempted some restoration work: "I remember sanding the fingerboard and in the process roughing up the frets. I also sanded the archtop and then put some varnish on it. It was not my best work."[4]

The brothers then fitted the guitar with some very cheap roundwound strings, and the result of all this work was a very thin-sounding guitar, with a very high action. Bobby remembers that both of them found it very difficult to play, not helped by the fact that neither of them had yet developed enough finger calluses.

As FZ described it: "It didn-t have a make on it—it had been kinda sandblasted! . . . It was an archtop, f-hole, ugly motherfucker with the strings about a half-inch off the fingerboard. I liked it because it was so tinny-sounding. It was just an acoustic guitar, but it was moving closer to that wiry tone I liked with Johnny 'Guitar' Watson, especially if you picked it right next to the bridge."[5]

Bobby gave this near impossible-to-play beast to his brother, and strummed chords on their father's guitar while FZ played lead lines: "Once I'd figured out that the pitch changed when you put your finger on the fret I was hell on wheels." However, after a while he realized that he needed to learn to play chords like Bobby could. Getting frustrated by the archtop, he took over his father's guitar. With Bobby's help, he studied photographs and other players to learn the basic chord shapes, and "finally got a Mickey Baker book and learned a bunch of chords off that."[6]

The next step was electrification. FZ bought a DeArmond soundhole pickup, and fitted it to his father's instrument. This design consisted of an electric pickup, sometimes with a built-in volume control, that had flexible clips to hold it in place in the round soundhole of an acoustic guitar. Not especially effective and prone to moving around from aggressive playing, these things were very popular in the 1950s and 1960s as a low-budget way of electrifying an acoustic guitar.

I remember fitting just such a device to my own first acoustic guitar, which I then played through a homemade tube amplifier

The Zappa brother's guitar. Detail from a photograph taken in FZ's apartment in 1966, I showed the photo to Bobby Zappa who confirmed, "That's the one."
(unknown)

The earliest known picture of FZ with a guitar, from his 1958 high-school year book
(unknown)

Hear It On:

Album: *The Lost Episodes*
Track: "Lost in a Whirlpool"

This is the only known recording of FZ from this time, with Don "Captain Beefheart" Van Vliet on vocal. FZ is playing lead on (presumably) the $1.50 archtop, while Bobby Zappa plays rhythm guitar.

that was basically just the chassis and speaker that I had salvaged from an old record player, but that is another story!

FZ did not consider that this was a real electric guitar, but in fact, soundhole pickups were used by many of the early blues guitarists who he revered. Lightnin' Hopkins was a particularly famous exponent of the DeArmond 210 model, which was made from the 1950s to the 1960s, and is most likely the design FZ used.

It had a built-in volume control, adjustable Alnico polepieces, and a reasonably solid fixing with a metal clip on one end and two folding arm clips on the other. According to ace bluesman and DeArmond aficionado Doug "Little Brother Blues" Jones, this single coil pickup has a loud fat feedback-resistant tone, which makes slide guitar "sound like a dream."[7]

Harry DeArmond invented the first commercially available attachable guitar pickup in the mid-1930s, and his pickups were manufactured and sold by Horace "Bud" Rowe's company from the 1940s to the 1970s. Fender acquired the DeArmond name in 1996. Such pickups now are highly prized by collectors, and FZ's would probably fetch more on eBay than the guitar it was fitted to.

One of the rare photographs of FZ from this period is from the Antelope Valley High School 1958 yearbook. A montage of pictures of students, it shows him playing a white Supro Dual Tone electric guitar. Supro was an offshoot of the Valco company, who also made National, Airline, and other budget guitar brands for various mail-order catalogs. When it was introduced in 1957, the 1524S Dual Tone was their top electric guitar, selling for around $150.

The guitar featured very cool art-deco styling; the Arctic White sculpted body was set off with a split-level black and white pickguard and brass-plated hardware. It had a pair of single-coil pickups (disguised as more expensive humbuckers), with a three-way selector switch and dual volume and tone controls (hence the name).

The bolt-on neck did not have an adjustable truss rod, but was built around an aluminum girder; Danelectro and Hagström used a similar concept. With large white block markers set into the rosewood fingerboard, the neck was finished off with an asymmetric headstock and Kluson Deluxe tuners. The strings passed over a carved rosewood bridge into a decorative "stair-step" plated tailpiece.

The Dual Tone was produced until the late 1960s; seminal rock and roll guitarist Link Wray used it on many records. Ry Cooder played one extensively in the 1980s, and David Bowie took one on his 2003–2004 tours.[8] Original Dual Tones in good condition are highly sought after now, and a modern version (with real humbucking pickups and a fully adjustable bridge) is available from Eastwood Guitars. FZ never mentioned owning such a stylish instrument, so we must assume he had only borrowed it from a friend.

A De Armond pickup in place in the soundhole of a guitar, showing the two fixing clips that swing into position to grip the guitar soundboard
(Doug Jones)

An original 1958 Supro Dualtone
(D.Alder/GuitarPoint)

ZAPPA GEAR

The First Telecaster

"I started off with a Telecaster...."

—FZ[9]

FZ's first real electric guitar was an early Fender Telecaster, which he rented for six months in 1961 while he was living in Ontario, California. As he recalls: "There was a music store not far from my house, and I rented this Telecaster for $15 a month. Eventually I had to give it back, because I couldn't make the repayments on it."[10]

The music store would have been Ontario Music on 215 West G Street, which was just a block away from his house at number 314. Ontario Music closed in July 2010 after fifty years.

First produced in 1950, the Fender Telecaster (originally named the Broadcaster) was the world's first commercially successful solid body electric guitar.[11] Leo Fender designed it to be easy to manufacture, with a separate neck that was bolted onto the body, a modular electronics panel holding the volume and tone controls and pickup selector, and a simple but stylish body shape that could be machined from a flat slab of wood.

It featured a large, angled single-coil pickup mounted in a steel plate bridge assembly and a smaller chrome-covered pickup next to the neck. At the bridge the strings passed over three adjustable brass saddles, then through the body, to be anchored at the back by six chromed ferrules.[12]

The guitar had an ash body with a plain blond cellulose finish, and a slim one-piece maple neck without a separate fingerboard. The angle of the larger and more powerful bridge pickup emphasized the treble tone of the higher strings; the neck pickup had a contrasting warm bassy sound.

On the original models the tone control was just a blend between the two pickups. In 1952 a conventional tone control was introduced, and it was not possible to combine the pickups until Fender introduced a third circuit design in 1967, which has remained standard ever since.

Most players tended to prefer the distinctive biting Telecaster sound produced by the bridge pickup. One can imagine that FZ would have gone for that.

The Telecaster was not an immediate success; its uncompromising functional design and clear biting tone was very different from the prevalent mellow-sounding Gibson "jazz boxes" of the time.

However, within a couple of years, word began to get around among working musicians and sales steadily increased. The guitar is still in production, almost unchanged after over sixty years. With this textbook example of form following function, Leo Fender showed (not for the only time) his ability to get a design right almost from the outset.

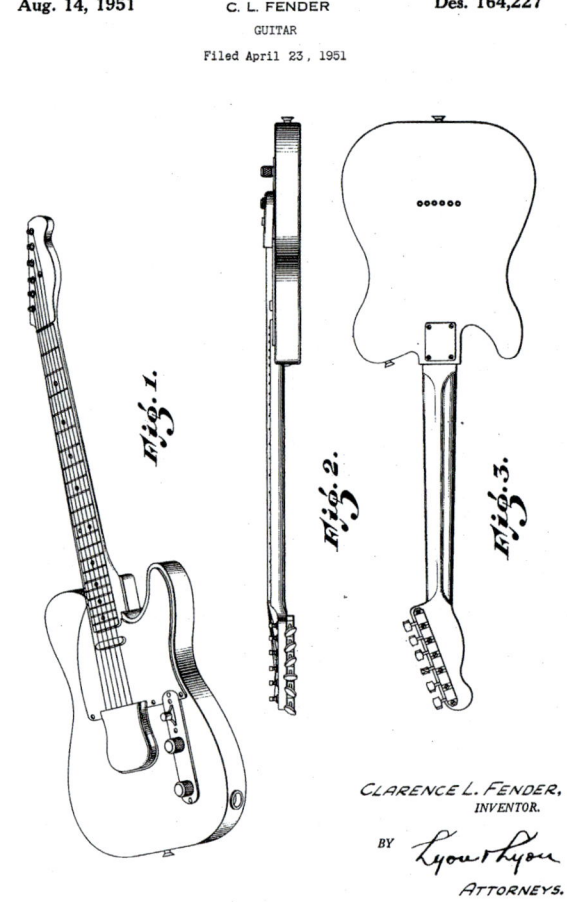

The drawings from Leo Fender's original Telecaster patent
(Public domain)

A cream 1969 Telecaster similar to the guitar in the 'Boogie Men' photograph.
(Micheil Grey)

A press kit booklet from 1974 contained an out-of-focus black and white photo dated May 1961 showing FZ with a Telecaster. FZ captioned it: "'The Boogie Men' rehearse Nite Owl for a high school weekend job. F.Z.'s garage, Ontario, California. Al Surratt-Drums, Kenny Burgan-Sax, Doug Rost-Rhythm Guitar, F.Z.-Lead, no bass player because we couldn't afford one."[13]

From the photo, it is just discernible as a blonde finish Telecaster with a white pickguard and a rosewood fingerboard. The fingerboard dates the guitar quite precisely as these were first introduced in 1959. However another 1961 photo of FZ with the band the Ramblers (same lineup plus Joe Perrino) clearly shows FZ holding an earlier model Tele with a maple fingerboard, we cannot be certain which is the rental guitar.

In his later career, FZ owned several Telecasters, although he rarely used them on stage or record, favoring guitars with considerably more controls than the volume, tone, and pickup selector switch. However, he did use one on the *Freak Out!* recording session and had some custom ones built in the 1980s, perhaps finding the functional simplicity a refreshing change from his more complicated instruments.

Fender Jazzmaster

"I put the guitar in the case, stuck it behind the sofa and didn't touch it for eight months."

—*FZ*[14]

Later in 1961, FZ somehow found enough money to purchase a Fender Jazzmaster, a very different guitar from the Telecaster he had used previously. His was a standard 1958 or 1959 model, with a gold anodized pickguard and a sunburst finish. It does not seem to have been modified in any way. The age can be pinpointed because Fender switched to red faux-tortoiseshell pickguards in early 1959.

When Fender introduced the Jazzmaster in 1958 it was priced at $329 (the Telecaster had a list price of $199); this was a definite move into the higher end of the market. Described by Fender as "America's finest electric guitar,"[15] it was the result of the design team's desire to build something even better than the top-of-the-range Stratocaster. Production manager Forrest White recalls, "Leo (Fender) was trying to get more of a jazz sound than the high piercing Telecaster sound."[16]

The Jazzmaster had a host of new features and some unusual electronics; given his later penchant for adding extra controls and circuitry to his guitars, this was likely to have been a big plus for FZ. The body had a striking shape with an offset waist (a patented feature repeated in the later Jazz Bass guitar) and a sculpted profile evolved from the Stratocaster. It was the first Fender to feature a rosewood "slab" fingerboard, and had a brand new floating vibrato system.

A well-worn 1959 Jazzmaster similar to FZ's
(Chicago Music Exchange)

Unlike the Strat vibrato, this was a separate unit from the bridge, with a locking facility and a long curved arm, which passed between the fifth and sixth strings. The bridge had six individually adjustable brass saddles; the scale length was the Fender standard of 25 1/2 inches.

The two large rectangular "soapbar" single-coil pickups were wound with wide and low coils. This was a different style to the usual Fender tall and thin coils, and gave them a markedly mellower tone. However, they were also more prone to picking up electrical interference, or "hum"; the large white plastic covers did nothing to remedy this.

There was a conventional master volume and tone control and a three-way pickup selector switch, mounted below the strings on the large pickguard. Above the strings were a second set of volume and tone controls, implemented as rollers inset into the pickguard, and a small slide switch.

In "rhythm" mode this selected the neck pickup only (overriding the lower selector switch) and brought the additional controls into the circuit. This feature of preset rhythm volume and tone settings was a first on production electric guitars; it was a concept originally developed by Forrest White in the 1940s.

The overall sound was much warmer than the previous Fender guitars and it did gain some success in jazz circles as well as being popular with surf groups such as the Beach Boys. Although it never achieved anything like the sales figures of the Stratocaster and Telecaster, it remained in the catalog until 1980.

Almost as soon as Fender discontinued the Jazzmaster, it started achieving cult status, thanks to its adoption by new wave artists, including Elvis Costello and Tom Verlaine of Television. In response to this, Fender has produced various vintage reissues since the late 1980s.

In late 1961, FZ got a regular gig playing with Joe Perrino and the Mellotones, who were the regular lounge band at the Club Sahara in San Bernardino. A photo of the band taken by a local newspaper can be seen in the booklet accompanying the *Mystery Disc* CD. FZ is holding the Jazzmaster, with a somewhat resigned "I don't really want to be here" expression on his face.

Although the Jazzmaster would have been well suited to the Mellotones' repertoire of easy-listening standards, FZ was not. He stuck at it for about ten months and then quit in disgust, shutting the guitar away for several months.[17]

Fortunately, FZ eventually picked up the guitar again, and used it regularly until 1964, playing in local R&B bands and recording various singles at Paul Buff's Pal studio in Cucamonga. There is some mystery about what finally happened to the Jazzmaster; in an interview in *Down Beat* in 1983,[18] FZ said that it was repossessed but most likely, he was thinking of his first Telecaster.

Paul Buff stated that it was part of the deal when FZ bought the Cucamonga studio from him: "I let Zappa use the studio for several months, then sold it to him for a little bit of money, his old drum set, his vibes, and his Jazzmaster guitar (which was later stolen from me at Original Sound)."[19]

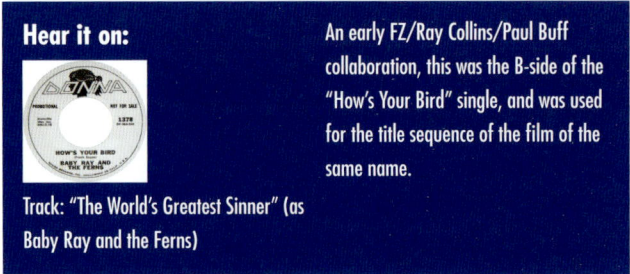

Hear it on: An early FZ/Ray Collins/Paul Buff collaboration, this was the B-side of the "How's Your Bird" single, and was used for the title sequence of the film of the same name.

Track: "The World's Greatest Sinner" (as Baby Ray and the Ferns)

Gibson ES-5 Switchmaster

"I used to really like that guitar; it had a nice neck on it."

—FZ[20]

FZ's next guitar was a Gibson ES-5 Switchmaster. It was to be his main instrument for several years, and featured on the first three Mothers of Invention albums. He purchased it sometime in the summer of 1964.

The triple-pickup ES-5 was introduced by Gibson in 1949; it was one of the first new designs produced under the auspices of the legendary Ted McCarty, who ran the Gibson guitar company from 1946 to 1965. The McCarty era was the most successful and creative period in Gibson's history since it was founded, and among many other innovations it also saw the introduction of the Les Paul, the SG, and the ES-355 guitars, all very significant instruments for FZ which feature later on in this book.

When it was launched, the ES-5 was Gibson's top electric model, and although aimed at jazz musicians, it also proved popular with bluesmen such as B.B. King.[21] It was based on the classic L5c acoustic archtop model, but with a veneered plywood top (aimed to reduce feedback) replacing the carved spruce top of the original.

It had three black P90 pickups, each with an individual volume control, and a single tone control. Although this arrangement provided total control over the blend of the three pickups, the lack of any form of selector switch made it awkward to switch from a rhythm to a lead setting quickly while performing.

In 1955, the Switchmaster version was introduced, with a new four-way toggle switch allowing selection of any single pickup, or all three. Curiously, the selector switch featured a Fender Telecaster–style Top-Hat tip. Three individual tone controls were added below the volume controls. It was justly labelled by Gibson as "a new high in versatility."[22]

The striking multicoil tailpiece was added in 1956, and in 1957, the black P90 pickups were replaced with the new Gibson

Guitars

The Switchmaster at the UMRK in 2012
(Mick Ekers)

PAF Humbuckers.[23] As became increasingly apparent during his career, FZ wanted the widest possible range of controls built in to his instruments; the Switchmaster was the first step on this path.

In late 1960, the final variant appeared with a sharp Florentine cutaway.[24] This was the model that FZ purchased sometime in 1964 with the money he got for producing the score for the *Run Home Slow* movie.[25] It is a very rare guitar: just forty-one were made in sunburst, and another eleven in the optional natural finish, before the model was discontinued in 1961.

Guitarist Del Casher, who had worked with FZ on some early recording sessions, and sat in on some gigs with the early Mothers of Invention, remembered: "When I first met him, he said he was interested in playing guitar, and asked me what was the most expensive guitar, and I told him that the most expensive one was a Gibson ES-5, like the one I had, so he went out and bought one."[26]

Eventually, as the Mothers started playing larger concerts and using more powerful amplification, the Switchmaster's tendency to feed back became a problem. " . . . The hollowbody was feeding back too much—we started working bigger and bigger places. The more the volume goes up, the more feedback you get, and I didn't want to stuff it full of Styrofoam in order to keep it from feeding back and so I switched to a Les Paul."[27]

FZ commented further, "I used to really like that guitar; it had a nice neck on it . . . the hollowbody had a nice feel and I liked the tone of it, but you could never use a fuzztone with it, and there was no way to tweeze it up and make it work. Remember, in those days there were no graphic equalizers or any other scientific equipment."[28]

Nonetheless, he did "tweeze it up" later on, and in September 1978, it reappeared in the hands of FZ's vocalist and sometime guitarist Ike Willis, who can be seen playing it on the German TV documentary *We Don't Mess Around*. Work had already been started on the guitar: a small square metal plate has been set into the lower horn, with three switches replacing the original pickup selector switch, and there are four new switches fitted between the control knobs.

The guitar was initially given to custom guitar maker Rex Bogue to work on (more on Bogue later), and the electronics were replaced with active electronics by Bogue's electronics specialist Jim Williams. A new shaped brass plate was inset into

Ike Willis on TV with the Switchmaster in 1978
(still from *We Don't Mess Around*, 1980)

7

ZAPPA GEAR

The replacement Yamaha machine heads
(Mick Ekers)

the lower horn replacing the original pickup selector with two small switches on either side of a rotary knob.

I asked Williams about this: "They could be a blend control and a volume in the preamp level . . . we did so much crazy shit, some of that stuff was 'Let's do this, let's try this. Let's make it do that.'"[29]

The body was further modified by cutting a large access hole in the back, which was covered with a black plate. Classic guitar aficionados are probably wincing at the last sentence, and Williams remembers: "That was one of those things that we would argue about, he'd want to cut the thing up and put it in all this stuff, and I was going 'Yeah, I wanna put in stuff, but I don't think I need to cut a big-ass hole in a really nice acoustic guitar to do it! I think we could poke and probe the stuff in there if we took our time or something.' He was like 'Nah, whack a big hole in it, put a plate on it, it'll be easy to get to and fix,' and I was going 'Oh man, I don't know about this!'"[30]

Later FZ sent the guitar to master luthier John Carruthers for some further work. Carruthers is something of a legend among professional guitarists. In the forty years he has been in business he has done work for an astonishing array of musicians (for example, Fleetwood Mac, Flying Burrito Brothers, Foreigner, Frank Sinatra are the four names immediately before Frank Zappa in the client list on his website).

When I visited his new premises in Camarillo, Carruthers showed me a small black and white photo pinned on the wall; it was the inside of the Switchmaster taken through the rear access hole! He remembered working on the electronics: "Frank had me put all those preamps in, there's like six of them that were chained together, and y'know, I thought it was a little excessive but with Frank you never knew, you'd come up with some way to make it work for what it was that he wanted . . . the preamps were just fitting in between the controls that were there so there was still a volume for each pickup and a tone for each pickup . . . it had all these gain boosts that you could switch in, it had like mini-toggles."[31]

Carruthers also noted that the preamp circuits had additional line outputs that could connect direct to a mixing desk. He also said that he was also less than impressed with the way the guitar body had been butchered: "It had a plate on the back so you could gain access to the inside of the body; somebody put that in before I got to it. I'd never do it that way, it's not my style. I would have fitted all the parts through the pickup holes and through the soundhole; it's like building a ship in a bottle."[32]

In its current state, the guitar pickguard has been removed, the machine heads are Japanese Yamaha gold-plated sealed units, and perhaps most controversially, the original PAF humbuckers (now worth a small fortune in themselves) have been replaced with three black Barcus Berry soapbar pickups.

The pickups don't even match; two bear the legend "barcus berry" and the third just has the letters "BBI" set into the three thin gold lines that run across the top of the pickups. Neither Carruthers nor Williams have any recollection of replacing the pickups.

There are four silver micro switches inserted between the original six volume and tone controls (presumably the gain boost switches mentioned above). The original Gibson knobs have been replaced with two silver and four black metal knobs. Two additional pots, also with black knobs, and a black toggle switch have been added near the edge of the body. We did find

John Carruthers at his factory in 2012
(Mick Ekers)

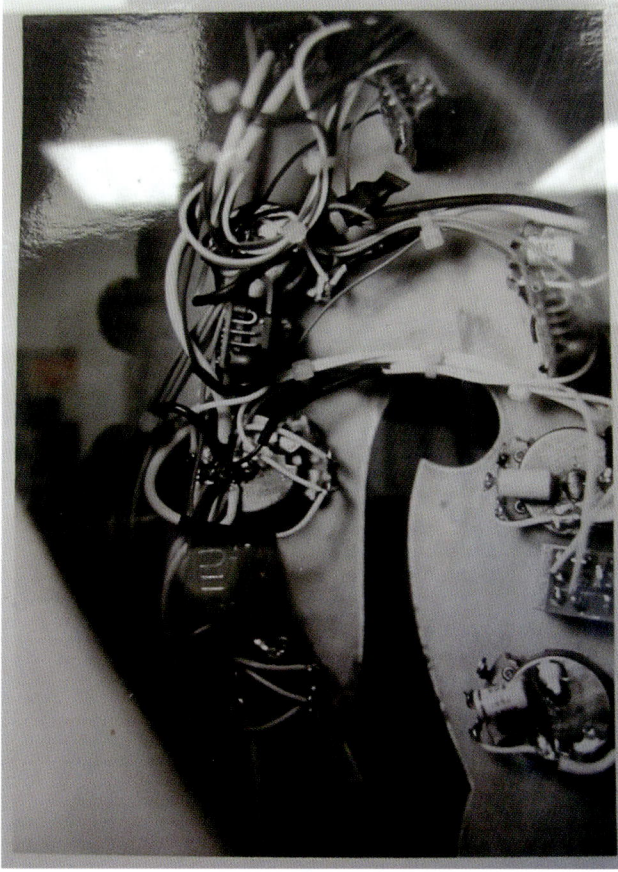

John Carruthers' photo of the inside of the guitar.
(Photo of polaroid by Mick Ekers; original by John Carruthers)

Frank these were just tools, Frank didn't look at these as investment guitars or anything like that, he probably would have put a Floyd on that if he could."35

Gibson reissued the Switchmaster in the 1990s. You can still buy a replica of the 1957 model today from the Gibson Custom Shop, but if you want to reproduce FZ's customized version, you will have to pay substantially more (and I mean a

Rear view showing the large plastic cover over the access hole
(Mick Ekers)

five of what could have been the original Gibson knobs in the accessory compartment of the big red Anvil flight case in which the guitar is stored.

The original bridge has been replaced with a gold-plated unit, with a Barcus Berry transducer screwed to it. Next to the output jack is a three-pin XLR socket, which is likely the mixing desk output Carruthers referred to, which may include a phantom power supply connection.

FZ said about the Switchmaster in 1980, "It's got a Barcus Berry on the bridge and one of those Seismic Sensors on the polepiece and three pickups in it and a quad output. It's got its own power supply to run everything—it's better than changing batteries."33

At the time of writing Dweezil Zappa was still trying to get the guitar working again (there is no trace of the Seismic Sensor), and had this to say about the guitar: "It's really kind of ugly actually, 'cause there are these brown Barcus Berry pickups with gold lines, and I don't know if he set it up for a stereo guitar but it seems like there's almost string-panners, there's an XLR output. I think he had set it up to use with a synth or something. I'm not sure; we couldn't make heads or tails out of the electronics in it . . . ."34

I asked DZ if he knew where the original pickups went: "They're gone . . . they're nowhere to be found. The thing is, to

ZAPPA GEAR

lot of money!) for one of the remaining forty (at most) sunburst models.

DZ told me "I would consider restoring that guitar as best as possible, to get it closest to what it used to be."[36] It certainly would be good to hear him using it again on some of the early Mothers of Invention material.

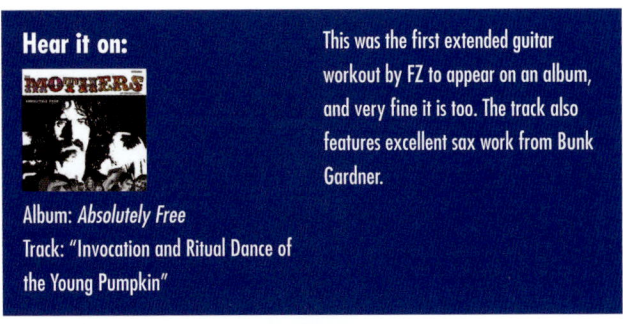

Hear it on: This was the first extended guitar workout by FZ to appear on an album, and very fine it is too. The track also features excellent sax work from Bunk Gardner.

Album: *Absolutely Free*
Track: "Invocation and Ritual Dance of the Young Pumpkin"

FZ with the Switchmaster in New York in 1967
(Frank Kofksy)

The distinctive ornate tailpiece
(Mick Ekers)

The neck pickup, and the stylish sculpted fingerboard end
(Mick Ekers)

The Switchmaster in 2012 at the UMRK, note the mess of wires behind the bottom f-hole!
(Mick Ekers)

Hagström Viking Deluxe

"That's a hot little number that we recorded using 35 Hagström guitars and a whole bunch of amplifiers."

— FZ[37]

If you look very closely at Ed Seeman's footage of the Mothers of Invention playing at the New York Garrick Theatre in 1967, you will see a few brief shots of FZ playing a sunburst finish semi-acoustic guitar with prominent white binding. Over the years, there has been a fair amount of speculation about the identity of this instrument, but close inspection of a still from the video shows it to be undoubtedly a Hagström Viking Deluxe.

This must have been given or lent to FZ by Merson Musical Products, the US distributors of Hagström guitars, as part of the advertising deal that FZ had with them. At this time, FZ was usually playing his Gibson Switchmaster almost exclusively, and this is the only record I can find of him using the Viking. Behind FZ's shoulder, bass player Roy Estrada can be seen holding a Hagström Concorde bass guitar; usually he played FZ's Höfner or his own Fender Jazz.

Hagström was originally an accordion manufacturer, founded in Sweden in 1925 by Albin Hagström. In the 1950s, they

FZ playing the Viking Deluxe at the Garrick Theatre in 1967
(still from Frank Zappa And The Original Mothers Of Invention, 1968)

started making electric guitars as the accordion market waned, basing their first designs on the Gibson Les Paul. Hagström guitars were generally rather cheap and cheerful and sold worldwide under various brand names such as Futurama in the UK and Kent in the US.[38]

In 1964, Hagström signed the US distribution deal with Merson, and launched a range of more upmarket guitars aimed at the American market. They made a feature of their slim necks, which they achieved by using an H section metal bar in place of the normal truss rod system.

FZ's Hagström advertising campaign came about when he formed an advertising agency in New York called Nifty Tough & Bitchin, and signed a promotion and advertising contract with Merson. FZ recorded a one-minute radio commercial featuring music from the *Lumpy Gravy* album, in which listeners were asked to write in to obtain a "pretty wild, way-out wigged-out poster" of the Mothers of Invention.[39]

The advert was allegedly a huge success, according to a news item in *Billboard* magazine; Merson vice president Bernard Mersky claimed that there had been over 15,000 responses, many of which had led to sales of Hagström guitars.

In the same issue, *Billboard* published a photo of FZ shaking hands with Mersky, FZ looking suitably businesslike wearing a jacket, shirt, and tie and a big smile.

FZ also appeared in a series of press adverts for Hagström, which were widely published in the music press, including one featuring a Series 1 Viking guitar, with optional Bigsby tremolo, with the slogan "Nifty." The Viking was, as far as I know, the only guitar from the adverts that FZ actually used.

Hagström introduced the Viking, their first semi-acoustic guitar, in 1965.[40] It had a distinctive Fender Stratocaster–style headstock with inline tuners, a birch neck with a rosewood

FZ and a VB-1 Viking - nifty advertising!
(Merson/Unicord)

fingerboard, and dot inlays. The neck was set into the 16" celluloid bound birch body in Gibson fashion; the scale length was 24 3/4". It had two single-coil pickups, with separate volume and tone controls for each, and a three-way pickup selector switch on the lower horn of the body. It had a shaped trapeze tailpiece with the Hagström crest at the base, an adjustable bridge, and a small black floating pickguard.[41]

In 1966, they brought out the Series 2 model number V2, which became known as the Deluxe. Essentially, it was the same as the Viking but with a maple or spruce body, gold-plated hardware, pearl block inlays and an ebony fingerboard, and bound f-holes and neck. The guitar was available in red and mahogany sunburst finishes, with an optional gold-plated Hagström-branded Bigsby vibrato unit.[42]

In 1968, the Viking received some wider promotion when Elvis Presley borrowed session guitarist Al Casey's red Deluxe and played it on his 1968 "Elvis Presley Comeback Television Special" for NBC.[43] Hagström continued making the guitar with some further design changes until 1979.

The Hagström name lives on in a range of guitars made in China; Dweezil Zappa appeared in a Hagström magazine advert recreating his father's pose, with the original photo in the background. He has a modern Viking guitar in his collection; the whereabouts of the guitar FZ used at the Garrick is unknown.

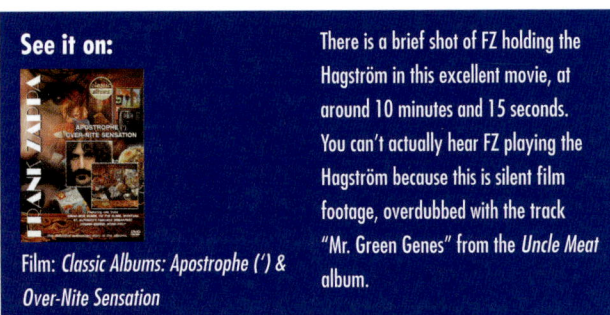

See it on:
Film: *Classic Albums: Apostrophe (') & Over-Nite Sensation*

There is a brief shot of FZ holding the Hagström in this excellent movie, at around 10 minutes and 15 seconds. You can't actually hear FZ playing the Hagström because this is silent film footage, overdubbed with the track "Mr. Green Genes" from the *Uncle Meat* album.

Gibson Les Paul Goldtop

"I switched to a Les Paul and somebody stole that."

— FZ[44]

FZ purchased a 1953 Gibson Les Paul Goldtop from Manny's Music in New York sometime in 1967. He did not immediately retire the Switchmaster; the photo inside the *Burnt Weeny Sandwich* LP shows FZ wearing his Switchmaster crouching over a guitar case, and the Les Paul neck can be seen over his shoulder. This was likely taken at the London Royal Albert Hall concert on 23rd September, 1967. However, the Les Paul soon became his main guitar and later went through a fairly radical series of customizations. The guitar was featured in the photo of FZ that graced the back of the *Mothermania* LP, released in 1969.

The Goldtop headstock
(Deepinder Cheema)

When Fender introduced the solid body Telecaster guitar in 1950, the Gibson guitar company soon realized that they had some serious competition, and started on the development of their own solid. They were determined to differentiate themselves from Leo Fender's mass-produced "planks," and eventually came up with a two-piece body consisting of a carved maple top laminated to a mahogany back. The guitar had a mahogany glued-in set neck, a rosewood fingerboard with large crown mother-of-pearl inlays, and a traditional Gibson "open book" symmetrical headstock.[45]

In 1951, Gibson boss Ted McCarty brought in celebrated guitarist Les Paul as an endorsee and design consultant, and the guitar was henceforth known as the Les Paul model. The first model came out in 1952, featuring a gold-finished top, and a trapeze-style combined bridge and tailpiece (both Les Paul suggestions).

The guitar had two Gibson P90 single-coil pickups, with an individual tone and volume control for each, and a three-way pickup selector switch. The trapeze tailpiece and bridge setup was not ideal: strings could not be palm muted and it could easily be knocked sideways, putting the guitar out of tune. In 1953, Gibson replaced it with a combined bridge and tailpiece, mounted straight into the body.[46] While retaining many elements of traditional Gibson design, McCarty and his team had come up with a modern classic electric guitar that would prove every bit as legendary as Leo Fender's Telecaster and Stratocaster.

FZ's Gibson Les Paul Goldtop in 2008
(Deepinder Cheema)

However, when FZ bought his Goldtop, the Les Paul was no longer in production, having been replaced by the SG in 1961 (see the Bath Festival SG section). I don't know what attracted FZ to this (at the time) unfashionable guitar. The P90 pickups were older and noisier than the humbuckers on his beloved Switchmaster, and it didn't have a fully adjustable bridge like the newer Gibsons. Quite likely he got it at a bargain price.

Photos of FZ on tour in 1968 show the Goldtop in more or less stock condition, the only exception being a strangely misshapen black shape surrounding the pickup selector switch; the original would have been cream plastic. By the summer of 1969, it had been changed quite significantly. Photos show that the cream pickguard and pickup covers had been removed, and a third pickup had been added next to the bridge pickup. The additional pickup is a Fender Telecaster bridge pickup.

An additional volume and tone control were added between the originals, with black Telecaster-style knobs. There is also an additional switch between the bottom two controls, and what looks like a black sliding switch next to the pickup selector (now minus the ugly black surround).[47]

A compact Bigsby B-5 Horseshoe vibrato had been fitted at the extreme end of the body. The original bridge was replaced with what appears to be a Gibson Tune-o-matic design. This resulted in a long gap between the front roller bar of the tailpiece and the bridge, and the vibrato arm would not have been easily accessible in a normal playing position.

In the late 1950s, Gibson supplied Bigsby B-7 models as an optional extra on the Les Paul. These had a longer tailpiece, which meant the arm end finished somewhere between the pickups, and there was only an inch or so between the string-retaining bar and the bridge.[48]

The choice and placement of the B-5 is puzzling. (Well, to me anyway!) The arm would have fouled the control knobs when depressed, and would only have been accessible when playing with the right hand almost on top of the bridge. Furthermore, the longer string length would have proportionally reduced the available pitch range of the vibrato (already limited in Bigsby units compared with Fender and other makes). Perhaps not surprisingly, I have yet to see a picture of FZ actually using the Bigsby.

All of this begs the question: who customized the guitar? The work has obviously not been done by a skilled luthier; it is clear from photographs that the cavity for the additional pickup was crudely hacked out. We may never know who did the work. It does seem likely that at this stage FZ was still not finished with modifying the guitar.

However, things took an unfortunate turn when the guitar was stolen from FZ, almost certainly in Belgium in October 1969, when FZ was hired as the compere of the Amougies pop festival. Photographs taken beforehand show him with a Les Paul case, but when he famously jammed with the Pink Floyd and other bands at the festival, he used borrowed guitars.

Nothing more was seen of the guitar until it turned up at auction in London in July 2006.[49] Inspection revealed that the original Gibson tuners had been replaced with early Schaller M6 machine heads. The case had been crudely covered in green paint, but there is an area where glue has percolated through the paint which is the same size and position as the original Mothers of Invention sticker seen on the 1969 photograph. My

Body and Bigbsy Tremelo
(Deepinder Cheema)

Switch detail
(Deepinder Cheema)

The green painted case
(Deepinder Cheema)

correspondent on this issue spoke to the seller and asked him how he came by the guitar and why the case had been painted. The seller claimed that it had been bought from an unnamed dealer in LA who had bought the guitar from FZ, and that the case had been painted because "that's what people did in the 60s." There appears to be no documentary evidence to support this.

The guitar did not reach its optimistic reserve price, and has appeared intermittently on various auction sites, most recently in March, 2018[50], but I have not found any evidence that it has been purchased. I understand that the ZFT made some preliminary legal steps towards recovering the guitar in 2012, but according to Gail, after all this time the original police report of the theft was lost and the process stalled.[51]

A photo of the guitar taken at the auction showroom shows the final state of the guitar: the slide switch has been removed leaving an empty cavity, the neck pickup has been replaced with what looks like a standard Gibson humbucker, and all the knobs have been replaced with a set of black Gibson "speed" knobs.

Detailed photos of the inside of the control cavity that appeared in the auction catalogue show that the wiring looks like it has been professionally done, and the additional two knobs were volume and tone controls for the third pickup, reminiscent of his old Switchmaster. The switch wiring cannot be seen but it has been labelled with the small white letters "S" and "M" applied to the body, so it is likely that this may have been a stereo/mono switch.

I believe that FZ may have had a second Les Paul, which he used as a live backup guitar. I base this assumption on an event that I witnessed during the earlier of the two shows when the Mothers performed at the London Royal Festival Hall on 28th October, 1968. Midway through a long guitar solo (probably "King Kong"), FZ made a hand signal to the band, who stopped playing instantly. Moving to the microphone, he announced, "I've broken a string on my guitar and I need to change it." FZ walked to the side of the stage and handed his Les Paul to one of his crew, who immediately gave him back what looked like an identical guitar.

The audience greeted this with laughter, in those days many guitarists did not run to a backup (let alone a matching model) and most were expecting to wait for the string to be replaced. He plugged the guitar in, quickly checked the tuning, and made another signal to the band, who started playing again, from exactly where they had stopped. The whole process had been slicker than a Formula 1 tire change!

Gail Zappa noted that this was fairly typical of FZ.[52] I asked percussionist Art Tripp about this and he had some memories of the occurrence but could tell me nothing about the guitar: "I only vaguely recall the guitar string episode from the Festival Hall show. I'm sure it was in the second half, when we played our typical concert show."[53]

There is a photograph taken in 1968 that may show this obscure instrument in its case on the floor on stage behind

Guitars

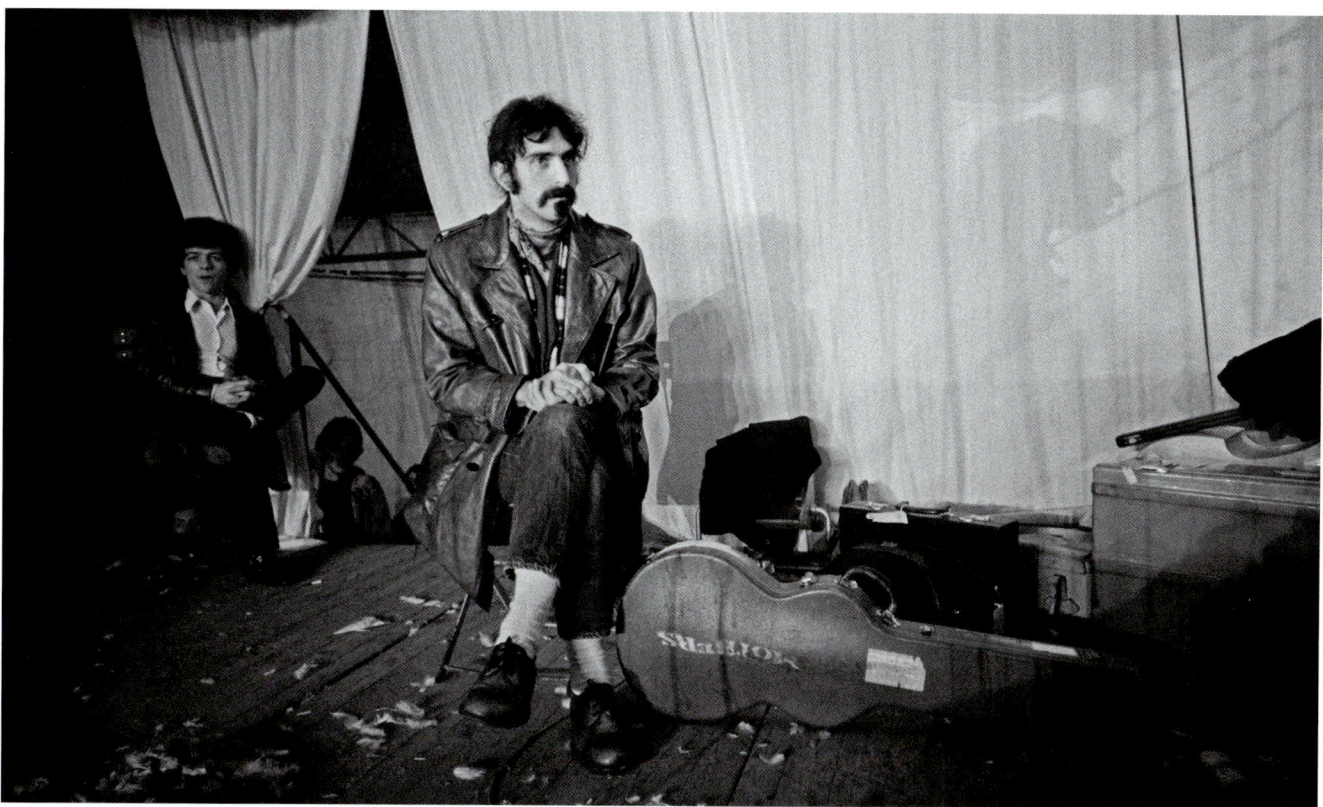

FZ and Gibson Les Paul Goldtop in case.
(Magnum photos)

Mothers of Invention drummer (and sometime trumpet player) Jimmy Carl Black. Marked with an X, this is a different-shaped case from the one that was put up for sale with the main Les Paul, so it could contain Les Paul X.

As with the Switchmaster, guitar fans have expressed dismay to see the way FZ had brutally customized this classic guitar. It is worth remembering that at the time the Les Paul was not in favor; it was just an obsolete model that could be purchased cheaper than the new SG guitar. John Townley (founder of Apostolic Studios in New York, where FZ often recorded in the 1960s) told me that FZ often left the Les Paul in the studio, and John played it a few times.

Townley didn't really like it, finding the neck too wide for his taste, and remembers it being " . . . just like the one I bought from John Sebastian for $100 and then traded to Pepe of the Blues Magoos for his Fender Mustang, which I used throughout the stint with the Magicians."[54] (A single sentence that tells a whole chapter of rock music history!)

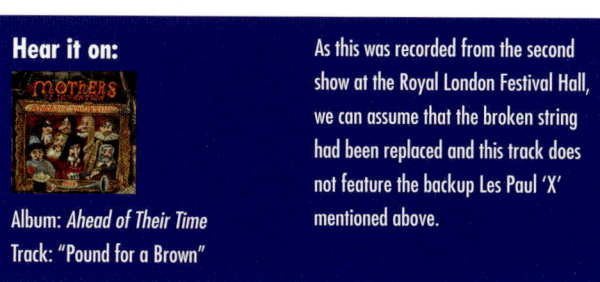

Hear it on:
Album: *Ahead of Their Time*
Track: "Pound for a Brown"

As this was recorded from the second show at the Royal London Festival Hall, we can assume that the broken string had been replaced and this track does not feature the backup Les Paul 'X' mentioned above.

FZ and Gibson Les Paul Goldtop, possibly the last times he used the guitar on stage
(Magnum photos)

THE BATH FESTIVAL GIBSON SG SPECIAL

"I got my first SG in 1970, after hearing one for the first time at a party on the Riviera."

—FZ[55]

From the 1961 Gibson Catalogue
(Scan from Gibson 1961 catalogue)

When FZ appeared at the 1970 Bath Festival in England, with his new lineup of the Mothers of Invention, he was playing a late 1960s model cherry-red Gibson SG Special with the vibrato arm removed. It looks like an unmodified stock instrument except for the non-standard bridge, which has what appear to be two oversized thumbwheels for adjusting the height.

In the late 1950s, the Gibson Les Paul range of guitars was not selling particularly well, and company president Ted McCarty decided that they needed a completely new design. The Les Paul range was discontinued, and replaced in 1960 with the new SG (Solid Guitar) Les Paul range. Paul had worked on the design of the new guitars but was never happy with the result, and after 1961 they were just known as SG guitars.[56]

All the SG models had a distinctive double pointed cutaway mahogany body, and a 24 3/4" 22-fret mahogany set neck with a rosewood fingerboard. The body was considerably thinner and lighter than the Les Paul, the neck was slimmer, and double cutaways gave unfettered access to the higher frets. The first two models introduced were the Standard and Custom versions, which had two and three humbucker pickups, respectively. The SG Special was introduced in 1961 and was essentially an economy version of the Standard model.

It had two black P90 single-coil pickups, dot inlays on the fingerboard, a pearl Gibson logo on the headstock, and nickel hardware. The electronics consisted of a volume and tone control for each pickup, and a three-way pickup selector switch, reverse mounted into the body.

The mahogany body was available in white or cherry-red, and originally featured a small black pickguard. In 1962, Gibson added the option of a Maestro vibrato unit in place of the wrap-around tailpiece.[57] In 1967, the design was modified slightly: the neck joint (a source of problems on the earlier guitars) was beefed up, and larger "batwing" pickguards surrounding the pickups were fitted.

Despite a certain tendency for the neck to dive while playing, due to the lightweight body and the position of the neck, players liked the improved playability of the new SGs and they were a great commercial success in the 1960s and early 1970s. Gibson sold over 30,000 SG Specials between 1961 and 1979, and it is still available today.[58]

Many guitarists preferred the tone of the P90 pickups to the humbuckers fitted on the other SG guitars in the range; notable

FZ and the SG Special in *Gitarist* magazine
(scan from magazine cover)

users in the 1960s and 1970s were Pete Townshend, Tony Iommi, and Carlos Santana. More recently, a white SG Special was featured by David St. Hubbins (actor Michael McKean) in the film *Spinal Tap*.

I don't know where or exactly when FZ bought his SG Special. The party he refers to in the heading quote was a jam session at the Byblos Hotel in St. Tropez, France, where the annual MIDEM convention was held in January, 1970.

FZ tended to favor his Gibson 335 (see the next section) during 1970–1971, but he was playing the same SG Special at the Montreux Casino in December 1971, on the night of the famous "Smoke on the Water" fire. The guitar was never seen again, and was almost certainly destroyed in the conflagration (see the Orange Matamp OR200 section for more on this).

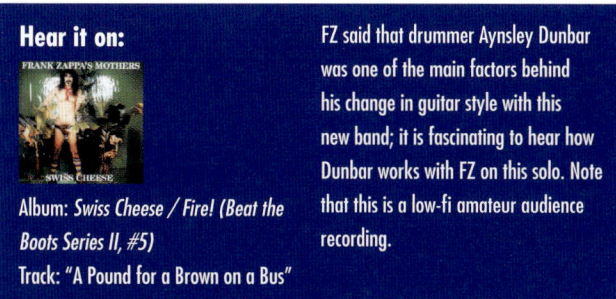

Hear it on:
Album: *Swiss Cheese / Fire! (Beat the Boots Series II, #5)*
Track: "A Pound for a Brown on a Bus"

FZ said that drummer Aynsley Dunbar was one of the main factors behind his change in guitar style with this new band; it is fascinating to hear how Dunbar works with FZ on this solo. Note that this is a low-fi amateur audience recording.

Gibson ES-355TD-SV

"I came up with the idea of putting a solid block of maple in an acoustic model . . . and we'd get a combination of an electric solidbody and a hollowbody guitar."

— Ted McCarty[59]

In 1970, perhaps missing using the Switchmaster on stage, FZ bought another expensive Gibson semi-acoustic guitar with complicated electronics: the top-of-the range ES-355TD-SV.

Until 1958, the only electric guitars Gibson sold were solid-body Les Paul guitars and large hollowbody instruments like the Switchmaster. Although many players preferred the mellower tone of the "jazz boxes," as they were known, they were notoriously prone to acoustic feedback.

This led Gibson boss Ted McCarty to come up with a brilliant compromise: the "thin-line" semi-acoustic guitar. The guitar was thinner than usual, and there was a solid block of wood running inside the length of the body. This greatly reduced the susceptibility of the guitar to feedback when amplified, yet

A 1970 Walnut ES-355 TD SV very like FZ's guitar
(Photo by Vintage-Guitar Oldenburg, permission given by JorgEisenhauer)

FZ with the 355 on a *200 Motels* cinema lobby card
(scan from author's collection)

The ornate pearl inlayed headstock with 'Stereo' on the truss-rod cover
(Photo by Vintage-Guitar Oldenburg, permission given by JorgEisenhauer)

ZAPPA GEAR

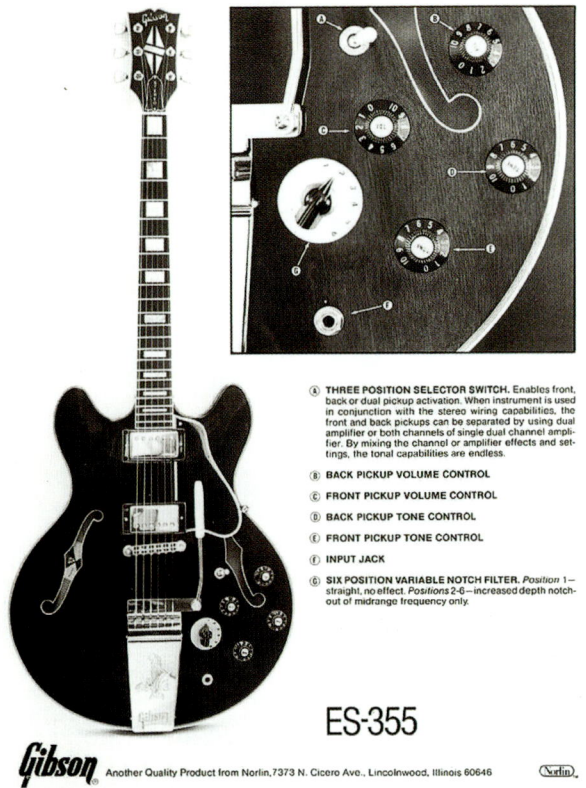

The ES-355 entry in the Gibson 1978 catalogue
(scan from private collection)

retained the traditional Gibson tone. The concept was launched with the ES-335 model in 1958.

They followed this with the ES-355TD-SV model in 1959.[60] It was essentially a dressed-up version of the standard ES-335, using the same basic construction, TD-SV standing for "Thinline Double cutaway Stereo Varitone."

The body top, back, and sides were all curly maple with thick white binding, and the center block was solid maple. The laminated low-action neck joined the body at the 20th fret. It had 22 frets and an ebony fingerboard with pearl block inlays. The 16"×19" body was 1 3/4' 'thin' (as Gibson put it), and the scale length was 24 3/4".

The hardware was all gold plated, and it had a Tune-o-matic bridge and a vibrato tailpiece. The twin humbucking pickups had separate tone and volume controls, and were selected by a three-way toggle switch.[61]

FZ was doubtless interested in the advanced electronics included in the SV version. The stereo jack socket was wired so that the output from each of the guitar's pickups could be routed to a separate amplifier. The Varitone switch was actually a "variable notch filter. Position 1: straight, no effect. Positions 2–6: increased depth notch out of midrange frequencies only."[62] This was achieved with a purely passive electronic circuit consisting of various capacitors and a pair of transformers mounted under the bridge pickup.

The circuit was designed by Gibson's chief electronic engineer and pickup expert Walter Fuller, but was not popular with most players.[63] The 3x5 series was a big commercial success for Gibson, and spawned many imitators as competitors rushed to bring out semi-acoustic models of their own. The guitars were particularly popular among R&B and blues guitarists, notably Chuck Berry and B.B. King, whose famous Lucille guitar is a custom 355-TDSV with a fixed tailpiece and no f-holes.[64]

The 355 sold in respectable quantities, averaging 2 to 300 guitars a year; however, few players made much use of the Varitone or stereo features and it was never as popular as the basic 335 model, which sold over ten times as many.[65] The 355 was discontinued in 1982, but is still frequently reissued by Gibson in various formats.

We know that FZ's 355 was a 1969–1970 model, because the walnut finish was only introduced in 1969, the year before he started using it on stage. At the time the retail price was around $900 (twice the price of the basic 335).[66] FZ played it almost exclusively when on tour with the Flo and Eddie band. He also played it during the making of *200 Motels*. It appears to be a stock guitar and unmodified in any way. It was completely destroyed in the fire at the Montreux Casino and was, as far as I know, the last Gibson 3x5 series guitar he owned.

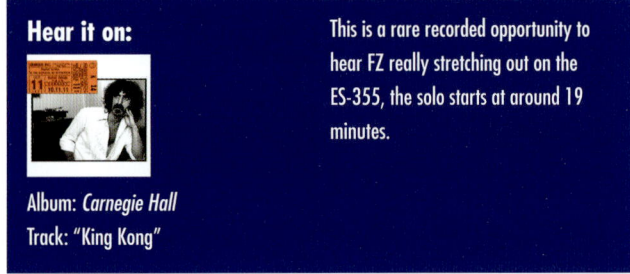

Hear it on: This is a rare recorded opportunity to hear FZ really stretching out on the ES-355, the solo starts at around 19 minutes.

Album: *Carnegie Hall*
Track: "King Kong"

The Rainbow Theatre Telecaster

"A stock Fender Telecaster with chubby strings"

—FZ[67]

FZ bought a Fender Telecaster in Paris in early December 1971, after the band lost all their stage equipment, including his guitars, in the fire at Montreux.[68] He used it at the Rainbow Theatre in London on 10th December, 1971, for what was to be the first and last time he played it on stage. FZ recalled in 1989: "The guitar I was playing (a stock Fender Telecaster with chubby strings) had a reasonable tone but was a nightmare to play."[69]

The concert famously ended in disaster, when a member of the audience pushed FZ off stage into the orchestra pit. Singer Mark Volman later traded his Martin D-18S with FZ for the Telecaster, which is still in his possession.[70]

The sunburst Telecaster with rosewood fingerboard was presumably a 1970–1971 model. In 1965, Leo Fender had sold his company to the CBS Corporation, who introduced a series of cost-cutting measures in the manufacturing process. It is generally agreed among guitar aficionados that by the 1970s this resulted in a marked deterioration in the quality of Fender instruments.[71] FZ was probably glad to see the back of it!

This was not the first time FZ had used a Telecaster in an emergency while in Europe—he borrowed one when he jammed with Pink Floyd at the Amougies festival in Belgium in October 1969, after his Les Paul Goldtop was stolen.

A 2012 Fender 'American Standard' Telecaster, FZ's would have looked much like this but would not have been as well made.
(Fender Musical Instruments corporation)

Hear it on:
Album: *Playground Psychotics*
Track: "Brixton Still Life"

You can also hear FZ playing this Telecaster on *You Can't Do That on Stage Anymore, Vol. 3* on the track "King Kong," which was the last guitar solo he played before he was pushed off stage.

Jacobacci Studio 3

"There is really no training for making a guitar . . . you have to learn to work the wood . . . ."

— Roger Jacobacci[72]

As far as we know, FZ bought his Jacobacci guitar in December 1971, after his band's equipment was destroyed in the "Smoke on the Water" fire in Montreux. The Mothers were scheduled to play a gig in Paris, which was cancelled in the end as it proved impossible to obtain suitable replacement equipment in time. While the band flew straight to London, FZ stopped in Paris for a day or so, and in a French TV interview recorded at Charles De Gaulle airport his assistant can be seen carrying a guitar case that likely contained the Studio 3.

The band convinced FZ to play the scheduled appearance at the Rainbow in London using borrowed equipment (FZ did not use the Jacobacci that night), where an even worse disaster was to happen: an audience member pushed Zappa off the stage into the orchestra pit, where he was seriously injured. In his own words: "I had a broken rib, I got a broken shin, tibia, I had a giant hole in the back of my head, the side of my face got mashed in . . . I couldn't even hold a guitar up by the time I left the place. It was too heavy for me."[73]

While still recovering in his wheelchair during early 1972, he used the Jacobacci guitar at the La Brea rehearsal hall when preparing the band for the *Grand Wazoo* recording.[74] He may have bought it as a quick replacement for his stage guitar, but he was obviously happy with it, and for the rehearsals he had it plugged directly in to one of his trusty Acoustic Corporation heads.[75] FZ probably appreciated the lighter body weight of the

FZ in rehearsal with the Jacobacci in 1972 on *Joe's Domage* cover

The stylish but shamelessly Gibson-like headstock of a 1970 Studio 3
(Christian Vaugeois — collection R. Gimenes)

Jacobacci while wheelchair-bound; a Les Paul gets quite heavy after a while.

Sicilian instrument maker Vincenzo Jacobacci moved to France in 1922, and set up the workshop at 7 Rue Duris in Paris in 1924, making guitars, banjos, and mandolins. He had twelve children with his wife Agathe, but it was only Roger (b. 1931) and André (b. 1934) who worked with their father, eventually taking over the business. Jacobacci had been pioneer makers of electric guitars in France since the early 1950s, and by 1970, the two brothers had established a reputation as the leading custom electric guitar makers in France.

The Jacobacci Studio 3 guitar (also available in a twin pick-up version as the Studio 2, with a slightly smaller body) was first produced in 1969 (there had been a couple of prototypes made in 1968). Visually the design owes a lot to the Gibson Les Paul, but it is in fact quite a different instrument in many ways.

The body is a development of that used for the Jacobacci Texas guitar produced in the 1960s, and is in fact largely hollow, making the instrument substantially lighter than the Les Paul. It was made from two 38 cm blocks of mahogany glued together; the cavities were then cut with a jigsaw. The arched top and the back are made of three-ply mahogany, finished with a maple or walnut veneer, and the final assembly was finished with a five-ply black and white plastic binding. Black was the standard color, although custom finishes were available.

The black headstock is edged with a plain white plastic binding, and has the Jacobacci logo and a tulip motif in mother of pearl. Gold-plated Schaller tuners were usually fitted. The two-piece mahogany neck had a built-in truss rod (adjustable at the headstock), and was joined to the body at the 16th fret, using the set-in neck method favored by Gibson.

A 1970 Studio 3, exactly like the guitar FZ bought
(Christian Vaugeois — collection R. Gimenes)

The ebony fingerboard was inlaid with large rectangular mother of pearl fret markers, and had a plain white binding. The neck had 21 frets and the scale length was 65 cm (approximately 25.6"), both features following Fender preferences.

The electronics consisted of a single set of passive volume and tone controls, and four switches on the upper bout—a simple on-off switch for each pickup and a "direct output" switch that connected the selected pickups straight to the output jack, bypassing the volume and tone controls. Intended as a simple but versatile arrangement for switching from lead to rhythm settings, this was not to everybody's taste, but I suspect it may well have appealed to FZ—he did like lots of switches on his guitars!

The pickups were made for Jacobacci by Michel Benedetti in Marseilles. The Golden Sound models fitted to the Studio 3 were powerful single-coil units. The 6.5k coil was wrapped round six ferrite polepieces attached to large (7×30mm) magnets supported in a Perspex molding. A self-confessed perfectionist, Benedetti aimed for the utmost clarity and purity of tone, which he admitted was not to every guitarist's taste of the time.[76]

The Golden Sound pickups (later rebranded simply as Benedetti) were conveniently made to exactly the same dimensions as a Gibson humbucker, and many players replaced at least one of them, but as far as we can see, the guitar FZ is holding is unmodified. This very attractive instrument was finished off with a gold-plated Schaller bridge and a handmade tailpiece.

Following the untimely death of André Jacobacci in 1991, all instrument making was stopped, and the workshop finally closed in 1994. I have not been able to trace the whereabouts of FZ's Studio 3 guitar; it is not in the hands of the ZFT and Dweezil Zappa has no memory of it.

FZ with a customized Fender Stratocaster at the UMRK in 1982
(Chris Walters — Getty Images)

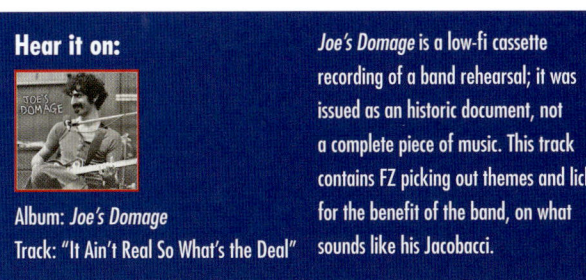

Hear it on:
Album: *Joe's Domage*
Track: "It Ain't Real So What's the Deal"

Joe's Domage is a low-fi cassette recording of a band rehearsal; it was issued as an historic document, not a complete piece of music. This track contains FZ picking out themes and licks for the benefit of the band, on what sounds like his Jacobacci.

Fender Stratocasters

"I definitely like a Stratocaster tone, especially when it's feeding back and with a midrange booster on it so it gets a real nasal sound."

— FZ[77]

In the early 1950s, Leo Fender began working on the design of a new guitar, which he expected would make the Telecaster obsolete. He wanted the new design to be better in all respects, with improved tonal range, intonation, and player comfort and with the additional feature of a vibrato unit. In 1951, local guitarist Bill Carson agreed to roadtest new designs in exchange for being allowed to pay $18 a month for his Telecaster. He complained that the squared-off edges of the Tele dug into his ribs when he played sitting down, and he scooped out the back of the body and beveled the front edge with a saw.[78]

Leo took note of this, rounding the edges of the new body shape, and contouring the front and rear. The guitar would have three pickups instead of the usual two; Carson had suggested four pickups, but Fender saw that the extra cost and complexity would give little benefit. Carson had a lot to do with the original prototype design, and recalled "the local guys would come borrow my guitar, which was known then as 'Carson's Guitar,' and they wouldn't bring it back. After Leo was convinced that the instrument was marketable, well that's what later became the Stratocaster."[79]

Carson specified that the vibrato should "not only come back to exact string pitch . . . but should also sharp or flat half a tone at least, and hold the chord." This was a tough requirement for Fender to meet, and one original design was completely scrapped at considerable cost.[80]

FZ with pre-CBS Strat in 1975 promo shot
(promo card — copyright ZFT)

The vibrato unit (incorrectly called a "tremolo" by Fender and pretty much everyone else) was an engineering breakthrough. Unlike the heavy bolt-on Bigsby units favored by Gibson and Gretsch, it was built as a single unit integrated with the special floating bridge, and most of the works were hidden inside the guitar body. Guitarists could remove one or more of the five tension springs accessible from the back of the guitar to adjust the feel of the unit, and although it requires careful set up, it still holds its own today against newer and more complicated designs.

Other innovations were special pickups with staggered height magnets to even out the string response, and a stylish recessed angled jack socket on the body face. The pickups, and all the electronics and controls, were mounted on the large pickguard; this single assembly could thus be built and wired up separately from the guitar body, which simplified production considerably.

The pickup selector was originally a three-way switch, with each position selecting one pickup. However guitarists soon found that the switch could be set halfway between positions, and the resulting combination of the two pickups gave a unique hollow sound. Although this became one of the signature Stratocaster features, Fender did not add a five-way switch until 1977, almost twenty-five years after the first design!

The Stratocaster finally went into production in late 1954, with a sunburst finish as standard, and an all-maple neck with the new signature Fender headstock shape. With its futuristic double-cut body, it looked so advanced that, like the Telecaster, it took a couple of years to really start selling. However, in 1956 early rock and roll stars like Buddy Holly and Gene Vincent took to the guitar, and its success was assured.

Although FZ mostly favored Gibson guitars as his main instruments until the 1980s, he used Stratocasters on and off throughout his career. The earliest photograph I have seen of FZ with a Strat is the 1968 picture overleaf, with a CBS-era sunburst model. As already noted, Fender guitars produced during this period were not always of the best quality.

FZ talked in 1982 about the different playing techniques required for Strats and Les Pauls because of the way the bodies sat: "When you hang a Strat around your neck, the 12th fret will hit your body at a certain point, but if you put the Les Paul on it will be in a different position."

He had this to say about the stock Fender tremolo: "It stays in tune to a degree and what you have to do if it doesn't come back right is to give it another yank and let it settle and if it comes back flat you have to press harder and intonate with your (left) hand. What you do is you don't start your solo off with a big wham. That would be dumb."[81]

FZ sometimes used a sunburst Stratocaster in 1975–1976, taking it with him on the Bongo Fury tour. He appeared with the guitar in publicity photographs with the original line-up for his winter 1975–1976 band (Roy Estrada, Napoleon Murphy Brock, FZ, Robert "Frog" Camarena, Novi Novog, Terry Bozzio, and Denny Walley, who only rehearsed and never actually went on tour). The guitar has the small headstock that marks it out as a pre-CBS model, and the logo identifies it as probably from 1965. FZ had this guitar modified with DiMarzio pickups, but otherwise it seems to have been pretty much standard. Certainly it had the classic Strat sound, very

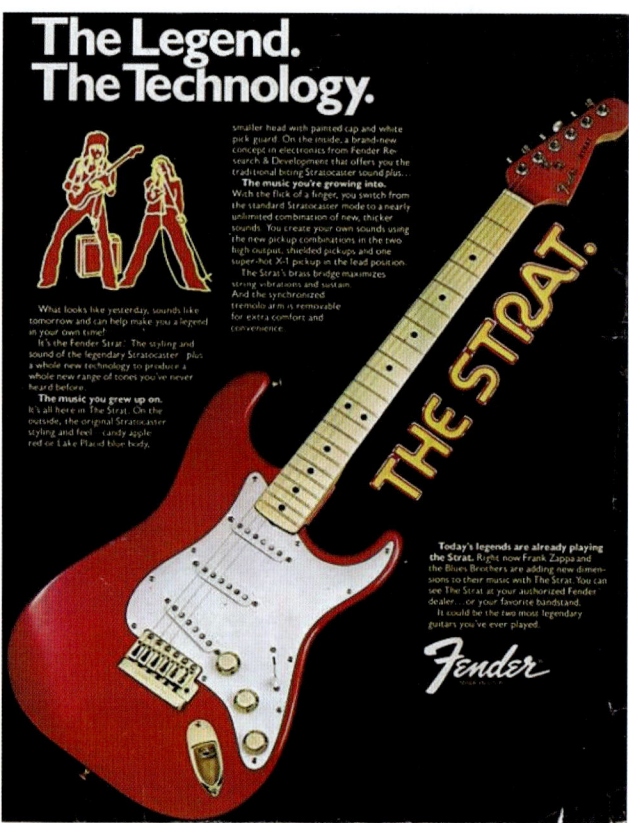

"Right now Frank Zappa and the Blues Brothers are adding new dimensions to their sound with The Strat"
(scan from private collection)

unlike the later guitars with their custom electronics. I don't know where and when the guitar was obtained.

In March 1977, FZ told *International Musician* that he had three Strats, noting that each one was wired differently. One of these would be the Hendrix Strat, one is presumably the sunburst, and the identity of the third one is not recorded. Fender gave FZ four Stratocasters in or around 1980; guitarists Ike Willis and Ray White each took one and FZ kept two, which he later customized. FZ was photographed with a natural-finish Strat in 1982 at the UMRK, presumably one of these. It has been fitted with a pickguard assembly containing a Carvin M22 pickup, a black humbucker, and a plain black pickup, and looks to have a parametric EQ setup. As part of the deal he was name-checked in 1981 adverts for The Strat, Fender's belated effort to catch up with the custom Stratocaster market, but I have found no evidence of FZ actually using one of these guitars.

Over fifty years after it was introduced, the Fender Stratocaster is the biggest selling, most copied, and almost certainly the most played electric guitar design in the world. Ask anyone to quickly draw you an electric guitar, and most likely their doodle will look like a Strat; for once it is probably correct to describe a design as "iconic."

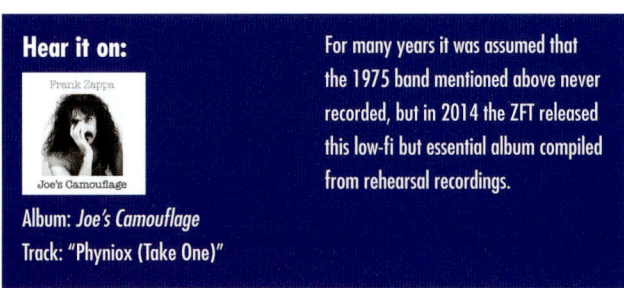

Hear it on:

For many years it was assumed that the 1975 band mentioned above never recorded, but in 2014 the ZFT released this low-fi but essential album compiled from rehearsal recordings.

Album: *Joe's Camouflage*
Track: "Phyniox (Take One)"

The Roxy Gibson SG

Then I got a real nice secondhand SG and played that from Apostrophe through Bongo Fury."

— FZ[82]

FZ bought his second cherry red Gibson SG Special in 1971 or 1972. The serial number 125063 dates it as having been manufactured in 1963.[83] I have been unable to discover exactly where or when FZ obtained it. It certainly had been well used, FZ said that when he first got it "The frets were all beat up on it, it was broken in just right."[84]

I've already covered the general history of the SG Special in the Bath Festival SG Special section; the main differences between this guitar and FZ's 1967 Bath Festival SG are that the original vibrato was a Deluxe model with the long metal tailpiece, it had the small pickguard, and significantly, the neck joint was the original low-profile design.

When FZ took the SG with him on the Petit Wazoo tour (October to December, 1972), the only modification that had been made was that the vibrato had been removed and the tailpiece replaced with a fixed unit (possibly before FZ bought the guitar).

Like many of FZ's guitars, the SG then went through a series of changes over the years, to such an extent that some people think it is two different guitars.

In 1973, FZ replaced the P90s with a pair of black DiMarzio Dual Sound humbucker pickups, and added two small toggle switches to the pickguard on the lower horn of the body. One was what is known as a "coil tap," which could change the humbuckers to single-coil operation like the original P90s, giving a sharper clearer tone. The other switch put the pickups out of phase with each other, resulting in a thin nasal sound. Such modifications are common today, but in 1973 they were cutting-edge.

Later on a Gibson Deluxe vibrato unit was fitted, with a flat vibrato arm, unlike the plastic-tipped rod that was originally fitted to these units. The cherry red lacquered finish was removed, showing the natural mahogany of the body; the black headstock paint was also removed. It is likely that this work coincided with the neck being shaved to a thinner profile. Apart from the switches, the electronics were left as standard.

It was in this form that the guitar appeared on the cover of the *Roxy & Elsewhere* album and FZ can also be seen playing it in *Roxy the Movie*. The guitar became known as the "Roxy SG" and it continued to be his main instrument for the next year or so.

I asked Napoleon Murphy Brock, singer and saxophone player with the band at the time, if FZ used any other guitars on stage at the time: "In my memory it was usually the Gibson. He loved the sound of that one. It was more versatile than a Telecaster, but could also do what a telecaster could."[85]

Dweezil Zappa remembers the guitar well from his younger days: "The SG was the most prevalent through the 1970s, so that was really the guitar that had the biggest impact on me . . . and he stopped playing that one 'cause he said it wouldn't stay in tune anymore, but that was the one that I saw him play the most before it got the mirror pickguard."[86]

FZ and the Roxy SG in its best-known incarnation on stage in Stockholm in 1973 *(still from Oppåpoppa, 1973)*

ZAPPA GEAR

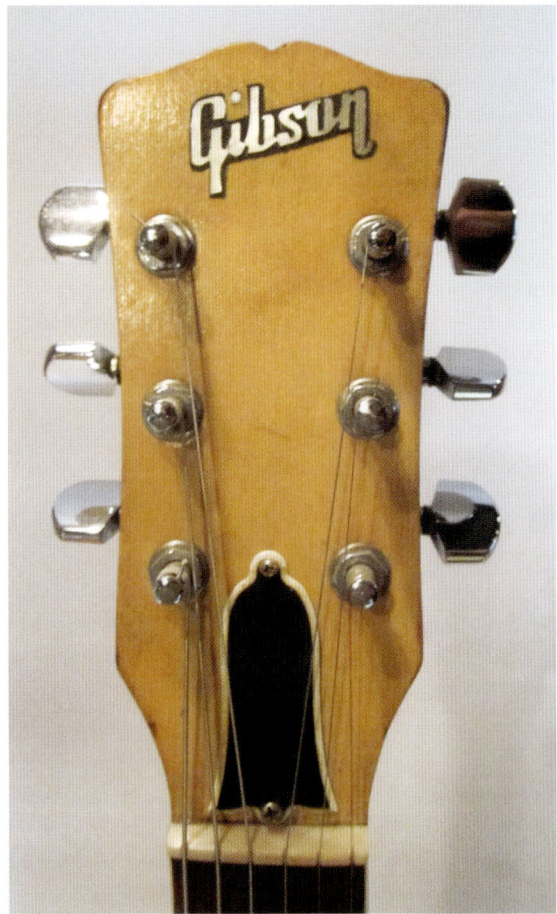

The stripped front of the headstock
(Mick Ekers)

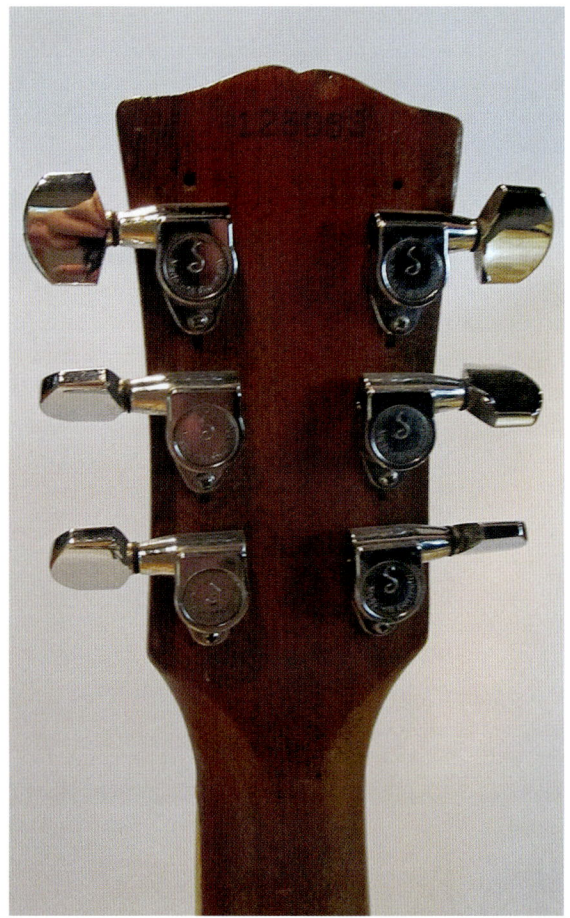

Rear of headstock showing replacement tuners and original screw holes
(Mick Ekers)

By 1977, the guitar was not in good shape, and FZ told *Guitar Player* magazine that he hardly ever used it any more: "The one that's on the *Roxy* cover has since been thoroughly injured by an airline company; they beat the hell out of it. They cracked the neck, and the most recent time it came back from Europe the binding was off the fretboard. I had the neck repaired, but it's never been the same."[87]

The body had also suffered: the controls had been pushed back into the control cavity.[88] FZ noted that the problems were not just the fault of the airline baggage handlers: " . . . the neck's been shaved so much that it's hard to keep it in tune; it flaps around like a piece of cardboard."[89]

To hide the damage to the bodywork FZ eventually fitted a full-size dark acrylic mirror scratch plate, which has caused some confusion as it can look like shiny black plastic in photographs. DZ again: " . . . apparently TWA had damaged the guitar and it had a crack through the body and all that stuff and so he [FZ] put a mirror pickguard over the thing. I don't really remember seeing him play it with the mirror pickguard too much but it was always around at the studio."[90]

The body and neck appear to have been restained back to a redder color (although still un-lacquered), and the electronics and hardware upgraded to FZ's typical 1980s preferences. The vibrato unit was removed and a fixed tailpiece and "harmonica"-style bridge were fitted. The original tuners have been replaced with sealed Schaller units (this may have been done earlier) and the black DiMarzios replaced with two white Seymour Duncan humbuckers, probably custom wound.

A new twin battery compartment with a black plastic cover was built in, to power an 18-volt active electronics circuit. The controls consist of four silver knobs: two parametric EQs for the bridge and neck pickups, a master volume, and a blend control. There is a small on-off switch for the EQ circuit and a large pickup selector switch with a star surround. The original white-tipped pickup switches have been replaced with plain metal ones.

After several years of rumors, Gibson finally got around to producing a replica of the Roxy SG in its 1974 incarnation in 2013. Dweezil Zappa took a prototype made by the Gibson custom shop on tour with his Zappa Plays Zappa band in 2012, and after exhibiting this at various music shows Gibson officially announced it in May 2013. The original guitar, when I saw it hiding away at the UMRK, put me in mind of an aging rock star, concealing his faded good looks behind a perpetual pair of dark glasses.

Guitars

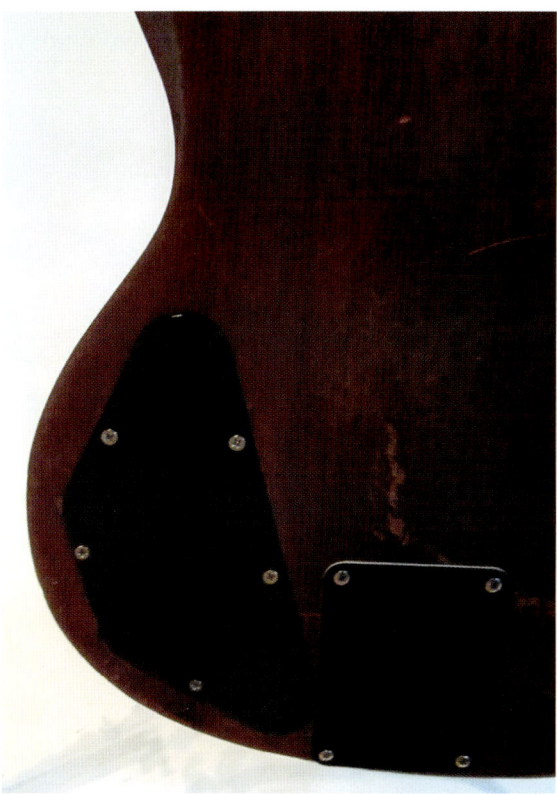
The back of the body showing added battery compartment cover
(Mick Ekers)

Detail of the Roxy SG showing the reflection of the UMRK in the mirror pickguard, not the easiest guitar to photograph!
(Mick Ekers)

The Gibson 'Roxy SG' prototype
(Dweezil Zappa)

The Roxy SG in its current state
(Mick Ekers)

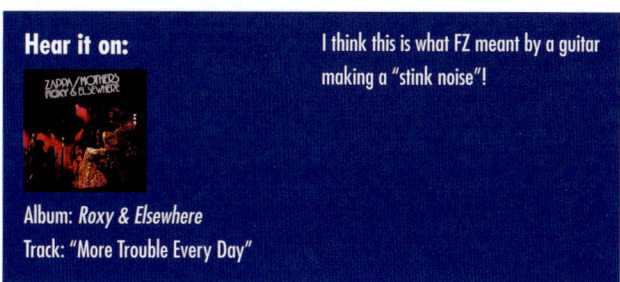

Hear it on: I think this is what FZ meant by a guitar making a "stink noise"!

Album: *Roxy & Elsewhere*
Track: "More Trouble Every Day"

ZAPPA GEAR

Acoustic Control Corporation Black Widows

"I've got two Acoustic Black Widows, made by the Acoustic Control Corporation."

—FZ[91]

The Mk1 Black Widow as found in a work area under the UMRK studio
(Mick Ekers)

FZ bought his Acoustic Control Corporation AC500 Black Widow guitar in 1969 (probably in early summer, based on the date of the photo on the right). {AU: photo on page X? ME: Yes - reference should be to wherever Fig01-13-01 gets placed } According to FZ, the Guitar Center store in Hollywood also sold him another model:

"At one time Acoustic manufactured a fretless guitar, they made a prototype and tried to interest people in it, but nobody wanted it. So the prototype ended up at Guitar Center. I walked in there one day and asked them if they had anything new, and they said, 'Have we got one for you!' And they brought out this thing, and it was really neat, so I bought it for $75. The only restriction was they had to take a chisel and some black paint and scratch off the word 'Acoustic' on the headpiece, because Acoustic didn't want anybody to know that they had made such a grievous error as to make a fretless guitar."[92]

The Black Widow range of guitars is a fairly obscure branch of electric guitar history. In 1968–1969, the Acoustic Control Corporation, best known for their solid-state guitar and bass amplifiers, decided to add a complementary range of guitars to their catalog. They commissioned veteran guitar engineer Paul Barth to produce an electric 6-string and bass. Barth had worked for Rickenbacker in the 1930s on the original electric guitar pickup design, ending up on the board of directors,

Back of the Mk1 showing the unusual red cushioned pad
(Mick Ekers)

leaving in 1956 to produce his own guitars.[93] Barth also worked for Fender for a while, setting up their automated production facilities, and in the mid-1960s, he founded Bartell, a small guitar production company in Riverside, California, in partnership with Ted Peckels.[94]

Bartell made the first series of Black Widow guitars for Acoustic in 1969.[95] They featured a black lacquered maple, semi-acoustic body with two large single-coil pickups, each with a volume and tone control. The control knobs were large flat aluminum units of the same style as those used on Acoustics amplifiers of the time. A pickup-selector toggle switch was mounted on the upper horn. The 22-fret bolt-on neck had a rosewood fingerboard, an aluminum string retainer, and a zero fret. The strings passed over an adjustable Tune-o-matic style bridge and ended in an aluminum block tailpiece. The body

FZ in 1969 with his Mk1 Black Widow (with head-stock logo and frets)
(Tony Frank)

Ray White and the Mk2 Black Widow, (also with head-stock logo and frets)
(still from Frank Zappa, Chorus, 1980*)*

and headstock were finished with a narrow three-ply white and black edging strip.

Bartell could not produce the quantities Acoustic wanted, and they soon transferred the manufacturing to Matsumoto Moko in Japan. The mark-two version had various design changes; most obviously, the position of the volume controls was moved nearer to the bridge.

Larger and more powerful pickups were fitted, the neck was extended to 24 frets, and the edge binding was made thicker and more prominent. Both versions of the guitar featured a large red leatherette pad on the back of the body attached by press-studs, with an embossed black widow spider design.

FZ told *Guitar Player* that he had a Barcus Berry transducer fitted to one of them: "I send the magnetic pickup to the left and the Barcus on the right. The thing that sounds like a slide guitar on 'The Torture Never Stops' is actually a fretless. It's also on 'San Ber'dino' and 'Can't Afford No Shoes' (both from *One Size Fits All*). It's different than a regular guitar; you don't push the strings to bend them, you move them back and forth like violin-type vibrato, which is a funny movement to get."[96]

FZ also stated in 1979 that he had one "souped up": "It's got a 24-fret rosewood neck, and I had two EMG pickups put in it, and new fret work by (John) Carruthers."[97] I found FZ's Mk-1 Bartell Black Widow in the basement workshop under the UMRK. It was in rather sorry condition, covered in dust and with no bridge or strings. The original aluminum control knobs have gone, and the bridge pickup has been crudely replaced with a large black pickup of unknown manufacture (possibly replacing the loop pickup referred to above).

Dweezil Zappa had previously told me that it had deliberately been left as it was: "The fretted one is in pieces in the same area where all things go to die under the studio, so no pickups in it, not been in a case . . . I never saw any pictures of Frank playing it."[98]

Since FZ's death, DZ has made sure that most of his guitars have been carefully preserved; "The ones that are all fucked up are doomed to stay fucked up. Like the Acoustic one, if it was a Gibson it may have gotten some better treatment. I might have considered getting it restored. The Acoustic had an interesting role in Frank's playing but it just didn't seem to be a guitar he

The cleaned up Black Widow as sold in auction
(Photo from ZFT)

cared that much about. I remember it had a horrible padded backside."[99]

However, the Black Widow guitars, although not considered a classic design, must have had some unique quality that FZ liked; Jimi Hendrix also used one for a while.[100] The dust-covered and neglected guitar we saw at the UMRK, cleaned up but unrestored, was sold in auction by the ZFT in 2016 for $12,500. The whereabouts of the other guitar(s) are not known. Ray White used the customized one with the EMG pickups on stage during the 1980 tour, and it is clearly a Japanese mark 2 model. In 1987, FZ said "Unfortunately, the fretless guitar was stolen several years ago."[101]

I have been unable to find any photographs or other evidence of the fretless neck with the removed logo and the special pickup that FZ referred to. Both the guitar I saw in the basement and the one White is playing have the Acoustic name on the headstock, and both are fretted. Therefore, either FZ had a third guitar, which was stolen, or he had the neck replaced with a fretted one at some time. Bartell did badge up a few Black Widows for Höfner, as they still owed them some instruments from a previous contract; this was around the same time as the

ZAPPA GEAR

Acoustic deal,[102] and they also made some similar fretless guitars for Höfner.[103] So possibly it was a Höfner logo that Guitar Center removed from FZ's guitar; we will probably never know.

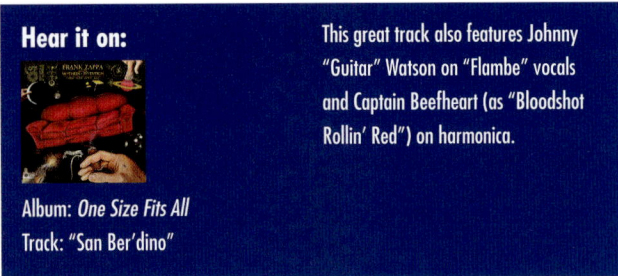

Hear it on: This great track also features Johnny "Guitar" Watson on "Flambe" vocals and Captain Beefheart (as "Bloodshot Rollin' Red") on harmonica.

Album: *One Size Fits All*
Track: "San Ber'dino"

The Hendrix Strat

"We had it hanging on the wall as a decoration for years and years, and then I met some guys who were capable of putting guitars back together."
— FZ[104]

This legendary instrument started out as a standard 1963 sunburst Stratocaster.[105] Jimi Hendrix played it at the London Astoria on March 31st, 1967; it was the first night of a package tour with the Walker Brothers, Cat Stevens, and Engelbert Humperdinck. Hendrix had only five numbers with which to make an impression, and at the suggestion of journalist Keith Altham it was decided to set fire to the guitar at the end of the set. Manager Chas Chandler got a roadie to obtain a bottle of lighter fuel and at the end of the song "Fire," the guitar was ceremoniously torched by Hendrix, to the amazement of the audience (and the ire of the Astoria management, who told him he would never play in one of their theatres again).[106] As far as I know, Hendrix only ever burnt one other guitar on stage, at the famous Monterey concert later that year (although he smashed many others).

The guitar was kept by his roadie Howard Parker, who gave it to FZ some time in 1968: "Well, there was this guy named Howard Parker—they called him 'H'—who was Hendrix's roadie, gofer, and general assistant. He stayed at our house for a couple of months in the late '60s, and he had this guitar which Hendrix had given to him. I thought it was from the Miami concert. He gave it to me . . . ."[107]

FZ's original assumption that it was from the 1968 Miami concert (at which FZ also played) cast some doubts on the guitar's authenticity, but it was later identified as the one from the Astoria show. "H" died at sea in 1974, and his body was never found. The story was further complicated when a burnt Strat purporting to be the Astoria model was auctioned in London in September 2008, and sold for £280,000 to a US collector.

However, comparison with the guitar Hendrix is holding in backstage photographs taken at the Astoria revealed it as an obvious fake; it even had two carefully melted volume and tone knobs which were missing on the original.[108] There is no reason to doubt that the guitar now owned by Dweezil Zappa is the genuine article.

FZ had the unplayable relic hanging on his wall as an ornament for several years, until in 1976 he gave it to luthier Rex Bogue to repair as a trial commission. Jim Williams, Bogue's assistant at the time, tells that they had visited FZ at the Record Plant to try and get to work for him:

"We showed him Rex's guitar and pictures of the McLaughlin double-neck and other stuff, and said 'We build really nice guitars, we're really interested in doing guitar work for you, because you're Frank Zappa, if you need any more excuse as a reason.' And he says 'Well, y'know, you guys sound like you got your shit together, you do some nice work here and stuff, but . . . I'll tell you what.' He walks over to a stack of guitar cases, digs through, pulls this one case out and says 'Here, you put this sucker together and we'll talk.' And that was it and he let us out of the room, we didn't even know what the fucking thing was!"[109]

Bogue and Williams took it back to the workshop and discovered what a challenge they had been given: "It's this fucking Stratocaster all broken in three pieces. The neck's missing a headstock, the pickguard's almost completely burnt off down to the last two tone controls, just a metal plate underneath, and the pickup cover's all black and bubbly. And it's completely

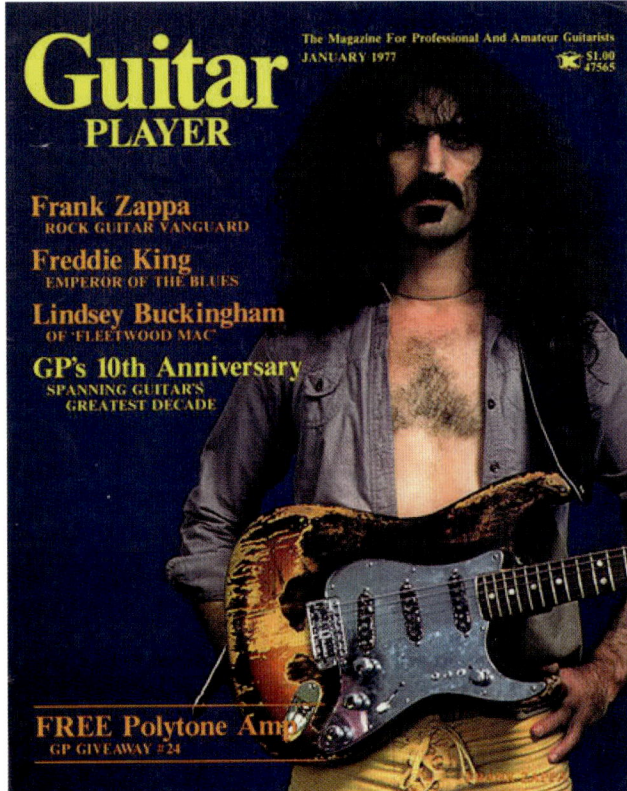

FZ as guitar hero, with the original 1976 Rex Bogue rebuild
(scan from author's collection)

The tremolo spring cavity in 2011; in 1978 FZ used four springs
(Mick Ekers)

Dweezil's 1991 rebuild
(Dweezil Zappa)

charred black and flaking, and it's like 'Okay! Hendrix! Let's put this fucker together!'"[110]

FZ told Bogue to "take your time and do what you wanna do." First Bogue glued all the loose pieces of the body back together with hide glue. The neck was deemed beyond repair and another Stratocaster neck was obtained. Amazingly the electronics still worked.

Williams told me: "All the pickups worked, everything worked, it was just there was no plastic left on the pickguard down to the metal shielding plate, which they had on those older models. We stuck new pickups in there, and shielded and screened it, put on a chrome pickguard, and inlaid a Barcus Berry into the headstock on the top side and then routed a little chamber on the side of the neck where the fingerboard was to tape the wire in."[111]

The pickups were basically stock 1970 Fender items, but the coils had been encased in some sort of resin compound to reduce feedback (a process known as "potting"). Bogue kept the neck and original pickups hanging up in his house as ornaments.

It was William's idea to put the Barcus Berry piezo pickup in the headstock; these had just come on the market and were designed for use on acoustic guitars: "We just decided to do something that would be wild, wacky, and might impress him. The neck of a Strat really moves physically, you can feel it vibrating in places; I thought that'd be a good spot to pick up the sound, because you get a lot of energy."[112]

The neck was finished in a pearl cellulose lacquer with an inlay to hide the wire cavity; new metal knobs were added including a blend control for the Barcus Berry on the lower horn of the body. According to Williams, the active electronics consisted of just a simple preamp to boost the signal with no special EQ features. The standard Fender pickup selector was augmented by three individual pickup switches. The guitar was finished off with a new bridge and the original blackened and distorted pickup covers.

After two or three months the guitar was delivered back to FZ. He was by all accounts very pleased and impressed with the results, and went on to commission Bogue and his team to work on many more of his guitars. He was famously pictured holding the results on the cover of *Guitar Player* magazine in January 1977.

FZ took it on the 1977 tours and gave it to band member Eddie Jobson to play during some numbers. Although a virtuoso violin and keyboard player, Jobson did not consider himself much of a guitarist, and told me he felt embarrassed to be holding such a legendary instrument on stage.[113]

Although FZ liked the guitar, he found it tended to feed back on stage, especially when using the Barcus Berry pickup, and had some radical changes made in 1978. The neck was replaced with a birdseye maple one with gold tuners. The chrome pickguard was replaced with a black plastic unit with a radical new set of pickups. The worst of the black charring body was gone, either flaking off or having been lightly sanded. A new gold-plated bridge was installed and FZ left the whammy bar in place; photos of the rear of the guitar show one of the five springs removed.

In 1978, FZ told *Record Review*: "on my Hendrix Strat I have a Dan Armstrong in the front position, I have a Seymour

Dweezil's 2011 rebuild
(Dweezil Zappa)

DZ and the Hendrix Strat body at his home
(Mick Ekers)

Duncan Strat pickup in the middle position, and a Carvin in the rear position."[114] The Carvin neck pickup was the newly launched M22, a unique 22-pole humbucker designed specifically to provide a more even magnetic field so that strings would not lose volume if the guitarist bent them out of line. The new neck was specially made to FZ's liking: " . . . it has a special size neck on it. It;s an SG-size neck. It does certain things that other guitars won't do. The width and depth of the neck is different from that of a Strat, so you can do all kinds of things that just don't feel right on another guitar."[115]

The guitar made a big impression on the young Dweezil Zappa: "that one always used to have the gold Maximus strings on it so when we were sitting around at the studio, it was all burnt up and it had the gold strings on it, of course that one had quite a bit of appeal!"[116]

FZ regularly took this version of the guitar on tour in the late 1970s and 1980s, even though it never was his main guitar. It would often be seen on stage on a stand next to FZ's amplifier and he would use it for occasional solos; sometimes giving it to other guitarists in the band to play.

Guitar tech Merl Saunders Jr. told me that FZ took it with him on his last tour in 1988, but never used it on stage: " . . . the guitar that never really saw the light of day, that I slept with . . . pretty much all the time, was the Hendrix Strat. He never played it live but it was out on the road."[117]

As Dweezil Zappa tells it, the guitar effectively disappeared in the late 1980s, until he found it in pieces under a staircase at the UMRK in 1991. "I grew up seeing it in the way Frank had it on tour in the 1981 period. It had a black pickguard on it and it had a gold tremolo system and it had three pickups; a humbucker in the back that was a Carvin and then two other single coils. It had this birdseye maple neck that had stars on the neck and actually stars on the tuners and regular fret markers. So I had played it when I was twelve and I remembered that guitar and then it sort of disappeared and I asked Frank 'What happened to the guitar?' and he said 'I don't know, I don't know where it is.'"[118]

According to Gail Zappa, the guitar had been sent back to Rex Bogue for some further work but he refused to finish it and refused to return it. "I had to drive out to his place to retrieve it—and not all the parts were returned." (Frightening experience!!!) What ultimately remained is what DZ found under the stairs.[119]

DZ remembers: "I just happened to look back there, and there was the Hendrix guitar in pieces, not in a case, just in pieces shoved in a corner. And it was like it had been raped and left to die. The electronics were stripped off the pickguard so it couldn't be put back together with the parametric that used to be in it and so I told Frank that I found it and he said, 'Where was it?' I said, 'Under the stairs,' he said 'I don't even know how it got there.' Of course I was glad to have found it and was hopeful that we could get it back to playing condition for him."[120]

DZ asked FZ if he would like him to rebuild it, and FZ agreed. As the electronics were missing and the neck was damaged he decided to restore it to something like its original condition in the late 1960s. He got Jay Black, master builder at the Fender custom shop, to make a maple neck with a flipped headstock as "a nod to Jimi" and fitted it with custom-wound Lindy Fralin single coil pickups. The guitar was finished off with a tortoiseshell pickguard and standard Fender white plastic knobs and DZ presented it as a birthday gift for Frank: "When he opened the case he smiled and played it for a while. A little later, he said, 'You know what, you should have this guitar.' Of course I smiled in disbelief."[121]

In 2002, DZ twice put the guitar up for auction but it failed to reach its reserve price; it was obviously not destined to leave the Zappa household. In 2011, DZ restored the guitar as close as possible to its 1977 configuration, complete with piezo pickup, mirror pickguard, and a new neck with a rosewood fingerboard. The work was done by the Fender custom shop and Performance Guitar in LA, and Dweezil intends to do some recording with it: "I plan to do some stuff with that guitar. Now that it's back to its former glory, why not?"[122]

Through all of its incarnations the guitar has possessed an almost mystical aura. Arthur Barrow said his hands were trembling when FZ gave him the chance to play it during the fall 1980 tour.[123] DZ has noted that guitarists have described the hair standing up on their arms when they picked it up.

DZ showed me the guitar when I interviewed him in his home studio in 2012. The neck was away having some further work done on it, but the body and all the electronics were complete. Despite the fact that all that remains of the original is the body, and it is now on its third owner, and fifth configuration, the instrument still has an indescribable presence, more so than any of the other FZ guitars I've seen.

Strap-peg hole on lower horn indicates that the guitar had a previous left-handed owner!
(Mick Ekers)

Dweezil is reflected in the mirror pickguard
(Mick Ekers)

The body is still raw and unvarnished
(Mick Ekers)

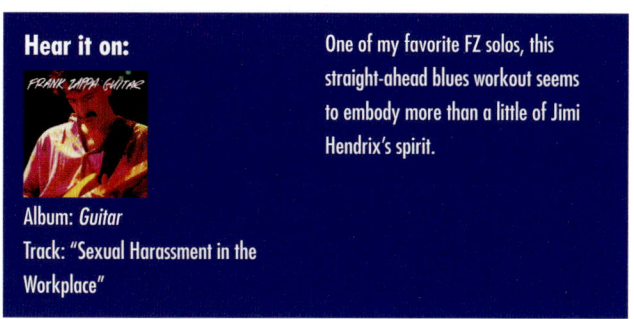

Hear it on:
Album: *Guitar*
Track: "Sexual Harassment in the Workplace"

One of my favorite FZ solos, this straight-ahead blues workout seems to embody more than a little of Jimi Hendrix's spirit.

ZAPPA GEAR

Rex Bogue Semi-Acoustic

"It's got two kinds of preamps in it and a mass of electronics. And it sustains for months."

— FZ[124]

In 1979, FZ took delivery of a very special guitar built for him by Californian luthier Rex Bogue. It was a beautifully finished semi-acoustic guitar with no f-holes in the soundboard, slanted frets, and an intricate tree of life design inlaid into the fingerboard. The guitar had a pair of humbucking pickups feeding into two separate active electronic circuits, each with treble, bass, and volume controls. The strings ran over a heavy brass adjustable bridge into a large brass tailpiece decorated with a heart-shaped cutout and the initials RB.

As it turned out, FZ had a major issue with the instrument, telling UK *Guitar Player* magazine: " . . . at the moment it doesn't feel right . . . . One of the reasons it's hard for me to play is because the dots on the neck are invisible, and I'm very neck-dot orientated. It's got that vine crawling up the neck and I can't tell where the fuck I am on it. I look down there and have to think too much where my hand is."[125]

Larel Rexford "Rex" Bogue was born in 1951, and grew up in the town of San Gabriel, California. Bogue was an eccentric but highly talented West Coast guitar maker, most famous for the double-neck guitar he built for John McLaughlin in 1973, known as the Double Rainbow.

He took a year to make this, while he was still an apprentice working for the Ren Ferguson Guitar Company in Venice, California, and when McLaughlin finally took possession of the guitar it was a sensation. As *Guitar Player* magazine said in 1974: "The word was out, 'McLaughlin's got a new guitar!' It obviously wasn't the familiar Gibson double-neck. In fact, it wasn't a familiar anything. But its beauty and sound were turning heads wherever Mahavishnu John McLaughlin performed."[126]

The publicity from this one instrument was enough to establish Bogue's reputation, and he set up on his own shop in San Gabriel, about ten miles east of LA, in the Guitar Ranch, a collection of wooden buildings he had inherited from his grandmother.

Operating from a small wooden shack, Bogue hired Jim Williams, who specialized in the electronics, and Michael Gnapp, who was a woodworker. As previously mentioned, Rex Bogue Guitars had already worked on many of FZ's guitars, including the initial rebuild of the Hendrix Strat and the (some would say sacrilegious) customization of the Gibson Switchmaster.

FZ told *International Musician*: "Rex Bogue, he was the guy that made that double-necked monstrosity for McLaughlin; he does most of the work on my guitars."[127] Although Rex Bogue Guitars had been FZ's preferred custom shop since 1976, this was the first time they had built him a guitar from scratch. If he had known FZ's opinion of the Double Rainbow, Bogue might have come up with a slightly less ornate design.

Gnapp remembers working on FZ's guitar with Williams: "as we worked on a very heavy guitar for Frank Zappa (think sustain), his band would come in and hang out. Steve Vai was Zappa's transposer at the time, and occasionally part of the crowd. Bogue's extreme approach to making guitars resulted in the very finest electric guitars of the period, if not still. But Rex was extreme in all he did. My first duty in the morning was to prepare a five-gallon water cooler full of piña colada, and it would be empty at the end of every day. The two of us didn't partake of the rum concoctions, but Rex did as he hosted his clients and their friends."[128]

According to Williams, the electronics were something special: "It had a metal plate on it, with all of the electronics mounted on it. The preamp in that one was a treble-bass job, and it was scary as I recall. Two channels, one for each pickup, that's why there's all those frickin' knobs and switches, and we put some LEDs on there to make it glow and do stupid things, that was the in thing back then, putting an LED in a guitar, made people go 'Ooohoooooo!'"[129]

Williams recalled that it was the position of the neck markings that was the issue: "The tree of life was originally designed so the leaf position marker would end up on D on the E string, not C sharp . . . . Now, I don't know how Frank missed it, the fact when he saw the guitar that it was that way, but he didn't

This murky Polaroid is one of the few known pictures of FZ with the guitar, taken at Performance Guitar in LA.
(Author's photo of polaroid courtesy of Kunio Sagai at performance guitars LA)

A Rex Bogue advertising card, with what appears to be the guitar that he built for FZ
(Rex Bogue website)

say anything about it. But when he got the guitar, he basically didn't like it because of that. And he ended up giving it back to Rex saying, 'Fix it.' And he [Bogue] was like 'Yeah, I'm gonna fix the fucking complex inlay and just botch it up!' "[130]

However, this seems at odds with FZ's statements that it was the overall lack of fingerboard dots that was the real problem. The UK *Guitar Player* interviewer continued by asked him if the slanted frets were an advantage, and FZ replied: "Well, I think they're good but the crawling vine is tough."[131] Williams told me: "to me it almost sounded like he was looking for something wrong with the guitar, he just had a bad attitude about it for some reason, I don't know what it was."[132]

At some point FZ took the guitar into Kunio Sugai's Performance Guitar shop in LA, where the Polaroid photo shown here was taken. Sugai remembers that they did some work on the guitar, but cannot recall exactly what was involved.[133] Although FZ doesn't look too unhappy with the instrument in the photograph, it obviously still didn't feel right, and eventually it was returned to Bogue's shop.

I asked Gail Zappa if she could recall anything about the guitar: "I remember that he built a guitar for Frank, which Frank absolutely rejected. I remember there was a big to-do because my recollection is, that in order to make good of it, he was going to do some other work, and this involved me having to go and pick up the Hendrix guitar that was in pieces."[134] FZ had always had a high opinion of Bogue's work (awarding him a special credit on the sleeve notes of the *Zappa in New York* album: "Rex Bogue – Guitar modifications"), but this marked the end of their professional relationship.

What happened next to the guitar is not known. The only other picture I have seen of the instrument is with the late Mike Gibbins (drummer with the band Badfinger) posing with it at an unknown Hard Rock Café with the words "Frank Zappa" written on the control panel. It is possible that the guitar was sold to the Hard Rock organization by Bogue himself; it was spotted in the Cayman Islands Hard Rock Café in 2013.

It is fairly certain that FZ never performed or recorded with the instrument. In 1982, when asked why he did not use custom guitars, he replied: "Well, I had one custom guitar built for me one time. And I didn't like it. And so, I'll never do it again."[135] Bogue died in 1996, aged only forty-five, from complications resulting from his diabetes, probably compounded by his lifelong enthusiasm for drinking rum. He left behind a small number of some of the most uniquely beautiful electric guitars ever built.

Vox Wah-Wah Guitar

"I got one real nice guitar in England; it's just a neck built onto a Vox wah-wah pedal for a body!"

— FZ[136]

During the European leg of the 1978 tour, FZ rented the big top of Circus Krone in Munich to rehearse and record a German TV program with his band. During the video FZ introduces band member Ike Willis as "Ike Willis on fake guitar." The "fake" guitar consisted of the neck and pickups from a UK-made Vox Phantom guitar, with the casing from a Vox wah-wah pedal as the body.

Willis remembers that FZ found the guitar in a secondhand shop in Germany.[137] Certainly FZ posed for a photograph with it in Munich, probably on the same day as the TV recording, as he is wearing the same clothes.

However, FZ's memory of it being purchased in England is borne out by Anthony Macari, who told me that FZ bought it from the famous Macari's music shop in London's Charing Cross Road, founded by his father Larry Macari. "I remember

Ike Willis playing the 'fake' guitar in Munich 1978
(still from *We Don't Mess Around*, 1980)

The guitar body as enhanced by Eddie Clothier
(photo provided by Thomas Nordegg)

Jennings Musical Instruments was the original company behind the Vox brand of amplifiers and instruments, founded by Tom Jennings in 1947, originally selling accordions and the early Univox electronic organ. Jennings hired guitar and electronics technician Denny in 1955, who designed the Vox AC 15 amplifier, which was subsequently developed into the legendary AC 30 amplifier.

By 1964, Vox had grown into a world-renowned brand, helped by the huge publicity from the Beatles' use of their amplifiers, but Jennings needed capital to increase production and he sold a controlling interest in the company to a holding company called the Royston Group.

A further deal giving US manufacturing rights to the Thomas Organ Company left Jennings and Denny sidelined; they were fired by Royston in 1967, and started a new company called Jennings Electronic Industries (JEI) at the old Vox plant in Dartford, Kent.[141]

The rear of the headstock showing Ibanez tuners
(photo provided by Thomas Nordegg)

it, because, as a kid, I wanted for myself! It was a really weird thing—the body was (if I remember rightly) three Strat-type pickups built into a Vox wah-wah case and then the neck stuck onto it!"[138]

The guitar was a concept prototype, probably produced in early 1967 by Vox lead engineer Dick Denny, who was photographed playing it, presumably at a trade show or exhibition as he is wearing an official blazer with a Vox badge on it.[139] Apart from the one FZ bought, only one other guitar is known to exist, which is in the collection of Strawbs guitarist Dave Lambert, who met Denny and discussed the guitar.

According to Lambert: "The pedals Vox were producing at that time were simply not doing very well. Dick was sitting one day with the body of a wah-wah in his hands trying to think of new ideas; his eyes were drawn to a guitar neck lying near his bench and he quite simply put the two components together for the heck of it."[140]

The 21-fret maple neck has a rosewood fingerboard and a zero fret, terminating in a natural finish "paddle" shaped headstock. The two pickups are Stratocaster-style single-coil units, known to have a fairly low output, and the original controls consist of master volume, bass, and treble, plus a pickup selector switch, placed along the top edge of the body. The strings pass over an adjustable bridge similar to a Gibson Tune-o-matic, terminating in a simple folded steel tailpiece.

In 1971, magazine adverts appeared introducing the Rifle range: two guitars and a bass, which featured built-in special effects and vaguely gunstock-shaped bodies, obviously inspired by the original wah-wah guitar.[142] These and the other JEI products did not prove to be successful—apparently only twelve rifle guitars were ever made, and the company went out of business in 1973. Some people (including Lambert) have confused the 1967 Vox prototype with the 1971 JEI Winchester model. However, they are not the same, and even rarer. Lambert's guitar may be the only one in the world in original condition.

In 1979, the guitar passed into the possession of guitarist Warren Cuccurullo, who had joined FZ's touring band and also contributed some guitar and vocals for the *Joe's Garage* album. Cuccurullo told *Guitar Player* magazine that Zappa presented him with it as part payment for his work on the album.

He had FZ's guitar tech Eddie Clothier add onboard active electronics, an LED power indicator, an overdrive unit, and various additional controls. The original tuners have been replaced with Ibanez star tuners, and a brass nut and a string clamp have been added. The neck has the serial number 76607 stamped on the back of the headstock. Cuccurullo said: "It's tiny and neck-heavy, but I love it. It has a great sound that's similar to a Fuzz Face."[143]

> **Hear it on:**
> There is no record of FZ ever playing this; it seems he bought it as a novelty. However, clips and recordings of the German TV broadcast are in fairly wide circulation if you want to see Ike Willis playing it. You can also see Cuccurullo playing it with his band Missing Persons in the video for their "Words" single.

The Baby Snakes SG

"This guy came to the dressing room after the show with this guitar he'd built and wanted to sell."

—FZ[144]

"This guitar" was the *Baby Snakes* customized Gibson SG (so called as it was featured in the film of the same name); it was to be FZ's number one guitar from 1975 through to the early 1980s.

"This guy" was actually Bart Nagel, an apprentice luthier working at the Juan Roberto guitar-making workshop (later to become the Roberto-Venn School of Luthiery) in Phoenix, Arizona. John Roberts (aka Juan Roberto) had been a lumberman in South America and on retirement had transported hundreds of board feet of exotic woods to his home in Arizona. These woods turned out to be perfect for guitar making: rosewood, mahogany, and ebony. Nagel remembers that the rosewoods in particular were highly figured.

The Baby Snakes SG in 2012 at the UMRK
(Mick Ekers)

As Nagel tells it, someone brought in a fire-damaged Gibson SG (probably a 1972 SG Standard). The neck was beyond repair but the body was still basically sound; and he decided to refinish the body and build a new neck from scratch.[145] He covered the front and back of the original plain walnut body with

ZAPPA GEAR

FZ with the SG in 1977 at Stamford University Palo Alto
(Eric Peterson)

Nagel's intricate mother of pearl 12th fret marker
(Mick Ekers)

The headstock with inlaid silver Gibson logo, note the star above the 'i'
(Mick Ekers)

The bridge pickup, note the worn bobbin
(Mick Ekers)

a handsome book-matched rosewood sheet inlay, and where there were voids in the rosewood he inlaid some ebony motifs, also putting a small rosewood inlay on the back.

He made a new three-piece neck with 23 frets (regular Gibson necks have 22) from two pieces of mahogany on either side of a rosewood center strip, which also provided the location for the truss rod. The neck features an ebony fingerboard with mother of pearl inlays, a star at the fifth fret, and an ornate design at the twelfth, the other fret markers being single dots. The white fingerboard binding has black dot fret markers.

Nagel says that the neck is "closer to a Les Paul neck in thickness, partly because I wanted to get up to that 23rd fret safely." The headstock has an inlaid Gibson logo cut from a sheet of silver; the "I" is dotted with a star, "so you'd know it was a special guitar".[146]

The neck was certainly to FZ's taste: "I like the neck that I used to have on the SG because it was a twenty-three-fret neck. And the fret spacing was more comfortable for my hand."[147] He later specified a similar fast, flat profile for the necks that Performance Guitar built for his Stratocasters.

The pickups and electronics included were stock Gibson, apart from the pickup selector switch, which was a tiny sculpted silver hand holding a clear glass ball; a switch for putting the pickups out of phase was also added. The tuners were gold-plated Schaller units, and the bridge and tailpiece were the original Gibson items.

Nagel first offered the guitar to Steve Howe of Yes, but he was more interested in hollowbody electrics. (He later sold Howe a Gibson ES-175 that he had refurbished, and went on to make him an electric lute.) A huge Zappa fan, Nagel decided to try the same trick he had used to meet Steve Howe. On the

17th of July, 1974, he waited by the stage door of the Celebrity Theatre in Phoenix around sound check time to see if he could get FZ's attention when he showed up.[148]

As Nagel told me: "It worked: he looked at the guitar in the case and quickly invited us inside. He messed around on it for a bit and decided to buy it and asked me to meet him at the hotel for breakfast in the morning and he'd give me cash." Bart remembers FZ giving him $600 the next day when he came back to meet him at his hotel.[149]

FZ said he got a slightly better bargain: "But one time we were working down in Phoenix, and this guy came to the dressing room after the show with this guitar he'd built and wanted to sell. He had copied a Gibson (SG) except he'd added one more fret so it went up to an E (FZ meant Eb), and it had an ebony fingerboard, humbucking pickups, and some inlay, and some real nice woodwork on it. He wanted $500 for it, and I thought it was a real nice guitar, so I bought it. I had (guitar maker) Rex Bogue do some stuff to it, add a preamp and snazz it up, and that's the one I'm using now . . . . "[150]

Bogue certainly snazzed it up. The original electronics were removed and replaced with 12-volt preamps; active bass and treble controls, each with a frequency range switch; pickup splitters to change each pickup from humbucking to single coil; and a phase change switch.

The circuit from a Dan Armstrong Green Ringer effects unit was also built in, with a separate on-off switch (more about this in the Green Ringer section of this book). Nagel met FZ again some years later in 1980, a suitably serious occasion that was photographed for posterity!

Some time later FZ had the pickups changed: "And on my SG I have a DiMarzio and an EMG. The EMG is wired up in a way they were never intended to be used; normally they're a real clean, clear pickup but if you hook them up the wrong way . . . . "[151] The "harmonica" bridge was replaced with a Tune-o-matic unit.

The Baby Snakes is one of the definitive top five guitars of FZ's career, and like his Hendrix Strat it was born of fire and its origins were originally shrouded in mystery. Even FZ seemed unaware that it was built around a genuine Gibson body; it is credited on the liner notes of the *Shut Up 'n Play Yer Guitar* album as just a "handmade copy SG."

Gibson were talking with DZ a few years ago about using this guitar as the basis for a signature Zappa SG, but in the end they decided the electronics and finish would be too complicated to replicate and they chose the Roxy SG as a more suitable candidate. The Baby Snakes SG remains (quite rightly) a unique instrument, and is still in the possession of the Zappa family.

Back of the guitar, note the three-part neck
(Mick Ekers)

The body of the Baby Snakes SG, showing all the typical signs of a much-used instrument
(Mick Ekers)

ZAPPA GEAR

The guitar is in what could be described as well loved condition, being fairly well covered with scratches and minor dings. It has a severe case of belt-buckle rash on the back, and you can even see that one of the pickup bobbins has been worn from repeated contact with a plectrum. However, it is still in good working order. No one knows what happened to the sculpted-hand selector switch, but DZ confirms that it still has the Green Ringer circuit inside.[152]

Bart Nagel is now a successful photographer with an established studio in San Francisco; he should be very proud of having created such an historic guitar.

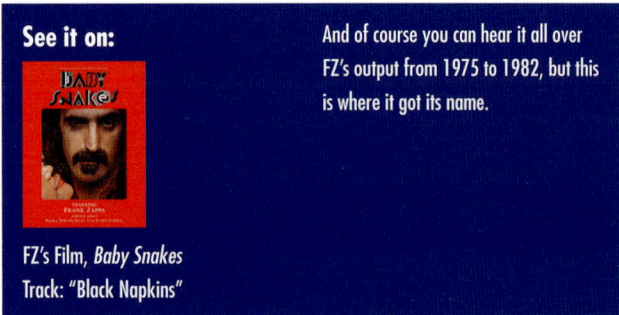

See it on:

And of course you can hear it all over FZ's output from 1975 to 1982, but this is where it got its name.

FZ's Film, *Baby Snakes*
Track: "Black Napkins"

FZ with the Baby Snakes SG in 1980
(Bart Nagel)

Les Paul Custom

"Most of the time I play a Les Paul Custom, with a lot of gadgets in it"
— FZ[153]

FZ bought his cherry sunburst Gibson Les Paul Custom guitar some time in 1979, probably from the Guitar Center store in LA: "It was a brand-new guitar when I bought it. It's not a vintage thing. It was a very well-made production-line Gibson Les Paul right off the rack."[154] The serial number 73197139 indicates that it was made at Gibson's Kalamazoo Plant in November 1977.[155]

The Les Paul Custom was introduced as the deluxe version of the standard Les Paul in 1954, tricked out with block pearl inlays on the ebony neck, striking seven-layer white and black binding on the body, and a bold split-diamond pattern mother-of-pearl inlay on the headstock.

It was the first Gibson to feature the new ABR-1 Tune-o-matic adjustable bridge, and it was fitted with very low flat fretwire, and advertised as the "fretless wonder." The slightly thicker body was all mahogany, which gave it a slightly mellower tone than the Goldtop.[156]

In 1957, the original twin P90 pickups were replaced with three of the new Gibson humbuckers. Although the Custom caused a brief uplift in the falling Les Paul sales figures, it was not enough. As I have mentioned earlier, Gibson discontinued all the Les Paul guitars in 1960, and replaced them with the new SG models.[157]

However, guitarist Eric Clapton kicked off a revival in the Les Paul's popularity, when he used one to great effect through an overdriven Marshall amplifier on the groundbreaking John Mayall album *Blues Breakers with Eric Clapton* in 1966. American guitarist Mike Bloomfield followed suit, using one with the Paul Butterfield band on *East West*, and soon more and more guitarists discovered what a wonderful noise they made when overdriving a tube amplifier. The Les Paul became the guitar to have in rock circles, demand for the old instruments rocketed, and they started changing hands for thousands of dollars.[158]

Meanwhile in 1967, sales of Gibson guitars had started to fall again. Les Paul renewed his association with the company, and the management took the obvious step of reintroducing the Les Paul range in June 1968. The first two models were the Goldtop Les Paul, and the less well-known twin pickup version of the Les Paul Custom. This was a good choice, as most guitarists preferred it to the three-pickup layout as it was easier to play, and the guitar has stayed in production ever since.[159]

When FZ bought his he had it "hopped up" by John Caruthers. The stock Gibson humbuckers were replaced with two cream-colored DiMarzio pickups and new active electronics were installed, as evidenced by an additional black knob that appeared in the middle of the stock Gibson knobs, next to a small toggle switch. A brass nut was also fitted. In all other respects the guitar appeared unchanged from its original condition. FZ took it on the road on his European tour in the summer of 1980, and appeared with it on the cover of the US Crush All Boxes autumn tour program.

The Les Paul complementing the color scheme of the Fall Tour 80 brochure
(Scan from authors collection — Copyright ZFT)

1982 *Guitar World* cover, the guitar has been fitted with Carvin and Dan Armstrong pickups
(Scan from author's collection)

The guitar went through some further changes during 1981, and FZ can be seen playing the revised version in the *Torture Never Stops* movie recorded on Halloween that year. The control knobs have been replaced with five gold-plated domed head ones, and a set of new tuners with pearl buttons are in place of the original Gibson tuners. The DiMarzio pickups are gone and there is a Carvin M22 (as described in the Hendrix Strat section) in the bridge position, and a black humbucker at the neck.

FZ made his first appearance on the cover of *Guitar Player* magazine in March 1982, and he talked at length about the Les Paul: "The Les Paul has a preamp and it has two different kinds of pickups, and it has a Dan Armstrong pickup in the neck position and it has a Carvin pickup in the bridge position. It has a Dan Armstrong gizmo called the Green Ringer built into it, which I can dial in. It also has an EQ circuit which in one position gives you about an 8 db boost at 8k and the other position gives you an 8 db boost at 500 cycles, so you can either go from a bright sound to a more midrangey wah-wah kind of sound, all built into the guitar.

And then it has a pickup selector switch that has nine positions. It changes the wiring between the pickups in a lot of different ways, so it's got a lot of tonal variation. I can make it sound just like a Telecaster if I want . . . . And then there's a little toggle

FZ's Les Paul Custom in 2012 at the UMRK
(Mick Ekers)

ZAPPA GEAR

The ornate headstock showing the 'split diamond' inlay
(Mick Ekers)

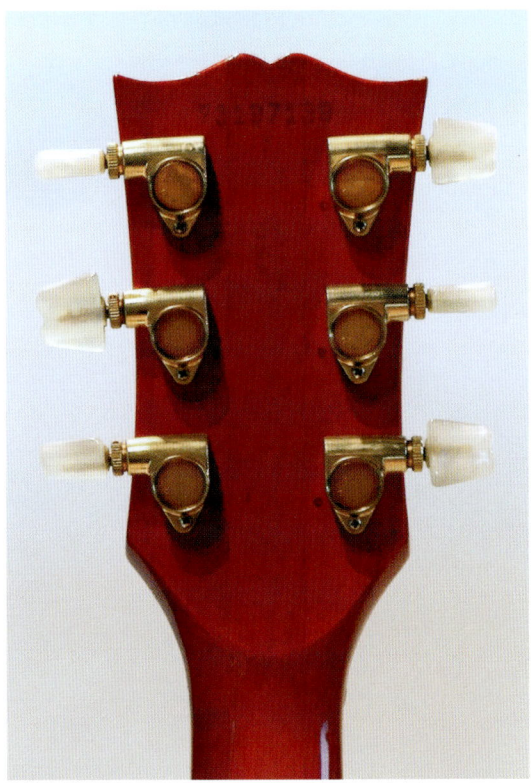

Rear of the headstock showing the replacement tuners, they are probably Ibanez
(Mick Ekers)

switch on it that goes from series to parallel on the pickups and depending on where the pickup selector switch is set that gives you yet another whole series of variations. And so, I have eighteen times three different tone selections on that guitar."[160]

Later that year the *Shut Up 'n Play Yer Guitar* box set was released, with FZ sitting at his Bösendorfer piano holding the Les Paul on the front. A picture from the same session was used on the cover of *The Frank Zappa Guitar Book*, of transcriptions of his solos by Steve Vai.

I talked to Dweezil Zappa about the guitar and he described the multi-position switch as: "a rotary of weird midrange stuff, like it's a wah-wah in a rotary so you can just choose which notch-frequency that you want." He wasn't sure what make the current pickups were. "He might have even at one point had EMGs in there . . . he switched the pickups in that guitar a lot." I asked about the Green Ringer: "Yeah, it might have been in the Les Paul at one time but it's not now."[161]

FZ had mixed feelings about the neck on the guitar: "The Les Paul, even though it has a thicker neck, for some reason you can play certain passages on it three or four times faster than you can on the Strat. But then again, you can't get the same type of sustain or vibrato, and you can't play those weird glissandos on the Les Paul. So, it just depends on what you want to say on the instrument. The Les Paul has more 200 cycles [bottom end] to it, so it's got a meatier sound."[162]

When asked what made the Les Paul unique among his guitars, he had this to say: "It's the sustain more than anything else.

You get a very warm sound and it also depends on how I have my amp set. But you can make notes ring for weeks on end on that thing. And there is no compression on it. It just sustains until you want to go home . . . Although the neck isn't as fast as the SG, it really slows me down, it's more cumbersome."[163]

For a couple of years in the early 1980s the Custom was FZ's main performing guitar, but then he started to favor his custom Stratocasters and it became rarely seen on stage. The guitar now looks little changed from the touring days. Although the back has some moderate buckle rash, the front of the body and neck are in excellent shape, and it still remains (in my opinion) FZ's most photogenic guitar. It now sports a matching pair of black humbuckers, probably DiMarzio Dual Sounds.

We found some scribbled notes on a loose piece of paper in the guitar case, including a diagram that shows how the controls are laid out. The electronics may have been simplified somewhat, the Green Ringer is no longer fitted and according to the notes the rotary control is now a six-position switch. The note also states "Parametrics set to really tight Q. Can adjust Q on board."

The guitar has a three-pin XLR socket next to the regular jack socket. It was good to discover no additional cut outs or other surgery in the back, with just the standard black covers for the control and pickup switch cavities present. The tuners look like they may be from an Ibanez Artist series guitar, but they have no name or markings.

DZ told me that Gibson had been discussing making a replica of the *Shut Up 'n Play Yer Guitar* Les Paul as well as the

Guitars

The pleasingly slightly worn but otherwise un-mutilated back of the guitar
(Mick Ekers)

The *Shut Up 'n Play Yer Guitar* Les Paul Custom at the UMRK in 2012
(Mick Ekers)

Roxy SG.[164] At the time of going to press the Roxy SG tribute guitar had just been released, but I suspect it may be some time before we ever see a Zappa tribute Les Paul Custom on sale. For now at least, this beautiful instrument, like most of the FZ guitars, remains unique.

The Frank Zappa Guitar Book cover, note the brass nut
(Scan from authors collection — Copyright ZFT)

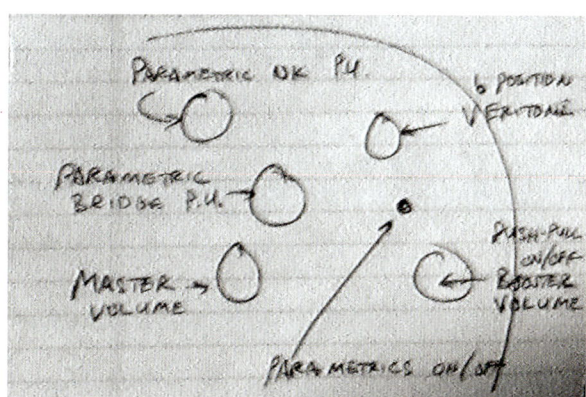

It's just as well someone took some notes, as there are no markings on the controls
(Mick Ekers)

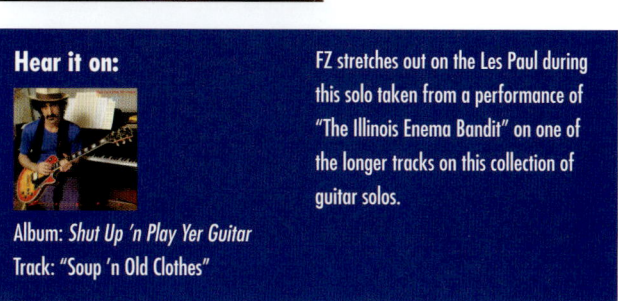

Hear it on: FZ stretches out on the Les Paul during this solo taken from a performance of "The Illinois Enema Bandit" on one of the longer tracks on this collection of guitar solos.

Album: *Shut Up 'n Play Yer Guitar*
Track: "Soup 'n Old Clothes"

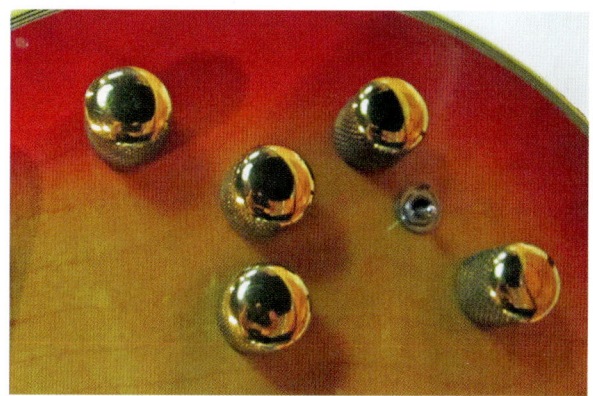

41

Bouzouki

"I'm playing the bouzouki, which is a Greek mandolin, and he's playing the baritone violin and it's really nice."

—*FZ*[165]

FZ was referring above to a session where he recorded some duets with violinist Jean-Luc Ponty in 1973. He went on to describe the instrument: "A bouzouki has a very long neck and it's tuned not like a violin, the way a mandolin is, but the same as the top four strings of a guitar down a whole step."[166]

The *Encyclopedia Britannica* entry for the bouzouki reads: "Long-necked lute used in Greek popular music. Developed from a Turkish instrument early in the twentieth century, it has a pear-shaped body and a fretted fingerboard. The modern instrument usually has four courses of strings, which are plucked with a plectrum, typically in a vigorous and agile style."[167]

I have been unable to find out much more about FZ's bouzouki except that at some time he had it fitted with a Barcus Berry pickup, as he remarked in 1977: "I also have an Ovation and a bouzouki with a Barcus on it. I've recorded some stuff with that, but it hasn't been released yet."[168]

One of the duets finally appeared on the *Shut Up 'n Play Yer Guitar* album. The only picture I have found of it is in a detail from Linda McCartney's well-known photograph of FZ in his office.[169]

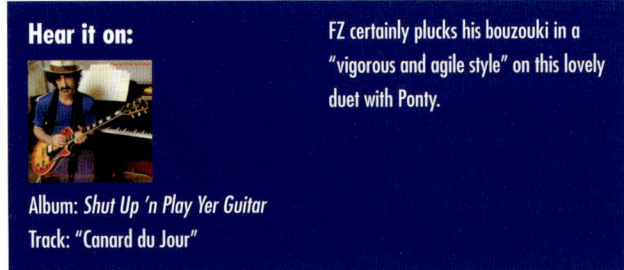

Hear it on:
FZ certainly plucks his bouzouki in a "vigorous and agile style" on this lovely duet with Ponty.

Album: *Shut Up 'n Play Yer Guitar*
Track: "Canard du Jour"

D'Mini Guitars

"You can't believe the noises that come out of that thing"

—*FZ*[170]

D'Mini guitars were a range of small guitars made in the early 1980s by a Hollywood-based company called Phased Systems, who produced a number of scaled-down versions of popular electric guitars. In 1982 the range included the 2/3-size Series II Explore, Flying Ve, Les Paule, and Strate models, and the 3/4-size Series III range, which were available with one or two pickups and adjustable bridges.

The names were subtly altered to avoid legal issues with Gibson and Fender, of course. They also produced a 3/4-size version of the Fender Precision bass. Bodies were of ash or mahogany, the mahogany necks had optional rosewood or ebony fingerboards, hardware was by Gotoh, and they used specially designed pickups.[171]

FZ appeared on the front cover of the February 1983 *Guitar Player* magazine clutching a Series III red Strat (we'll take the additional "e" as read from now on; sadly, Phased Systems are long since beyond the risk of legal action). He is also pictured inside with a 2/3-size Les Paul model. The necks had a normal profile, but the scale was shortened by approximately the same factor to 16 3/4" for the Les Paul (with 17 frets), and around 19" for the Strat with 21 frets.

In the interview, FZ speaks at length about his D'Mini guitars; he had two Les Pauls and one Strat, with another Strat on order with a deeper body to allow the fitting of a locking

FZ with the red D'Mini Strat
(Scan from author's collection)

The 'St Etienne' sunburst D'Mini Strat
(Mick Ekers)

The D'Mini Les Paul, somewhat dwarfed by the guitar stand
(Mick Ekers)

vibrato unit. He had the Les Pauls tuned up to A, and the Strat to F#. No expense was spared on the strings: the Strat was fitted with Gold Maxima strings, the Les Pauls with Teflon-coated Black Maxima strings and platinum-plated unwound strings. FZ said the Strat was fitted with Seymour Duncan pickups, and most likely so were the Les Pauls.

The Red Strat had obviously already endured some serious usage on the road, as FZ remarks that one of the parametrics had failed and had been replaced by a silver plug. Dweezil Zappa told us that this guitar was in pieces somewhere in the house, and we didn't get to see it. Both Les Pauls were also in the hands of the Zappa family, but only one was available to photograph.

All the guitars had custom electronics installed by Midget Sloatman (FZ also credits Eddie Clothier and David Robb with some of the work). The stock controls on the Red Strat were replaced with a pair of dual-concentric parametric EQ controls, with an additional mini toggle switch to select between the two. A master volume was installed below the neck pickup; the three-way pickup selector was stock.

FZ had similar parametric EQ controls fitted to most of his later guitars. He used them to tune the feedback characteristics of his guitars and to optimize them for the specific acoustic environment of each show. Being able to switch between two presets would have allowed FZ even more control while playing.

The Les Paul I saw at the UMRK was similarly modified, with a master volume, a pickup selector, what I assume is a concentric high frequency boost/cut and frequency control (based on similar circuits on his other guitars), and another knob which is possibly a pickup blend. (I wasn't in a position to try it out!)

The control cavity cover was missing, exposing the twin 9-volt batteries, but the details of the circuitry were not visible under the mass of wiring and insulating tape. The original tuners have been replaced with Schaller-style tuners. The mahogany body is finished with a beautiful bright sunburst closely matching FZ's full-size *Shut Up 'n Play Yer Guitar* Les Paul. The ebony fingerboard appears to have been varnished, and there are two cream humbucker pickups.

The second Strat that FZ mentioned as being on order in the *Guitar Player* interview is also still at the URMK, with a handsome sunburst finish and black pickguard. The neck is maple, and there are two unnamed black Stratocaster-type pickups, presumably Seymour Duncans, as FZ had fitted to the other Strat. The guitar appears to have the same electronic circuitry as the Les Paul, with a three-way Fender-style pickup selector switch.

The Strat showing the large cover for the vibrato unit
(Mick Ekers)

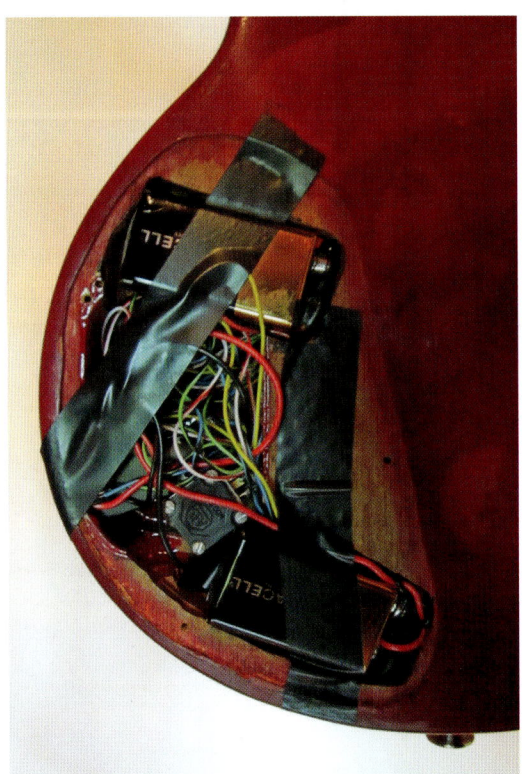

The crowded control cavity of the Les Paul
(Mick Ekers)

A suitably tiny D'Mini advert

The tuners look like stock Gotoh units, and the guitar has been fitted with an early model Floyd Rose vibrato unit and locking nut. On the back of the guitar is a white plastic cover for the vibrato cavity, which looks like a standard Fender item offset to fit the 3/4-size body, and a small black cover for the battery compartment.

During the 1982 tour FZ played both the Strats and at least one of the Les Pauls. FZ was fulsome in his praise of these tiny guitars: "The D'Mini Strat that I have is unbelievable; you can't believe the noises that come out of that thing. It's ridiculous."[172] In passing, he also noted that the light weight of these was an important comfort factor when playing live. FZ can be seen playing the sunburst Strat with the Floyd Rose on "St. Etienne," in the *Video from Hell* video.

In the light of all this great publicity, Phased Systems were obviously powerless to resist the pressure from the *Guitar Player* advertising sales team and splashed out on a tiny 1/6-page black and white advert in the magazine, not even placed anywhere near the article.

As well as FZ, the advert name-checks legendary session musician Carol Kaye, who played 12-string guitar on the *Freak Out!* and *Absolutely Free* albums. Carol used one while recovering from a serious accident, and recalls "I used the D'Mini because it was the best-made little easily played instrument that got good bass sounds (I experimented with strings for the low E and finally hit upon the right ballsy sound) and was easy to play."[173]

However, FZ would later refer to one of the Strats in less than glowing terms in the notes to *You Can't Do That on Stage Anymore, Vol. 3*: "The 1982 solo from Dijon is played on a customized mini-guitar tuned to F#. It had a nasty sound and absolutely refused to stay in tune. Throughout the '82 tour I struggled to get something useful out of it during the solo sections in 'King Kong.' I got close twice. The solo included here is the more deranged of the two."[174]

The red Strat as sold in 2016
(ZFT)

Nonetheless, it is obvious that FZ had a lot of time for these attractive little guitars and the solo mentioned above has a very distinctive sound, quite unlike almost any other recorded solo on the official CDs. Perhaps because of the higher pitch of the instrument the structure of the solo is also somewhat atypical (or "deranged," as FZ puts it).

Anyone fortunate enough to come across one of these great little guitars will recognize that it is a serious musical instrument; not a children's toy like most similar guitars made today. There is an historic precedent for such instruments: as well as the half-size apprentice pieces produced by many traditional Spanish guitar makers, Les Paul himself once had a similar scaled-down guitar made for Mary Ford. Phased Systems were honorable (if short-lived) upholders of this tradition.

The red Strat, minus all the electronics, was sold in the 2016 auction, fetching $4,800, as was the Les Paul shown here, which sold for $15,000.[175]

Hear it on:
The D'Mini comes in at around 18 minutes into the track, but best to take your time and listen to it all.

Album: *You Can't Do That on Stage Anymore, Vol. 3*
Track: "King Kong"

The D'Mini logo
(Mick Ekers)

The D'Mini Les Paul, almost life size
(Mick Ekers)

ZAPPA GEAR

Coral Electric Sitar

"I have a Coral sitar which has been modified"

—FZ[176]

The Coral Electric Sitar was arguably the coolest instrument ever produced by the Danelectro company. Launched at the Chicago Music Show in May 1967, under the company's up-market Coral brand name, it sold for $295, the most expensive instrument in their range.[177] For a couple of years it sold fairly well on the back of the raga rock craze inspired by the Beatles; customers included Jimi Hendrix, who had a unique left-handed model made for him.[178]

Nathan "Nat" Daniel was born in New York City in 1912, the son of Lithuanian immigrants escaping the Tsarist Russian Empire. As a teenager he developed a keen interest in radio and electronics, leaving college to start manufacturing amplifiers as Daniel Electrical Laboratories in lower Manhattan, and soon became the exclusive amplifier supplier to Epiphone guitars.

During World War II, Daniel worked as a designer for the US Army Signal Corps, and when he reopened his amplifier business, at new premises in Red Bank, New Jersey, he renamed it the Danelectro Corporation. After a year or so, he had won contracts to make Silvertone and Airline brand amplifiers for the giant retail chains Sears Roebuck and Montgomery Ward.

1967 advert for the sitar (dated in so many different ways!)

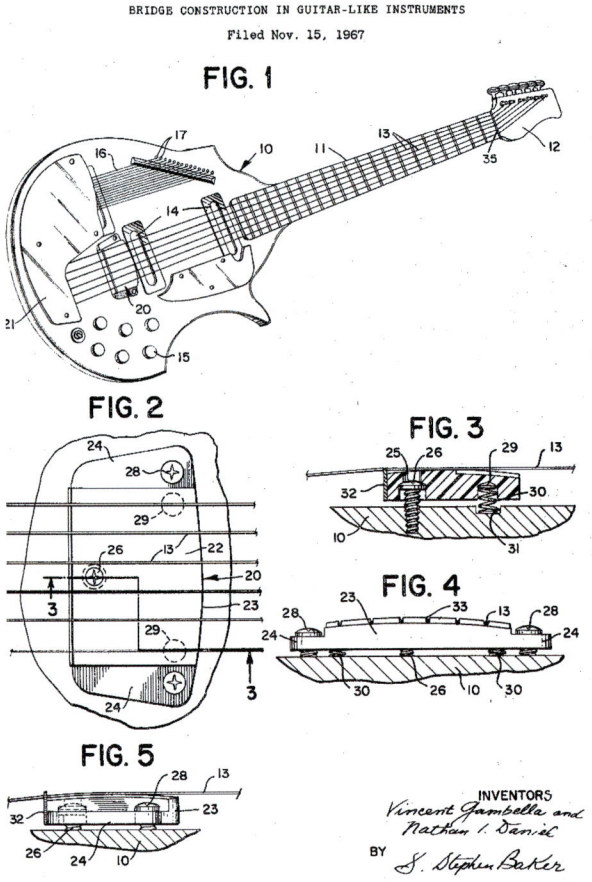

Drawings from Bell and Daniel's 1967 patent
(Public Domain)

In 1954, Danelectro started making electric guitars, and from the start Daniel's mission was to produce instruments a beginner could afford, but of a quality that wouldn't discourage them from progressing on the instrument. To this aim he developed some manufacturing innovations which enabled the retail price of "Dano" guitars to start as low as $69. Bodies were made of a Masonite shell on a pine frame, necks had fixed non-adjustable truss rods, and bridges were simple metal plates with movable rosewood bridge saddles.

Daniel's most celebrated invention was possibly the "lipstick tube" guitar pickup, an all-purpose design that was used on almost every Danelectro instrument. The pickup consisted of a single coil wrapped directly around an Alnico bar magnet; the whole was then wrapped with insulating tape and inserted into the two halves of the tubular chromed lipstick tube pickup cover. As well as being the lowest-cost guitar pickup in the industry, they had a unique tone that gave the Danelectro guitars a sound all of their own; they also looked cool and gave the guitars a distinctive branding.[179]

The electric sitar was the brainchild of session guitarist Vincent "Vinnie" Bell (born Vincent Gambella), who came up with the idea while thinking of the practical difficulties of

Guitars

transporting and recording the regular Indian sitar that he was using. Bell produced a couple of prototypes and worked on the design with Daniel, and both their names appear on the patent.[180]

The advertisements for the guitar featured Bell wearing a turban, accompanied by the slogan, "You don't have to be Hindu to play the Coral Electric Sitar." A colorful character who played with almost all of the big names in the music industry, Bell claims that once he was working on an early Mothers of Invention recording, and because he was the only conservatively dressed musician in the studio, FZ told him to take his shirt off during the session.[181]

Unlike most of the Coral range, which had poplar bodies made in Korea, the Sitar had typical Danelectro Masonite and pine construction. The body was a teardrop shape with two asymmetric horns and a lower cutout, finished in a striking crinkled Bombay Red paint finish.

Bell said this came about by accident when he sprayed a second coat of lacquer on one of the early models before the first coat had dried.[182] As well as the six standard guitar playing strings, it had thirteen short drone strings mounted on the top half of the body, which were intended to vibrate in sympathy with strings.

There were two lipstick tube pickups for the play strings and a third for the drones, each of which had a separate volume and tone control. The 21-fret neck had a rosewood fingerboard with white plastic fret markers, "never warp" fixed truss rods, and an Action Adjustment neck tilt adjusting screw.

Tuners were Kluson Deluxe for the main strings, and piano-style friction pegs for the drone strings; a special tuning wrench for these was supplied with the instrument. The guitar was finished off with a clear plastic cover over one end of the drone strings, designed to stop the player accidentally muting

The Coral Sitar, still with Steve Vai's strap attachment
(Mick Ekers)

THE FIRST ELECTRIC SITAR is shown here by Nathan I. Daniel, president of Danelectro Corp. which is introducing the instrument, and Magnus Hendell, director of marketing. It will be displayed at the Chicago Music Show.

Nat Daniel promoting the sitar in 1967
(scan from private collection)

47

ZAPPA GEAR

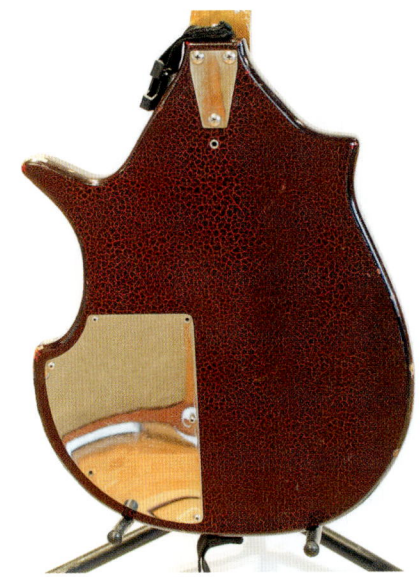

Rear view of the sitar showing the typical Rex Bogue metal control cavity cover and neck plate
(Mick Ekers)

The somewhat dusty Coral Sitar in 2012, at the UMRK
(Mick Ekers)

them, and a pickguard bearing the legend "Vincent Bell signature design electric sitar."

The drone strings were not particularly effective; it was the patented SitarMatic bridge that produced the sitar-like sound. The bridge consisted of a slightly curved rosewood plate, which could be adjusted so that the strings buzzed against it, resulting in a sitar tone. Although surprisingly effective, it tended to make the guitar hard to tune, and chords were particularly difficult to intonate.

FZ got the sitar in 1978–1979, perhaps specifically for the *Joe's Garage* album: "The only time I go shopping is if I need a special sound. I got that Coral electric sitar that's used throughout Joe's Garage. Actually, Denny Walley found it for me."[183]

At some point FZ gave the instrument to Rex Bogue to modify. Bogue replaced the stock tuners with Ibanez units, and added a drilled brass string guide to the headstock. A new chromed-brass cover was fitted at the back over the control cavity, and a replacement chromed neck plate was also installed. This was shorter than the original, leaving the hole for the neck-tilt adjusting screw uncovered. Three battery-powered preamps were fitted, each with individually toggle switches. The control panel also had a master on-off/bypass switch for the active circuitry, with a yellow LED indicator.

I have been unable to find any pictures or recordings of FZ playing the Coral himself; he generally got his "stunt" guitarists Steve Vai or Warren Cuccurullo to use it, to add color to particular tracks.

FZ lent the guitar to Vai in the mid-1980s, who used it during his time with the band Alcatrazz. Vai's guitar tech of the time, Elwood Francis, remembers that, "in typical Frank fashion, there were little switches that did various things. I honestly do not remember what they controlled. I do remember that they all had to be off in order for Steve to use it."[184]

Vai returned the guitar to the Zappa family some years after FZ died. The active electronics do not work anymore, and the body is somewhat road-worn, with a crack and a missing piece noticeable on the plastic tailpiece guard, but it is still in playable condition. Vai's preferred DiMarzio ClipLock strap fittings are still attached.

During our photo session at the UMRK, Zappa Plays Zappa bass player and the then–ZFT "Scoremeister" Kurt Morgan picked the sitar out of its case and idly started playing the introduction to "Outside Now"; even unamplified, the distinctive tone was so evocative of the original recording that everyone in the room stopped in their tracks.

The original Coral sitar ceased production in 1969, when MCA, who had bought Danelectro in 1966, closed down the company. Later in the 1980s, Nashville guitar maker Jerry Jones produced a technically improved version, but Jones retired and sold his factory in April 2011,[185] making the copies potentially just as hard to come by as the originals.

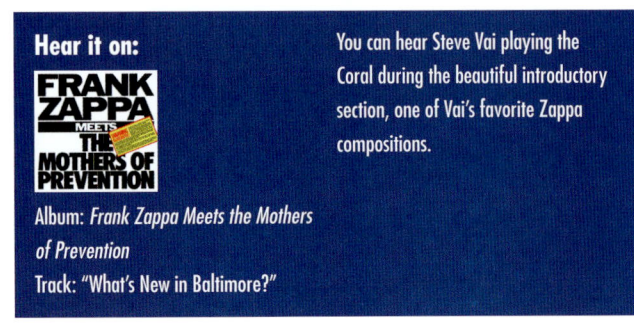

Hear it on: You can hear Steve Vai playing the Coral during the beautiful introductory section, one of Vai's favorite Zappa compositions.

Album: *Frank Zappa Meets the Mothers of Prevention*
Track: "What's New in Baltimore?"

Rickenbacker 360 12-String

"I've also got a Rickenbacker 12-string and a Fender 12-string, both of which are a little tweezed."

— FZ[186]

Although he was sometimes disdainful of the instrument ("folk-rock 12-string swill" was one expression he used)[187], FZ had a few 12-string guitars, although he rarely recorded with them. In 1966 he owned a natural finish solidbody Rickenbacker 350 12-string. He attempted to teach Gail to play guitar on it. (Not the easiest instrument for a beginner to learn on!) This guitar was stolen by a guest staying at his Laurel Canyon house.[188]

FZ later got a semi-acoustic sunburst Rickenbacker 360-12, which makes a tantalizing appearance in the *Baby Snakes* movie. You can see it on a stand at the beginning of "Jones Crusher," but I have been unable to find any pictures of him playing it.

The Rickenbacker company was originally formed in LA in 1931 by Adolph Rickenbacker, Paul Barth, and George Beauchamp, who invented the famous "frying pan" electric steel guitar—the first modern electric guitar.[189] The frying pan was so-called because that was just what it looked like, with a small round cast-aluminum body, and it featured what was probably the first successful electric guitar pickup, with two large horseshoe magnets wrapped round the pickup coil and strings. The company prospered, mainly selling lap steel guitars, until 1953, when Rickenbacker retired and sold the firm to Fender distributor Francis Cary Hall.

Hall recruited Roger Rossmeisl from Gibson as head designer, and the two of them revamped the company, introducing the stylish semi-acoustic 360 model with a bold "slash" soundhole, two "toaster" pickups, and a bright sunburst finish.

Acoustic 12-string guitars were popular with folk singers in the early 1960s, and Hall saw a market for an electric version. In 1963, they built the first prototype 12-string versions of the 360. Designer Paul Burke cleverly avoided the oversize headstocks resorted to by some manufacturers, adding a set of six additional tuners set at right angles to the main ones, with the tuning barrels accessible by two slots cut into the headstock like a Spanish guitar. The Rickenbacker company, still privately owned, continues to make 360-12s unchanged from the original design.

When I met Dweezil at his studio in January 2012, he thought that the Rickenbacker was still at the Zappa house, but when we visited the UMRK it was not available to photograph. DZ remembered "It never stayed in tune; I tried playing it a couple of times."[190]

The 360 was indeed still in the possession of the ZFT and appeared in the 2016 auction. FZ's Rickenbacker 360 was a 1966 model, serial number FD 1433[191], with stock Rickenbacker pickups. From the auction photograph there are no obvious signs of extra controls or switches, so it is hard to tell in what way it had been tweezed; possibly it had some active electronics installed. Most of the adjustable bridge saddles are at the extreme of their range, which does indicate that there may have been intonation problems with the guitar. It sold in the 2016 auction for $16,000[192].

The 360 12-string making a cameo appearance in Baby Snakes
(still from Baby Snakes, *1979)*

FZ's Rickenbacker 360 as it went for auction, looking in very good condition
(ZFT)

ZAPPA GEAR

Fender Electric XII

"I've got a Fender 12-string that I've only had a chance to play in concert once. I put heavy-gauge strings on it and tune it weird ways."
— FZ[193]

For those of you who might not know, the 12-string guitar has its strings grouped in pairs, or "courses." Usually the guitar is tuned like a conventional 6-string guitar: the top two or three pairs are each tuned to the same note, but the bottom courses consist of a normal guitar string and a thinner string tuned an octave higher. As you will see, FZ had some other ideas about this. The Fender 12-string electric guitar was introduced in 1965, in a somewhat belated attempt to compete with the hugely successful Rickenbacker. The Fender Electric XII, as it was called, was immediately recognizable by the bizarrely shaped headstock, which became known for obvious reasons as "the hockey stick."

Unlike most other models of the time, Leo Fender designed a purpose-built instrument, not just a 6-string with a 12-string neck. The guitar had an offset-waist body, similar to the Jaguar and Jazzmaster, and two unique split pickups in plain black plastic casings. Controls consisted of a four-way rotary pickup selector switch (bridge, neck, and both together, in and out of phase) and master tone and volume controls. The bridge was a Telecaster-style unit, with 12 individual barrel-type bridge saddles allowing for precise adjustment of intonation, and through-body stringing to enhance sustain.

The bolt-on 21-fret neck was made of maple with a rosewood fingerboard, later enhanced with white binding; block markers replaced the dots in 1966. Strung with two unison and four octave courses, with the high-octave strings at the top in the traditional fashion (unlike the Rickenbacker), this functional (if not particularly elegant) guitar was available in sunburst, or plain color finishes with a matching headstock face.[194]

The fully adjustable bridge and the versatile electronics made it the preferred instrument of many session musicians of the time (such as Carol Kaye), but the heyday of the electric 12-string had already passed, and despite achieving reasonable sales, it was discontinued in 1968. Ignominiously, the remaining stock of bodies and necks were cut down and used for the notoriously ugly Fender Custom (also called the Maverick) 6-string design, a regrettable decision by Fender's new cost-conscious management. Unsurprisingly, these were a complete commercial failure.

From the plain dot-marked neck, we know that FZ's sunburst XII was an original 1965 or early 1966 model; the serial number 128312 confirms this date.[195] As usual FZ had his customized: when I asked Dweezil Zappa about the guitar he said, "That one has one of his preferred parametric EQ circuits in it. I saw him play it a few times live on stage. I would like to listen

The Fender XII at the UMRK in 2012
(Mick Ekers)

through the vault and find some 12-string solos as well as solos where he used other unusual guitars like the minis, and make another *Shut Up 'n Play Yer Guitar*."[196]

There are a few photographs of FZ playing the guitar in the early 1980s, which show the original split Fender pickups replaced with a pair of angled cream soapbar units. The original Fender faux tortoiseshell pickguard and chrome control panel have been replaced with a one-piece black pickguard, and two toggle switches replace the stock rotary pickup selector.

Today the guitar is fitted with a pair of brown Barcus Berry pickups, similar to the ones fitted to his Gibson Switchmaster, although they still have the cream surrounds. Otherwise, the guitar looks much the same as it did in in the 1980s.

There is a four-pole XLR socket set into the body near the controls. As Terry Bozzio notes below, the guitar was wired for stereo, with another output for the Barcus Berry transducer that FZ had mounted in the neck, so this could be for that purpose. There are three sets of black dual concentric controls, one with the inner knob missing, and a pair of small preset knobs.

The distinctive 'hockey stick' headstock
(Mick Ekers)

One of the Barcus-Berry pickups and the bridge, which allowed individual string length adjustment
(Mick Ekers)

These are typical of the parametric EQ setups that FZ had fitted to most of his guitars at the time, so we can assume that the first set are the master volume (with possibly a missing blend or stereo pan knob), with the others allowing control of gain, center frequency, and "Q." According to Terry Bozzio, the guitar was wired for stereo.

A black plastic cover on the back opens up to reveal a compartment with two 9-volt batteries. The stock Fender tuners have been replaced with sealed Schaller units with a twin-screw fitting; the original screw holes have been filled with darker wood and are clearly visible. Apart from a few dings to the bodywork, the guitar is in excellent condition; the bridge and neck plate are original.

FZ explored the full harmonic potential of having 12 strings.

Body of the Fender XII, note the four pin XLR socket (three or five pin connectors are more common)
(Mick Ekers)

DZ told me: "I remember he had it tuned weird at times. I can't recall the tuning, but some strings were harmonized."[197]

In an interview with Andrew Greenaway in 1992, Bozzio confirmed this when he talked about FZ's use of this guitar on the track "The Ocean is the Ultimate Solution": " . . . he played it on a real interesting Fender 12-string that had a Barcus Berry in the neck. He had the bottom strings turned to major 7ths . . . I think he had every string tuned to a different interval, so it was like a major 7th then a minor 7th. The next ones were, you know, a tritone major 3rd and a minor 3rd. And he had the low strings panned left, and the high strings panned right, and the Barcus Berry panned center; he had this glass-shattering 12-string sound. It was really unique."[198]

The guitar was sold in the 2016 auction for $16,000.[199]

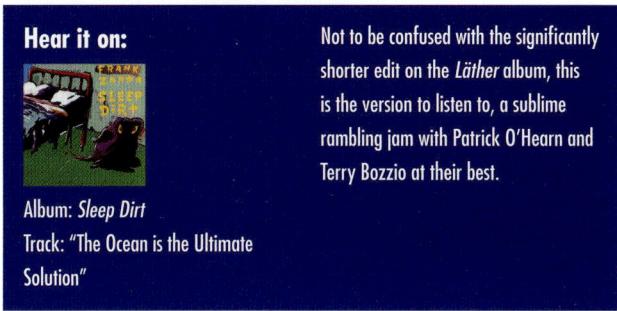

Hear it on:
Album: *Sleep Dirt*
Track: "The Ocean is the Ultimate Solution"

Not to be confused with the significantly shorter edit on the *Läther* album, this is the version to listen to, a sublime rambling jam with Patrick O'Hearn and Terry Bozzio at their best.

ZAPPA GEAR

Performance Blonde Stratocaster

"There are sounds which come out of my Stratocaster which don't come out of anything else on the face of the earth."

—*FZ*[200]

In July 1984, FZ took delivery of the yellow custom Stratocaster that was to become his main guitar, and the one he played almost exclusively for the remainder of his life. The guitar had been customized by Performance Guitar, a small guitar shop in LA owned and run by Kunio "Kenny" Sugai. Sugai started out as an aircraft mechanic in Japan. When he came to the US, he worked for Fender guitars for some time, eventually setting up his own workshop in the mid-1970s.

The guitar was probably as close as FZ ever got to his perfect guitar. In 1982, he said: "My ideal would be a combination of a bunch of different kinds of guitars. I like the vibrato bar if it's on a Strat, but I don't like a normal Strat neck because the curve is wrong for my hand. I like the neck that I used to have on the [Baby Snakes] SG. I like the tone quality and sustain that I get out of the Les Paul, which is due to the bulk of the guitar. And so, if I could get all of that together in one instrument that didn't weigh a million pounds I would be a happy guy."[201]

The "Blonde Strat," as he called it, covered all those bases and more. Performance made the body from heavy maple wood, built him a custom neck with the same slim low profile as the neck on the Baby Snakes SG, and fitted it with the latest Floyd Rose vibrato unit. FZ also had it fitted with what was his definitive active electronics setup, the culmination of his years of experimentation starting with the hacked-around Les Paul Goldtop.

The circuit was designed and built at the UMRK by FZ's technician (and brother-in-law) Arthur "Midget" Sloatman,

FZ with his new Blonde Strat in New York in August 1984, from Does Humor Belong in Music
(*still from* Does Humor Belong in Music, *1985*)

Neck detail showing the wide frets
(Mick Ekers)

to FZ's specification. FZ explained it in a 1988 interview for *Musician* magazine: "It's got a gain stage and two parametric EQ circuits built into it. It's set up so that you can have either EQ or gain plus both of these concentric [EQ] pots. The pots give you variable frequency selection and variable boost and cut at the different frequencies. And then there's a screwdriver adjustment for the Q of the filter: how peaky it will be. This allows you to tune right into the feedback point of that room. You can find out where it's going to squeal, locate it, and that's it."[202]

Sloatman gave *Guitar Player* magazine some more technical details in 1995: "They were identical parametric filter circuits. One of the filters was set for the bass frequencies from about 50 Hz to 2 kHz, and the other one was set for the top end, from about 500 Hz up to 20 kHz. The filters had a variable resonant frequency independent from the EQ gain. The Q ranged from .7 to 10, or a very wide dynamic range to a very narrow one."[203]

The circuit ran off two 9-volt batteries and developed a phenomenal amount of gain, which was ideal for overdriving his Marshall amplifiers; however, as Merl Saunders Jr. remarked, this also caused problems as the guitar could overload the radio transmitter that he used on stage: "The sound coming off his guitar was really hot . . . so we had to put caps on the input of his wireless just so it wouldn't be too distorted."[204]

The pickups probably changed around at first. Eventually FZ settled on custom-wound Seymour Duncan models; the bridge and middle pickup are what are known as "rail" pickups, with a single bar magnet spreading across the strings, and the neck pickup has the more usual six-magnet configuration. FZ again: "Seymour has wrapped some special pickups for me from time to time. I believe that what live in the Strat now are pickups that have an 8k boost."[205]

The Blonde Strat in 2012 at the UMRK
(Mick Ekers)

Rear view showing the skunk stripe on the neck. The black square on the headstock is a piece of velcro
(Mick Ekers)

As FZ said about the guitar: "The only thing that is 'Strat' about this Strat is the shape of the body. I think that the original body was a heavy Fender Stratocaster body."[206] However, Sugai was adamant that they built that body: "that yellow one, we made everything."[207] FZ may have been thinking of his other Performance Strat (see the next section).

FZ was very pleased with the results, saying in 1984: "I just starting using this particular guitar in July, and usually when I go on tour I take a number of guitars and I change them during the show. The ones I brought on the '82 tour I changed a lot. On this tour I just play this one guitar." From then on FZ hardly ever used any other guitar on stage. He played it in his last-ever public performance in Budapest in 1991.

When I saw the guitar at the UMRK in 2012, it was in excellent condition all around, with a handsome wood grain visible through the yellow varnish. The high-gloss maple Performance Guitar neck is fitted with 22 low wide frets, and has a redwood "skunk stripe" at the back.

The headstock is fitted with a chrome Floyd Rose locking nut assembly and string-retaining bar, and the unmarked tuners look like regular Gotoh sealed units. The pickguard is three-ply black plastic; the jack socket plate is brass and the vibrato unit is a regular chrome Floyd Rose unit.

The controls consist of a volume control, a pair of concentric gain and frequency controls, and two small preset pots for the Q. There is also an additional toggle switch. Merl Saunders had this set to completely bypass the preamp circuit: "There was a switch on his Strat that went straight from the pickups, just line in to the JV8 [Roland effects unit], which gave an acoustic sound because there were no preamps. I remember the only way he could control it was the volume pedal on the board."[208]

The back plate is missing, revealing that the vibrato unit is set up with three springs, and there is a plain metal cover for the battery compartment. The plain chrome neck plate has the mock serial number 00001 punched into it. Photographs do not

ZAPPA GEAR

The body of the Blonde Strat, a very striking and beautiful instrument
(Mick Ekers)

Kunio Sugai in his shop, 2012
(Mick Ekers)

do it justice, in my opinion. The "Butterscotch Strat," as it is sometimes known, is probably the finest of FZs guitars that I have seen, aesthetically and technically. Some lucky owner paid $70,400 for it in the 2016 auction.[209]

I visited Performance Guitar in 2012 to meet Mr. Sugai, and discovered a small shop full of gorgeous custom guitars, with photographs of customers, including Dweezil Zappa, pinned to the wall. There was a counter with a tiny cluttered office beyond and a doorway to what I assumed would be an equally small workshop.

I was astonished when Sugai showed us that he has a complete mini guitar factory out the back, complete with a CNC machine, woodworking rooms, a drying room, and a sanding room with some machines built specifically by Sugai. He proudly showed me his own horizontal belt sander, which he said, was his own improvement on a Fender factory design, and also a photograph of himself with legendary Fender engineer George Fullerton.

Sugai told the story about his first commission for FZ in 1979. He got a phone call from FZ, who asked him if he could come by his studio and look at some guitars that needed attention. "I asked him if he could bring them to the shop as I was busy right now, and Frank said 'Well, I'm busy too!'" (Sugai laughs at the memory.) Eventually he dispatched one of his staff to FZ's studio, who returned with thirteen guitars that needed fixing in a hurry for a tour that was starting imminently.

It was to be the start of a working relationship that was to continue right up to FZ's final days in 1993. Sugai said that the last project FZ asked him to do was just one month before he passed away. He told me that he visited FZ at his house around then and FZ said to him "I'm very sick, I need many kinds of doctor. One kind I need is a guitar doctor. You!"

Hear it on:

Movie: *Does Humor Belong in Music*
Track: "Whippin' Post"

You can hear the Blonde Strat all over the *Guitar* album and on almost all of FZ's live recordings from 1984 onwards, but I've chosen this clip because it seems to me that FZ is really trying to see just what he could get out of this relatively new guitar. I can imagine him thinking, "Right, let's see what this sucker can do."

The Fretless Stratocaster

"Have you seen the fretless Strat yet? You're gonna hear it in a minute."
— FZ[210]

I have no information on this guitar other than to confirm that it really did exist! There is a recording of FZ at a rehearsal that keeps popping up on the Internet, in which you can hear him changing his own guitar strings and talking about his new Floyd Rose vibrato on a Stratocaster with a fretless neck fitted. He then plays a five-minute solo, which is to my knowledge the only time the guitar was recorded.

I asked tech Merl Saunders about this and he thought that it might have been one of the various guitars that were taken on the 1988 tour but never got played. "I think I had a fretless Strat. He had had twenty guitars on the road with me; most of them never saw the light of day but I do remember a fretless Strat. It wasn't Performance Guitar; the guys from Valley Arts may have made it."[211] I have no idea what happened to the guitar or what it looked like. Possibly it was a short-lived experiment and the neck was later replaced with a fretted neck.

> **Hear it on:**
> Rehearsal tape, possibly 20th April 1982
> Track: Untitled solo
> Perhaps there are some recordings of this beast lurking in the ZFT vaults, for now that is all I can offer you!

Custom Stratocasters

"I definitely like a Stratocaster tone, especially when it's feeding back and with a midrange booster on it so it gets a real nasal sound."
— FZ[212]

Although he used the Blonde Strat almost exclusively on the 1988 tour, FZ also took a backup sunburst Stratocaster, although he did not use it very often. Merl Saunders told me he "rigged up the sunburst Strat with Valley Arts parts." I said that I thought both Strats were from Performance Guitar: "The guitars weren't identical, that was one thing. I think the electronics were identical, but the guitars themselves weren't. The neck on the sunburst was a smaller neck; it felt more like a Tele neck, it wasn't like the maple one."

Saunders also recalled: "I remember the sunburst guitar only had like two springs in it, and the two springs could hardly keep the guitar in tune. One of the other reasons why he didn't change back and forth was because the guitars' weight was a lot different. The blonde one was a lot heavier than the sunburst. So he only used it occasionally. There were a couple times the blond guitar went down, and I had to pull out the other one."[213]

When I spoke to Dweezil Zappa about the sunburst Strats, he remembered: "Well, he had a Performance that was a sunburst one, and then there was another one that was like a tobacco sunburst. I don't know if that was a Fender body or it could have been Valley Arts, but it didn't have a Fender logo on the neck, so it could have very well been a Valley Arts guitar, but that one's missing."[214]

Kunio Sugai told me that for the sunburst Strat they used a Fender body, and in 1985, Performance Guitar's Bob McDonald said it was an alder body, possibly from the 1960s. "The neck is one of ours, very thin with a flat back and a very flat maple fingerboard. We've made about four or five Strat and Tele necks for Frank and Dweezil; he swaps parts like crazy."[215]

When I visited the UMRK, things became a little clearer. As well as the three-color sunburst Strat, the tobacco sunburst Strat had also been found. The tobacco burst body looked like the backup guitar FZ used in the 1980s, as pictured in the 1988 tour program, and the sunburst looked like the one FZ used on the 1988 tour.

Photos of FZ rehearsing for the tour in 1987 show him using the tobacco burst, with a set of plain black-covered pickups. Something was still not quite right as the tobacco burst now had a humbucker pickup at the bridge with two other regular Fender-style pickups. It had a Performance Guitar neck and a Fender neck plate, and was most likely the 1960s Fender body McDonald mentions above.

The sunburst had a plain neck without a skunk stripe, so probably this was the Valley Arts neck I'd heard of; the make of the body is not known. It wasn't until I started sorting out my photographs from the UMRK session that I realized that at some stage the pickup assembly from the Performance tobacco burst must have been swapped with the one on the sunburst body. This explained why the main Blonde Strat and the sunburst Strat had such different necks and bodies but the same electronics. Although the sunburst was his primary backup guitar, FZ also used the tobacco burst on at least one occasion on the 1988 tour: see photo on the following page.

I should not have been surprised at all this; as Performance Guitar's McDonald noted, FZ was notorious for getting his techs to swap parts around. When FZ changed to mainly using Stratocasters, their modular design meant that he could switch necks and pickup assemblies around at will. DZ had told me that it was common practice for his techs to replace a faulty component with one from another instrument, rather than buying a new one or repairing it.[216] FZ would not necessarily have known the source of these parts.

The following descriptions are of the guitars as I found them at the UMRK in 2012.

Tobacco Burst Strat

The tobacco burst body is fitted with a maple Performance Guitar neck with 22 jumbo frets very similar to the one on the Blonde Strat. The headstock is fitted with a chrome Floyd Rose locking nut assembly and string-retaining bar, and Fender American Standard tuners.

The vibrato unit is a chrome Floyd Rose system. The bridge and middle pickups are standard Fender-style pickups; the neck pickup has been replaced with a twin black humbucker. The control panel is much simpler than the other custom Strats, with just a volume control and a single dual concentric control. Several pickguard screws are missing, as is the pickup selector switch-tip.

The front of the body is in very good condition, with only a few minor dings; the back shows some signs of use but the finish is still largely intact. The back plate is held on with just two screws, as is the battery compartment cover. This has four holes

FZ and the Tobacco burst, Paris 20th May 1988
(Alain Benainous — Getty Images)

allowing screwdriver access to preset controls. I would suspect that these varied the center frequency and Q of the EQ circuits, with the front control knobs varying the gain of the high and low circuits. The neck plate is a plated Fender four-screw item with signs of corrosion and the serial number FZ001 has been added. See page xii for a full-page photo of this guitar.

A very handsome guitar
(Mick Ekers)

Rear view of the Tobacco burst Strat, more missing screws!
(Mick Ekers)

Sunburst Strat

The sunburst has a handsome one-piece solid maple neck, fitted with 23 medium-gauge frets (one more than the Performance necks). The headstock is fitted with a gold-plated Floyd Rose locking nut assembly and string retaining bar plus two Fender-style string trees and gold Gotoh tuners. The vibrato unit is a gold-plated Floyd Rose and the black pickguard is fitted with plastic-covered Seymour Duncan pickups. The control layout is almost identical to that fitted to the Blonde Strat but without the on-off switch. There is a black master volume nearest the bridge (this was a silver knob when the pickup assembly was fitted to the tobacco burst Strat), and there are two sets of concentric knobs for the high and low frequency EQ circuits, each with a separate preset Q control.

The front of the body is in very good condition, with only a few minor dings; the back shows more signs of use but the finish is still largely intact. The back plate is missing, showing three springs fitted to the vibrato unit, and the plastic cover for the battery compartment has an ICA inventory sticker #017. The neck plate is plain metal with no markings or serial number. As a minor detail, the top strap button has been fitted at a more horizontal angle than normal for Stratocasters. It is worth noting that FZ did not seem fussy about strap fitting systems. As far as I can tell, he rarely used any type of strap locking system; certainly none of his guitars I saw had anything but regular metal buttons (with the exception of the Coral Sitar, as noted).

Erstwhile Rex Bogue tech Jim Williams did some electronics work on FZ's guitars in the 1980s. He remembers working on one of the Strats: "As I recall, this Strat had a really clean two-band sweep EQ circuit. I put little mini pots in to fit and it was high EQ, low EQ and then a frequency knob. Like swept mids on a nice recording console. And I remember Gail called me up and says, 'Frank is not happy with the guitar.' And I said 'Really? Why?' And she says, 'He thinks it sounds too clean.' And still to this day I go 'That's the best compliment I ever got from Frank!' It really was. That was a good compliment. (Laughs)"[217]

Front and rear views of the Sunburst Strat
(Mick Ekers)

ZAPPA GEAR

The body of the Sunburst Strat, signs of wear around the neck joint indicate that replacements have been made.
(Mick Ekers)

Custom Telecasters

"I also have a Telecaster.... It's a real good blues guitar."

—FZ[218]

The guitar FZ was talking about was a 1980s reissue, as he described it "one of the copies of the originals that Fender put out about a year ago."[219] We found two custom Telecasters at the UMRK in 2012, both fitted with non-Fender maple necks.

Dweezil Zappa told me that FZ had at least three custom Telecasters: "One of them was what he called the 'Butterscotch Telecaster' and that was made by Performance. But I don't know where that one is, it's sort of disappeared. There's another one that probably started its life as a standard Fender Telecaster but it's got a Performance neck on it."[220]

The Stripped Telecaster

Dweezil told me that this started out as a cream-colored guitar but at some stage, the paint was stripped off. "And that one has two humbuckers in it and it's got a black pickguard on it. Mike Keneally played that one on tour with Frank."[221] This was one of the two I found; just as DZ said, the guitar body has had the finish stripped off. The pickguard has two small holes drilled in it for two screwdriver preset pots, which would most likely control the frequency and the Q of the parametric EQ.

The pickup selector switch has a small white tip, the volume control has a regular Fender knob, and the tone control has a black plastic one. The bridge assembly is a modern, fully adjustable model with individual saddles for each string. The one-piece neck is fine varnished maple, with medium gauge frets.

The stripped Tele at the UMRK in 2012
(Mick Ekers)

I suspect it is not from Performance Guitar; possibly another Valley Arts neck. The guitar looks like it is a work in progress; at the rear the unfinished roughly cut battery compartment was covered with a piece of gaffer tape! Despite its rough appearance it sold in the 2016 auction for $11,250.[222]

The stripped Tele's unfinished battery compartment
(Mick Ekers)

The Yellow Telecaster

DZ also spoke about the other Tele that we were to find: "And then, there was another one that was kind of like a butterscotch one that I think also started as an original Fender, but it had a different neck on it as well."[223] This Tele was in much more pristine condition. The neck is a beautiful example of a Performance Guitar neck, in heavy varnished maple with a skunk stripe up the back and 22 fat wide frets, very much like the one on the Blonde Strat. The body is finished in an attractive pale-yellow varnish, and the pickguard is white pearloid, held on with just two screws.

The bridge assembly is a Fender unit with three brass saddles and a serial number 20827, and the pickups and control assembly all look like original Fender units. There is no sign of a battery compartment or other custom electronic work, so this most likely has a standard Telecaster control setup.

Kunio Sugai at Performance remembered making a Telecaster for FZ, and told me that they did a lot of changing pickups around; mostly they were Seymour Duncans.[224] This was most likely the missing Butterscotch Tele that DZ mentioned. The guitar did not fare as well as its unfinished brother

The stripped Tele body; I wonder what the intended finish was?
(Mick Ekers)

The body of the Yellow Telecaster; someone really should put some screws in the pickguard!
(Mick Ekers)

ZAPPA GEAR

Front and rear views of the yellow Telecaster at the UMRK in 2012
(Mick Ekers)

in the 2016 auction, and sold for $9,600. Apart from Mike Keneally's use of the stripped one, I have been unable to find any information on where or when FZ used these guitars.

Ovation Acoustics

"... an Ovation gut string acoustic plugged directly into the board..."
— FZ[225]

In October 1975, FZ appeared on TV with Australian comedian Norman Gunston, cradling an Ovation 1613-4 Classic electric acoustic guitar. Introduced in 1973, the Classic had a Spanish pine top, a plain ebony fingerboard, and a standard 5 13/16" deep fiberglass bowl body. It had a pickup built in to the bridge and a discreet volume control mounted on the body near the neck.

After a hilarious interview, Gunston (real name Garry McDonald) played some blues harmonica accompanied on guitar by FZ, who invited him to come and jam with his band. FZ kept this promise, and Gunston can be heard on *The Torture Never Stops* on the *FZ-OZ* double CD set, recorded at the Hordern Pavilion in Sydney on 20th January, 1976. Gunston is credited as "a fine, fine TV show host & very reasonable harmonica player with exceedingly funny persuasions."[226]

Ovation Guitars are made by the Kaman Music Corporation, which was founded in 1964 by inventor, aerospace engineer, and guitarist Charles Kaman. As a teenager in the 1930s, he won a national guitar-playing competition, the prize being a position in the Tommy Dorsey Orchestra. Dorsey offered him a $75-a-week contract, but Kaman decided to concentrate on his engineering studies.[227] He graduated from university in 1940 with a degree in aeronautical engineering, and after a stint designing propellers for United Aircraft, founded helicopter design company Kaman Aircraft. The innovative Kaman helicopters

FZ with Norman Gunston on his TV show
(still from Norman Gunston Show, 1975)

were adopted by the US military and the company grew into a major corporation.

In the 1960s, prompted by losing a government contract, Kaman decided it was time to diversify. He had kept up his interest in the guitar, and around that time he took his Martin guitar to the Martin factory for repair. He was given a tour of the factory and was shocked that the guitars were still being hand-built using hammers and animal glue. Itching to modernize Martin's manufacturing methods, Karman twice offered to buy the company. However, C.F. Martin would not sell, so he founded his own Ovation Instruments.

Kaman wanted to build a better acoustic guitar, using contemporary materials and production techniques, and he tasked his R&D team with determining if the guitar could be sonically improved by modifying its shape and construction. By 1966, they had proved that a semi-parabolic shape yielded the most efficient and responsive guitar body. Using aerospace technology, they developed a fiberglass and resin composite called Lyrachord to build this shape, which became the trademark Ovation Roundback body. [228]

The first Ovation guitar, the Ovation Balladeer, was launched in 1967, and they soon found a high-profile endorsee in John Denver, at the peak of his career and with a national TV show. In 1970, Denver was seen on TV playing a borrowed Baldwin nylon-string classical guitar with a built-in pickup. He liked the freedom of movement this gave him, as he did not have to keep his guitar pointed at a second microphone while singing.

His sponsors were less than happy to see this, and worked with Denver to produce their own pickup. In 1971, they introduced a range of their guitars with piezo pickups built into the bridge, and a battery-driven preamplifier set into the guitar body. This was the first commercially successful pickup of its kind, and despite Charles Kaman's initial skepticism, electro-acoustic guitars eventually accounted for over seventy percent of Ovation sales.[229] FZ's 1613-4 Classic was one of these first-generation models, as always he was keen to try out a new musical technology.

Dweezil Zappa told me that FZ had another two Ovations: "And he has some hideous Ovation that was probably given to him; he had two Ovations, one was a brown one. He always had really light strings on that guitar, and then the other one was this, it's just so ugly it's like a grey-green color with weird, I want to say roses or something on it. He always had really light strings on that guitar."[230]

The ugly Ovation to which Dweezil is referring was an Ovation Adamas. Developed in the late 1970s, these had a carbon fiber body with two sets of eleven varying-size holes replacing the traditional round hole in the center of the body. It can be briefly seen, leaning against the wall of the UMRK, at the beginning of Henning Lohner's *Peefeeyatko* German TV documentary.

The brown one was a steel-strung 1712 Custom Balladeer with a non-standard brown top, possibly koa wood. This was a more conventional-looking instrument with a traditional inlaid round soundhole, introduced in 1975. FZ took it on tour in 1979, giving it to guitarist Warren Cuccurullo to play. It can

An Ovation Classic like FZ's
(Ovation website)

ZAPPA GEAR

FZ's Adamas; note fine detail on fingerboard markers and figuring on bridge and body edging
(ZFT)

also be seen on the couch beside FZ at the start of his 1981 TV interview with Trooper Charles Ash of the Pennsylvania State Police.

Steve Vai recalled recording "Theme from the 3rd Movement of Sinister Footwear," the first thing he ever recorded with FZ and an incredibly difficult piece: "Yeah. I did it on an acoustic guitar, he gave me this Ovation . . . "[231] Tommy Mars remembered that when they were touring "I would always seem to be able to find a piano in a hotel. And a few times each tour, I would say 'Pops, I got the piano, are you ready to jam?' And he would, with his Ovation guitar, real blues style."[232]

In early 1975, FZ put his Ovation Classic to good use, recording the band tracks for "Revised Music for Guitar and Low-Budget Orchestra" at the Record Plant in LA. The Ovation, although clearly sounding like a nylon-string guitar, is accompanied by what appears to be a synthesized brass effect. Den Simms asked FZ how this was done, during a lengthy interview for the US *Society Pages* fanzine. FZ explained: "Well, I played the solo. It's an Ovation gut-string acoustic plugged directly into the board, and it was transcribed by Bruce Fowler, and he wrote it down, and he doubled it with four trombones . . . . in harmony. [With all the bent notes?] All the bent notes. [My ear says "brass"] It is brass. [. . . but my mind says, "brass can't do that'"] Brass can't, but Bruce can! (Laughter)"[233]

I did not get to see any of the Ovations during my UMRK visits, but the Adamas turned up in the 2016 Auction. The catalog entry describes it as "A 1978 Ovation Adamas acoustic guitar, serial number 354-90, model 1687-7, signed by Charles Kaman."[234] It sold for $10,240.[235] Fender Musical Instruments Corporation acquired the Kaman Music Corporation in 2008, and Charles Kaman died in 2011, but Ovation are still making their unique style of acoustic guitars.

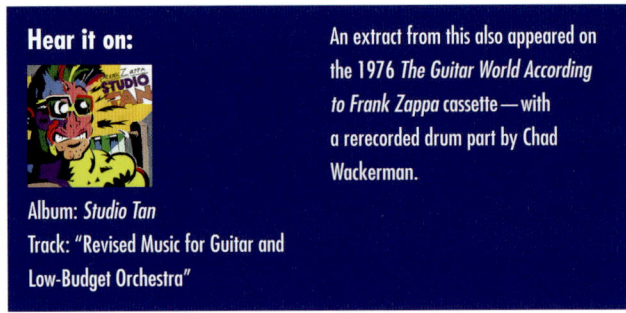

Hear it on:
Album: *Studio Tan*
Track: "Revised Music for Guitar and Low-Budget Orchestra"

An extract from this also appeared on the 1976 *The Guitar World According to Frank Zappa* cassette — with a rerecorded drum part by Chad Wackerman.

Gibson Super Jumbo J-200N

"Zappa has used a Stratocaster, a Les Paul, and a Gibson J-200."
—Guitar Player *magazine*[236]

The original Gibson Super Jumbo was a custom special, made in 1937 for the Hollywood singing cowboy Ray Whitley, complete with inlaid western scenes on the neck position markers.[237] It entered the catalog the following year, designated as the Super Jumbo 200, the number referring to the retail price of $200.

It had a super large 17"×21"×4 1/2" body, with a round semi-circular end, unlike most jumbo guitars, which had a body that was flattened around the endpin. The guitar was aimed very much at country and western musicians; the bridge was intended to look like a pair of cow horns, and is now generally known as a "moustache" bridge as it more closely resembled a handlebar moustache.

The fully bound body had a simple rosette of black and white rings, and a large brown celluloid pickguard with an engraved flower design. The sides and back of the guitar were made of rosewood and the top was of red spruce. The "slim fast low action neck" was made of laminated curly maple with an adjustable truss rod; the scale length was 25 1/2" with 20 frets.[238] The bound ebony (later rosewood) fingerboard was inlaid with a new design called the Crest, and had an ornate pointed end. The headstock had a crown inlay and a pearl Gibson logo. It was intended to be the world's biggest and fanciest guitar in production.

None were manufactured from 1944 to 1946 during World War II. When production resumed the guitar had maple back and sides as standard. This may have been as a result of economic or supply factors, but it gave the guitar a brighter, cutting sound. During the 1950s, the model number was changed to simply J-200 and the body depth gradually increased to 4 7/8", but otherwise the design was little changed. In 1961, Gibson replaced the bridge with a fully adjustable metal Tune-o-matic design, and in 1963, the pearl tulip-shaped tuning pegs were replaced with a triangular metal design.[239] It was mostly made in a sunburst finish, but was also available as the J-200N natural finish version.

The J-200 was another of those guitars that I had only seen mentioned once, and I was beginning to doubt its existence, until I saw a video clip of FZ accompanying the late Larry "Wild Man" Fischer in his home in Hollywood. FZ is quietly picking out lines on a big blonde J-200N, while Fischer sings and bashes out random chords on FZ's Gibson J-160E.[240]

Apart from the wartime break, the J-200 has been in continuous production in one variant or other. It is one of the most famous acoustic guitar designs, as well as FZ it has been used by musicians as diverse and celebrated as Elvis Presley, Bob Dylan, Pete Townshend, and Jimmy Page. The whereabouts of FZ's guitar is unknown: as DZ told me, "Quite a few guitars from those days are missing."[241]

FZ and his J-200 in 1970, from the VPRO TV documentary
(still from Frank Zappa, 1971)

A recent Gibson J-200 reissue
(Gibson catalogue)

ZAPPA GEAR

Guild Aragon F-30R-NT Acoustic

"I also have Martin, Guild, and Gibson acoustics."

—FZ[242]

The above quote is the only I have seen in which FZ mentions his Guild F30R. FZ can be seen strumming the guitar on the tour bus in *The Official Mothers of Invention Tourbook 1971*, with Mark Volman accompanying him on another acoustic guitar, probably the Martin D18S that he was later to trade with FZ (see next chapter).

The serial number (53468) shows that it was made in 1971[243], so FZ most likely bought it new. The original tuning machines have been replaced by Gotoh units, and the truss rod cover has been replaced upside down. The Julien's auction catalog entry for the guitar states that there was a jack socket on the lower bout that has been removed and the body repaired.[244] I confess we did not notice this in the short time we had to photograph it at the UMRK. I have not found any evidence of it being used on stage, but it has all the marks of being played often, and I like to think that FZ was quite fond of this very attractive guitar.

The original Guild story belongs to Alfred Dronge, born Avram Dronge in Warsaw in 1911, whose parents emigrated to the USA in 1916 and settled in New York. Alfred had an interest in music from an early age, working in music stores and learning to play banjo and guitar. Dronge worked as a professional guitarist in his 20s, but when he married he settled down and opened a musical instrument shop in Park Row, New York.

Guild Guitars Inc. was founded by Dronge and ex-Epiphone executive George Mann in 1952, following Epiphone's decision to move out of their New York factory. The new company employed several skilled Epiphone workers who did not want to move. Mann left after a year but Dronge continued,

The Guild F30 in 2012 at the UMRK
(Mick Ekers)

building up the company's reputation for producing high quality instruments.

Guild originally worked out of a small workshop in Pearl Street, but soon outgrew these premises and in 1956, they moved to a new factory in Hoboken, New Jersey. The company continued to grow, and in 1966, Guild was purchased by Avent Inc., a large American conglomerate, who kept Dronge on as president.

In 1967, the company opened another production facility at a factory in Westbury, Rhode Island, eventually transferring all production there.

Dronge regularly commuted to Rhode Island from his home in New York, flying his own plane. Tragically, his twin-engine Beechcraft Baron crashed while landing in bad weather on 3rd May, 1972, killing Dronge instantly. Guild continued, however, and kept up their reputation for producing quality instruments at a time when competitors Fender and Gibson were in decline.

FZ and Guild F30 on the bus in 1971
(from The Official Mothers of Invention Tourbook *1971*, ZFT)

The model F30 flat-top acoustic guitar was introduced by Guild in 1954, when it was the smallest flat-top guitar they produced. In 1959, it was redesigned with a slightly larger body, and mahogany back and sides. It became very popular during the folk boom of the 1960s, and Guild made over 2,500 F-30s between 1965 and 1969. [245]

Their 1976 catalog described it thus: "With a body smaller than most the F-30 is a guitar that's comfortable to play without tiring. It has . . . the sensitive, personal tone so desirable in folk playing."[246]

The F30R-NT (the R suffix indicates that the sides and back are made of rosewood, while NT stands for Natural Top) did not actually make it into the catalog until 1973. However, a small number of F30s were made for Paul Simon in 1967, with Brazilian rosewood back and sides, and FZ's must also have been a special order.[247]

The headstock features the Guild "Chesterfield" inlay design, so called because it is strongly reminiscent of the design on the Chesterfield cigarette packet. The 25 1/2" scale neck has an ebony fingerboard with plain white dot markings; the spruce-top body is 15 1/2" wide by 19 1/2" long by 4 7/8" deep.[248] The guitar is finished off with a "cloud"-style rosewood bridge, a tortoiseshell pickguard, white binding at the front and back of the body, and three decorative circle inlays around the soundhole.

When it was first introduced, the F-30R-NT version sold for $450; it was briefly dropped from the line in 1975 but reappeared with a new deluxe neck in 1976. Guild went through various changes of ownership and some difficult financial times in the 1980s and 1990s, and the company was purchased in 1995 by Fender Musical Instruments. In 2014, Guild was acquired from Fender by the Cordoba Music Group and the company is now based in Oxnard, California, making a range of acoustic and electric guitars inspired by the company's early Hoboken days. The mahogany-sided F-30 was produced for some years under the Fender ownership, although at time of writing was not in the catalog.[249] FZ's guitar was sold in the 2016 auction for $16,000.[250]

The headstock with the 'Chesterfield inlay, a scrap of paper has been placed over the nut, presumably to correct loose fitting strings
(Mick Ekers)

The Guild F-30 body at the UMRK in 2012
(Mick Ekers)

Martin D18S

"I have a real nice Martin."

— FZ[251]

The original Martin Factory circa 1900
(public domain)

In an interview with *Guitar Player* in 1977, FZ described the Martin guitar that he got from Mark Volman as follows: "I have a real nice Martin—I don't know what the model number is, but it has a classical-width neck that joins the body right at the 12th fret, in a jumbo shell."[252] FZ's Martin is in fact a model D18S 12-fret standard Dreadnought, with a slotted headstock; Brazilian rosewood fingerboard, headstock, and bridge; and mahogany back and sides, manufactured in 1969–1970.

The Martin Guitar Company is one of the most highly regarded acoustic guitar manufacturers in the world. It can trace its heritage back for 200 years, when founder Christian Friedrich Martin left his family home in Germany at the age of fifteen and started an apprenticeship in Vienna with guitar maker Johann Stauffer.

Martin emigrated to America in 1833 after a long and wearying dispute with the guild of violin makers, who were attempting to restrict the right to make guitars. Originally he opened a small music store and guitar workshop in New York, but he and his wife were not happy there, and in 1838 he moved to Pennsylvania and set up shop in the small town of Nazareth, which has been the home of Martin guitars ever since.

C. F. Martin Sr. died in 1873, and ownership of the company passed to his son C. F. Martin Jr. and then to his son Frank Henry Martin in 1888 at the age of twenty-two, when his father died unexpectedly. F.H. Martin was responsible for much of the subsequent development of the company until he retired in 1945.[253]

In 1931, the model D steel string guitar was launched, named after the British Dreadnought class of World War I battleships. The D18 was the plainest dreadnought Martin offered, with mahogany back and sides and simple binding, unlike the more elaborately finished D28 and D45 models.

Originally, these were produced with the neck joining the body at the 12th fret and a slotted headstock, but in 1934 the D series design was modified so that the neck joined at the 14th fret and had a solid headstock. These guitars were revolutionary at the time, with the large body and extended neck range immediately finding favor with blues and country musicians, and they went on to become the industry standard.[254]

Martin started making the 12-fret D-28 again in 1954, in very limited numbers, but in the early 1960s these became popular with many of the new generation of folk singers (notably Peter Yarrow of the folk trio Peter, Paul & Mary). In 1968 Martin added the D-18S, D-28S, and D-45S to their regular line.[255]

On the sleeve notes to *The Guitar World According to Frank Zappa*, FZ notes: "The tune itself ("Sleep Dirt") was composed in a hotel room in Stockholm, Sweden, sometime in November, 1971, as a result of borrowing the Martin guitar (owned then by Mark Volman) and experimenting on a day off during the tour. I eventually traded Mark a Telecaster for the Martin. It now sits unused in a dark corner of the studio."[256]

FZ's Martin case at the UMRK
(Mick Ekers)

Guitars

FZ's Martin D18S
(Mick Ekers)

Former Mothers of Invention singer Volman was happy enough to make the trade, remembering: "The D-18 had a wide neck and he had much bigger hands so it fitted him better."[257] FZ made few recordings playing acoustic guitar, but as well as "Sleep Dirt," he also used the Martin on the track "Blessed Relief" on *The Grand Wazoo* album.

The S series Dreadnoughts are still sought after by many guitarists because of their supposedly richer tone, caused by the bridge being placed further down the body than the 14-fret versions. The Martin Guitar Company is still producing instruments in Nazareth, Pennsylvania, under the direction of Christian ("Chris") Frederick Martin IV, the sixth generation of Martin to run the organization.

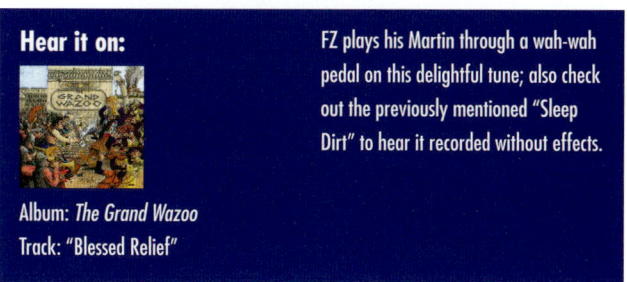

Hear it on: FZ plays his Martin through a wah-wah pedal on this delightful tune; also check out the previously mentioned "Sleep Dirt" to hear it recorded without effects.

Album: *The Grand Wazoo*
Track: "Blessed Relief"

Gibson J-160E

"I also have a Gibson round-hole acoustic with a pickup right next to the fingerboard."

—FZ[258]

The guitar FZ was talking about was his mid-1960s Gibson J-160E, described by Gibson in their 1964 catalog thus: "Here it is—the popular jumbo flat top that's electric—and the only guitar of its type with the adjustable bridge that gives perfect action plus much more power and sustaining quality to the tone. An exceptional amplified instrument popular with Country and Western artists."[259]

The J-160E was introduced in 1954. It was in fact Gibson's second attempt to produce an electrified acoustic guitar; the smaller cutaway CF-100E had made its debut in 1951, but never achieved great popularity and was discontinued in 1959.

Gibson based the J-160E design on the company's best-selling J-45 jumbo acoustic guitar, adding a single-coil magnetic pickup (based on the P-90) at the end of the fingerboard and fitting volume and tone controls on the lower bout of the body.[260]

The back and sides were made of Honduras mahogany, with decorative "ivoroid" binding. The "slim fast low-action" neck, as Gibson described it, had a bound rosewood fingerboard with large pearl inlays. The neck had 20 frets and the scale length was 24 3/4". The round-shouldered dreadnought body was 16 1/4"×20 1/4"×4 7/8".

To make room for the pickup between the end of the fingerboard and the soundhole, the neck joined the body at the 15th fret (instead of the usual 14th fret). The J-160E also featured a height-adjustable bridge, originally operated by two large thumbwheels. These were later replaced by less obtrusive screws, as on FZ's guitar.[261]

Larry 'Wild Man' Fischer with FZ's J-160E from the 1970 VPRO TV documentary
(still from *Frank Zappa, 1971*)

67

ZAPPA GEAR

There is a story that the Gibson J-160E was originally going to be the "Les Paul Flat-top," but Paul considered that the original solid spruce top would feed back too much. Whether Paul instigated this or not, in 1955 Gibson replaced the solid top and back with plywood, and substituted ladder bracing for the original cross bracing. The intention was to deaden the guitar's tone and reduce its susceptibility to feedback when plugged in. Paul never endorsed the model, in any case.[262]

The effect of these design modifications was to produce a guitar with what is generally considered a flat and uninspiring acoustic tone, and a nondescript electric tone. The main reason for the continued interest and collectability of the J-160E is because John Lennon and George Harrison famously used a pair of them when they were in the Beatles.

FZ's mid-1960s J160-E has been modified with a Barcus Berry contact pickup screwed onto the bridge, and the original machine heads have been replaced with Schaller M-6 tuners; the G tuner has been knocked out of alignment. There is some

The Gibson J-160E in 2012, at the UMRK
(Mick Ekers)

The headstock with typical Gibson 'pineapple' inlay
(Mick Ekers)

cracking to the varnish behind and below the bridge, but it is in generally sound condition, and does not appear to have been played too much.

However, the "slim and fast" neck obviously worked for FZ, as in 1977, he stated: "I also have a Gibson round-hole acoustic with a pickup right next to the fingerboard; I don't know what model number it is either. I like that guitar; it's got a good neck on it. I just lucked out, because I don't think all the necks are good on Gibsons. In fact, they're usually a little too pudgy for my hand; I like to get them shaved down."[263]

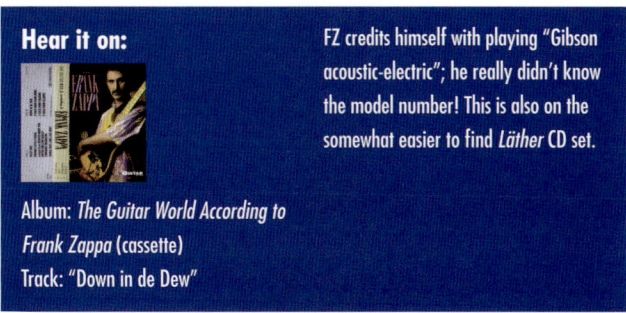

Hear it on:

FZ credits himself with playing "Gibson acoustic-electric"; he really didn't know the model number! This is also on the somewhat easier to find *Läther* CD set.

Album: *The Guitar World According to Frank Zappa* (cassette)
Track: "Down in de Dew"

Close-up showing Barcus Berry contact pickup fitted to bridge
(Mick Ekers)

The single coil pickup
(Mick Ekers)

The Gibson J-160E in 2012, at the UMRK
(Mick Ekers)

ZAPPA GEAR

Candelas Flamenco Guitar

"And then he's got an unnamed classical nylon-string guitar."
— Dweezil Zappa[264]

The nylon-string guitar that DZ refers to was one of the more enigmatic instruments I found at the URMK, but at least I was able to put a name to it. The maker's label inside has been partly obliterated with black ink, but the words "Guitarras Candelas" and "Tijuana" can be made out.

I spoke to Tomas Delgado, who now runs Candelas Guitars in LA, who confirmed it was one of their guitars but was unable to verify the date of manufacture.[265] For a while, Candelas originally had shops in Tijuana and Los Angeles, but the shop in Mexico was closed in the 1970s, so the address may have been marked out deliberately.[266]

It has a traditional Spanish guitar body, a typical nylon-string rosewood bridge, natural light wood top (spruce, most likely), and darker sides and back. There is a typical decorative rosette around the soundhole made of wood inlays and the top and bottom edges of the body are protected with predominantly black edging. The 19-fret flat classical neck joins the body at the 12th fret.

The headstock is painted black with no visible maker's mark, and is in the flat flamenco style, rather than the slotted style usually found on nylon-strung guitars. The gold Schaller tuners are not original (they are regular metal-string type) although it has been strung with nylon strings. The D string was already broken when we took it out of its battered shaped case. When the guitar was auctioned the catalog description noted that the original tuners are in the case, which is labelled "Flamenco FZ."[267]

The guitar looks to have been played a fair bit, with some wear visible on the frets and the varnish on the body worn away below the strings. Most intriguingly, a jack socket has been drilled into the bottom edge of the guitar, but there is no trace of any pickup having been fitted. Presumably, this connection would have been for some sort of contact pickup like FZ's favorite Barcus Berrys, as a magnetic pickup would not work with the nylon strings, but there is no trace now. Bill Gubbins' excellent book on the recording of *Hot Rats* shows FZ with the Candelas in Witney Studios in August 1969, but it is not certain what tracks he played it on.[268] The guitar sold in the auction for $7,680.[269]

The Candelas in 2012 at the UMRK
(Mick Ekers)

Guitars

The defaced label
(Mick Ekers)

The unexplained jack socket
(Mick Ekers)

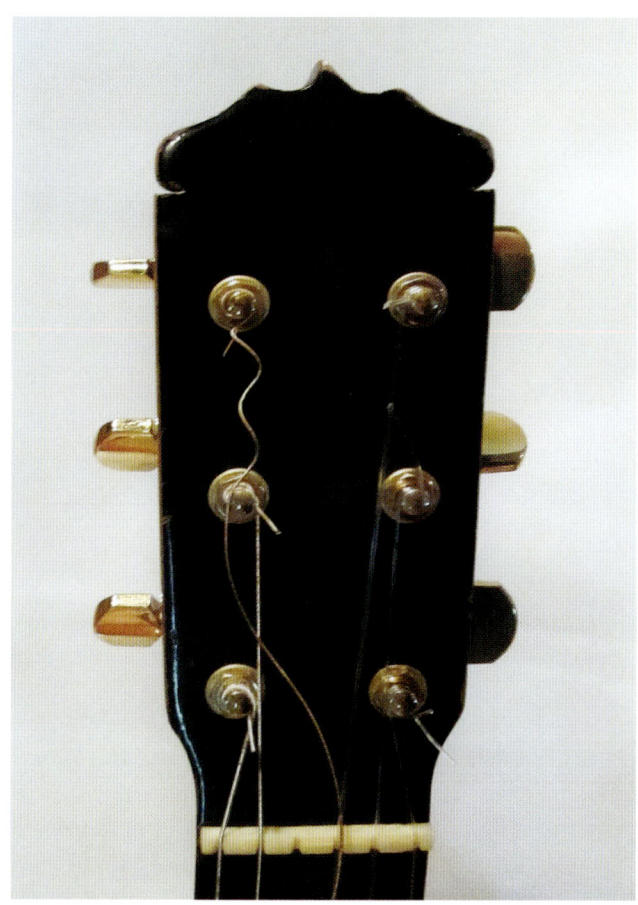

The headstock with steel string tuners
(Mick Ekers)

Nice guitar, one broken string
(Mick Ekers)

ZAPPA GEAR

Höfner 500/8 BZ Bass

"It's got a fuzz circuit in it that's pretty cool; that one is a good sounding bass."

—*Dweezil Zappa*[270]

During the early years of the Mothers of Invention, bass player Roy Estrada would usually be seen playing a large-bodied, natural finish semi-acoustic Höfner bass guitar. This was actually FZ's instrument; presumably Estrada was using it because FZ preferred the tone over Estrada's Fender Precision.

By 1969, Estrada had reverted to playing his Fender, and the instrument was (as far as I know) not used on stage again. FZ used it occasionally during his career for recording purposes, on the rare times when he played bass. It was also used by Arthur Barrow on the triple-tracked bass-guitar instrumental "Tink Walks Amok," on the *Man from Utopia* album.

The Höfner company was founded in 1887 by violin maker Karl Höfner in Schönbach, Germany. Karl brought two of his sons, Josef and Walter, into the business just after World War I, and they quickly began to expand the business, making violas, cellos, and double basses. By the mid-1930s, they were also making steel-strung archtop guitars, and the company employed thirty staff in the factory and around 300 outworkers.

WWII saw the company producing wooden crates and boot soles for the army, and after the war Schönbach was once again part of Czechoslovakia, where the company was nationalized by the communist government. In 1948, they were allowed to move to West Germany, where they restarted the business, and by 1950 they had built a new factory at Bubenreuth in Bavaria, complete with a housing estate for the displaced workers from Schönbach.

Höfner steadily rebuilt its reputation, and when rock and roll came along in the 1950s, they quickly capitalized on the increased demand for guitars, which soon accounted for over fifty percent of turnover, building a second factory in nearby Hagenau. By the early 1960s, they had a wide range of electric

The Höfner in 2012 at the UMRK
(Mick Ekers)

Estrada and the Höfner at the BBC in 1968
(still from Late Night Lineup, *1969)*

guitars and basses, which were particularly popular in Europe, where they were considerably cheaper and easier to find than US-made Fenders and Gibsons.[271]

The 500/8 was Höfner's bass version of the Ambassador guitar (model number 4578) and was the only bass that Höfner produced with a double Florentine cutaway. It was produced between 1968 and 1977, and was a typical Höfner mixture of high-quality traditional craftsmanship and cheap mass-production techniques. The body has a solid spruce arched top, maple sides, and an arched maple back with a cutout for the battery compartment.

The body was finished with ivoroid binding around the back, top, and f-holes, with ornate mother-of-pearl inlays on

The control panel, the different style knobs are original
(Mick Ekers)

The inlaid headstock
(Mick Ekers)

the headstock. The short scale (31 1/2") neck has a rosewood fingerboard with stylish mother-of-pearl block markers. The bridge is a typical Höfner bridge made of slotted black-stained wood, with short strips of fret wire fitted in the slots acting as bridge saddles; the strings are anchored by a simple trapeze tailpiece.

The guitar was fitted with two special Bass Sound pickups;[272] these were type 512B blade single coil pickups, each with two ceramic magnets either side of a metal blade around which the coil was wrapped. The adjustable pole pieces just screwed into the pickup frame next to the coil bobbin,[273] so probably had little effect in adjusting the individual string levels. The 500/8 was sold with various active electronic options. These were indicated by the model number suffix: "M" for mixer, "B" for bass boost, and "Z" for fuzz.[274]

FZ's model was the BZ, combining bass boost and fuzz; the electronic circuits were basically the same as in Höfner's Bass Boost and Buzz Tone effect pedals (branded as Selmer in the UK). By all accounts the Buzz Tone was notoriously bass-heavy, and it never achieved much popularity among guitarists, although it would have been well suited to bass-guitar use.

The bass has a three-way pickup selector switch above the neck pickup and a sizeable control panel below the bridge, with master tone and volume controls, bass and fuzz boost controls, a rotary effect selector switch, and a battery on/off push button.

FZ was possibly attracted to the bass because it had a similar body style to his beloved Gibson Switchmaster, but it is also likely that he was more interested in the advanced circuitry; this may well have been the initial inspiration for his later experiments with onboard guitar electronics.

The instrument was in excellent condition for its age, with hardly a mark on the body, and still possessing both the serial number sticker on the headstock (55176) and the sticker on the control plate next to the on/off button, which sternly advises "URGENT Keep push button in OUT position to conserve battery." It sold for $10,880 in the 2016 auction.[275]

Despite the publicity from Paul McCartney's high-profile use of a Höfner bass guitar, Höfner guitar sales declined in the 1960s, as US guitars became more readily available, and the company returned to producing primarily orchestral instruments.

The Höfner 500 at the UMRK looking remarkably well for its age
(Mick Ekers)

ZAPPA GEAR

During the 1990s and 2000s, Höfner suffered a bewildering and disruptive series of takeovers and sales, but eventually in 2004 became an independent company again as a result of a management buyout led by former general manager Klaus Schöller. The company is still making guitars and orchestral string instruments at the Hagenau factory, with a second factory in China making student instruments.[276]

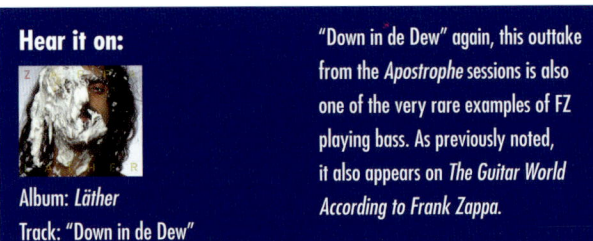

Hear it on:
Album: *Läther*
Track: "Down in de Dew"

"Down in de Dew" again, this outtake from the *Apostrophe* sessions is also one of the very rare examples of FZ playing bass. As previously noted, it also appears on *The Guitar World According to Frank Zappa*.

Fender Jazz Bass

"Well, it's like a car, you know; you come out with a standard model, then you have a deluxe model, a Cadillac version."
—Leo Fender[277]

One of FZ's lesser-known instruments is this handsome natural-finish Fender Jazz Bass, manufactured in 1977–1978, according to the serial number (S857938).[278] It has a maple neck with a fretless rosewood fingerboard and white binding connected to the body by a three-bolt neck joint.

The body has a natural finish with high-gloss polyester "thick skin" varnish, a black pickguard, and screw holes indicating it was originally fitted with the standard Fender thumbrest and pickup and bridge covers.

Fender introduced the Fender Jazz Bass in March 1960. They positioned it as an upmarket alternative to their hugely successful Precision Bass guitar, with the name and offset body shape marking it as a companion to the Jazzmaster guitar.

It featured a slim and fast bolt-on neck and twin single-coil pickups, which were wired out of phase to provide a noise-cancelling humbucking effect when used together. The pickups had twin pole pieces for each string, like the Precision Bass. Originally the electronics consisted of a concentric volume and tone control for each; later they were replaced with a simpler design consisting of an individual volume control for each pickup and a master tone control.[279]

The thinner neck made it easier to play than the Precision Bass for most people, and the twin pickups produced a brighter, more cutting tone, which gave the bass a more prominent role in a band.

It was another huge success for Fender, and disregarding its name, it was especially popular among rock bass players. The Jazz Bass has been in continuous manufacture since it was introduced, and the basic design is unchanged.

The Fender Jazz Bass at the UMRK in 2012
(Mick Ekers)

FZ in the UMRK in 1991, Jazz Bass in background
(still from Profile, *1991)*

Guitars

The unpopular 3-bolt neck fixing
(Mick Ekers)

The Jazz bass showing screw holes where the original bridge and pickup covers, and thumb rest were fitted
(Mick Ekers)

What looks like the same guitar can be seen propped up next to the wall of the UMRK control room in an interview with FZ for the Dutch *TROS* TV show in 1991. In the video, the bass has a maple fretted neck with white block markings (a standard Fender option in the late 1970s);[280] otherwise it appears identical to the instrument I photographed.

Assuming it is the same guitar, my guess is that FZ had the fingerboard replaced with a fretless one for the purposes of sampling it into the Synclavier, possibly around the time of rehearsals for *The Yellow Shark* in 1992. The bass is in beautiful condition, and looks as if it has hardly been played. The electronics and pickups appear to be standard, with no sign of any other customization having taken place.

I don't know when or where FZ came by the instrument; but his tech Arthur "Midget" Sloatman has said that Fender gave him a couple of basses in 1978, so most likely it is one of those.[281] I asked FZ bass players Arthur Barrow (1978–1981) and Scott Thunes (1981–1988) about the bass; neither of them remembered ever using it. Thunes told me that it was always hanging around the studio but he never saw anyone playing it, certainly not FZ.[282]

The late 1970s are generally considered among the darkest years for the Fender brand, with inferior-specification instruments being produced with poor quality control due to parent company CBS's desire to cut costs. The three-bolt neck fittings (the original design had four) and the heavy, dull-sounding ash bodies are among the reasons why many bass players look down on Jazz Basses from this period.

However, Fender did still manage to produce some good basses around this time; famed jazz musician Marcus Miller still favors his signature 1977 Jazz Bass. Maybe FZ found something special in this particular instrument.t sold for $5,760.[283]

Picks

"I also do some stuff where I use the pick on the fingerboard."

—FZ

The type of guitar pick (or plectrum) used by a guitarist can make a significant difference to the tone produced. FZ didn't always use his conventionally; in 1977, he told *Guitar Player* magazine, "I also do some stuff where I use the pick on the fingerboard, pressing down and hitting the string at the same time. It gets kind of a Bulgarian bagpipe sound."[284]

FZ elaborated on this in *Down Beat* in 1983, when interviewer Bill Milkowski asked about the "Bulgarian bagpipe technique": "You mean with the pick on the strings? With your left hand you're fretting the notes and with your right hand you're also fretting the notes with a pick. Instead of plucking the string you're fretting the string, you hit the string and then that presses it against the fret so it actuates the string and also determines the

ZAPPA GEAR

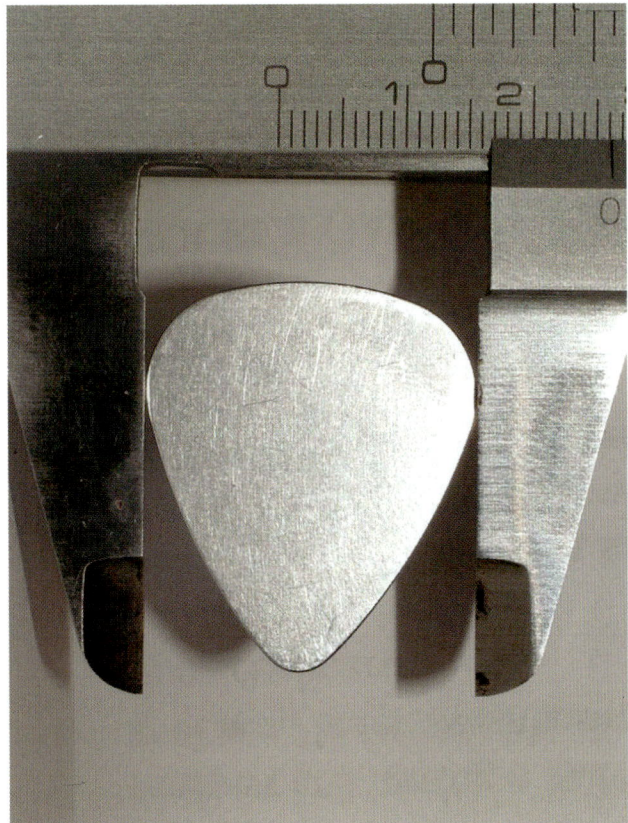

One of FZ's stainless-steel picks from the 1988 tour
(Deepinder Cheema)

Phased Systems advert and a Landström Sharkfin pick
(Author's collection)

pitch, and you can move back and forth real fast that way.... The first time I ever used it in concert was in Vienna in '72 or '73. I decided I would try it, and I've done it ever since."[285]

FZ started out playing the small plastic teardrop-shaped Gibson picks popular with many jazz guitarists. Dweezil Zappa remembers: "When I first started playing guitar, the only picks that were around were the kind that Frank was using which were these little Gibson teardrop ones, the little teeny-tiny ones."[286]

DZ continues: "They ended up being too small for me and I got heavy Fender-style picks and Frank ended up just using those; later he switched to Fender medium and then heavy picks and then he got into using some of those shark-fin picks that had the serrated edge sometimes."[287]

Sharkfin picks were invented by Swedish guitarist Stig Landström in 1964, and were imported into the US in the 1980s by Phased Systems,[288] makers of the D'Mini guitars that FZ liked; presumably they introduced them to him.

In the 1980s, DZ became friends with guitarist Warren De Martini (lead guitarist with the band Ratt), who used metal picks. De Martini used to visit the house to play guitar with DZ, and FZ liked his playing, and they sometimes talked technique: "Warren gave him some of those metal picks and then he started using them, which ate up the strings really fast."[289]

FZ was to favor metal picks for the rest of his career. If you look closely, you can see him using one on the *Does Humor Belong in Music* DVD recorded on 26th August, 1984. Likely this was supplied by Performance Guitar in LA. Performance's Bob McDonald talked to *International Musician* in 1985, and mentioned that FZ was using stainless steel and copper picks.[290] I have been unable to find any photographs of FZ with a copper pick; it seems that stainless steel was his preference.

Deepinder Cheema (see the wah-wah section) showed me one of FZ's metal picks that was given to him by guitar tech Merl Saunders Jr. in Genoa on 9th June, 1988. The pick is around 0.7 mm thick and just under 26mm wide, and is shaped

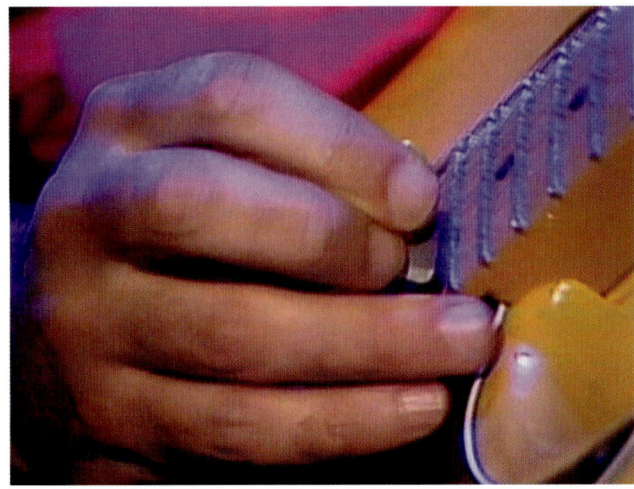

FZ's hand holding metal pick in characteristic style
(still from Does Humor Belong in Music, 1985)

like a Fender teardrop. It appears to be stainless steel, and apparently is slightly magnetic, which suggests it has been work hardened.

Saunders told me that for the 1988 tour he bought several hundred from Tour Cure in Minneapolis, in varying thicknesses. The amiable Mr. Saunders gave many away to fans on the tour, but noted "They were all silver-plated [presumably nickel silver] but here's the deal: If they're silver, they were never used. That's the thing. The ones he actually used are oxidized, because it was so much acid that eventually the oxidation would turn the silver total bronze; now they are not silver at all."[291]

Hear it on:
Album: *One Size Fits All*
Track: "Inca Roads"

FZ uses the "Bulgarian bagpipe" technique at around 4 minutes and 20 seconds into the track, but listen to it all — this is a wonderfully rich piece of music. FZ also noted that you can hear it on "Gee I Like Your Pants" and "Variations on The Carlos Santana Secret Chord Progression" on the *Guitar* album.

Strings

"I use a different set of strings for each guitar, and I have about twenty-two guitars."

—FZ

FZ used a wide range of guitar strings during his career, often mixing different brands and types on a single instrument. He was happy to tell guitar fans what type and gauge he used. In 1975, he described the set he currently had on his SG as follows "... a mixed set of strings: the top string is a 009 Ampeg string, the B-string is a Gibson E-string, and the G-string is an Ernie Ball 15, and the D-string is a Rickenbacker D-string. And the A-string is a Rickenbacker E-string, and the low E-string is a Gibson 340 A-string."[292]

In the 1960s, it was nigh-on impossible to find light-gauge guitar strings with an unwound third string in your local music shop. Building a custom set of your favorite brand using different gauge strings was unheard of. To get an unwound third string, players would often resort to using a banjo string for the top E, and moving the rest of the strings down one (known as "slack stringing"). To build a custom set you had to mix and match from different makes, as FZ was still doing in 1975. This situation was changed by Ernie Ball, yet another West Coast innovator who had a major influence on the music industry.

Born in 1930 in Santa Monica California, Roland Sherwood Ball, encouraged by his father, learned to play pedal steel guitar in his teens. He soon found himself playing professionally in local combos, and at nineteen was touring with the Tommy

The distinctive Ernie Ball 'Slinky' packet design — essentially unchanged for 50 years (Copyright Ernie Ball; used with permission)

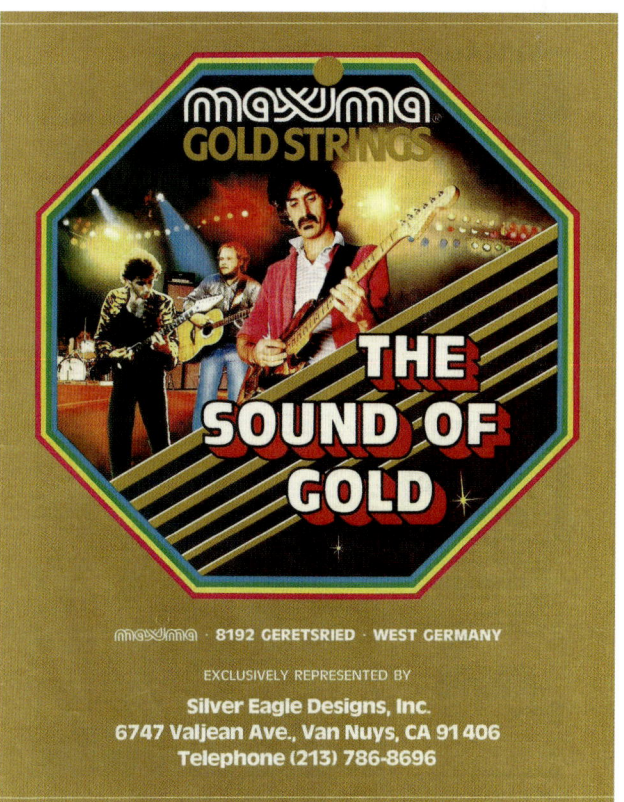

Maxima strings advert featuring FZ, also Warren Cuccurullo with the Vox Wah-wah guitar! (Author's collection)

Duncan band, adopting the stage name "Ernie." After his military service he gained a place in the house band on the *Western Varieties* TV show, which gave him a featured spot. This led to studio work and teaching, and a deserved reputation as a top-class performer on both steel and regular electric guitars.[293]

ZAPPA GEAR

In 1957, Ball opened a specialist guitar-only shop just outside Hollywood in Tarzana, a revolutionary idea at the time that proved very successful, despite warnings from conservative members of the music trade. He noticed that many of his guitar students had trouble fretting the roundwound third string of the Fender #100 medium gauge strings—standard issue on Fender electrics at the time. He tried to persuade Leo Fender to use a lighter gauge plain third string instead, but Fender was concerned that it might cause fret-buzz and didn't want to re-engineer his guitars to compensate.

Undeterred, Ball ordered some custom sets from a string manufacturer with a plain 24-gauge third string. These were very popular with local musicians, who started talking about "Ernie Ball" strings. With the rock and roll era, and the growth in popularity of solidbody electric guitars, came a demand from players for lighter gauge strings than were generally available. Noting this, he again tried to persuade Fender to produce such a set, and was again rebuffed; he also contacted Gibson, who were equally uninterested.

Once again Ball ordered a custom set from the manufacturer, a 10-46 set with a plain third, which he called Slinky strings. To accommodate the guitarists who wanted to make up their own custom sets, he also sold individual strings—a range of gauges from a homemade rack in his store. He later started selling them via mail order and they soon gained a reputation among leading musicians as the strings to use.

By 1967, the strings side of the business had grown to such an extent that the shop was sold and Ernie Ball became a full-time string manufacturer. During the 1970s and 1980s, the company grew into a multimillion-dollar turnover organization, expanding to include an industry-standard guitar volume pedal, Music Man guitars and amplifiers, and other products. Ernie Ball died in 2004, but the company remains an independent family business run by his son Sterling. The Slinky range of strings is still one of the most widely used worldwide.

In 1977, FZ was using just Ernie Balls: "I use either an .008 or .009 on top [E], an .011 or .012 on the B, a .016 or .017 on the G, a .024 on the D, anywhere from a .032 to a .038 on the A, and anywhere from a .046 to a .052 on the low E . . . and they're mainly all Ernie Balls."[294]

FZ continued to experiment with strings, usually favoring very light top strings and medium gauge for the bottom strings. In 1979, he discovered the German-made Maxima gold-plated strings. He told *UK Guitar* magazine's John Dalton, "I've found a good combination of strings for the SG, (Fender) Super Bullets for the top three and Maximas for the bottom three."[295]

Traditional electric guitar strings are secured to the guitar by a "ball end," one end of the string being wound around a small metal cylinder too large to pass through the hole in the guitar bridge or tailpiece. Fender invented the "bullet" string, with a bullet-shaped metal end that fit snugly in the Stratocaster vibrato unit, to mitigate the problem of strings going out of tune when the ball end moved slightly under the vibrato action (see FZ's comments on the Fender vibrato in the Fender Stratocasters section). Later designs of vibrato units like the Floyd Rose locked the strings in place, effectively solving this issue.

The Maxima strings were gold-plated, the theory being that they would resist corrosion and stay bright-sounding longer, which would compensate for their high price compared to conventional nickel-plated strings. Maxima went out of production in 2002, but the strings are now being produced again under the Optima Strings brand.

In the early 1980s, FZ endorsed Maxima gold strings, and appeared on the packaging. Despite the corrosion resistance of the Maxima strings, FZ used to change them as frequently as any other string. "I change them about every four or five days, sometimes sooner for the upper ones because they get bent more and get little notches in the back."[296] Remarking that guitar magazines *always* asked him what size strings he used, he told *Guitar World* in 1982: "OK, on the Les Paul, the top E string is 8, the B string is 10, the G string is 13, the D string is 24, the A string is 32 and the E string is 46. And they're Maximus [sic]."[297]

Later in the 1980s, FZ mostly played his custom Stratocasters made by Performance Guitar, who fitted them

Standard 'Ball-End' on an Ernie Ball .009 string
(Mick Ekers)

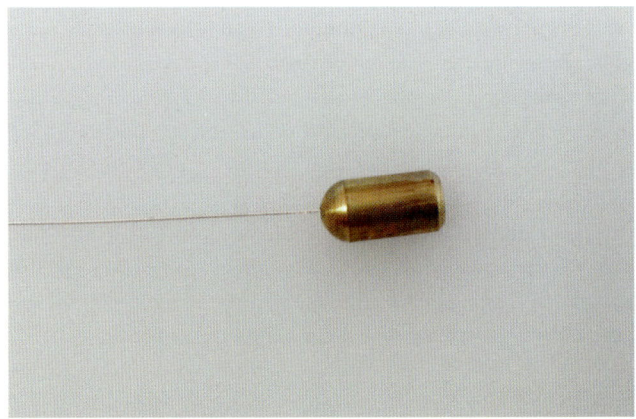

Fender 'Bullet' end on a .016-string
(Mick Ekers)

with Ernie Ball stainless-steel strings.[298] These are made of regular steel wire with a stainless-steel winding for the wound strings and are described by the manufacturer thusly: "Made from stainless steel wire wrapped around tin plated hex shaped steel core wire. These guitar strings provide brighter sound and extra string life."[299]

On FZ's final tour in 1988, ace guitar tech Merl Saunders Jr. changed his strings every day. Saunders told me he used Ernie Ball Super Slinkys, and only broke one string on the whole tour, a tribute to Saunders' skills as much as FZ's technique (according to the book *Zappa the Hard Way*, this happened during "Sharleena" at the Brighton show).[300] Percussionist Art Tripp, who played with the original Mothers of Invention and later Captain Beefheart, also noted: "I don't recall Frank breaking strings very often. He probably didn't punish the strings like the guys in Beefheart did!"[301]

Ever the perfect guitar tech, Saunders told me that sometimes he would go against FZ's instructions and change the gauge of his strings: "And there were nights where it looked like he was struggling, and then the next day I would change the gauge of the strings and not tell him. So I would do the top end of the strings, I would change the E and the A string to lighter gauges and then he would just sort of look over at me and smile like 'Yep. Gotcha!'"[302]

Floyd Rose Vibrato

"Floyd Rose. It changes the way the instrument plays. Everything feels springy."

—FZ [303]

Along with many other guitarists, FZ's style of playing was profoundly affected by the invention of the Floyd Rose vibrato system. He told *Down Beat* magazine in 1983 that "I've got a Floyd Rose apparatus on my Strat, and it just changed the world for me. Basically, it's a vibrato bar apparatus that doesn't go out of tune . . . I had this thing installed so that you could not only bend way down but bend up on it; it'll take you up a whole step or drop it down below an octave, so it gives you the possibility to play glissandos and other types of sounds that you can't get any other way."[304]

Vibrato systems ("whammy bars," as FZ called them) for guitars were nothing new, but before the invention of the Floyd Rose they all shared a common problem: if you depressed the bar to lower the pitch too much, the strings would loosen, and the windings around the tuning pegs and the position of the string ball-end in the bridge would often move slightly.

The result was that when you returned the vibrato to its normal position, some strings may have gone out of tune. The Fender bullet-end strings mentioned in the previous section

Eddie Van Halen with Floyd Rose in an early advert
(Author's collection)

were designed to stop the movement at the bridge, but that only solved half of the problem.

In the late 1970s, guitarist Floyd Rose (like many players) was trying to emulate the heavy use of vibrato employed by Ritchie Blackmore and Jimi Hendrix, and was frustrated by the resultant constant retuning required on his Stratocaster. He realized that holding the strings in place was the solution, and came up with a design for a clamp that locked the strings at the nut and a vibrato bridge design that clamped them at the other end. He soon found that getting prototypes built was expensive, so he obtained his own bench mill and taught himself how to use it.[305]

Because Rose's system clamped the strings at both ends, the movement that caused them to go out of tune was eliminated. To enable tuning of the guitar without undoing the lock nut, it had fine tuners built into the bridge. The design also allowed the vibrato to vary the string pitch over a much wider range than was possible with other units.

While he was still refining the design, Rose was working as a tech for guitarist Randy Hansen. One day he showed Hansen a guitar with one of his units fitted, and challenged him to put it out of tune. Hansen gave the vibrato unit a full-on assault, including throwing the guitar to the ground and jumping on the bar, and was astounded when he found it was still in tune. This became Rose's standard method of demonstrating the unit to guitarists. In 1979, Eddie Van Halen was similarly impressed and had one fitted to his guitar. Soon after this, an article in *Guitar Player* magazine mentioned Van Halen's vibrato units; this was enough to start spreading the word. Dismissed by Fender and Gibson guitars, Rose struck a deal with Kramer guitars, who were fast establishing a name for themselves, and before long, a Floyd Rose was mandatory equipment for any serious rock guitarist.[306]

ZAPPA GEAR

Just before the advent of the Floyd Rose, FZ had been mostly playing his fixed-bridge Gibson guitars, but that was all to change: "At the time, I wasn't playing guitar with a whammy bar. So another important thing would be when I changed over and started using Strats instead of Gibsons. Before the Floyd Rose tailpiece came along, the old Strats were just so out of tune that I could never stand to listen to them."[307]

The Floyd Rose vibrato unit became an essential element of his guitar playing, and typically FZ took it to its limits: "On the last tour I used it to excess. Because the Floyd makes it possible to come back in tune after you go down to the subsonic regions. You can dump all the strings slack and come back up and be in tune. And the way my Floyd is set up, you can go down two octaves practically, then back up to normal position, and then bend up a whole-step and sometimes even a third. It's balanced so well that I can just wiggle it a little bit and get a real nice vibrato."[308]

Merl Saunders Jr. remembered: "He would do the dive-bomb thing and I would just sit there and cringe (laughs), I'd be like 'God dammit, I hope it comes back into tune.' And he would do the thing where he would pull it too, it would go up three or four steps, and stay in tune!"[309]

Thirty-five years later, the Floyd Rose vibrato is still the biggest-selling floating bridge system on the planet, and is offered by almost every electric guitar manufacturer. It was justly recognized by *Guitar World* magazine as one of the ten most earth-shaking guitar innovations, and it has become so established that is referred to by most guitarists as simply a "Floyd."

Floyd Rose patented locking nut on FZ's Sunburst Strat
(Mick Ekers)

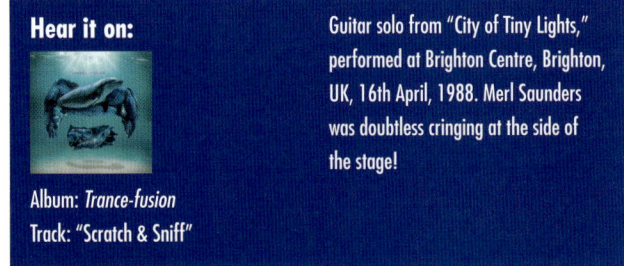

Hear it on:
Album: *Trance-fusion*
Track: "Scratch & Sniff"

Guitar solo from "City of Tiny Lights," performed at Brighton Centre, Brighton, UK, 16th April, 1988. Merl Saunders was doubtless cringing at the side of the stage!

Floyd Rose vibrato fitted to FZ's Tobaccoburst Strat
(Mick Ekers)

CHAPTER TWO
AMPLIFIERS

"Well, last tour I was using a three-amp setup. I had a Carvin that I kept fairly clean—it was my precise line amplifier, and I use a Marshall 100-watt for squealing high-end, biting fuzz stuff that's in the 2k [2.000 cycles per second frequency range] register. I also had an Acoustic that was centered more between 100 and 500 cycles, with a peak around 300 for the kind of grunty Les Paul-type roaring sound. The three of them together gave a pretty good balance."[310]
—FZ

Fender Champ

Standel Combo

Fender Combos

Acoustic Control Corporation

Acoustic Control Corporation 270

Marshall Amplifiers

Pignose 7-100

Orange Matamp OR 200

Oberheim Studio Practice Amp

Mesa Boogie Mk I

Acoustic 165 Combo

Carvin X-100B

Seymour Duncan 100-Watt Convertible

Vox Beatle Amplifiers

Vox 4×12 Cabinet

Note
Having got this far, you may be wondering if there is any significance in the ordering of the sections in this book. The original intention was to proceed chronologically, but FZ did not always follow a linear path with his gear! Some pieces of equipment were first used many years after they had been made; others were tried out as prototypes long before they went into production. Still others were re-tired, modified and then re-used, and it soon became clear that keeping to an ordered structure would be impossible. Therefore, I have taken approximate chronological order as my starting point, but I have also grouped items by type or manufacturer, or in some cases just to avoid page breaks.

If it seems I have been following FZ's watchwords "Anything, Any Time, Anywhere—for No Reason at All," that is not strictly the case, and I hope the reader will bear with me. There is an Index at the back, which may be of some help!

ZAPPA GEAR

Fender Champ

"A cheesy little amp with a sign on the front said 'Fender Champ'"
— FZ[311]

The above words from the title track from the *Joe's Garage* album bring smiles and nods from countless numbers of American men of a certain age, who were teenage guitarists in the 1950s and 1960s. The Fender Champ was the *de facto* standard beginner's guitar amp—small, cheap, surprisingly loud, and with a good clean tone that would distort satisfyingly once the volume was turned up past seven or so. It was (and still is) a popular studio amp.

The Fender Champ was introduced in 1948 as the Fender Champion. It was the smallest and cheapest Fender amplifier, developing just five watts of power with a single 6-inch (later 8-inch) speaker. It had two inputs, a volume control, and an on-off switch.[312]

The circuit was very simple, a 6SJ7 preamp tube and a 6V6 power tube. In 1954 it was officially renamed the Champ, and in 1964 was redesigned in the new Fender "blackface" style, with the addition of a treble and bass control. This was the first model that actually had the word Champ on the front—earlier tweed-covered models just had the Fender logo—so we can assume that this is the model that Joe and his band had in his garage.

The Champ was produced more or less unaltered (briefly changing to the "silverface" style for a few years in 1968 before reverting to blackface) until it was discontinued in 1982.[313] Fender brought out a reissue in 2006.

There is no record of FZ ever recording with a Fender Champ, although if the Pignose amplifier (of which more later) had not been invented, things might have been different. Nonetheless, it is almost inconceivable that FZ never used one when playing and rehearsing with his various pre–Mothers of Invention bands. In 2008, Fender placed an appropriate advert for the Fender Champ in the program of the stage production of *Joe's Garage*.

Fender advert from the *Joe's Garage* program

An original 1960s Blackface Champ
(John Shults, Truevintageguitar.com)

> **Hear about it on:**
> A rollicking live version from 1984, the original was released as a single and is also on the *Joe's Garage* album, of course.
>
> Album: *You Can't Do That on Stage Anymore, Vol. 3*
> Track: "Joe's Garage" (live version)

Standel Combo

" . . . it was a Standel, about the same size of a Fender Deluxe . . . "
—FZ

Not very much is known about this amplifier, but it obviously meant enough to FZ for him to write a song inspired by it. In 1969, FZ said in an interview, "I get kind of a laugh out of the fact that other people are going to try to interpret that stuff and come up with some grotesque interpretations of it. It gives me a certain amount of satisfaction. You can imagine how insane that must get on a song like 'Electric Aunt Jemima,' which was written about an amplifier. Yes, it's a Standel amplifier, about this big, that I used on a couple of sessions."[314]

In a later radio interview, FZ recalled that it was originally owned by New York singer David Blue: " . . . he used to work in Greenwich Village in the early 1960s when we were working there. And he had an old amplifier, it was a Standel, about the same size of a Fender Deluxe and he donated it to our cause when we were short of equipment. And that's the amplifier that turned out to be Electric Aunt Jemima."[315]

The Standel brand was established in 1953 by electronics engineer Bob Crooks (named after his repair shop Standard Electronics) in Temple City, California. He was originally hired by Paul Bigsby (inventor of the Bigsby vibrato unit) to design an amplifier, but the first prototype was not a success and Crooks continued independently. Eventually he came up with an innovative design that included many revolutionary features for the time. The 25L15, as it was known, featured separate preamp and power amp units, with the power unit located in the base of cabinet. The 22-watt tube amplifier had a 15" JBL speaker, separate bass and treble controls with illuminated dials, and luxury padded cream Naugahyde upholstery.

Crooks then decided to take the amplifier to the musicians, rather than wait for them to come to him. Hardcore FZ fans will be amused to note the following, from *The Standel Story* by Deke Dickerson: "Bob began making the rounds to some of the local Los Angeles–area country music shows. The first place he went to was Cliffie Stone's Hometown Jamboree which was held at the El Monte Legion Stadium, just blocks away from Bob's backyard workshop in Temple City."[316] The El Monte Legion Stadium is mentioned in the song "Dog Breath" from the *Uncle Meat* album, which also features "Electric Aunt Jemima." FZ once described the El Monte stadium as having "the worst acoustical environment in Southern California."[317]

With a great tone, advanced features, and a high volume for its size (partly due to the high-efficiency JBL speakers), the Standel quickly gained a reputation as one of the best amplifiers of the day. Crooks soon found his hands full building luxury custom units to the clients' individual requirements, with different size speakers, bright or mellow tonality, and custom color finishes. The first seventy-five ended up being sold to some of the top guitarists of the time, including Merle Travis, Cliff Gallup, and Chet Atkins. Crooks moved to larger premises in 1958 and started mass producing the amps. Further innovations included moving the control knobs to the front and then early hybrid tube/solid-state models. The company went out of business in the early 1970s; its all-transistor amps were not that successful, and the final nail in the coffin was the production of a bad batch of circuits that could not be repaired because Crooks had them encased (potted) in epoxy resin to stop anyone from stealing his secrets.

FZ used his 1960s C15 during the *Hot Rats* recording sessions, as can be seen in the photo below from Bill Gubbins' excellent *The Hot Rats Book*.[318] Doubtless it sounded rather special—let's hope it is in a good home now. High-quality reproductions of the classic early combos are still being produced by the company Standel Musical Instrument Amplifiers.

FZ sets up his C15 in the studio. The smaller amp is a Gibson Les Paul Junior. *(Bill Gubbins)*

Hear about it on:
We don't know what tracks FZ used his C15 on, but this song about the amp.
Album: *Uncle Meat*
Track: "Electric Aunt Jemima"

ZAPPA GEAR

Fender Combos

"What equipment did you use on Freak Out? *Just a Fender Deluxe amp, that's all"*

—FZ[319]

Fender Deluxe

In the early days of the Mothers of Invention, FZ's amplifier was a small blackface Fender Deluxe. Although he later upgraded to the more powerful Fender Twin, he kept the Deluxe for recording purposes, at least up until the *Hot Rats* sessions in 1969.

The Deluxe was another classic small amp design from the Fender factory. Based on the original tweed-covered model from the 1950s, the Deluxe was reintroduced in 1963, in a new black Tolex finish with a silver grillcloth. This range became known as the blackface series, to differentiate it from the 1968 redesign introduced under CBS ownership, which featured a silver control panel.

This compact combo amp had two input channels, one labelled Normal, with Volume, Bass, and Treble controls, and one labelled Vibrato, which had additional controls for Reverb and tremolo Speed and Intensity. To the presumed dismay of musical lexicographers, once again Leo got his terminology mixed up; the amplifier contained a tremolo unit that rapidly varied the volume of the output ("vibrato" means to vary the pitch of a note, and is what he should have called the "tremolo" units on his guitars).

The 12" speaker (usually a Jensen C-12Q) was powered by what has become a classic low-powered amplifier circuit. The 22-watt amplifier had two 6V6GT power tubes, four 12AX7 preamp tubes, one 5AR4 rectifier tube, and two 12AT7 tubes driving the reverb and phase inverter circuits. It was point-to-point wired, and the reverb and tremolo effects could be switched on and off by a footswitch.[320]

Apart from the use of the word "vibrato," there is almost nothing to criticize about this amplifier. Simple, compact, and versatile, it had a great clean sound, but could deliver an excellent overdriven tone when the volume was turned up. The ability to do this at relatively low volume made it an ideal studio amp. More than one guitarist has voted it their desert island amp,[321] and Fender still sell a reissue of the 1965 model, little changed from the original.

FZ described how the amp was hooked up during the recording of "Willie the Pimp," and also told the tale of an unwelcome control room guest: "I was overdubbing the solo while standing in the control room. The guitar was going into the board, out of the board, into the studio, into the amp, picked up by a microphone, and back into the board. I'm playing my wah-wah pedal and wailing away, and this guy from the union comes in. He's standing behind me, tapping his pencil on his clipboard, waiting for me to get done so that he can ask me whether or not I've filed some kind of union paper about how many musicians I'm using. That's the solo on the record, and the whole time there was this union pood-head standing behind me."[322]

Fender Twin Reverb

FZ mainly used a Fender Twin Reverb on stage during the rest of the 1960s, with two 12" speakers and an amplifier rated at 85 watts; it offered him considerably more volume than his Deluxe.

The Twin Reverb, another blackface model from the same period (1963–1967) as the Deluxe, also had Normal and Vibrato channels. The Normal channel had two inputs; Volume, Treble, Middle, and Bass controls; and a Bright switch (which would compensate for the loss of treble when the volume was at low levels). The Vibrato channel had the same controls as the Normal, plus Reverb, and tremolo Speed and Intensity controls.

The 85-watt power amplifier had four 6L6GC power tubes, and six preamp tubes (four 12AX7 and two 12AT7), and drove a pair of 12" Jensen speakers. It had a pair of chromed tilt back

An immaculate Deluxe from the mid-1960s
(Wikipedia Commons)

A 1965 Twin Reverb
(Ben Bove, Retro Rentals)

Amplifiers

legs that enabled the amp to be angled slightly upwards for better sound dispersion when on stage.

Of all the blackface series, the Twin Reverb was undoubtedly the most successful commercially, and was standard equipment for almost every guitar-based band in the late 1960s, until the Marshall amps began to take over. Although considerably louder than the Deluxe, the Twin was known more for its clean tone than its distortion, which tended to be mellower than the Deluxe.[323] Both amplifiers are still available from Fender as part of their vintage reissue range.

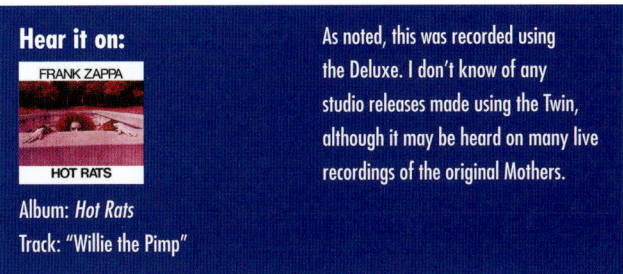

Hear it on:
FRANK ZAPPA
HOT RATS

Album: *Hot Rats*
Track: "Willie the Pimp"

As noted, this was recorded using the Deluxe. I don't know of any studio releases made using the Twin, although it may be heard on many live recordings of the original Mothers.

Fender Super Reverb

The 2016 Julien's auction catalog listed a 1979 silverface Fender Super Reverb amplifier, serial number A992424. It had four 10" JBL speakers, and tape marked "Ray."[324] Used by singer and guitarist Ray White during the 1980s Zappa tours, it was on the storage shelves in the UMRK when we visited.

The Super combo was introduced by Fender in 1963 and was in production until 1982. Originally rated at 40 watts, the later versions had a master volume control and a 70-watt power amplifier with two 6L6GC power tubes, and six preamp tubes (four 12AX7 and two 12AT7). This version, made during Fender's period of CBS ownership, had what was known as an Ultralinear circuit design with a solid-state rectifier.[325] Notably used by blues guitarist Stevie Ray Vaughan, these combos were favored for their rich scooped tone when distorted; the Ultralinear versions allegedly had a cleaner, harder, and thinner-sounding tone. Heavy and very loud with the custom JBL speakers, this doubtless helped Ray White to cut through and contrast with FZ's huge Marshall sound. The Super sold for $3,840.[326]

Acoustic Control Corporation

"Meet our friends . . . the Mothers, they use Acoustic Amplifiers"[327]

In their early days, the Mothers of Invention struggled with their motley collection of onstage equipment. FZ said that at one time, part of their rig was "a Harman Kardon hi-fi amplifier hidden inside a peach box."[328] In 1968, all that changed when they took delivery of a number of the new Acoustic Control Corporation 260 amplifiers and matching 261 and 262 cabinets. For the first time, they were loud!

The Acoustic Control Corporation (ACC) was founded in 1967, by Steven L. Marks and his father Robert Marks. From the start, their aim was to produce the best musical instrument amplifiers in the world.[329] In those days, PA systems were very puny affairs, used just for vocals and the odd wind instrument, and the bulk of a band's live output came from the onstage amplifiers (or "backline," as it is known). At the time, there was no serious competition for the loud stadium-filling tube-based guitar amps manufactured by UK firms Marshall and Hiwatt.

Marks decided to go for a more modern approach: the amps were all solid-state transistor designs, with built-in effects such as fuzz, tremolo, and reverb, and featured a modular computer style design so that individual circuit boards could be replaced relatively easily on the road. Rather than going for the square-profile Marshall style, the Acoustic speaker cabinets

The Fender Super Reverb used by Ray White
(ZFT)

FZ with Acoustic amps at the BBC
(*still from* Late Night Lineup, *1969*)

ZAPPA GEAR

Cal Shenkel's cartoon of the Mothers, for a concert advert in 1968, shows his impression of their Acoustic amps and cabinets
(From the Frank Zappa Beat the Boots Scrapbook *—ZFT)*

were tall and high-tech looking; with their distinctive black, baby-blue, and aluminum finish, the systems had a unique and stylish image that set them apart from the rest.

The 260 amplifier, with "62 all-silicon transistors and diodes," as the 1968 catalog boasted, was a highly versatile unit that could be used for keyboards and electrified wind instruments as well as guitar. It had two input channels, each with volume, bass, and treble controls, and a Variamp semi-parametric equalizer.

There were controls for fuzz, tremolo, and reverb, and a connector for a four-way footswitch that enabled selection of the input channel and effects. The 260 had an optional stereo output for connection to an additional amplifier, and even included an electronic tuning fork switch, which produced a tone that you could tune your guitar to. The built-in power amplifier produced 125 watts RMS.

Two speaker units were available: the 261, with four 12" Altec speakers, and the distinctive 262, with two 15" Altec speakers and a bright blue high-frequency horn. The 262 could be supplied with a built-in power amplifier, enabling bands to connect as many as they wanted to a single instrument amplifier.

The Mothers of Invention were one of the first groups to use Acoustic Corporation gear, and Acoustic placed adverts in the press with the slogan "Meet our friends . . . the Mothers." Very much in evidence during their 1968 European tour, videos and photos show various 260/261/262 combinations in use for guitar, keyboards, and the electrified horn section. FZ also used the built-in fuzz unit; at the time all he had on the stage floor was the Acoustic footswitch next to his trusty Vox wah-wah.

They also used Acoustic amps for their PA system. FZ noted: "In 1968 the 'monitor system' . . . had not yet been invented. Our PA system for the 1968 European tour was a nasty-sounding mono appliance, which consisted of twelve 100-watt guitar amplifiers wired together . . . There was no 'house mixer.'"[330]

It may have been primitive by modern standards, but when I heard this system in action at the London Royal Festival Hall in 1968, I thought it sounded pretty good compared to most live rock performances of the time.

In 1969, FZ lent some of his Acoustic gear to Don Van Vliet (Captain Beefheart), so that his band could rehearse the music for the *Trout Mask Replica* album. Drummer John French was not impressed: " . . . we used Acoustic brand amplifiers. They were, I think, part of Zappa's stage gear. Acoustic is a terrible name for these amps as they were totally solid-state and had no warmth or acoustic tonality at all, with the exception of the bass amp, which I thought was exceptional. 'Hair Pie' was done with these amplifiers."[331]

The bass amp French liked was the 360/1 bass amp and cabinet, used at one time by Mothers of Invention bass player Roy Estrada. These remained popular with many top bass players, including John Paul Jones and Jaco Pastorius, and would carry the company's reputation long after the 260 series fell out of favor.

In 1978 Acoustic introduced the massive 408 bass cabinet containing four 15" speakers (two forward-facing and two internal-horn loaded), which was rated at two ohms.[332] One of these beasts, complete with wheeled road case, used by FZ for touring in the late 1970s, turned up in the 2016 Julien's auction.[333] The catalog description described it as having two 15" speakers and a horn (possibly this was an error and nobody had opened it up to see the additional pair of internal speakers). It sold for $3,125.[334]

The 260/261 from an Acoustic catalogue ca 1970

The 260 series was listed in the catalog until 1971; it was replaced by the new 270 series the following year.[335] The suggested retail price for a 261 amp/speaker combination in 1970 was $1,195. The price FZ paid is not known; in the early days Acoustic only sold their equipment direct to the bands that used them. Apart from the Mothers, they were used by several big-name bands of the time, including Traffic and the Doors, who had a massive onstage Acoustic rig. For a time they had a considerable reputation, but eventually most bands tired of their rather harsh and piercing tone, and they were rarely seen in the 1970s.

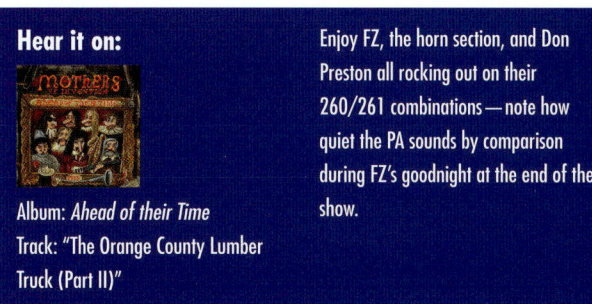

Hear it on:
Album: *Ahead of their Time*
Track: "The Orange County Lumber Truck (Part II)"

Enjoy FZ, the horn section, and Don Preston all rocking out on their 260/261 combinations—note how quiet the PA sounds by comparison during FZ's goodnight at the end of the show.

FZ's mighty 408 bass cabinet
(from auction catalogue—copyright ZFT)

Acoustic Control Corporation 270 Amplifier

"I'm real fussy about equalization...."

—*FZ*[336]

Although the Mothers of Invention stopped using Acoustic Control Corporation amplifiers as their main stage and PA gear in the late 1960s, FZ kept a 270 lead amplifier in his onstage rig, alongside one or more Marshall amplifiers, throughout the mid-1970s. The 270 was Acoustic's second-generation flagship guitar amplifier, introduced in 1972 as a replacement for the 260 that FZ had used previously.

Aimed very much at professional users, it had a recommended retail price of $770.[337] Its power was very optimistically advertised as 375 watts RMS in the 1972 catalog; it was later more conservatively rated as 275 watts. Realistically, it probably should have been rated at about half that. Regardless of the advertising hype, it continued the Acoustic tradition of being loud and clean-sounding.

The 270 featured high and low gain inputs; Volume, Bass, Midrange, and Treble rotary controls; a bright switch; a five-band graphic equalizer; and built-in reverb/fuzz and tremolo. There was a switch to select reverb or fuzz, and a rotary fuzz/reverb control, which varied the level of distortion or the reverb mix accordingly. The tremolo section had a rate and intensity control, and as with all Acoustic amps the intensity had a huge range, with the maximum setting producing an extreme on/off effect.

With typical lack of modesty, the user manual states: "The name Acoustic on your amplifier is synonymous with the ultimate in professional amplification. Your Acoustic 270 is the standard by which all others are judged."[338] The manual also

An apparently unmodified 270 sits below FZ's Marshall amps in 1974
(still from The Dub Room Special!, *1982)*

ZAPPA GEAR

The modified Acoustic 270 at the UMRK in 2012
(Mick Ekers)

offers users a lifetime guarantee provided the product is not misused or mishandled.

Characteristically, FZ recalled the precise control settings that he used on his amp in an interview in 1977: " . . . and on the 270 the volume will be on four, treble all the way up, the bright switch is on, the midrange will be on about 75%, the bass will be about 80%, the graphic equalizer is all the way up at 80 cycles, about 80% at 160, all the way up at 320, just about flat at 640, and maybe a little bit of boost at 1250."[339]

FZ seems to have had a lot of time for this amp. The booklet that comes with the *Joe's Domage* CD shows the wheelchair-bound FZ in 1972 (after the Rainbow accident) with a 270 set up on a table next to him during the *Grand Wazoo* rehearsals; the graphic EQ settings look similar to the above. In the movie *The Dub Room Special*, the 1974 recordings, made at KCET studios in Los Angeles, show the 270 manfully supporting the weight of two 100-watt Marshall heads.

We saw FZ's trusty 270 on a shelf in the control room of the UMRK, with the above EQ settings written down on a piece of card taped to the top of amp. An additional knob has been added beneath the reverb/fuzz level control; possibly this is another level control to allow simultaneous use of the fuzz and reverb effects. There is a multipin connector beneath the output jacks at the back, the purpose of which is unknown. The serial number is GA-1004.

FZ must have originally had at least two of these amps; the additional knob fitted to the amp at the UMRK can just be made out in the rehearsal video of the band at the Hordern Pavilion in Australia in June, 1973; however, the amp shown in the 1974 KCET recordings appears unmodified.

The 270 stayed in production until 1978, when it was superseded by the new 330 amplifier. These days the Acoustic brand is best known for its bass amplifiers, but back in the 1970s, the 270 had several other high-profile users, including Mahogany Rush virtuoso Frank Marino[340] and Ernie Isley (who also blended his with a Marshall amp).[341]

The rear of the 270 showing added multi-pin connector
(Mick Ekers)

Serial number GA-1004
(Mick Ekers)

Amplifiers

EQ settings taped to FZ's amp at the UMRK (not FZ's handwriting)
(Mick Ekers)

FZ in Sydney in 1973, with the modified 270 in the background
(screen grab from video)

Marshall Amplifiers

"I wanna have a Marshall tonight . . . I don't want a 'spin-off' of a Marshall, I want a Marshall"

—*FZ*[342]

Around the time of the *Over-Nite Sensation* album, FZ's guitar playing style went through a marked change, and *Guitarist* magazine asked him about this in 1973. FZ put this partly down to the high standard of musicianship of his current band, but also due to his equipment: "But it also changed because of the guitar and the amplification. Prior to that time I'd been using a Goldtop Les Paul or an ES-5 Switchmaster through a Fender amp or an Acoustic amp with a fairly nondescript tone . . . But by the early 1970s I was playing a Gibson SG and I switched over to Marshalls."[343]

Although FZ already had a reputation as no slouch when it came to guitar playing, this period marked the start of his establishment as a recognized virtuoso. From then on FZ would hardly ever appear on stage without at least one Marshall amplifier in his rig. The heading quote above was in response to a suggestion from his tech that he use a substitute amp that night, as his Marshall needed repairing.

The man who would be responsible for these amplifiers, James Charles Marshall, was born on July 29, 1923, in North Kensington, London. At the age of five, he was diagnosed with a rare brittle bone condition and spent most of his childhood immobilized in a full-body plaster cast. He was kept immobile until he was twelve and a half, when he was finally discharged from the hospital. He left school soon after, determined to get on with life and make something of himself. While still in his teens, it was discovered that he had a great talent for singing, and before long was working most nights of the week crooning with dance bands. During World War II, Marshall was not allowed to join the armed forces because of his medical history and worked as an engineer, useful training for what was to come.

Continuing with his singing, Marshall found he also had a talent for drumming, which made him even more in demand. By the time the war ended in 1945 he was one of the top working musicians in the country, playing in and leading bands behind the drum kit. Marshall found it hard to hear himself singing over the volume of a big band and his drums, so using his basic engineering knowledge he built his own PA speakers, which had an open back to allow some of the vocals to be heard on the stage.

By 1949, he had enough of a reputation to give up his day job and supplant his income from performing by giving drum lessons. Before long Marshall was making more money from teaching than playing; at one time he had sixty-four students, all having weekly lessons. One notable pupil was the young Mitch Mitchell, who later found fame with Jimi Hendrix.

Marshall gradually gave up performing, and by 1960, he had saved enough money to open a small drum shop at 76 Uxbridge Road, West London. The shop was a great success, and was especially popular with the up and coming rock and roll musicians, and he soon branched out into selling electric guitars, amplifiers, and his own speaker cabinets. Momentously,

FZ adjusting his 1970's pair of Marshalls
(Bob Lilly)

ZAPPA GEAR

FZ with his Marshalls in 1974 (still from The Dub Room Special!, 1982)

the young Pete Townshend asked Marshall if he could make something bigger and louder than the Fender amps he had been using.

Marshall instinctively knew that the time was right for the world's first rock and roll amplifier. At his electrician Ken Bran's suggestion, he poached the highly regarded young engineer Dudley Craven from EMI, who came up with a modification of the Fender Bassman circuit that was louder and grittier sounding. The first production Marshall amp—the JTM 45—was put in the shop window in September 1962. They took orders for twenty-three in the first day and couldn't make them fast enough. By 1964, the first Marshall factory was opened in Silverdale Road, Hayes, Middlesex.

One problem with the JTM45 was that it was too powerful for the 2×12 speaker cabinets of the time, and Marshall came up with his signature 4×12 slant-top speaker cabinet design. Pete Townshend and John Entwistle from the Who were the first customers, but Townshend wanted still more power.

He persuaded Marshall to build a 100-watt amplifier and an 8×12 speaker cabinet. This last was too heavy for even the Who's burly roadies, and Marshall came up with the classic twin 4×12 cabinet design. The "Marshall stack" had arrived! Before long almost every British guitarist of note was using one. Apart from Townshend, other significant users included Eric Clapton, Jeff Beck, and Ritchie Blackmore. Marshall's former pupil Mitch Mitchell had narrowly beaten later Zappa sideman Aynsley Dunbar for the job as drummer with the coincidentally named James Marshall Hendrix. Mitchell introduced Hendrix to Marshall and he soon showed the world just what could be achieved with these great amps and cabinets.

The earliest record I can find of FZ playing using a Marshall amplifier is at the 1967 Albert Hall concert in London, when he had a 100-watt head and a single 4×12 cabinet on stage. He was still using his Switchmaster for live gigs at that time, and favored a relatively clean tone, so presumably he didn't see the potential. When he returned to the UK in 1968 he brought his Acoustic Control Corporation backline with him. It would be a couple more years before FZ discovered what he could do with a Marshall amp.

FZ started using Marshall amplifiers in 1970, when he started touring with his new lineup of the Mothers. He paired a Marshall 100-watt with an Orange Matamp 200, starting a habit of blending the sound of different amplifiers together that he was to continue through the years. Both amps were destroyed in the Montreux Casino fire.

In the mid- to late 1970s, FZ tended to use a pair of 100-watt Marshalls in conjunction with his Acoustic 270 amp. From the footage of the 1974 KCET TV show included on the *Dub Room Special* DVD, we can see that the amps are a pair of early 100w Super Lead "Plexis" (so called because the front panels were made of plexiglass, unlike the later models, which had metal control panels).

These didn't have master volume controls, and this caused FZ some problems during that show: "Science has come a long way since 1974. With that band I was using Marshalls, and in those days if you wanted Marshalls to distort, you had to turn them up all the way. But since that segment was originally intended for a TV show and was shot in a small place—like 200 people in the audience—I had to turn it way down. No sustain . . . a very old-fashioned kind of sound."[344]

In the 1980s, FZ started putting his Marshall amps under the riser at the back of the stage mainly used by the drums and keyboard players. As a result, the amps were less noticeable to the audience, but the band were well aware of their presence, as bass player Arthur Barrow told me: "I was up there, Tommy was up there . . . the riser was where all his amps were and it seems like pretty much it was guitar amps underneath the whole fucking thing! You know, spanning about thirty feet! And you know, the whole thing shook when he played."[345] Guitarist Steve Vai described Zappa's 1981 sound as "Godzilla meets Mothra. It was devastatingly loud, heavy, and feedbacky."[346]

Dweezil Zappa remembered trying out FZ's Marshalls; at the time he was used to playing Van Halen–inspired modified Marshalls with a very high input gain for maximum distortion. He discovered that FZ did not use much gain because the signal from his modified guitars was so high: "I tried playing through them and found them to be difficult to play on because they were so loud and piercing. They had a good crunch but didn't have any saturated gain. It made sense for Frank's playing because his guitars had huge amounts of preamp gain. He could hit the front of the amp with that and control things from his guitar with a very good signal-to-noise ratio. This allowed him to have a very dynamic sound. I think that may be the reason his guitar rigs never had a huge amount of hiss."[347]

I asked DZ if they were modified at all: "He had a few amps that had master volume mods. One of those did have a high-gain sound similar to Edward Van Halen, but based on the amp markings it was never used for that sound. To get the sustain Frank loved he used the preamp and EQ in his guitars. I believe Midget (Sloatman) said his main guitars had 50 db of gain."[348]

At least one of FZ's Marshall Plexi heads was stolen. According to Alain Dister, there was a disastrous gig in Rome in September, 1974, where a new American 110-volt TycoBrahe mixing desk was destroyed when a roadie plugged it directly into a European 240-volt supply. During the confusion of unloading the van, one of FZ's amps went missing and was not recovered.[349]

On the 1988 tour, FZ used a combination of 100-watt and 50-watt heads: "And the rest of the dirty sound was made by four Marshall amplifiers, two 100 watts and two 50 watts. Most of the speaker cabinets were hidden underneath the stage and miked. And that's what's going to the PA. At the end of the tour I started using one Marshall cabinet onstage, powered by one of the 50-watt heads, just so I could have a little more presence right behind me."[350] Merl Saunders Jr.: "He had Marshalls packed underneath, his main cabinets were Marshall slant cabs." I asked Saunders if the amps were new or vintage: "they were vintage, and they were all tricked, they were all tweaked. I know I bridged the inputs to give them a little more power."[351]

FZ was never specifically sponsored by Marshall, but seems to have had a good relationship with the company. Ike Willis told me that FZ and the band visited the Marshall factory in Milton Keynes at least once when they were touring in the UK. His name was featured in the list of notable users in the 1982 twentieth anniversary adverts, and on the 1988 tour, he was presented with a couple of Silver Jubilee amplifiers. Dweezil Zappa thought one of the heads was still around in the Zappa house somewhere,[352] but I didn't see it during my visit.

The basic design of the Marshall 100-watt tube amplifier has changed very little over the years. The front panel has four tone controls: Presence, Bass, Middle, and Treble, and two volume controls, one for each of the two input channels (bright and normal). There are separate power on-off and standby switches. Tubes need to reach a certain operating temperature before they start working; this takes ten seconds or so. The standby switch turns off the main circuits but passes current through the heater circuits of the tubes to keep them warm. There are two pairs of input jack sockets; high and low sensitivity inputs for each of the two channels. FZ used a small jumper lead connecting two input sockets to allow the guitar signal to be blended across the channels.

The amplifier was built on a heavy steel chassis with two massive transformers, a set of ECC83 tubes for the preamp and tone control stages, and then a set of four EL34 power tubes. At the back would be a couple of speaker outputs, fuse-holders, a speaker impedance matching selector, and mains voltage selector. Eventually Marshall introduced the Master Lead series; these models had just one input channel and a Master Volume control in place of the other channel volume control. This enabled the amplifier input stage to be overdriven to get the distorted Marshall sound without requiring the amplifier to be working at full volume. Marshall introduced this by popular request, as it was a common modification applied to the earlier models.

When we arrived at the UMRK in January 2012, the good people of the ZFT had made available seven of Frank's Marshall amplifiers for us to photograph. Most of them had been labelled with various notes on tape describing their tonal characteristics; the control positions had been marked in red and yellow. Four of these subsequently were sold in the 2016 Julien's auction.[353]

1974 Lead 50

This amplifier appears to be an unmodified Marshall 50-watt Lead amplifier and is both the best kept and least remarkable of the Marshall amps at the UMRK, its good condition, perhaps, suggesting that it had not received much live use. The impedance selector is missing and a notation in marker beneath the impedance selector socket reads: "4Ω OR 8Ω ONLY!" The blue tape legend on this amplifier reads: "Bright—clean Quite #1." ([Sic]—presumably the writer meant "Quiet.")

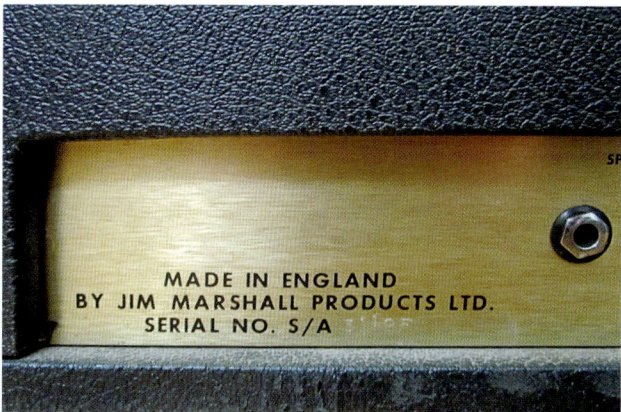

Detail of the Lead 50—"Made in England"
(Mick Ekers)

1976 Super Leads (R12 and Spare)

These are two similar 1976 Marshall Super Lead amplifiers. The spare amp is what is known as a transitional model: with modern "elephant grain" vinyl and the larger plastic logo from later amps, but still lacking the protective corner caps. They both have what appears to be a master volume control added to the front panel. They have four speaker outputs (possibly a modification), modern style impedance selector switches, and non-removable mains leads with no voltage selector.

Both bear Custom Audio Electronics stickers on the back; the input sockets have been marked with tape indicating that the channels were to be jumpered. The amp marked "Spare" has a strip of blue tape on the back bearing the legend: "Real Smooth—LOUD BUZZ"; this could well explain this amp's status as spare.

There is a faded label affixed to the top of the other amplifier, from a company called Sound Service, indicating that they modified the amp in 1978 (the date reads 1/23/78). The remains of another label reads "R12," implying it may have been used with the R18 Major. It has strips of white tape affixed to the front of the amplifier and marked: "LOW GAIN BREAK UP," "EXTRA GAIN JUMPED," and "STRAT FENDERS." On the rear, a legend on blue electrical tape reads: "Killer #2—AWESOME ALL OVER." Sold in the 2016 auction as Lot #492, it went for $18,750.[354]

1974 Super Lead

This 1974 Super Lead is the most heavily modified amplifier in the collection at the UMRK. It started life as a standard Marshall 100-watt Super Lead but has since been modified with an effects loop on the rear panel with a send, a return, and a send level control, and four speaker outputs. It has a new mains voltage control knob with settings for 110V, 120V, 200V, 225V and 245V, and a disconnected impedance selector (a label has been attached below the rightmost pair of speaker outputs reading "16 OHM ONLY").

A plugged hole in the front panel indicates that this amplifier was probably given a master volume modification that has since been removed; the channel II input sockets are blocked. The amplifier is the only one without a description on blue electrical tape. Sold in the 2016 auction as Lot #476, it went for $4.800.[355]

The input section of the 'Spare' 1976 Super Lead, with plenty of markings that must have meant something!
(Mick Ekers)

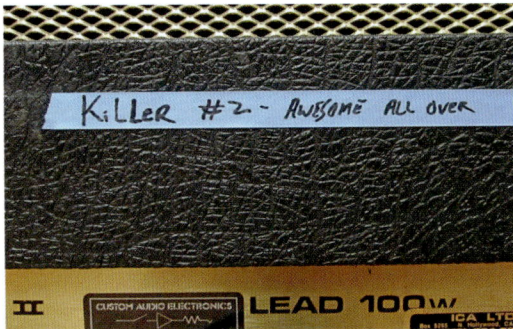

The verdict on the 'R12' amp, note the Custom Audio Electronics sticker
(Mick Ekers)

The power end of the 1974 Super Lead control panel, showing signs of removed master volume mod
(Mick Ekers)

1972 Major (Rear 18)

This is a 1972 200-watt Marshall Major, the oldest and most powerful amplifier in the UMRK Marshall collection. An additional knob on the front panel suggests that this amplifier was also modified with a master volume control. The power cable has been removed, and a modern three-pin socket installed in its place. Settings are marked on the front panel in red and an old, damaged label on the top of the amplifier reads "R18." A smaller label on the front reads "Rear 18." The amplifier's back panel had been removed, but a matching panel was discovered at the UMRK with a small label attached marked "Bass Model," almost certainly confirming that this amplifier is the rare bass guitar model. This is reinforced by the legend on blue tape, which reads: "AWESOME—Real WARM—Lots of PWR—EXTRA Bottom #3." This was almost certainly the amplifier used by FZ for the low signal from his octave divider pedal, driving an 18" speaker; see the section on the Mu-Tron Octave Divider for more on this. Sold in the 2016 auction as Lot #481, it went for $6,250.[356]

The front panel of 'Rear 18'
(Mick Ekers)

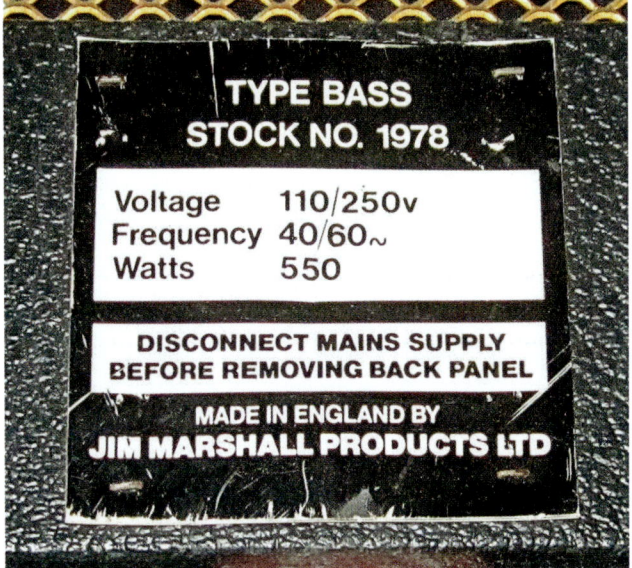

The rear-panel label identifying it as a Bass model
(Mick Ekers)

1978 Master Volumes (Frank Left and Frank Right)

Two 1978 Marshall Mk II Master volume amplifiers, these have consecutive serial numbers and ICA inventory numbers and were obviously bought as a matched pair. Both appear unmodified apart from the lower sensitivity inputs, which appear to have been disabled. The rear panels are missing, enabling the interior to be inspected. Frank Left has Ruby Tubes EL34L power tubes, and Frank Right has a set of four Tesla EL34L power tubes (possibly FZ wasn't too picky about tube brands). The factory inspection labels inside are dated 18/12/78. Frank Left bears the legend "Bottom is Mud—& Muffled—WICKED TREBLE," an additional blue label on top reads: "PWR HEAD #1." The blue tape legend on Frank Right reads: "HENDRIX ISH—High Gain." This one was sold as Lot 490 in the Auction for $4,800, its partner was not listed.[357]

FZ hooked his amps up to a variety of speaker cabinets. He often used Marshall 4×12 cabinets, but mostly he had the stock Celestion speakers replaced with more powerful and efficient JBL drivers. DZ: "In the mid- to late 70s I think he was getting his best sound, especially when he had the Ma Bell rig. (See the Rack System section for more on Ma Bell.) The cabs had the JBLs; they were loud but had great clarity."[358] FZ never had his 4×12s placed in the traditional Marshall stack configuration, concerned that having a speaker cabinet behind him at head height would damage his hearing: "Here's one good piece of advice: don't go for the Marshall stack/pile syndrome. It has two bad effects: One, it makes the feedback harder to control, and two, it rips your head off."[359]

To this day, Marshall amplifiers remain the benchmark against which all other rock tube guitar amplifiers are compared. In 1989, Harmon Instruments offered Jim Marshall (then sixty-six years old) £100 million for the company, plus a fifteen-year retainer of £1million for himself. He turned it down with the reason, "It's my name, and I wouldn't want to be told what to do by somebody else."[360] Jim Marshall OBE died in 2012 at the age of eighty-eight. Although they now have international manufacturing facilities, Marshall are still making hand-wired 100-watt tube amplifiers at their UK factory in Milton Keynes.

Front panel detail of 'Frank Right'
(Mick Ekers)

All seven Marshalls on the floor at the UMRK, with Spare at the front
(Christopher G. Ekers)

Three of the 'Ruby Tubes' power valves in 'Frank Left'
(Mick Ekers)

Six of FZ's Marshalls at the UMRK, , from the top: 'Frank Left', 'Frank Right', Lead 50, Super Lead, R12 - 'Killer #2', 'Rear 18'
(Christopher G. Ekers)

Pignose 7-100

"I have used a Pignose extensively on the last five albums. It's a very reliable sound source for the studio"

— FZ[361]

The Pignose 7-100 amplifier (to give it its full name) was invented in 1969 by Richard Edlund and Wayne Kimbell, who were working in Hollywood as photographers and graphic designers in the music industry. After seeing a five-watt amplifier in an electronics shop, Edlund had the initial idea for a portable rock guitar amp. The prototype was built in a cedar English Leather men's cologne box.

The Pignose name and concept was born and an initial batch of sixty-five was made with a rubber pig nose volume knob and real pigskin covering. The design skills of the inventors are clearly evident; the funky logo and chunky metal corner protectors gave the amp a great look that was very resonant with the Woodstock spirit of the time.

Edlund and Kimball proceeded to give these away to the good and the great of the rock world, including FZ, George Harrison, Mick Taylor, Keith Richards, Warren Zevon (who was the first to record an album using it), and Terry Kath of the band Chicago. Kath and Chicago's management group went on to form a partnership with the inventors and the first production amps made their appearance in 1973 (as the Legendary Pignose) at the NAMM music industry convention in Chicago.

Designed to be worn while playing, it had two buttons to fit a guitar strap, and could run on six AA batteries. The amp produced around five watts (peak) into its single 5" speaker and had a satisfying distorted sound when overdriven. As a marketing bonus, the 9"×6"×4" dimensions meant that it could be illustrated "actual size" in magazine adverts.

The little amplifier was a big success; Edlund notes that they made 50,000 units in the first year.[362] As well as finding many fans in the 6-string world, it gained popularity with harmonica players seeking a distorted Little Walter blues sound.

The five-pound amp featured just one control: the "Pignose" volume on/off knob (the original rubber knob had been replaced by a more practical metal "nose"). The box was hinged to allow storage of the optional power supply, leads, etc., and owners soon found that partially opening the box could be used to vary the tone. There was an auxiliary preamp output at the rear that could be used to drive a larger amplifier.

Quite a few other guitarists had experimented with the Pignose (Eric Clapton, Joe Walsh, and others), but in typical fashion, FZ stretched it to the limit of its capabilities, using it in many different ways that the inventors had never thought of. Its small size and ability to distort at low volumes allowed for a lot of versatility in placement and recording situations.

FZ and Pignose, partly obscured by microphone
(still from The Mike Douglas Show, 1976)

Terry Kath of Chicago in an early advert
(Author's collection)

One technique FZ used was to lay it on its back on the studio floor with a single microphone suspended vertically above it (probably a Shure SM57). Known as "half-space orientation," this greatly enhances the bass frequencies of a speaker, making the amp sound more like a large Marshall cab.

FZ would also mic it up in a live room with a single close Electro-Voice RE-20, and would often use two mics with one further back in the room to capture a larger, ambient sound. It is likely that this is what you hear during "Dirty Love" on the

Amplifiers

Front and back views of FZ's 'Special' Pignose
(Mick Ekers)

Over-Nite Sensation album. (Dweezil Zappa plays the individual close and far microphone tracks on the *Classic Albums— Apostrophe (') /Over-Nite Sensation* DVD.)

As FZ explained it: "We've put the Pignose in a 'live' chamber to simulate 'live' sound and to get a really large sound. Instead of just mixing it and sending the mic signal into the echo chamber, you can get a completely different effect by actually having the amplifier in the chamber, and sending the guitar through the echo send into the Pignose and picking it up with the microphone in the chamber room."[363]

In an interview in *Mix* magazine, engineer Davey Moire recalls that at one time FZ placed a Pignose on some foam, face down on the harp of a Bösendorfer grand piano. He put a sandbag on the sustain pedal, and selectively placed rubber piano tuner's mutes to silence the strings he didn't want to resonate.[364] This must have created an astonishing harmonious reverberant effect.

On the title track of *Apostrophe,* FZ recalled, "On that solo on *Apostrophe* I'm using an SG with a Barcus Berry on the bridge, and that's being sent to one of the channels, then the other side is coming out of a Pignose. And there's an attack differential between how fast the Barcus Berry speaks and how fast the Pignose speaks. So you've got a sharp attack on one side and then the rest of the note following it on the other."[365]

In a later interview he notes that the guitar solo on "Purple Lagoon" from *Live in New York* was overdubbed using the Pignose and an Eventide Harmonizer set at 99 (see the Eventide Harmonizer section).[366]

Singer Napoleon Murphy Brock remembers that he always used a Pignose in the dressing room for warmup and practice before each show.[367] FZ used to take more than one with him on the road; violinist and keyboard player Eddie Jobson recalled that when he auditioned for FZ in a dressing room in Chicago, he was given a Pignose to use for his electric violin while FZ played guitar through another.[368]

In 1976, FZ made a notable TV appearance on the *Mike Douglas Show* in which, he performed "Black Napkins" with the house band through a Pignose using the Baby Snakes SG. This was probably one of the only times he used it in a live situation. FZ was obviously happy with the outcome, mentioning the show during the introduction to "Black Napkins" on the *Philly 76* CD. The Pignose also makes a brief appearance during one of the backstage interludes in the *Baby Snakes* DVD.

Howard Edlund soon became bored with amplifiers (despite good sales, the inventors had received little revenue from the project) and returned to photography. This turned out to be a good career move, as Edlund went to on to receive Oscars for his special effects work on *Star Wars* and other films. Wayne Kimbell now runs a successful graphic design company. In 1982, the company passed into the ownership of Howard Chatt, whose company manufactured the original hardwood pigskin covered cases. Chatt still runs Pignose Gorilla (as it is now known) from Las Vegas, and the 7-100 is still being made today.

We last saw FZ's Pignose in residence in the control room of the UMRK. From the front it looks like a standard model apart

ZAPPA GEAR

The tiny Pignose speaker
(Mick Ekers)

The mystery XLR connections
(Mick Ekers)

from the fact that FZ has written "SPECIAL" underneath the input jack. At the rear FZ has written his name and the address and the word SPECIAL again. Two 3-pin male XLR sockets have been mounted on the back. I thought when I saw these that FZ must have had these hooked in some special way to the Pignose circuit so that he could connect the signal from the echo send on the mixing desk as he described.

This may have been the original use, but when the back was opened, it was clear that the two sockets were connected to two short cables, terminating in two XLR mic plugs, not connected to anything and zip-tied up in the corner of the case. The battery holders have been removed, so the amp must have been used purely with an external power supply. The preamp output connector just below the power input socket on the back is blanked out. The speaker and small amplifier circuit show no signs of any modifications, and there is nowhere to connect the XLR plugs. So all we have now is effectively a totally standard Pignose, and the original configuration of the connections remains an enigma.

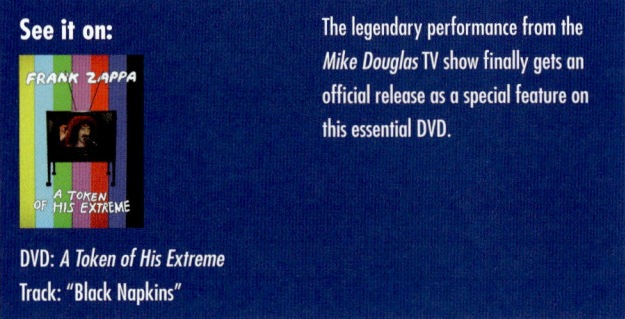

See it on: The legendary performance from the *Mike Douglas* TV show finally gets an official release as a special feature on this essential DVD.

DVD: *A Token of His Extreme*
Track: "Black Napkins"

Orange Matamp OR200

"Every 200 watter . . . was tested down in the basement, running for 100 hours in order to burn in the KT88s . . . . Now to do that for each amp is very expensive and time consuming."[369]

Sometime in 1971, FZ took delivery of several Orange Matamp amplifiers. One can clearly be seen on the floor in various photos of John Lennon and Yoko Ono jamming with the Mothers of Invention at the Fillmore East in New York on 6th June, 1971. FZ was using the Orange paired with a Marshall amp, but he let Lennon use the Orange when he joined them on stage.

Orange Musical Industries was started by designer, musician, and entrepreneur Cliff Cooper in London in 1968, when he opened the tiny Orange Recording Studios in New Compton Street, Soho. To raise some urgently needed cash Cooper put some of his band's equipment up for sale in the window; everything sold that day, and this success prompted him to diversify into music instrument retailing.

He started the Orange music shop on the premises, advertising in the underground newspaper *International Times* and

Amplifiers

optimistically offering a free demo disc recording service for any band who spent over £200. However, although there was a steady supply of secondhand guitars at the time, he was unable to find suppliers prepared to provide him with new equipment for sale. Cooper decided to make his own guitar amplifiers, and he engaged a small Huddersfield firm called Matamp to build him some 100-watt heads.[370]

Matamp had grown out of a small radio repair company called Radio Craft, which was owned by the self-taught electronics engineer "Mat" Mathias. Born in 1923 of Jewish parents in Germany, Hans Alfred Mathias was evacuated from Berlin in 1939, just days before the outbreak of WWII. Described on his passport as a "refugee from Nazi Oppression" (sadly, his parents both died in the Holocaust), he worked in a variety of jobs before settling in Huddersfield and joining the staff of Radio Craft in 1945. Mathias gradually bought out the company from his employers, and soon established a reputation as a top electronic engineer and repairman.

By 1963, he had expanded the business, selling early PA systems to local bands and building a small demo studio in the back room of the shop. Unimpressed with the early Vox and Watkins amps that guitarists were bringing into his studio, Mathias teamed up with hi-fi design engineer Tony Emerson to build something better. In 1964, they came up with the Matamp 2000, a 20-watt hi-fi quality guitar amp, which had been specifically designed to produce an undistorted clean sound. The unique amps gained a local reputation, but were little known outside the North West of England.

Cooper wanted his amps to stand out; he specified heavy-duty wooden cases covered in bright orange vynide fitted with contrasting black corner protectors. The Matamp white front panel was retained, with large black plastic knobs that looked like something from a 1950s science laboratory, and two sturdy metal grab handles that protected the controls. Cooper added bold simple graphics, and the overall effect was an appealing combination of psychedelic chic and military-spec solidity and reliability; the Orange amps looked loud in more senses than one. Orange quickly picked up two high-profile endorsees, the band Fleetwood Mac and the British Broadcasting Corporation, both attracted by the clean sound and reliability of the OR100.

After the success of the 100-watt amps, Cooper commissioned an all-purpose 200-watt amp from Matamp, which became known as the OR200. Fleetwood Mac took the first ten prototypes on a US tour in 1968. After this tough road test, the design was refined and the chassis strengthened, and they went into production in August 1969. FZ must have bought some of the very earliest models, which were still being made by Matamp; they had to subcontract later in the 1970s, as they could not keep up with demand.

The Orange Matamp OR200 was a very high-powered amp, with four KT88 valves like the Marshall 200-watt amps, but with very different preamp and tone circuitry, using two 12AX75 valves. The front panel had two input jacks, two large rotary switches for Depth and Drive, two small Bass and Treble tone controls, and two more large Boost and Volume knobs. Internally there was a strong orange enameled steel chassis and three massive (and expensive) custom Partridge transformers.[371] Inside the chassis was a small masterpiece of meticulous military-standard hand wiring. The relatively compact unit measured 21.5" wide × 16" deep × 11" high (55 x 40 x 28 cm), and at 70 lb. (32 kg) in weight, certainly needed its two carrying handles on the top.

The F.A.C. (Frequency Analyzing Control, as Orange called it) preamp design was different from anything else on the market; the Depth and Drive switches selected various high and low frequency boost and cut settings that worked in conjunction with the bass and treble controls, the Boost control affecting the midrange. The whole was designed so that you could achieve high volume with minimal distortion, and tailor the response to suit guitar, bass, or keyboards. Before the completed amp was shipped out it went through a rigorous test regime, including 100 hours of burning in the valves. Each unit left the factory with a waterproof cover, a set of leads, and an individual logbook. OR200s were often referred to as the Rolls Royce of British amplifiers.

The combination of the hi-fidelity Orange sound with the overdriven roar of his Marshall Plexi 100 obviously worked well, and FZ continued to use various combinations of clean and dirty amps on stage throughout his career. Photos of the band at the time show two other Orange amps on stage, along with some Orange speaker cabinets; likely these were being used for keyboards.

FZ was using his OR200 when the Mothers of Invention played their infamous gig at the Montreux Casino, Switzerland on 4th December, 1971. As documented in Deep Purple's song "Smoke on the Water," the casino burnt down completely when a fire started during the Mothers' set, caused by someone letting off a flare gun. The solid construction of the OR200s had a

1968 advert from 'underground' paper the *International Times*

ZAPPA GEAR

critical part to play in this tale; in a French TV interview recorded a couple of days after the incident, FZ stated that when the audience was evacuating the building they found that the fire exit was locked, and they broke the door down by throwing Orange amplifiers at it![372] Fortunately, everyone got out alive, with only a few minor injuries recorded.

Along with the rest of the band's gear, the Orange amps were burnt to cinders during the fire. FZ told the French TV crew that the only piece of kit that was salvaged was a cowbell, and as far as we know, he did not use Orange amps again.

The Orange/Matamp partnership was dissolved in 1975, mainly due to the Matamp philosophy of low-volume, boutique production conflicting with Cooper's ambitions for mass production and global sales. Orange was forced into liquidation in 1979 when two international distributors folded, owing the company a large amount of money. However, the Orange brand returned in the mid-1990s, at first licensed by Gibson with the amps once again being made by Matamp. Orange is now enjoying considerable success as a fully independent company, still run by Cliff Cooper, and still includes traditional valve guitar and bass amplifiers in its catalog. "Mat" Mathias died in 1989, but Matamp continues to produce high quality hand-built amps in Huddersfield. Their current GT200 model is based very closely on the OR200 design.

A pair of OR200s—one with additional custom controls, one made for Jimmy Page (Luc Henzig, Tune Your Sound)

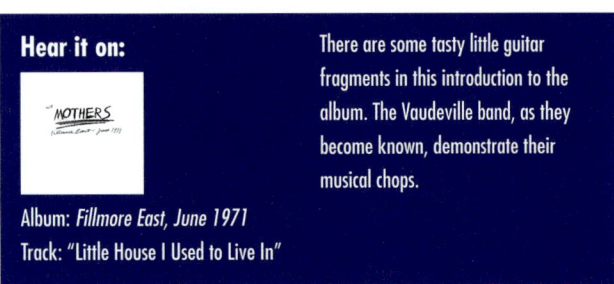

Hear it on:
Album: *Fillmore East, June 1971*
Track: "Little House I Used to Live In"

There are some tasty little guitar fragments in this introduction to the album. The Vaudeville band, as they become known, demonstrate their musical chops.

Oberheim Studio Practice Amp

"He had a little practice amp that he used, I can't remember who made it . . . sounded like a battery-operated amp."

—Dweezil Zappa [373]

The amp that Dweezil was talking about was the Oberheim Studio practice amp that FZ took with him on the 1988 tour, forsaking his trusty Pignose. Oberheim Electronics were primarily a synthesizer and electronic effects manufacturer (see the section on the Oberheim VCF-200), but in 1975 they produced the solid-state five-watt Studio amplifier. Their aim was to make a portable amplifier of professional quality that was both AC- and battery-powered.

Housed in a solid oiled oak cabinet, it had an angled control panel with knobs for volume, distortion, bass, middle, and treble; to the right of these there was a switch and a speed control for the built-in phaser circuit. Below the controls was a small red LED, the words "Oberheim Electronics," and the famous Oberheim logo, which depicted an aggressive looking pair of musical notes marching along with fists swinging.

On the top were high and low-level inputs and clean and dirty line-level outputs. Originally produced with an elliptical speaker, the amplifier was later fitted with a circular speaker. The Studio retailed for $170.[374]

By all accounts Oberheim succeeded with their intentions, *Guitar Player* magazine describing it as "a neat sturdy and remarkably versatile five-watt model . . . it demonstrated that all the functions found in amps many times larger were possible in a mini-amp."[375] However, it was not a commercial success and was soon discontinued. Tom Oberheim described it as " . . . an interesting experiment. It incorporated a nice fuzz preamp, the circuitry of the Maestro Phase Shifter, which was the first phase shifter on the market, a ten-watt amp, and a nice oak case. We built less than 50 of these."[376]

FZ took a massive amount of equipment with him on the 1988 tour and could have chosen anything he wanted for a dressing room amplifier; he must have liked the little Oberheim. Its tone was probably closer to the clean sound he was going for on stage at the time, as opposed to the distorted output of his old Pignose.

The whereabouts of this amp is unknown; probably it was sold after his death. The late Rory Gallagher also favored one of these rare and little-known amplifiers.[377] They must have had something going for them; so if you ever find one in a second-hand shop, it could be well worth investigating.

Amplifiers

Mesa Boogie Mark I

"Depending on the year it was either a Marshall or a Boogie"

— FZ[378]

The above quote comes from a *Record Review* interview where FZ was talking to about the amplifiers used on the *Shut Up 'n Play Yer Guitar* album. In 1979, FZ kept a Mesa Boogie Mk I on stage with him, next to a pair of Marshall heads, and we can assume from the above that he used it for a lot of his solos. It was a stock plain wood finish Mark I with a graphic equalizer and (assuming FZ didn't economize) the optional reverb unit.

The Mesa Boogie story started in 1967, when Randall Smith and a friend set up an alternative music shop called Prune Music in Berkeley, California. They soon built up an impressive clientele among the groups in the burgeoning San Francisco scene, including the Grateful Dead, Jefferson Airplane, Santana, and the Steve Miller Band. In 1969, they decided to play a joke on Barry Melton, guitarist for Country Joe and the Fish. Randall took a tiny 12-watt Fender Princeton combo, replaced the circuit with one based on a Fender Bassman, installed large transformers to handle the power, and replaced the 10" speaker with a state-of-the-art 12" JBL D-120.[379] All of this would make the tiny old amplifier stupidly loud compared with its regular sound.

Smith took the completed unit into the front of the shop to find Carlos Santana had dropped in. Santana tried out the amp and as Smith tells it, "When he stopped playing he just said, 'Shit man. That little thing really boogies!'" Word spread and Smith sold boosted Princetons to many name guitarists. Eventually Fender became suspicious of the number of replacement transformers he was ordering and cut off his supply. Smith had already named his company Mesa Engineering; at this point realized he needed to build his own amp, and the Mark I Mesa

Oberheim advert ca 1975
(Author's collection)

FZ backstage in 1988 with his trusty Performance Strat and the Oberheim Studio
(Linn Goldsmith)

Early Mesa advert with Randall Smith and his then wife Rayven

A Mark I Boogie, similar to FZ's
(Hendrix Guitars)

Boogie was born.[380] Of course, at the time it was just called a Boogie; the Mark I tag was only applied later after Smith introduced the Mark II version.

The Mark I drew heavily on the design of the original Boogies. It had a single 12" speaker (usually an Altec or Electro-Voice unit) and a Fender-inspired 100 or 60-watt valve amplifier. What made the Mark I truly revolutionary was Smith's brainwave: a high-gain cascading preamp, multiplying the normal amplifier gain by a factor of fifty. The combo had a high-gain Input 1 channel and a clean Input 2 channel.

The front panel had controls for Volume 1, Volume 2, Treble, Middle, Bass, and Master, with Bright and Boost pull switches on the volume controls. FZ could switch between channels and select the boost function via his pedalboard. On stage, FZ drove his into a 4×12 cabinet as well as the internal speaker.[381]

There was also a five-band graphic equalizer and switches for 100/60 watt modes, EQ in/out, standby, and power. The body was light-colored hardwood (probably koa) and the grill was cream wicker. In 1979, the cost would have been around $1,290.[382] This was a very expensive little amplifier!

Around 3,000 Mark I Boogie combos were made between 1971 and 1978, when it was replaced by the Mark II version.[383] Most of these would have been hand made by Randall Smith, and with his avowed attention to detail and quality, most are probably still working. Good condition Mark Is sell for several thousand dollars these days.

Dweezil Zappa told me that FZ only ever had one Boogie: "That was the only Boogie that he had, that's not around anymore."[384] The serial number was A1647 and it was sold to Guitar Oasis, Huntington Beach, California on 19th July, 1994.

Acoustic 165 Combo

"On the last tour I used . . . two small Acoustics to run my three MXR digital delays through."

— FZ[385]

In 1980, Acoustic Control Corporation launched their first valve amplifier, the Model 165 combo. It was a direct response to the success of the Mesa Boogie, and had many similarities in design. As they described it in their catalog: "'State of the Art' is the only apt description for the Acoustic models 164 and 165 all tube guitar amplifiers. Innovative engineering provides features such as a switchable FET or tube front end, 60 or 100-watt RMS power output, dual master volume controls, five band graphic EQ, and a built-in reverb."[386]

The engineering was not exactly innovative, but it was a handsome, well-built unit, with a single Electro-Voice EVM 12L speaker and a two-tone solid oak and walnut cabinet. The power amplifier stage featured four 6L6 valves, which could be run at 60 or 100 watts output. There were two footswitchable channels, each with concentric gain and master volume controls.

The switchable preamp stage used a 12AX7 valve, and had regular bass, mid, treble, presence, and reverb controls, as well as the graphic EQ on the front panel. The back panel contained main and extension speaker outs, an FX loop, and three footswitch jacks for channel switching, reverb, and EQ in/out.

FZ on the cover of the 1980 Acoustic catalog
(Author's collection)

Hear it on: The Boogie was probably used on most of the 1979 recordings on this album—take your pick!

Album: *Shut Up 'n Play Yer Guitar*

Amplifiers

The 165 catalog page
(Author's collection)

Although a compact 20"×22"×10.5" size, it weighed a hefty 65 lbs. thanks to the 3/4"-thick wood cabinet and the heavy EV speaker. The original retail price was set at $1195,[387] but within two months was increased to $1495.[388] (Yes, that was a lot of money in 1980.) A slightly cheaper model, the 164, was available in a vinyl-covered cabinet.

An Acoustic endorsee from way back, FZ was featured on the cover of their 1980 catalog playing the Hendrix Strat with a 165 in the background. In 1983, he told *Guitar Player* magazine: "I also had an Acoustic that was centered more between 100 and 500 cycles, with a peak around 300 for the kind of grunty Les Paul-type roaring sound."[389]

On later tours, FZ had a couple of 165s in his stage rig, fed by his stereo delay signal. Merl Saunders Jr. remembered how he used them: "There was a left and right, that could play against each other. He would strum a rhythm, and then he would just stop the left one, then he would start another rhythm on the right side, and then he would solo over."[390] Other FZ guitarists, most notably Steve Vai, also used the 165s on some tours.

Acoustic also manufactured a matching extension speaker cabinet, the model 465, with the same overall dimensions but a full-depth, flat top without a handle so the 165 could sit on top of it. FZ had several of these, which he liked to spread along the stage on his early 1980s tours, probably liking the open-back design which would have helped the drummers and keyboard players on the riser behind hear the guitar parts.

I was sent some pictures of a pair of these cabs, which had been sold in the Joe's Garage sale in the early 1990s. They were in a single flight case marked DSR (downstage right, presumably). Interestingly, they are not a matching pair; one of these is a stock model with an EV speaker, and the other has been fitted with a 15-ohm Celestion G12-50 speaker and a flying jack socket. The label "4 ohms" suggests that these were linked together on stage in a set of four.[391] Merl Saunders remembered some small open-back cabinets being used under the drum riser on the 1988 tour; most likely these were 465s.[392] The Celestion/Electro-Voice combination was also used in FZ's 4×12 cabinets

on that tour; possibly, the speakers were swapped around between the cabinets.

The 165/465 series were only produced for a couple of years. These were the last days of the Acoustic Control Corporation, which was desperately diversifying into valve amplifiers and even budget-price equipment as their solid-state range went out of favor. In 1983, the ailing company was bought by the Wagner Corporation and the 165 was never manufactured again.

Custom 465 with 15-ohm Celestion speaker
(Peter Jay)

Stock 465 with Electrovoice speaker
(Peter Jay)

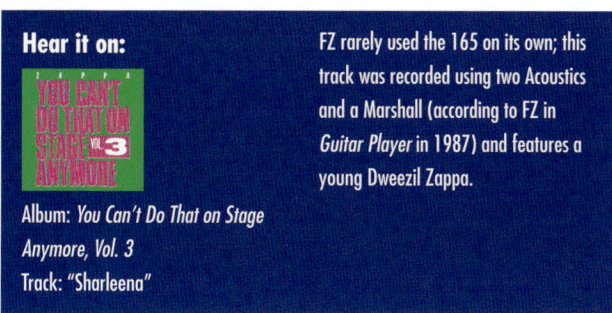

Hear it on:
Album: *You Can't Do That on Stage Anymore, Vol. 3*
Track: "Sharleena"

FZ rarely used the 165 on its own; this track was recorded using two Acoustics and a Marshall (according to FZ in *Guitar Player* in 1987) and features a young Dweezil Zappa.

101

ZAPPA GEAR

Carvin X-100B

"What I've been using on the road on this tour was a pair of Carvin Heads for the clean sound."

— FZ[393]

A 2012 X100-B reissue
(Carvin)

In 1981, FZ signed a sponsorship deal with Carvin and he started using their guitar amplifiers on stage. As part of his massive multi-amplifier rig on the 1988 tour, FZ fed the clean signal from the Roland GP-8 effects unit into two Carvin X100-B amplifiers, each driving a Marshall 4×12 cabinet.[394]

In 1946, Hawaiian steel guitarist Lowell Kiesel, the son of a Nebraska farmer, formed the L.C. Kiesel Company in Los Angeles, starting out by winding electric guitar pickups on an old sewing machine. In 1949, he changed the name of the company to Carvin, after his two eldest sons, Carson and Gavin. The company soon extended their range of pickups and other accessories to include amplifiers, guitars, basses, and other gear. Many early Carvin instruments were made by Lowell Kiesel himself.

Originally they advertised in magazines such as *Popular Mechanics*, sending out product information sheets on request. They published the first Carvin mail-order catalogue in 1954, establishing the direct-selling business model that they used throughout their existence. The company expanded throughout the 1950s and 1960s, with a popular range of guitars, basses, mandolins, and steel guitars. After several relocations, Carvin moved to Escondido in California in 1975, which remained their base for twenty years.[395]

Carvin introduced a limited range of solid-state guitar amplifiers in the 1960s, but they expanded their range in the late 1970s and started offering various-sized transistor and tube-powered models. They launched the X-100 100-watt tube amplifier in 1981, which by 1982 had metamorphosed into the X-100B. Carvin pitched the amplifier as a more flexible alternative to Marshall amplifiers, offering both clean and overdriven sounds. The look of the X-100B was very much in the style of Marshall; Carvin described it as "a rugged British styled head."

The X-100B used four 6L6GC valves in the power stage, with three 12AX7 valves in the preamp circuit, and it was certainly a very versatile piece of equipment. A switch on the rear panel allowed it to be switched from 100 to 50 or 25-watt operation using only two or one of the power valves, enabling the cranked tube sound to be obtained at lower volumes.

It had a clean Rhythm channel with a single volume control that could be pulled out to switch in a bright mode. The Lead-Drive channel passed through a pair of 12AX7 valves in series for extra gain and featured separate drive and master volume controls, again with a pull switch for Hi-Lead Drive that promised to deliver the bright Marshall sound. The control panel featured a five-band graphic EQ that could be applied to either of the channels; presence, bass, middle, and treble tone controls; and a reverb control for the built-in Hammond spring reverb unit.

The rear panel had two speaker outputs with variable impedance, an effects loop, and a balanced line output from the preamp for recording and direct connection to a PA. The optional footswitch allowed switching of input channels, plus volume boost and reverb. The original price for the X-100B was $579. It was also available in various combo formats.[396]

Although almost entirely a mail-order organization Carvin had a few shops in the US, and I visited their branch in Hollywood where I talked to Carvin's Moshe Albarez. He told me that "the first rig he (FZ) scoped from us that he really liked was the original X100B 100-watt amplifier. It had 6L6 tubes at the time, and the thing he liked about the X100B was that it had a very loud, clean tone. A distorted tone was important to him,

FZ Carvin advert in 1988
(Carvin)

but the main thing above all else was the clean tone that he was looking for, which he got in abundance with this head here."[397]

Carvin partnered the X-100B with a range of matching 4×12 speaker cabinets. Like Marshall they made these in straight and angled cabinet versions; they were supplied fitted with Carvin's own MagnaLab speakers or optionally Celestion speakers. FZ took delivery of several of the amps and 412C cabinets (with Celestion speakers).

Of the two cabinets illustrated (photographed in the Guitar Oasis store in 1994), the angled cab has a closed back, and the straight cabinet has an open back and was fitted with two Celestion G12T-75 speakers and two G12-50s. Many of FZ's cabinets on the 1988 tour had mixed speaker combination, usually pairing the G12-50s with Electro-Voice units.[398]

This cabinet has the pairs set horizontally with the G12-50s at the bottom; most likely two speakers had to be replaced at some stage with whatever was at hand. According to Merl Saunders, on the 1988 tour FZ "drove a pair of Marshalls into two open-back 4×12 cabs with Celestion speakers,"[399] almost certainly a pair of the Carvin cabs.

FZ appeared in a Carvin advert in 1988 with two X-100Bs and a single square-front cabinet; I have never seen a picture of him using an angle-front model. In general, FZ had a dislike of the Marshall stack twin cabinet configuration, well aware that having an overdriven speaker at head height behind you was not going to do your hearing any good.

FZ's collection of Carvin amplifiers were sold in 1994; the sale included six X-100Bs and six 4×12 cabinets. Also sold were a selection of small solid-state combo amplifiers: two SX-100s, two X-100s, and a tiny X-60.[400] I have not seen any photographs of FZ using these, but of course any of them could have found use hidden under the touring band stage riser at some point in the 1980s.

Lowell Kiesel died in 2009 at the age of ninety-four, but his name lives on in Kiesel guitars, which was formed when Carvin split off its guitar making business.

Carvin stopped making the X-100B in 1994, but launched a reissue around 2010, based on the 1980s model and endorsed by Dweezil Zappa, who says "I used one exclusively on my very first album. I asked nicely to borrow it from my Dad."[401] I found DZs new X-100B on display on a shelf in the UMRK control room in 2012. Carvin audio stopped making guitar amplifiers and closed down the factory in 2017.

Hear it on:

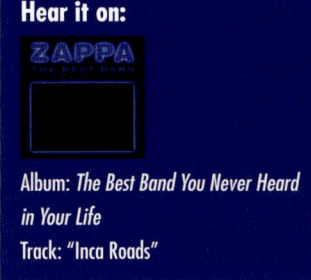

Album: *The Best Band You Never Heard in Your Life*
Track: "Inca Roads"

What you are hearing is probably a combination of the X-100Bs and the Acoustic 165s that FZ used on this tour. The solo on this track certainly has a very different tone from the warm wah-wah fuzziness of the version on the *One Size Fits All* album recorded fourteen years earlier.

Seymour Duncan 100-Watt Convertible

"What would I have done without my Marshalls or my Seymour Duncan amps? I'm perfectly content to be in this time and place."

—FZ[402]

In 1988, FZ started enthusing about his new Seymour Duncan Convertible amp; in fact it was Dweezil Zappa's to start with: "That was mine originally and then he was trying it out. It was one of those ones where the idea was that you had these different little things that you could pull in or out, they were these little circuit board things, that could change . . . 'Okay, it's a Fender sound,' or 'it's a Marshall sound.'"[403]

Primarily known for their guitar pickups, Seymour Duncan introduced the Convertible amplifier in 1984. The concept was simply to build the most versatile amplifier possible, with modules to make it sound like a Fender, a Marshall, and so forth. Effectively this was an analogue version of today's modelling amps; Duncan said, "I wanted an amp that could duplicate the distinctive sounds of all the great amps, all in one amp."[404]

The combo had a 100-watt power stage containing four Sovtek EL34 tubes, and was fitted with a 12" Celestion or Electro-Voice speaker. The sturdy cabinet was made of 5/8" plywood, covered in black Tolex, and it came fitted with a built-in cooling fan. The amp had two switchable channels, each with overdrive, master volume, treble, mid, bass, and reverb

Seymour Duncan 100-watt combo
(Mill River Music and Guitars)

Detail from 1984 advert showing module being fitted
(Author's collection)

controls. To the right of the panel was the Variable Power control, graduated from 5 to 100 watts. Not an attenuator, this varied the power amplifier current to reduce or increase power amplifier wattage and could be operated by a volume pedal on stage. The power stage valves could be switched from pentode to triode operation, which brought the maximum power down to 60 watts. (A normal amplifier valve has five electrical connections; if you use three, you more or less halve the power.) The rear panel also had a continuously variable speaker damping control, and the front panel had an RCA phono socket for special resistor plugs, which let you to set the input impedance to match your guitar.

At the top of the amplifier was a panel that slid back to reveal the compartment for the plug-in modules. The amps came supplied with Classic and Normal, Hi-Gain and Presence modules. Duncan listed fourteen different modules for sale, including some solid-state units but most with a tube, including Low-Cut Normal, Classic-Distortion, and Hi Gain Hybrid, ranging in price from $60 to $150.[405]

Merl Saunders Jr. remembered that FZ tried these out in the rehearsals for the 1988 tour, but they were not used on stage: "They were ones that you could take out modules and put 'em in. And I had those on the road but I never used them. We tried in rehearsal and I think it was his thing to try them every once in a while. Because every once in a while he would just come in and go 'I want something different,' I'm like, 'No you don't.' 'Yes I do.' 'No you don't!'"[406]

At one time endorsed by Jeff Beck, the amp was also available as a freestanding head, and later a smaller 60-watt model was introduced with only two modules. Unfortunately, the amps gained a reputation for being unreliable. DZ told me that although the concept was cool, " . . . the contacts weren't good, so you had this crap out kinda thing."[407] Seymour Duncan eventually stopped making amplifiers in the early 1990s; however the Convertibles still have a great reputation for sound and versatility. Guitar hero Joe Bonamassa is a big fan. [408]

Vox Beatle Amplifiers

"He still had a couple of the old 'Super Beatle' Voxes that he used to use, those were all solid-state."

— Dweezil Zappa [409]

When DZ mentioned this I was quite surprised. At the time, I was not aware of FZ ever having used these, although I knew about his old Vox 4×12 cabinet (see the next section). When I got to the UMRK, I found both a Beatle and a Super Beatle, both in somewhat road-weary condition. I suspect that they probably need attention; DZ continued: "I think a lot of that stuff just became unreliable, it would break all the time."[410]

When the Thomas Organ Company signed an agreement with the UK JMI company in 1965 to distribute Vox amplifiers in the US, they included clauses allowing them to manufacture Vox amps in the US if JMI could not meet the demands of the American market. Almost before the ink was dry, Thomas Organ had started developing the designs of their own VOX amps. Although they started out by making a couple of tube-based amps, Thomas Organ decided that solid-state transistor amps were the way forward.

Thomas Organ kept using the Beatle name, but by the time Sergeant Pepper was released they had abandoned touring, and would not be seen using Vox amps again

 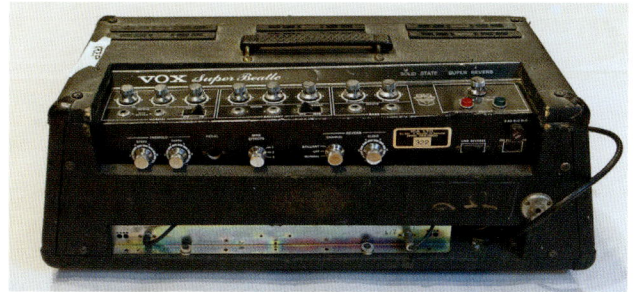

Front and rear views of the Super Beatle, looking somewhat the worse for wear
(Mick Ekers)

They hired the brilliant electrical engineer Sava Jacobsen, who had previously worked for Fender, to design transistor circuits that would recreate the Vox tone. Initially he came up with a three-channel Vox AC30 clone that they called the Viscount. The preamp stages were then combined with a 120-watt power amp section and mounted into a trapezoid shaped cabinet similar to the Vox AC30SRT, and this was named the V-14 Super Beatle, which was launched in 1966. It was the flagship model in their range and effectively forced the UK-made Vox AC100 out of the US market.

The Super Beatle went through a bewildering series of design changes over the next few years, model numbers changing to 1141, 1142, and 1143 and the name changing to just The Beatle for some variants. All used essentially the same three-channel preamp, coupled with a variety of effects and footswitches. Over the years various cost-cutting measures were introduced into the design: the case was made of fiberboard instead of plywood, the solid aluminum nameplate at the rear of the amp was replaced with a thin stamped metal unit, and so on.[411]

Despite the difference in name, FZ's two amps are essentially the same. Both have three input channels. The Bass channel has a volume and tone control; the Brilliant has volume, bass, and treble controls plus a midrange boost control; and the Normal channel has volume, bass, and treble controls plus a top boost switch and a tremolo effect. There is a built-in reverb unit, which can be switched to the Normal or Brilliant channels.

FZ used one of these on stage as part of his multi-amp set-up in the late 1970s, usually placed on top of his Mesa Boogie combo. According to the *Bluebox for Bimbos* notebook, the amp was used for the Dirty Left stage output from FZ's effects rack. The signal went in to the Normal channel, which was connected via a jumper cable to the Brilliant channel. Both channel volumes were set to ten, bass and treble to eight/nine, and the top and middle boost circuits were switched on. The Bass channel controls were set to zero.[412]

Apparently FZ sometimes used the Vox footswitch that could switch on the Tremolo and MRB (Mid-Range Boost) effects. The power output would be connected to his Vox 4×12 cabinet (see next section) and a custom 4×12 stage cabinet, or sometimes to the inner speakers of a pair of split 4×12 cabinets.

As I have described in the Vox wah-wah section, it was the "MRB" circuit of the Super Beatle that was the inspiration behind the invention of the wah-wah pedal. With FZ's love of using a midrange boost on his guitars, it may have been this feature that led him to use these early solid-state amps. I have been unable to find any record of how or when he came by them, presumably at the same time as his Vox 4×12 cabinet. Both amps were sold in the 2016 auction.[413] The Beatle amp sold for $5,937.50 and the Super Beatle fetched $5,120.[414]

The Beatle amp was discontinued in 1970, the same year the Beatles broke up. Thomas Organ went out of business in 1979,[415] although the company was reborn in 1997 as a specialized organ maker.[416] Sava Jacobsen went on to invent the cassette-tape telephone answering machine in the 1980s; he died in 2007, at the age of eighty-seven.[417]

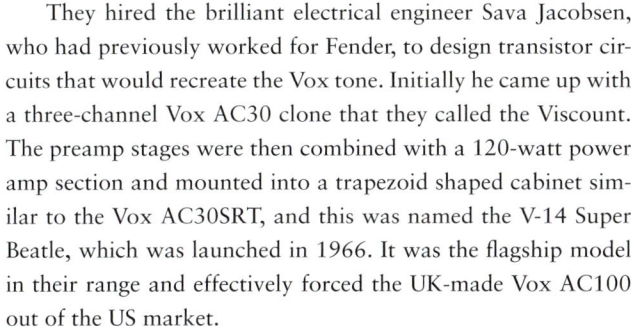 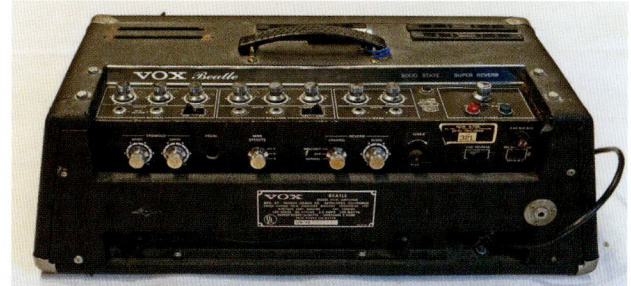

Front and rear views of FZ's Vox Beatle amp
(Mick Ekers)

ZAPPA GEAR

Vox 4×12 Cabinet

"I have a Vox cabinet with four JBLs in it (12" each)."

—FZ[418]

This distinctive speaker cabinet, with its chrome pivoting stand, was originally developed in the UK in 1964, specifically for John Lennon and George Harrison to use with their new Vox AC100 amplifiers, and was in evidence at the famous Shea Stadium concert. The design was effectively a pair of small format VOX AC50 cabinets stacked one on top of the other, but with the depth increased to accommodate the Midax high frequency horns that augmented the 12" speakers.

The Baltic plywood cabinet was 40" high by 27 1/2" wide by 11" deep, and sat in a handsome chrome-plated swivel trolley. The cabinet was divided internally into two compartments, each holding a Midax horn and two 8-ohm Celestion T1088 speakers, painted silver and with Vox badges affixed.[419]

Although sold in the UK as the Vox AC100 cabinet, in the US Thomas Organ marketed it as the Super Beatle cabinet, introducing it in 1965 as model number V1242, with a retail price of $499.[420] By 1968, the US Vox catalogue referred to it as the Beatle Deluxe cabinet, model number V4141, and it was offered as the 4141J with optional JBL D120F speakers, with a price of $1234 (as opposed to $884 for the standard unit). By 1970, Vox had fallen out of favor and the catalog price had dropped to just $764 for the 4141J. The company went out of business in 1971.

It is not known if FZ bought the JBL version, or replaced the speakers himself. Certainly, in the 1970s many guitarists, especially in the US, were using high-powered JBL speakers in their cabinets in place of the supplied models. It is probable that FZ got hold of it in 1975; I haven't seen any earlier pictures of him using it. Possibly FZ obtained this cabinet at the same time as his Vox Super Beatle amplifier, as they were commonly sold as a pair.

In the 1977 *Guitar Player* interview FZ continued: "On *Zoot Allures* about the only thing I used the Vox bottom and the Marshall top for was to get feedback on a song called 'Filthy Habits.'"[421] Note that "Filthy Habits" is not a track on *Zoot Allures*, although it was recorded around the same time; it eventually appeared on the *Sleep Dirt* and *Läther* albums.

FZ eventually covered the cabinet in the red-carpet material that was used for a lot of the band's stage gear, but kept the chrome trolley. He probably liked the ability to angle it to control the amount of projection; it can be seen prominently on stage next to FZ's rack in his film *Baby Snakes*. The cabinet, minus speakers, in very road-weary condition was sold in the 2016 auction for $2,187.50.[422]

The Vox cabinet as sold in auction, looking suitably post-apocalyptic
(Auction catalog—ZFT photo)

From the 1965 Vox UK catalogue

Hear it on:
Album: *Sleep Dirt*
Track: "Filthy Habits"

You will also find the same track on the *Läther* set.

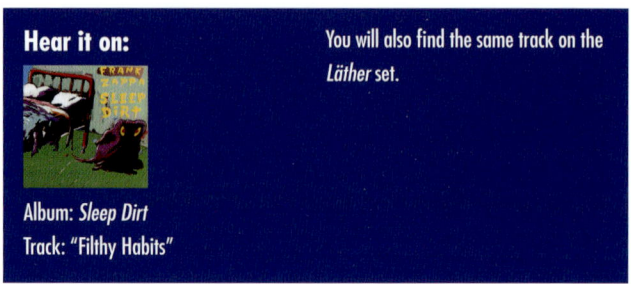

CHAPTER THREE
EFFECTS UNITS

"I work with effects every day, trying to optimize the sound I want to get at any one time, trying to set things up so that I can go from one sound to another really quickly. As every guitar player knows, getting the right amount of sustain and distortion at the right moment in the line that you're playing is a difficult thing to achieve. You've always got to mess around with the knobs. My idea is just to step on a footswitch and get the noise you want, on the beat."

— FZ[423]

Vox Wah-wah

Maestro Boomerang and other wah-wah pedals

Arbiter Add-A Sound

Rack Systems

Electro-Harmonix Big Muff

Electro-Harmonix Small Stone

Dan Armstrong Green Ringer

Ibanez FL-303 Flanger

MXR Flanger

MXR Distortion+

MXR Digital Delays

DBX Boom Box

Alembic F-2B Preamp

Electro Wagnerian Emancipator

360 Systems 20/20 Frequency Shifter

Morley Rotating Wah Volume Pedal

EBow

Systech Harmonic Energizer

Mu-Tron III

Mu-Tron Bi-Phase

Mu-Tron Octave Divider

Oberheim VCF-200 Voltage Controlled Filter

Roland GP-8

MicMix Dynaflanger

ProCo Rat

Note
When people ask me, "What effects pedals did FZ use?" my first answer is "Probably all of them!" FZ would try out any new piece of technology that came his way, and in later years, manufacturers were continually bringing him their latest wares to evaluate. Some made it into regular use, others were discarded almost immediately, and others were ripped to pieces and incorporated in rack systems but may not have been used in practice. Accordingly, I am in general only covering items that FZ specifically mentioned, or that are of specific or historic interest. In some cases the onstage effects that FZ used were primarily pieces of studio equipment, and are covered in that section.

ZAPPA GEAR

Vox Wah-Wah

"I was one of the first guys to use one . . . I loved the noise"
— FZ[424]

Early Vox advert for the Wah-wah

The electronic wah-wah effect was created, more or less accidentally, by Brad Plunkett in 1966. Thomas Organ Company had recently bought the rights to manufacture the Vox brand of amplifiers in the US, riding high at the time due to their association with the Beatles. Plunkett was working for them as a junior electronics technician, and had been tasked with redesigning the midrange-boost circuit of the new Vox Super Beatle.

He built a prototype circuit and after testing it with an oscilloscope, asked his colleague John Gennon to try it with a guitar through an amplifier and speakers, at which point several of the Vox engineers sat up and took notice of the sound. The circuit was quickly housed in the case of a volume pedal from a Vox Continental organ, and guitarist Del Casher tried out his electric guitar through it—the wah-wah pedal had been born![425]

It could hardly have been named anything but a "wah-wah"—as that exactly describes the sound. For those of you who need to know such things, R.G. Keen explains how it works: "It is either a band-pass filter or an over-coupled low-pass filter that exhibits a resonant peak just at its low-pass roll-off frequency. The resonant peak can be moved up and down in frequency by the player, and this makes for a striking emulation of the human voice making a 'waah' tone, or its tonal inverse, 'aooow.'"[426]

Vox launched the pedal in February 1967, originally marketing it for general use with keyboards, horns, and vocals, and calling it the Clyde McCoy wah-wah pedal after the jazz trumpeter, who was famous for his wah-wah trumpet mute technique. They later just called it the Vox Wah-wah, and for marketing purposes also sold it as the Cry-Baby Wah-wah.

Del Casher was convinced that its future was with the electric guitar, and recorded a demonstration record to be given away in guitar stores. In *Billboard* on the 8th April, 1967, Vox US president Joe Benaron announced that it would result in major changes for the sound of music. "The wah-wah pedal can be used with guitar or any amplified instrument or microphone," he explained. "It offers startling effects . . . its possibilities are unlimited." Indeed, it would find use with almost every amplified instrument (although few vocalists ever recorded with it), but the guitarists were the first to catch on to the pedal.

Casher had done some early session work for FZ at his Cucamonga Studio Z, and he also played guitar on some early Mothers of Invention shows.[427] He recalls telling FZ to get hold of a wah-wah pedal. Which FZ duly did—likely from Manny's Music store in New York. As well as using it on stage, FZ used it on the track "Stuff up the Cracks" recorded that July, 1967, at Mayfair Studios in New York, and also on various tracks for *We're Only In It for the Money* recorded later that summer.

The story goes that FZ introduced the wah-wah pedal to Hendrix. Certainly in July, 1967, Hendrix was playing sets in the Scene club in New York while FZ was playing the adjacent Garrick Theatre with the original Mothers of Invention. He came and saw the show and reportedly was fascinated by FZ's recently purchased wah-wah pedal, and bought one from Manny's Music store the very next day.

Hendrix would have been well aware of the track "Tales of Brave Ulysses," which had recently been released by Eric Clapton's band Cream; it featured heavy use of the new wah-wah pedal. Doubtless he was somewhat piqued at his archrival stealing a technological march on him, and small wonder that he was so intrigued to see FZ making the same sounds on stage.

Original Mothers of Invention drummer, the late Jimmy Carl Black, used to tell how he had been present when Hendrix tried out FZs wah-wah at the Garrick, using FZ's Gibson Switchmaster, which is corroboration enough for me!

Definitely a VOX! From the Mothers of Invention appearance on BBC TV
(still from *Late Night Lineup,* 1969)

Effects Units

Maestro Boomerang and other Wah-Wah Pedals

"I moved to the Boomerang . . . it added a certain amount of distortion, and I liked that"

— FZ[429]

A vintage VOX pedal from the 1960s
(tonehome.de)

Hendrix started using it right away on the sessions for both sides of his new single "Burning of the Midnight Lamp," which was recorded on the 7th and 20th of July, 1967, at Mayfair Studios, and slightly later, on several jams recorded at Ed Chalpin's studio.

By the end of the year, it had become the guitar effects pedal to own, its use having been showcased by Clapton and Hendrix (FZ's recordings with it would be delayed until 1968). The pedal was marketed under the name Cry Baby in the US, but it was never fully patented under that name, and before long there were many other manufacturers making similar pedals.

A Vox wah-wah pedal was clearly visible on the studio floor when the Mothers recorded "King Kong" for the BBC *Late Night Line-Up* TV show a year later in 1968.

According to Alice Cooper guitarist Michael Bruce, one day backstage at a gig with Zappa he noticed that Zappa's wah-wah pedal was a Vox like his own; and as his was worn out he decided to swap his one with FZ's, a secret he kept for many years.[428] Apparently the story doesn't end there; later on, that same pedal was swapped again with Eric Clapton's wah-wah! It would be nice to know who's got it now.

Hear it on:
You can also hear the original vinyl mix of this song, and an alternate take with an extended guitar solo on the *Greasy Love Songs* package.

Album: *Cruising with Ruben & The Jets*
Track: "Stuff Up the Cracks"

As I have mentioned, there were a lot of copies and variations of the original Vox wah-wah around in the 1960s and 1970s. FZ probably tried most of them—as Napoleon Murphy Brock said, "Many companies that built and designed effects pedals would bring their new gear and have Frank try them, and check if they could hold up on the road."[430]

FZ considered that each of the different makes had their own distinct sound. One that he certainly tried was the Morley wah-wah pedal; he later went on to use their Rotating Wah/Volume pedal (see the separate section for more about the Morley brand). In the 1970s, the wah-wah pedal that FZ mainly used was the Maestro Boomerang.

The Boomerang wah-wah pedal was one of a range of effects sold by Maestro during the 1960s. Maestro were a subsidiary of Gibson; perhaps their most famous (or influential) pedal was the original fuzz box used by Keith Richards on the Rolling Stones' "(I Can't Get No) Satisfaction" single. Like all the other units on the market, the Boomerang was a variant of the original Vox circuit.

The original version was a plain wah-wah pedal called the BG-1. However, Maestro soon brought out a revised version called the BG-2, which worked as a volume pedal when the wah-wah effect was switched out. The BG-2 instruction manual stated, with a certain economy of truth:

"WHAT IS THE BOOMERANG? It's Maestro's super wha-wha [sic] and volume pedal. It received its name from the fact that it always returns to the exact original setting after scanning

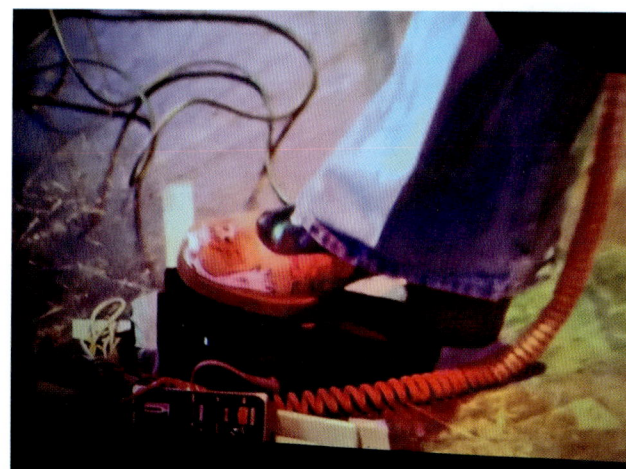

FZ's snazzy footwear and and a Boomerang pedal, Mutron III also visible
(still from Roxy, the Movie, 2015)

ZAPPA GEAR

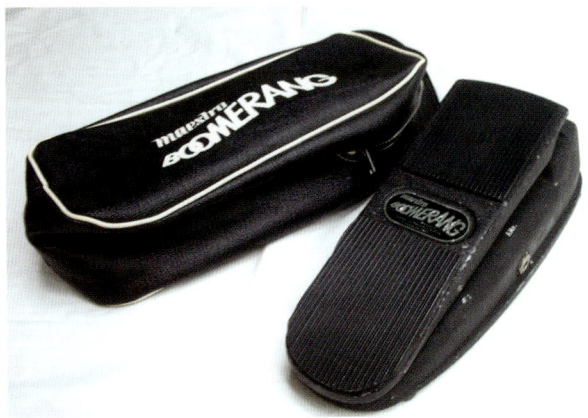

An original boomerang pedal and bag
(Joe Gagan)

The distinctive metal cased Morley wah-wah-wah pedal
(Ben Bove, Retro Rentals)

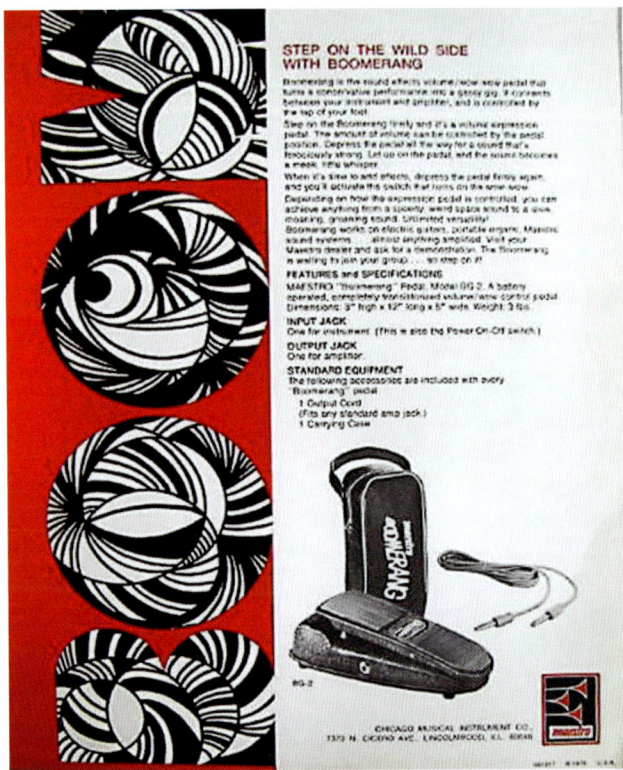

Maestro 'Step on the wild side' advert for the Boomerang

FZ in 1988 holding the wah-wah pedal given to him by Deepinder Cheema
(Deepinder Cheema)

a wide range of harmonics. 'Boomerang' was the first wha-wha on the market, and is currently the most reliable and effective. The Boomerang circuit is responsible for what is known as the 'Shaft' sound."[431]

Despite its larger case, it was quite a lot lighter than the Vox, and the dual use as a volume pedal was a useful innovation.[432] The Boomerang enjoyed considerable sales success in the US during the heyday of the wah-wah pedal, and was manufactured from 1968 to 1979, when Maestro production was stopped by Gibson's parent company Norlin.

Geoffrey Teese, classic wah-wah restorer and boutique pedal manufacturer and probably the world's expert on wah-wah pedals, says that the original series Boomerang are his second favorite pedal (after the original McCoy). Teese now sells his pedals as The Real McCoy range.[433]

FZ switched to the Boomerang from the Vox because he liked the distortion it added to his sound. However, like almost all wah-wah pedals, it couldn't cope with the high output from his later guitars with built-in preamplifiers, and he eventually stopped using a wah-wah pedal on stage.

In *Guitar Player* magazine, FZ gave some useful advice on how to use a wah-wah pedal, explaining that controlled and minimal foot movements give the best results: "The first thing you don't do is tap your foot on it in time with the music. The two basics are to locate a notch in the pedal so it gets a mid-range sustain that is tuned properly to the amp EQ that you have, so you get a nice boxy sound out of it . . . and the other thing is to move it very slightly and put most of the action in the rear half of the pedal, because that's where you get most of the speaking type sounds out of it."[434]

There was one last wah-wah pedal that passed through FZ's hands; it originally belonged to uber Zappa fan Deepinder Cheema. In 1988, he followed FZ throughout Europe to every gig on what was to be his last tour, carrying a Jim Dunlop Cry Baby Wah pedal in his baggage. Cheema explains: "I was listening to a lot of 1974 Zappa in '88; also I remembered "Dog Breath" from the 1971 LA live LP, the one with "Billy the Mountain." The former had a great solo by FZ with wah-wah all over the place . . . . So that is the reason why I carried my wah-wah to Europe. I was young and I liked the Maestro's wah sound of yesteryear, which had been absent for a long time. Who knows, perhaps I was naive to think that FZ would stick his guitar though my wah if I happened to bump into him."[435]

At the Mannheim show, he met up with Dutch fan Nico Otten, who knew all the tunes and all the words of the songs. When "We're Turning Again" started, Otten knew that there was a line about "Jimi and his wah-wah," and excitedly told Cheema that he should hand the pedal to FZ when he was about to sing that line. So precisely at that very moment the pedal was handed to FZ, who was habitually on the lookout for the unexpected from the audience.

Cheema continues, "He spotted it immediately, and sang the line staring at this new object whilst the rest of the band looked agog—yet he remained steady without missing a beat. The look on Ike's face was a picture. That was it; and the wah was placed next to FZ's mike stand for the remainder of the gig."

Later on in the tour Cheema learned from technician Bob Rice that he had lobbied FZ hard to try to acquire this as a souvenir of the tour. The final part of the story: "I met FZ himself in Rome and handed him the Jim Dunlop case belonging to the pedal; he immediately tossed that case to Merl Saunders, his very cool guitar roadie, and said 'Merl, put it with the wah-wah.' Luckily, Merl was walking past. I have to say FZ took all these moments in his stride, as if these events were the most natural thing in the world."[436]

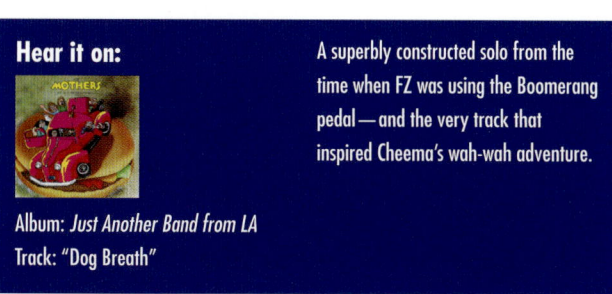

Hear it on:

A superbly constructed solo from the time when FZ was using the Boomerang pedal — and the very track that inspired Cheema's wah-wah adventure.

Album: *Just Another Band from LA*
Track: "Dog Breath"

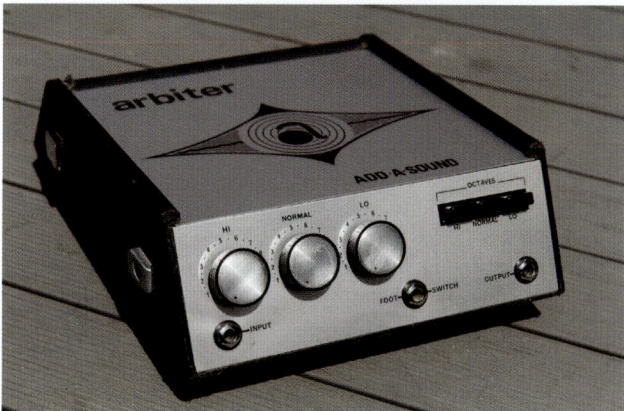

An original Add-A-Sound unit
(Raphael Tidas)

Effects Units

Arbiter Add-A-Sound

"Groups were invited to test and if possible destroy some of our prototypes; to be absolutely frank, the groups were successful in their destruction in some cases."

—*Dallas Arbiter* [437]

On the 24th September, 1967, at the Concertgebouw in Amsterdam, FZ was photographed cradling a rather large electrical box of tricks. This was the Arbiter Add-A-Sound, a very early octave-splitter effects unit.

Ivor Arbiter was born in London in 1929, and first made his mark in the 1950s as the proprietor of Drum City, one of the first shops in London specializing in percussion equipment. Arbiter opened a second shop in the late 1950s called Sound City, which specialized in guitars and amplifiers.[438] In the 1960s, Arbiter decided to have his own guitar amplifiers and effects units made, using the brand names Sound City and Arbiter Electronics.

Arbiter Electronics most famous product was the Fuzz Face distortion unit, as used by Jimi Hendrix and many other guitarists, although not, as far as I know, by FZ. Arbiter had his products made at various locations; some were built at the back of the Sound City shop, and other units were manufactured by various OEM suppliers.[439]

In 1967, Arbiter Electronics merged with the long established musical instrument distributor and manufacturer John E. Dallas and Sons (makers of the Jedson range of budget guitars, among many other things), to form Dallas-Arbiter Ltd.

The Add-A-Sound took the input signal and from this generated two additional signals, an octave above and below the original. It was a purely analogue device; indeed, in 1967 the word "analogue" was not used in this context, as there were no digital electronic devices to be differentiated from.

The front panel features three push buttons, which select the High, Low, and Normal outputs, and three corresponding knobs, which allow full control of the mix of sub octave, clean, and high octave outputs. Also on the front are input and output jack sockets and a footswitch socket. The unit also features a handy carrying handle on one side, and a look inside reveals some clean-looking 1960s solid-state circuitry. The mains electricity–powered Add-A-Sound featured a voltage selector at the back of the unit and a lift-up flap where the supply cable could be stored. Multi-voltage use would have been a key selling point for FZ, as it would still work when he took it back home to the States.

The unit can be seen perched on top of FZ's Marshall amp, with a footswitch attached, in the inside cover sleeve of the *Burnt Weeny Sandwich* album (taken while the band were setting up at the Albert Hall in London on 23rd September, 1967).

ZAPPA GEAR

The Add-A-Sound was featured in the Dallas Arbiter catalogue for 1968–1970 with a list price of £40 and 5 shillings (£40.25), but it had disappeared from the range by the time their 1970–1973 catalogue appeared. Forty pounds was quite a lot of money in those days, and it does not seem many were sold. FZ most probably bought it from Arbiter's Sound City music shop at 22 Rupert Street, London, just before the Mothers played the Albert Hall. The Amsterdam picture was taken the day after (24th September), you can see in FZ's expression that this was still very much a new toy that he was not quite sure what to do with! He never mentioned the unit by name to my knowledge, and I have no evidence that FZ used it on any other gigs. What became of this very rare and historic effects unit is not known.

Rack Systems

"The reason for putting the rack together is that if I do something on record and there is an opportunity to make the same sound on stage, I want to be able to do it."

—FZ[440]

FZ tunes up in front of his rack in 1977
(Eric Peterson)

With the above aim in mind, FZ invested a significant amount of money in getting a succession of touring rack systems built, each filled to the brim with a mixture of studio equipment and effects pedals, most of which were selectable from a custom pedal board. The first major system was built in 1973. Nicknamed "Ma Bell," it was a giant refrigerator-sized rack with a similarly huge pedal board. It was put together by tech Claus Wiedemann. As FZ put it: "It's a specially built thing that looks a little like a small version of the G.P.O. Tower around here. It has all the normal fuzz and phasing switches taken from their little boxes and put on this thing."[441]

The circuits and controls for the effects pedals were removed from their casings and mounted on cards in vertical modular units, which fit into a specially built rack unit with a power supply and connections for each. The pedal board consisted of four sections, each with a set of six or seven footswitches and large indicator lights, and a narrower center unit with a wah-wah pedal. The section combined to form a radial setup, around 5' wide.

When asked if it wasn't perhaps a little confusing, FZ responded: "It's hard to dash over sticking one leg out to hit just the right button out of twenty-seven, and hope that the levels you set during the sound check, say the level of fuzz versus the normal guitar, is gonna come out right. You can step on a button and get a horrible surprise!"[442]

Eventually Ma Bell was replaced by a twin rack system that was called the "Blue Box." Engineer David Gray was responsible for a large part of the design and helpfully wrote some fairly detailed notes about setting it up for FZ's road crew called *The*

One of the sections from FZ's 1970s pedalboard
(Mick Ekers)

Effects Units

The 'Effects/Junk' flight case as we found it at Joe's Garage
(Mick Ekers)

FZ rack unit with various cased effects units
(Mick Ekers)

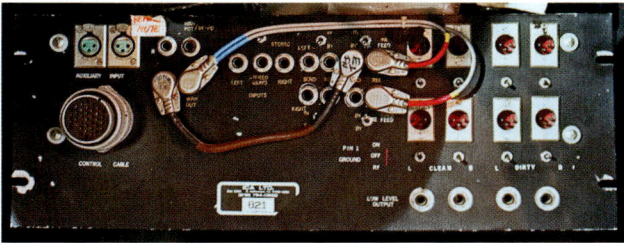

The main connection panel
(Mick Ekers)

Warning label found on one of the rack units
(Mick Ekers)

Blue Box for Bimbos! (see appendix). This included an even wider selection of effects units, an Alembic preamp, a custom preamp designed by Gray, and more sophisticated switching and routing.

The system had four stage outputs, each of which could be routed to different amplifiers, which were selectable via the pedal board. Gray notes that the foot switches were connected to the rack via a snake (heavy multicore cable): "Thick black job with Amphenol connectors," adding: "Please be careful and don't cross-thread them suckers, they're a bitch to wire!"[443]

FZ described the system in some detail in 1979: "Well, actually it's not all that complex. It's got a pair of Dynaflangers, a pair of MXR Flangers. It's got one input and four outputs, two dirty outputs and two clean outputs, all stereo. There's also two Big Muffs, Systech Harmonic Energizer; all these things are in pairs. Oberheim VCF, Eventide Harmonizer, MXR DDL, Mu-Tron, DBX 162 compressors, Gain Brains, Kepexes, a theremin, and a (Mu-Tron) Bi-Phase. That's about it, and there's about twenty-four switches on the floor. I add to it every year. The Dynaflangers are the newest thing. Oh yes, there's a Mu-Tron Octivider and a DBX Boom Box."[444]

Dweezil Zappa researched the rack systems when he was putting together his original rig for his Zappa Plays Zappa band. He told me: "It was a crazy system; he had spent over 30,000 dollars to build his guitar rig back in the mid-70s, and that's like 300,000 dollars in today's money." DZ noted that as well as all the guitar effects pedals, he also incorporated various expensive pieces of studio equipment including Telefunken and DBX compressors and an Eventide 949 Harmonizer. I asked what became of the racks: "All that stuff doesn't really exist, unfortunately. That big rig in the middle 70s was when he had the best guitar sound, I thought. But that whole rig was disassembled and none of it really works."[445]

When I visited Joe's Garage in March 2012, the first evidence I found were some of the sections of the pedalboard. The sections consisted of a wooden base and sides with a top metal plate into which the lights and switches were mounted. The connections were made via five-pin XLR connectors mounted on the side. The wiring inside was not especially tidy but functional, and the units showed a considerable amount of road wear.

Then we discovered an old flight case labelled "Effects/Junk," containing a jumble of bits and pieces, including two of the modular units and two large complicated devices that appeared to be preamps of some kind. These were in very grubby condition; many modules were loose in the case with pieces of perished flight case foam sticking to them. The whole looked like remains from the film set of a mad scientist's lab. At least some of the modules came from FZ's main rack unit from the 1988 tour.

The modules were in a variety of styles; some had the faceplates finished and engraved, others were raw metal marked with stickers, and some retained the knobs from the original pedal. Each consisted of a combined metal base plate and front panel supporting a computer-style card upon which the original circuit board was attached. Each card slotted into a connector at the back of the unit, which had connections for the inputs, outputs, and power supply.

The 1988 touring rack was considerably simpler than previous versions, containing two MXR Delay System II units, a Roland GP8 multi effects unit, and one 3U modular unit containing the circuits from two MXR Flangers, two Mu-Tron IIIs, a Big Muff fuzz, and what appears to be a pair of limiters. The pedal board was also stripped down, consisting of just twelve footswitches.

Even so, it could cause problems in a live situation. FZ's tech Merl Saunders Jr. kept a close eye on which buttons FZ had pressed, remembering one time when he had to rescue the situation: "But he did something out there . . . and it had this feedback that was just wailing and he looked at me like the curse of death. Bob Rice was just cracking up because I stood up, I didn't run out there, I just walked out and pressed a button and it stopped and I turned around and walked back. And Frank just looked at me . . . and I'm like, 'Dude, I just gotta watch you to make sure you don't kill yourself on this stuff!'"[446]

Electro-Harmonix Big Muff

"So he had taken a Big Muff and put it on this card, it was this crazy system"

— Dweezil Zappa[447]

Although I knew that FZ had used one or two Electro-Harmonix Big Muff pedals in various touring setups, it seemed unlikely any trace of them could be found. When I spoke to DZ before I visited LA, he told me: "I think the Big Muff was taken apart and put onto this card but now there's no power supply for it. It could be brought back to life but I don't think there was anything too special about it." I replied optimistically, "Sad people like me would probably want to see the circuit board if it still exists, just so I could figure out which model Big Muff it was."

A couple of months later when I visited Joe's Garage, I discovered part of FZ's pedal board, with a switch in the top of the unit labelled "Muff," so here was some concrete evidence. The position in the board highlights the relative importance of the Big Muff to FZ's sound at the time. As the day wore on, there was no sign of the pedals, but when we started examining the "Effects/Junk" case, I noticed a single grubby circuit board loose in the case.

To my astonishment, it was the board for a Big Muff! After some initial research, and consulting with expert Kit Rae, this has been identified as a 1977–1978 Mark 3 Big Muff circuit, with an AC connector and BC 239 transistors. The circuit has

Electro-Harmonix advert from the late 1970s
(Author's collection)

been modified to use the power supply from FZ's rack unit, and there have also been some changes made to the input/output sections. According to Kit, a couple of the resistors have been changed to values that would have reduced the gain in the clipping sections, so it is likely that it had a softer distortion than usual.[448]

The Electro-Harmonix Big Muff is one of the most famous and instantly recognizable guitar effects pedals ever made. It created a new voice for the electric guitarist in the same way that the first fuzz boxes and wah-wah pedals had done previously. Electro-Harmonix was founded in New York by Mike Matthews in 1968, at first selling the LPB-1 linear power booster by mail order. This was a simple unit designed to boost the output of a guitar so that it would drive an amplifier into distortion. Then followed the Muff Fuzz, a basic guitar distortion pedal. Matthews maintains it was so named because it sounded "muffled."

In 1969, Matthews and codesigner Bob Myer came up with the Big Muff Pi. Myer deliberately designed the basic circuit to have a very long sustain, and Matthews recalls: "I also worked a lot with the filters to get the notes to sound less raspy and more sinusoidal and smooth."[449] The Electro-Harmonix publicity material described the pedal as "the finest harmonic distortion-sustain device developed to date," and this was no exaggeration. As Kit Rae puts it on his marvelous Big Muff Pi website:

"The Muff had monstrous loads of gain and sustain, and a monstrous sound to go along with it, from thunderous mud to hammering treble. It was the first fuzz pedal with such a huge bottom end, and it stepped on just about any typical fuzz pedal out there. There is a characteristic underlying harmonically doubled octave mixed into the Muff tone, sometimes described as the Muff's 'buzz' or 'fizz.' It was quite different from what was a common 'fuzz' tone at the time. The tone sweep ranged from huge, dark, bassy sludge to thick, piercing, buzzsaw treble, all with a deep mid scoop. Somewhere in the middle was a sweet spot that just about anyone could dial in for the signature Big Muff tone."[450]

Effects Units

The 'Muff' button and light from FZ's effects board
(Mick Ekers)

The Big Muff circuit board I found at Joe's Garage
(Mick Ekers)

The author's 1977/8 Big Muff pedal, coincidentally the exact same version that FZ used
(Mick Ekers)

It had a large sheet metal case (nobody had pedal boards in those days, and something too big to accidentally kick over on stage was a good thing); controls for volume, tone, and sustain; and a single footswitch—it looked like it meant business. The relatively advanced electronics meant that unlike many earlier fuzz boxes, it performed well in combination with other effects units, and didn't stop working if it got hot.

The Big Muff was a huge and immediate success, and pretty well every guitarist of note got hold of one. The buzz among musicians about this new pedal was so great that FZ would almost certainly have tried one (and probably bought one) very early on, although the earliest mention I can find of him using a Big Muff was in 1979, when describing his onstage rig for *Guitar* magazine.[451]

Electro-Harmonix (EHX) had some serious problems in the early 1980s. According to Matthews, an intimidating campaign by a trade union (which he says only six out of the 200 employees actually wanted to join) disrupted the business, and led to him filing for bankruptcy in 1982. Undaunted, he sold some property and repurchased the company, which was soon back in production again. However, EHX then began to suffer from competition with imported Japanese products. The last straw was when their Japanese supplier stopped sending the critical bucket brigade chips used in their delay pedals; unable to meet demand, they were giving local Japanese companies preference for the limited supply. EHX filed for bankruptcy again in 1984.[452]

Matthews turned his back on New York, and with the end of the Cold War, seized the opportunity to start a business based in Russia called Sovtek, selling vacuum valves and circuit boards back to the US. By 1989, many major guitar amplifier companies were buying the Sovtek valves, including Marshall, Mesa Engineering, Peavey, and Fender. Matthews bought back the Electro-Harmonix name, and seeing the demand (and high prices) for vintage EHX items, started manufacturing versions of the Big Muff and other classic pedals in Russia.

However, demand for the US models continued, and in 2000 the fully revitalized Electro-Harmonix company reissued the US Big Muff Pi. Based on the three-transistor, late-1970s version, it had a revised circuit designed by Fran Blanche, who went on to found Frantone, the highly regarded boutique pedal manufacturer. Today the pedal is available in various formats, most of them packaged in smaller cases, with specific variants for bass guitar and heavy metal guitarists; but the classic

> **Hear it on:**
>
>
>
> **Album:** *Guitar*
> **Track:** "Watermelon in Easter Hay"
>
> At the time, FZ was using a very complicated set of effects devices, and only he knew which ones he was using at any point in a solo. However, the sustained notes in this sound distinctly Big Muff—like to me, so I'm going to stick my neck out here.

sheet-metal case Big Muff Pi is still in production, and using more or less the same design as FZ's model.[453]

In the late 1970s, FZ had a pair of Big Muffs installed in modules in his Blue Box double rack unit, and also in the later system used on the 1988 tour. It's no accident that alongside an ever-growing array of sophisticated (and considerably more expensive) studio effects units, FZ always had at least one $50 Big Muff in his rig, and it was a key element in many of his signature guitar solos.

Electro-Harmonix Small Stone

"We had great designers, the greatest of whom is an English dude, David Cockerell."

—Mike Matthews[454]

Another discovery at Joe's Garage was FZ's Electro-Harmonix (EHX) Small Stone phase-shifter module, which was barely attached to the main rack unit when we found it. In this instance, the mounting plate had been helpfully printed with the name, and the reused original knob identified the unit as being a 1970s model.

Many people do not realize that phasing is a different effect to flanging; although the results may sound broadly similar, they are produced in different ways, and phasing tends to sound more subtle and ethereal. For the technically curious: a phase-shifter splits the input signal into two separate signals, one of which is passed though filter circuits that vary the phase of certain frequencies. When the filtered signal is blended with the original, the result is a series of peaks and troughs at different frequencies, known as a "comb" filter. Most phase shifter units will continuously vary the amount of shift, causing the comb to move up and down through the frequency spectrum, creating the familiar phaser sweeping sound.

The Small Stone story starts in 1974, when EHX president Mike Matthews hired engineer David Cockerell, who was formerly chief designer for EMS, the UK synthesizer pioneers. His first design for EHX was the Small Stone, basing the circuitry on his previous work back in 1971 on the EMS Synthi Hi-Fli guitar synthesizer. For the very technical among you, it rather uniquely uses Operational Transconductance Amplifiers (OTAs), unlike rival MXR's Phase 90, which used FETs (Field Effect Transistors) that needed to be matched in pairs. This made the Small Stone considerably cheaper to manufacture, and it swept the market, selling even more than EHX's flagship Big Muff pedal.[455] The unit was housed in a typical EHX folded steel case, and ran off a single 9-volt battery.

A late 1970's Small Stone pedal
(Pedal Area)

FZ's Small Stone module—note the trim pot at the bottom
(Mick Ekers)

Effects Units

Apart from the on-off switch, the only controls are a Rate knob, which varies the speed of the phase modulation, and a Color switch, which adds feedback to the circuit, resulting in a deeper and stronger-sounding effect. FZ's rack module has an additional small preset potentiometer at the bottom of the unit; this would most likely be a volume trim control, used to balance the output between the on and off states.

You can see from the markings that FZ preferred the Rate control set at 11 o'clock, and the Color control on (up). The Small Stone was introduced in 1975, and went on to become one of EHX's biggest sellers. According to Matthews, at the time the factory could barely keep up with demand, running at nearly 7,000 units a month.[456]

When EHX ceased operations in the 1980s, Cockerell went to work for Akai, working on their legendary samplers such as the S900. He returned to work for EHX in the 2000s, designing pedals such as the HOG and Micro-POG. The Small Stone is still being manufactured by EHX, in a smaller nano format, but using more or less the same circuitry as the original design.[457]

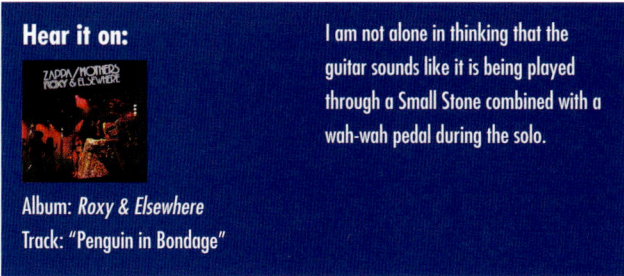

Hear it on:

Album: *Roxy & Elsewhere*
Track: "Penguin in Bondage"

I am not alone in thinking that the guitar sounds like it is being played through a Small Stone combined with a wah-wah pedal during the solo.

Dan Armstrong Green Ringer

"We wanted it so that when the effect is called for, you just reach down and flick a switch."

—Dan Armstrong[458]

The Green Ringer was one of a range of modular effects units designed by the American guitarist, luthier, and designer Dan Armstrong, most famous for the clear-bodied guitars that he designed for Ampeg in 1968. After leaving Ampeg, Armstrong moved to London, England, in the early 1970s, where he was to develop his own range of guitars and amplifiers.

In 1973, he met fellow US expatriate George Merriman, who was the electrician at the London Rainbow Theatre at the time. In 1971, Ampeg had given Armstrong a prototype effects unit called The Scrambler, which was an unusual combination of a ring modulator and distortion pedal (which had not achieved any commercial success). He told Merriman about the device and to his surprise, he knew all about it and built Armstrong a copy. Armstrong recalled, "Together we changed it some, tweaked it until we got it to play an octave up, and like two octaves down as well as other neat sounds—all depending on what note was originally played."[459]

They decided to put it into production and Armstrong had the idea of making the unit small enough to fit straight onto a guitar. The unit had a built-in jack plug at the back, and a socket and small on-off switch on the front panel. By switching two internal wires, the signal path could be reversed and the box plugged into the input of an amp. The unit was named the Green Ringer and was the first of a series of color-coded effects

The Musitronics version of the Green Ringer
(Mark Schnoor)

The backplate, with instructions on reversing the plug and socket, soldering iron required!
(Mark Schnoor)

ZAPPA GEAR

The circuit board, about the size of a 9-volt battery and not too difficult to fit inside a guitar! (Mark Schnoor)

units (known as Sound Modifiers) including the Blue Clipper (fuzz) and the Purple Peaker (parametric EQ). The aluminum boxes had interlocking tabs so the units could be joined together in various configurations.

Originally made by Wareham Electronics in the UK, they were subsequently made at various times by Musitronics in the US and Maxon in Japan. Armstrong's idea of making them to fit directly on to the guitar or amp had some drawbacks; the units could not be easily used in combination, and might not fit to a guitar or amp without a suitable amount of space around the jack socket. (Fender Stratocasters were out of the question!)

After being out of production for over twenty years, they were reintroduced in 2006 by Grafton Electronics in the US (cofounded by Armstrong's son, guitar pickup designer Kent Armstrong). The effects units were made available in a standard footswitch-operated effects pedal configuration as well as the original compact case, but the company suffered a factory fire in 2009[460] and appears to have ceased trading.

FZ would likely have had tried one of the mid 1970s Musitronics versions, and he liked the sound so much that he asked his electronics technician Arthur "Midget" Sloatman to install the Green Ringer circuit permanently into his guitars. As the circuit was so small, and he already had battery-powered electronics fitted to the guitars, this was a fairly straightforward task. A small on-off switch was fitted to the body, taking Armstrong's concept of an effect that could be controlled on the guitar to its logical conclusion. In the end, Sloatman fitted one to both the Les Paul and the Baby Snakes SG, and possibly the Hendrix Strat at one stage. I asked Dweezil Zappa about this: "Yeah, it might have been in the Les Paul at one time but it's not now, but the Green Ringer is definitely in the Baby Snakes one."[461]

Sloatman explains that the Green Ringer "is a low-pass filter into a DC rectifier circuit. Because it's trying to convert AC to steady DC, it produces an abundance of a second harmonic. It kind of feels like it's feeding back, because you play a note and instantly hear the octave. But any time you play more than one note, it does this horrible modulation stuff, which Frank loved."[462]

IBANEZ FL-303 FLANGER

"Until very recently this effect could only be achieved by actually using two tape decks, or through expensive digital processing"

— Ibanez[463]

Another find that was discovered inside the Effects/Junk flight case at Joe's Garage was an empty case from a first-edition Ibanez FL-303 Flanger. Flanging is the sound effect produced when a signal is played back simultaneously through a pair of tape recorders and the speed of one is adjusted very slightly; the two signals interact producing a whooshing "jet plane" type of effect. Although pioneered in the 1940s, the effect was most popular in the latter half of the 1960s, used on recordings such as "Lucy in the Sky with Diamonds" by the Beatles and "Itchycoo Park" by the Small Faces.

It was not until the advent of suitably powerful integrated circuits in the late 1970s that (as Ibanez state) it became possible to reproduce the effect using a small effects unit suitable for on stage use. Ibanez (following the lead from Electro-Harmonix and MXR) introduced their first flanger pedal, the FL-303, in 1977. It had three controls for Speed, Width, and Regen, and ran on two 9-volt batteries. The FL-303 was restyled in 1979 with black knobs, and was replaced with the smaller-cased unit, the FL-301, in 1980.[464]

Hear it on:
Album: *Shut Up 'n Play Yer Guitar*
Track: "Hog Heaven"

It sounds to me like the first minute of this track could involve the Green Ringer.

FL-303 in mint condition
(Jan Atze de Vries)

Effects Units

The case from FZ's FL303
(Mick Ekers)

Like all the Ibanez branded effects units of the time, it was actually designed and manufactured by the Maxon (Nisshin Onpa) company in Japan. Maxon was established in the 1960s, at first supplying guitar pickups to various companies including Ibanez. When they brought out their first range of compact effects units, Ibanez licensed the designs and sold them worldwide under the Ibanez brand until 2002. Maxon is still in business and has reissued many of the classic Ibanez pedals under its own name, but at the time of writing the FL-303 is not available.[465]

The FL-303 is one of the few surviving effects unit cases from this period in FZ's career. Presumably the circuit board and controls found their way into a rack unit, but we did not find it. Many people consider the FL-303 one of the best effects of its type, with a considerably wider range of effects than its contemporaries; whether FZ actually took it on stage or recorded with it is lost in the mists of time.

MXR FLANGER

"I'm using the MXR Flanger on a few of the guitar sounds."

— *FZ*[466]

FZ had a pair of MXR Flanger circuit boards mounted in his late 1979 rack unit. The location of the original cases and knobs is not known (Gail Zappa believed they were still around in a box somewhere in the Zappa estate).[467]

It is popularly assumed that the term "flanging" derives from the original method of achieving the effect: the signal is played back simultaneously on two tape decks and the speed of one is varied. Supposedly this was done by the recording engineer placing their finger on the rim ("flange") of the tape reel. In fact, the effect was invented by engineer Ken Townsend, while the Beatles were recording *Revolver*, by electronically varying the tape speed of one machine. George Martin asserts that the term was originated by John Lennon, a private joke between the two after a nonsense technical explanation that he gave Lennon, saying they had used a device called a "double-bifurcated sploshing flange."[468]

FZ's Stereo pair of MXR Flanger circuits - rack mounted. Note the red marks indicating his preferred settings: Manual 10 o'clock, Width 11 Speed 10, Regen 3
(Mick Ekers)

An original 1970's AC powered flanger
(Garret Park Guitars)

ZAPPA GEAR

MXR (from "MiXeR")[469] was founded in 1972, in Rochester, New York, by Keith Barr, Michael Laiacona, and Terry Sherwood to sell the Phase 90 pedal designed by erstwhile hi-fi repairman Barr. A range of other units soon followed. Incorporated under the name MXR Innovations, they immediately differentiated their product from the extravagantly named and packaged units produced by rival companies such as Electro-Harmonix.

All their pedals were contained in heavy-duty compact cast metal cases, with a minimal number of controls and simple graphics. The pedals had unpretentious names like "Flanger"; the look was seriously businesslike. Early adverts used slogans such as "this is not a toy," and they soon gained the reputation as being the premier effects units for professional musicians.[470]

The original MXR Flanger (model number M-117) was introduced in 1977, and stayed in production until the company ceased operating.[471] Packaged in a typical sturdy MXR compact box, the unit was AC powered. Many competing designs struggled to provide enough electricity for the hungry ICs with two 9-volt batteries. The MXR featured a Manual control for the delay range, as well as an oscillator that continuously varied the effect—controlled by the Speed and Width controls. With the Speed set to zero, this allowed the flanging effect to be operated manually. The Regen control varied the amount of the processed signal fed back into the circuit, giving an increased depth to the effect. The flanger weighed in at a hefty seven pounds and retailed at $127.50 in 1980.[472]

By the early 1980s, MXR had become the largest US effects company, but, like competitor Electro-Harmonix, they could not withstand the onslaught of imported Japanese pedals from companies such as Boss and Ibanez, and the company closed down in 1984. Barr moved to Los Angeles and went on to found Alesis Studio Electronics; he died of a heart attack in 2010.[473] Sherwood remained in Rochester and cofounded Applied Research and Technology; Laiacona founded Whirlwind USA, the audio interface company. He died in 2013.[474] The MXR name was purchased by Jim Dunlop in 1987, and they still sell the MXR-117 Flanger little changed from the original.

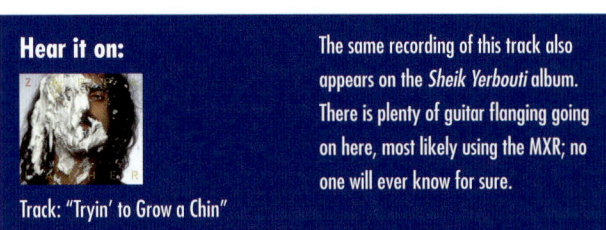

Hear it on: The same recording of this track also appears on the *Sheik Yerbouti* album. There is plenty of guitar flanging going on here, most likely using the MXR; no one will ever know for sure.

Track: "Tryin' to Grow a Chin"

MXR DISTORTION+

"I mean, to me, MXR was an art project. Yeah, it was a business, and yeah there was the little game to see how cheap we could make a unit, but . . . we had this idea collectively that what we were doing was an artistic expression."

—*Keith Barr*[475]

Another discovery we found rattling around loose in the Effects/Junk case at Joe's Garage was a small effects module. The two distinctive black knobs on the front marked it as an MXR product, and I was later able to identify the circuit board as coming from the final 1981 version of the Distortion+ unit.[476]

The Distortion+ (model number M-104; the word "plus" was never used in packaging or marketing) was designed by MXR founder Keith Barr, and introduced in 1973. In typical MXR less is more style, he developed a simple but effective circuit, with only two controls: Volume and Distortion.

At a time when most distortion pedals incorporated a significant amount of fuzz, the unit actually provided less distortion than most, producing a manageable amount of gain better matched to the new generation of valve amplifiers.

Unlike the silicon transistors at the heart of most of the 1960s fuzz boxes, the Distortion+ used a pair of germanium diodes and a basic IC op-amp to provide the smooth overdrive and moderate gain characteristics that were just what many

A 1981 Distortion+ like FZ's. The rubber knob cover enabled the control to be foot operated (Pedal Area)

120

MXR Digital Delays

"I took three MXR Digital Delays — two with minimum memory storage, and one with tons of it."

— FZ[480]

The distinctive black MXR knobs on the unit
(Mick Ekers)

The simple circuit board, showing the interior construction of FZ's effect modules
(Mick Ekers)

In the quote above FZ was referring to the second edition MXR digital delay, the Delay System II (see below); originally he used a single MXR Digital Delay rack unit in his touring rack in the late 1970s. The original MXR Digital Delay (model number M-113) was introduced in 1976, and became a common fixture in guitarists' rack systems. Its rugged construction and relatively simple control panel made it far more suitable for touring than more sophisticated units that had been specifically designed for recording studio use (of which FZ had several, as you will see).

Price was also a significant factor. When the M-113 was released, it cost $1,000 with one memory card installed; up to three additional cards could be fitted, which cost $250 each. At the time, the cheapest studio units cost $4,500. In 1975, FZ was asked if he used digital delay on stage. He replied: "No. It's an expensive piece of property to drag around with you, and it's not really too roadable."[481] When the MXR came out, it was just what he (and many other musicians) needed.

1980 MXR advert featuring the digital delay

guitarists were looking for (notably Jerry Garcia and Randy Rhoads, who used the pedal extensively).[477]

Housed in a standard 2 3/8"×4 3/8"×1 1/4" MXR case and finished in a mustard yellow color, the earliest versions of these pedals had the legend "Hand built by guitar players" printed on the circuit board, and they sold for around $40.[478] In the 1970s, MXR used the cases as a promotional paperweight, without any electronics inside but with working knobs and a pen holder where the footswitch would be.[479]

Again we can only conjecture if this module was used in the studio or on stage; FZ never mentioned it specifically, but we can assume that he must have tried it out and asked for it to be racked up at some point. It would have provided a useful contrast to the Electro-Harmonix Big Muff pedals that he was also using at the time.

Like many MXR pedals of the time, it is considered a classic, and is still being produced by the Jim Dunlop company. However, the reissue is regarded as having a slightly less smooth tone than the originals, which are still much sought after.

ZAPPA GEAR

The black faced MXR Delay System II
(Patrick Gaumond)

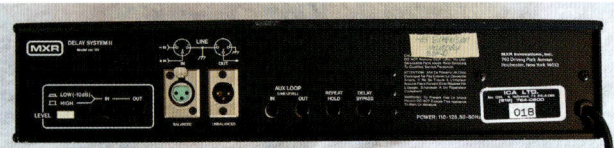

Back panel of the System II, with ICA inventory sticker as used on most of FZ's gear in the 1980s
(Patrick Gaumond)

Built into a two-unit rack case, the M-113 had a distinctive bright blue front panel (it is now commonly referred to as the "Blue Face" delay), with a row of push buttons that selected the delay time. Beneath these were controls for further adjusting the delay time, Mix, Regen, and Level, plus Sweep Width and Frequency.

Pulling the Mix knob reversed the phase of the output signal, which combined with the sweep controls allowed for a variety of chorus, flange, and phase effects to be produced in addition to standard delay and reverb.

Even fully loaded with memory cards, the M-113 could only produce 160 milliseconds of full-frequency-range delay, and a maximum of around 1.25 seconds with the frequency range going up to just 2.5khz. (For the non-technical: this means that longer delays would have sounded very muddy indeed.) Nonetheless, it served FZ's purposes, and was favored by many other notable musicians, including bassist Jaco Pastorius and Pink Floyd guitarist Dave Gilmour.

In 1981, MXR introduced the M-151 Delay System II, which was a significant improvement in quality and features, and with the maximum amount of memory on board had a continuously variable maximum delay of 3 seconds. FZ, as noted, put two fully-loaded units in his rack. Possibly, FZ was talking about the third unit here:

"I was also using an MXR Digital Delay with a small amount of vibrato in it and a short delay. That was responsible for the difference between the Marshall and the other amps, and it gave a good stereo perspective."[482]

MXR made the Delay System II until the company closed down in 1984. FZ kept a pair in his stage rack right up to the last 1988 tour, feeding the signal into a pair of small Acoustic amps.[483] The digital delays were sold in the Joe's Garage sale in 1996, and I didn't find any remaining at the UMRK in 2012.

Thankfully, Patrick Gaumond was kind enough to send me pictures of the unit he purchased; UMRK inventory number 018, which has a sticker confirming that it has expansion memory board. The MXR is still in full working order.

DBX Boom Box

"Oh yes, there's a . . . DBX Boom Box."

— FZ[484]

The above quote is the only mention of the DBX Boom Box by FZ that I have found, when he was describing the contents of the current version of his onstage rack in 1979. I feel it is still worthy of mention, if only to avoid confusion, as otherwise some readers might assume that FZ had a large portable cassette player in his system!

DBX originally introduced the DBX 100 Boom Box in 1978 as a small wooden-sided hi-fi accessory, with domestic RCA (phono) connectors. Its purpose was to add more bass to a music signal, which it did by taking low frequencies in the 50–100 Hz range and synthesizing a signal one octave below them, which was then blended with the original. The effect was warmer and more natural sounding than a regular octave divider. Controls consisted of an operate/bypass switch and rotary controls for low frequency boost and subharmonic level.

DBX also produced a professional version, the DBX 500, which was essentially the same unit in a metal rack case with 1/4" jack socket connectors. This is the model that FZ used, and his appeared in the 2016 auction.[485] For their professional series DBX called the unit a Subharmonic Synthesizer; however, FZ's has the words "BOOM BOX" boldly added to the front panel label, presumably added by his crew. It seems that he liked the name. In his 1978 setup, FZ had the Boom Box switchable from his pedal board and it was patched into the Clean Left channel feeding one of his Marshall amps. It sold in the auction for $1,562.50.[486] The DBX 500 was only produced between 1978 and 1980,[487] when it was replaced with the 120 series, which become particularly popular with DJs. The current model DBX 120a is still in production.[488]

FZ's 'Boom Box'
(ZFT)

Alembic F-2B Preamp

"... at one point he also had this Alembic preamp thing that was just for a clean signal"

— *Dweezil Zappa*[489]

The "Alembic preamp thing" was a model F-2B stereo preamplifier, a top-quality handmade rack unit containing two sets of volume and tone controls, designed to boost and modify the signal from an electric guitar, for subsequent output to an uncontrolled power amplifier.

FZ personally ordered two F-2Bs from Alembic in 1973–1974, one for himself and one for his new bass player Tom Fowler, who was using an Alembic bass guitar at the time.[490] FZ had his fitted in the top position in his Blue Box touring rack, wired in to the dirty channels. It can be seen in the photo in the Rack Systems section.

Alembic was founded in 1969 by Ron and Susan Wickersham; originally it was a consulting firm working closely with the Grateful Dead and other West Coast bands such as Jefferson Airplane and Crosby Stills Nash & Young. The company was joined by guitar maker Rick Turner in the same year, and they developed early mobile multi-track recording systems and built the legendary Wall of Sound live-sound system used by the Grateful Dead. They also worked on improving the electronics of the band's guitars and amplifiers, and started making custom guitars and basses in 1972.[491]

The circuit of the F-2B is based on that found in the Fender Dual Showman guitar amplifier, known for its exceptional warm but clean tone. Ron Wickersham had done some work on the Grateful Dead's Fender amplifiers, taking separate outputs from the preamp stages to feed the band's high-power McIntosh power amplifiers; the next stage was to rack-mount the Fender circuitry. As Turner put it, "Ron took the front-end preamp stage of the Dual Showman, put it on a modern printed circuit board and loaded it with military-grade parts, put it in a single-rackspace box, and that's what became the Alembic F-2B."[492]

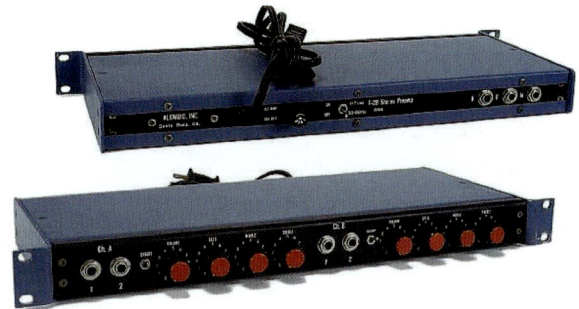

The F2-B, front and back views
(Alembic)

The original F-2B was built into a blue single-unit rack case, with a plain black front panel. The Alembic name and model number were on the back panel only. Two pairs of input jack sockets connect to two independent sections, each with identical Volume, Treble, Middle, and Bass controls and a Bright switch. At the rear are separate outputs for the two channels plus a combined mono output. Each channel uses a single 12AX7 valve. Although designed primarily for bass, many other top guitarists have made good use of the F-2B, including David Gilmour; it has been referred to as the "secret ingredient" of his tone.[493] This is not the first time that Gilmour's name has cropped up in this book—he obviously had similar ideas on guitar amplification to FZ.

DZ remembered FZ's preamp as only having one knob; I checked with Alembic and they confirmed that they only built their standard models which all had multiple controls, but the early versions had red caps on the knobs which used to regularly fall off, so it may be that FZ's unit had lost all the caps but one; on a dark stage it would look like it only had the one control. Dweezil also noted: "I saw this unit in Scott Thunes' live rig on stage in the 80s. Frank was very interested in getting the best recordings possible and probably specifically requested Scott use that as part of his sound. Scott does have a good sound on those recordings."[494]

Susan Wickersham remembers that one time, FZ returned the two units for a checkup prior to a tour: "Everything checked out fine and we sent them back."[495] Turner left Alembic in 1978, and the Wickersham family is still running the business. Although mainly known for their famous high-end bass guitars these days, Alembic are still making the F-2B to the same high standards as ever, and the basic design is almost unchanged since the original, although less modestly there is now an Alembic F-2B badge on the front, and the all-black knobs don't have caps that fall off!

Hear it on:

Scott Thunes is not positive that he used the Alembic in 1988, but as DZ says, he does have a good sound.

Album: *The Best Band You Never Heard in Your Life*
Track: "Bolero"

Electro Wagnerian Emancipator

"There's one thing a guy named Bob Easton constructed for me called the Electro Wagnerian Emancipator"

— FZ[496]

The Electro Wagnerian Emancipator (or EWE) was a one-off guitar synthesizer device that was built for FZ by Bob Easton, founder of the audio-electronics company 360 Systems. Easton says, "I worked with a lot of musicians, but the main difference with FZ was that he was pretty technical, in terms of the detail of what went on inside boxes, or why they might sound a particular way if you were to build some specific idea. That is how the EWE (his words, obviously) came to be."[497]

Easton remembers having a lot of midnight-to-breakfast "yak sessions" with FZ in the basement of his house, during which the subject of automating parallel harmony came up. Easton knew how to do this, and the first (and only) EWE was built. FZ described the EWE as follows: "It's a very attractive little device that combines a frequency follower with a device that puts out harmony notes to what you're playing. You can have your choice of any twelve chromatic notes in four parts following your runs. You can't play chords with it, but linearly it'll follow you whether you bend or whatever. Its main drawback is that the tone that comes out of it is somewhat like a Farfisa organ."[498]

The EWE had momentary push buttons that selected a range of plus or minus one or two octaves. It had a keypad that selected the interval in semitone increments, a number of synthesizer modules to alter the tonality, a low-pass filter connected to an envelope generator (triggered by a pick-detector), and a mixer to combine the guitar signal and various EWE outputs. For the early 1970s, this was pretty advanced stuff. And it actually worked—the only problem was the timbre of the synthesizer sound it produced was, according to FZ, "fairly unattractive." Easton admits, "It did sound like a Farfisa, and 'weaselly'!"[499]

According to the 1986 *Guitar Player* interview, FZ planned to use it on "Big Swifty" from the album *Waka/Jawaka*, but Easton is certain that he made the EWE in 1974–1975, and *Waka/Jawaka* was recorded in 1972. It may be that FZ is confusing the EWE with the Moog pitchshifter mentioned in the album sleeve notes. In any case, the EWE never ended up on any final record, and it was relegated to gather dust in the warehouse. No pictures of the device are known to exist.

360 Systems 20/20 Frequency Shifter

"Frank tried it on his own mike just to be weird. It was"

— Bob Easton[500]

The 20/20 Frequency Shifter was another innovative product from Bob Easton's company 360 Systems. Unlike the Electro Wagnerian Emancipator, this design made it into general production. It was similar in function to the earlier Frequency Shift module invented by Harald Bode and used in the Moog modular synthesizers (mentioned by FZ on the *Waka/Jawaka* sleeve notes).[501]

Designer Bob Easton describes it: "The 20/20 is a single-sideband frequency shifter (not a multiplicative harmonizer) which produced simultaneous upper and lower sidebands from separate outputs." So now you know (well, some of you, anyway)![502]

Oversimplifying considerably, you input a musical signal into the 20/20 and select the shift signal frequency using the dial on the front, and it will produce two additional signals: the up shift and down shift sidebands, one higher in frequency and one lower than the original. The sidebands are a result of the sum and difference of the input signal and shift frequencies, and because these are shifted from the original by an absolute frequency (rather than a harmonic multiple) they are not harmonically related.

The result is similar to that produced by a ring modulator, but the two sidebands are separate outputs, which can be used separately or combined. Depending on the amount by which the frequency is shifted this can range from a relatively subtle chorus effect to extreme robot-like vocal sounds. The frequency shift on the 20/20 could be controlled by a foot pedal as well as from the front panel.

FZ's favorite use was to mix the lower sideband with his spoken voice to add a deep undertone effect, on numbers such as "Stink-Foot" and "I'm the Slime." Easton remembers that as well as being used by FZ to modify his voice, keyboard player George Duke also "worked over his Rhodes '73 notes with the 20/20."[503]

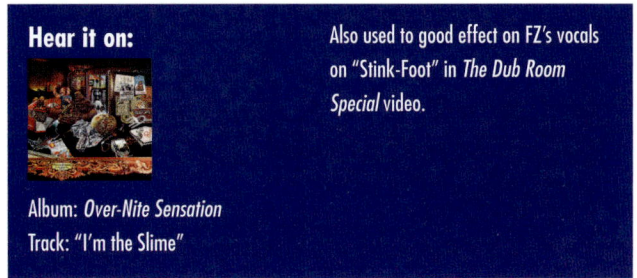

Hear it on:
Album: *Over-Nite Sensation*
Track: "I'm the Slime"

Also used to good effect on FZ's vocals on "Stink-Foot" in *The Dub Room Special* video.

Effects Units

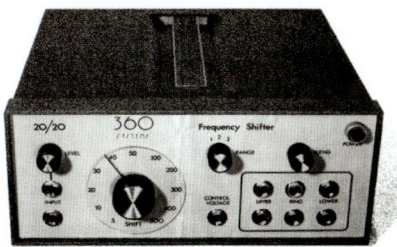

An advert for the 20/20 (360 systems)

Morley Rotating Wah Volume Pedal

"I just bought a Morley rotating sound pedal. Have you seen that? It's pretty interesting."

—FZ[504]

Morley effects pedals had their roots in a company called Tel-Ray, founded by brothers Raymond and Marvin Lubow in Los Angeles in the 1960s. Raymond designed an echo unit that used a motorized rotating disc inside a small metal can filled with electrostatic fluid. Without any magnetic tape to break, the Adineko unit, as it was called, was considerably more reliable and more compact than other units on the market, and the device was bought by many companies, including Fender.[505]

Raymond also designed a variant of the Adineko unit that simulated the sound of the Leslie rotating speaker cabinet, beloved by Hammond organ players and some rock guitarists of the time. The name Morley was originally a pun that the brothers made: "more-lee" rather than "less-lee," get it? The Morley range was launched with the rotating sound pedal, which was soon followed by a range of volume and wah-wah pedals.

They all shared the signature design features of the original unit; they were powered directly by mains electricity and the cases were large, heavy-duty, chrome plated affairs, with a large rubber covered treadle. Some of the heavier units needed a built-in carrying handle. With their trademark Morley Man logo (a wild guitar-playing hippie with Morley pedals for feet), they perfectly fit the style of American 1970s rock.

The other unique feature of all the pedals was that the treadle controlled the effect optically, moving a shutter between a light source and a Light Dependent Resistor. This system meant that there was no potentiometer in the signal path to get crackly with time, and no mechanical linkage to wear out.

In 1974, FZ talked to *Hot Flash* magazine about his new Morley pedal. "You've seen the Morley wah-wah pedal? It's not battery-operated; you plug it into the wall. It's chrome; it's about this long, about that wide. It's got a real big pedal on it . . . . It's got a motor and some other weird stuff on it and it's got a few adjustments. It can either sound like a Leslie or it can do a thing that's roughly equivalent to a Cooper time cube . . . . You know, a real short echo . . . . Anyway, what this box does is in one position, if you pull it back, if you hit one note on the string, you'll hear the original note you hit and then a very slight delay of it. It just thickens the tone. It's pretty interesting."[506]

The pedal FZ was so pleased with was the Morley Rotating Wah Volume, model RWV. It featured two footswitches either side of the pedal: the one on the right switched the unit between wah-wah and volume, and the other independently turned on the rotating sound. There was an intensity knob on the side, which varied the blend between the rotating sound and the direct signal. The Variation lever on the top of the box housing the oilcan unit allowed the intensity of the effect to be altered between a Leslie effect and a short echo.

In 1979, Morley were actively trying to sell to the European market, with a six-page spread in *International Musician* magazine's special Frankfurt Trade Show issue, which listed FZ (as well as almost every other major rock star of the day) as a "Friend of Morley."[507] During the 1980s, Morley, like many other US effects manufacturers, had a hard time coping with changing musical styles and competition from smaller and cheaper pedals from Japan (the RWV retailed at around $250 in 1977). The company was sold in 1989 to the Illinois based Sound Enhancements Inc., who still manufacture the Morley brand. Morley pedals of today use essentially the original treadle design and optical-electronic circuitry of the originals, although they use internal LEDs rather than flashlight bulbs and run on 9-volt batteries. Sadly, there is no chrome plating or oilcan echo unit in evidence.

The Tel-Ray period Morley pedals were engineered and built to the highest standards, and justly gained a reputation for ruggedness and reliability. They still have many fans today, and replacement light bulbs and oil are still available.[508] In recognition of their heritage, the new Morley Pedals company still keep user manuals and schematics for the old Tel-Ray units on their website.[509]

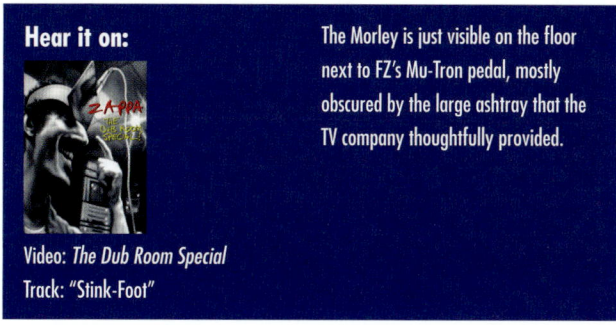

Hear it on:
Video: *The Dub Room Special*
Track: "Stink-Foot"

The Morley is just visible on the floor next to FZ's Mu-Tron pedal, mostly obscured by the large ashtray that the TV company thoughtfully provided.

ZAPPA GEAR

The EBow

"I went to the EBow to get the kind of sustain that the guitar wouldn't normally produce"

—FZ

The EBow (short for "Energy Bow") is a unique handheld electronic device that enables a player to produce indefinitely sustained notes from a guitar (or other metal-stringed instrument). Powered by a 9-volt battery, it vibrates the strings with an electromagnetic field, producing a sound somewhere between a sustained feedback tone and a bowed violin.

The EBow was invented by Greg Heet in Southern California in 1969, when he developed a prototype designed to be built into the guitar. In his words, "I marveled at how singing into an acoustic guitar would vibrate the strings sympathetically. I made a device I called the Voicitar that did just that, electromagnetically, to a set of twelve strings tuned to a scale. One day I plugged the output of the Voicitar into its input and voila, the strings began to vibrate themselves."[510]

Heet had a thriving pretzel cart business, and he used the proceeds from this to finance the patents for his invention and set up the tooling to make the device. In 1974, Heet developed a handheld version of the EBow, which was launched at the NAMM trade show in Chicago in 1976.[511]

The photo used for the original EBow adverts
(Greg Heet)

The EBow was marketed as a high-end professional item; it had a chrome-plated finish and was supplied with a real leather holster. It was not cheap, *Synapse* magazine commented: "At $125 list, it's one of the most expensive distortion devices you can buy for a guitar."[512]

Always keen to try anything new, FZ bought a couple of EBows, but like many players he found that the EBow requires a completely new playing technique, and cannot just be plugged in and switched on like an effects pedal. It has a similar learning curve to attaining proficiency in playing guitar with fingerpicks or a bottleneck.

FZ told *Guitar Player* magazine in 1988 that he wasn't getting as much sustain as he wanted out of his Gibson SG, and tried out the EBow to overcome this. He noted that the EBow was not reliable enough onstage in his unskilled hands: "If you pick it up and stick it on your guitar and go for the sound, you better know what's coming out and if it's not a predictable quantity I couldn't really make it fit into the stuff I do. . . . I like the texture of the EBow, my problem has more to do with my manual clumsiness than with the box itself. I just don't have the skills necessary to make it perform but I think it's a neat little device."[513]

Heet more or less stopped producing the original EBow for a while in the early 1980s. "We struggled to make money for a half-dozen years. Everybody loved the EBow, but nobody could play it as well as my original demonstrator Geoff Levin."[514] There were also various production issues: "The automatic power-on portion of the EBow circuit was more complicated than the EBow 'bowing' circuitry and ninety-five percent of our rejects were due to this auto-switch. There were other problems with the "hot" chrome-plating process, which often deformed a whole batch of plastic parts. We never really stopped production. We just slowed down for a spell."[515]

Full production was resumed in 1983, with a new version in plain black plastic with a mechanical on-off switch. The EBow is still being made today by Heet Sound Products; the current model is an enhancement of the original design called the Plus

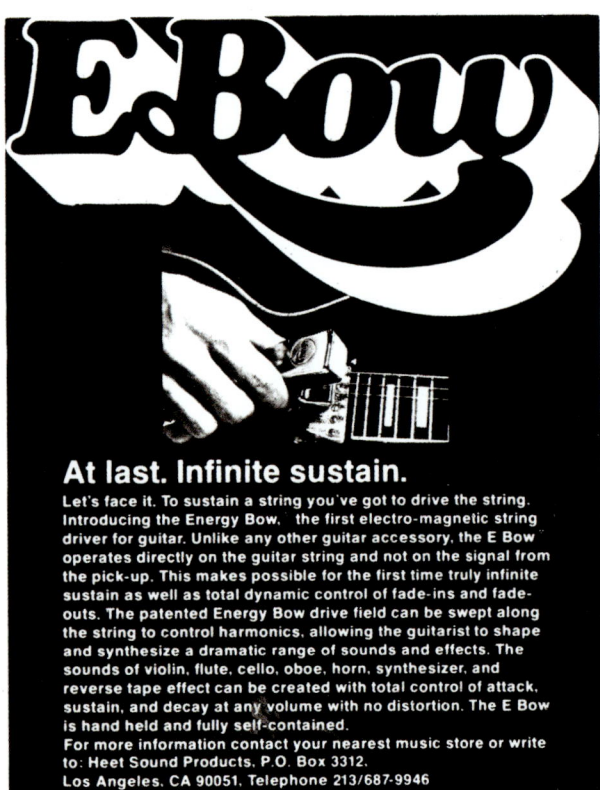

An EBow advert from 1977

EBow, and has an additional mode that produces a higher harmonic sound in place of the fundamental note.[516]

The EBow has been used by many high-profile bands and musicians, including ex-Zappa guitarist Adrian Belew (on *Lone Rhino*), R.E.M. (on the track "E-Bow the Letter"), and even composer John Cage in his 1982 piece for mass harps, *Postcards from Heaven*, where the instructions state: "The improvisation . . . should begin and end with use of all harpists of the EBow, for a period of between one-tenth and one-sixth of the total time length."[517]

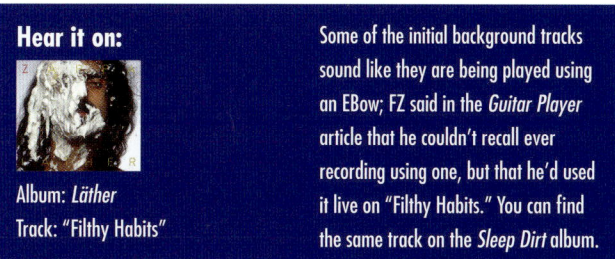

Hear it on:
Album: *Läther*
Track: "Filthy Habits"

Some of the initial background tracks sound like they are being played using an EBow; FZ said in the *Guitar Player* article that he couldn't recall ever recording using one, but that he'd used it live on "Filthy Habits." You can find the same track on the *Sleep Dirt* album.

Systech Harmonic Energizer

"Sometimes it's actually a wah-wah, while in other cases it's a thing called a Systech Harmonic Energizer"

— FZ[518]

A significant element of FZ's guitar tone (especially in the 1970s) was his use of a wah-wah pedal cocked in the middle position to give a midrange boost to his guitar, but as he told *Guitar Player* magazine, he often accomplished this with a Systech Harmonic Energizer pedal, which gave a similar midrange frequency boost but with more peak. "A wah-wah pedal sweeps between, say, 300 cycles (per second) and 700 cycles, making a peak right there. And it's movable. The Systech Harmonic Energizer, on the other hand, allows you to select a frequency that you want a peak at, and lets you crank up the juice so that you get a lot of feedback at that particular frequency."[519]

Systech was the brand name for a company called Systems and Technology in Music, Inc., based in Kalamazoo, Michigan, in the 1970s. The company was formed by Greg Hochman, Charlie Wicks (later to found ProCo), and ex-Chess-records engineer Bryce Roberson (aka "Uncle Dirty.") They established the business, comprising Wicks' Sound Factory, Hochman's

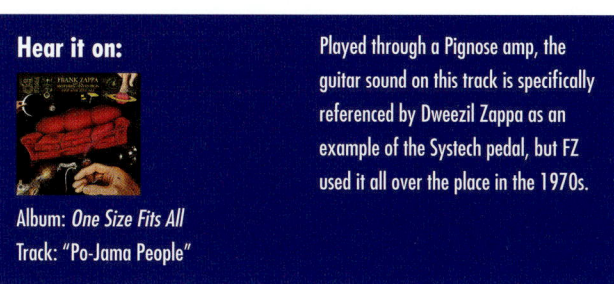

Hear it on:
Album: *One Size Fits All*
Track: "Po-Jama People"

Played through a Pignose amp, the guitar sound on this track is specifically referenced by Dweezil Zappa as an example of the Systech pedal, but FZ used it all over the place in the 1970s.

Front and back panels of FZ's Systech Harmonic Energizer, in a 'lunchbox' case for rack mounting
(Mick Ekers)

SysTech, and Roberson's Uncle Dirty's Recording Studio, in an old factory site on Kalamazoo Avenue.[520]

They produced a small range of high-quality pedals, including an envelope follower, a phaser, a couple of overdrive units, and the Harmonic Energizer.[521] All the pedals I have seen share the same large-format aluminum case with three rotary controls, a top mounted battery compartment, and a distinctive ridged section below the footswitch. Most had a plain aluminum finish but some were also manufactured in black.

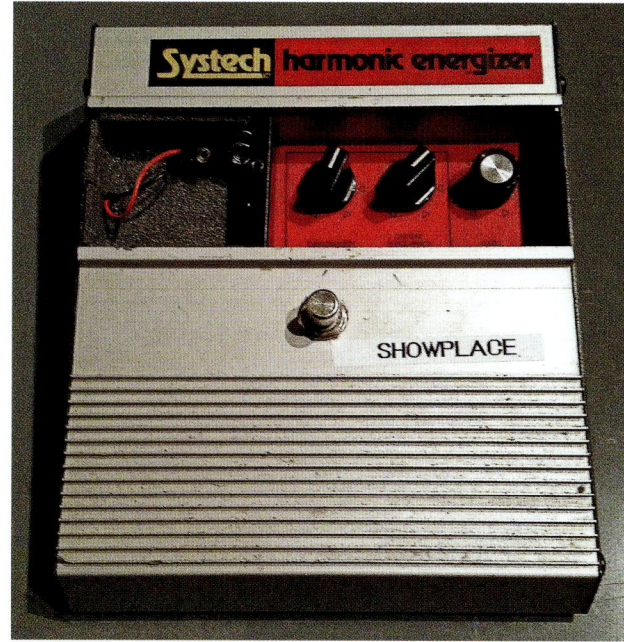

An original Harmonic Energizer, not cheap these days
(Josh Gannett Showplace Studios)

FZ usually had a Harmonic Energizer circuit board built into his touring effects racks. In March 2012, I found one on the remnants of his 1980s rack at Joe's Garage and also discovered a fully enclosed module in the workshop beneath the UMRK; the original case was not in evidence. Systech are long since out of business, and original pedals are very rare, with good quality items selling for over $1,000.[522] However, there are various clones of the design available, including the Triskelion Harmonic Energizer, which has been used by Dweezil Zappa.[523]

Mu-Tron III

"Well, let's see. I think the Mu-Tron is a good box"

— FZ[524]

A key element of FZ's effects toolkit in the 1970s was the Mu-Tron III envelope follower, produced by the Musitronics Corporation in the 1970s. FZ used it on several recordings and built the circuits from two Mu-Tron III units into his touring rack system.

The Musitronics story started when Mike Beigel, the first MIT double-major graduate in electrical engineering and electronic music, developed a prototype synthesizer with some of his fellow MIT students. This attracted the attention of Guild president Al Dronge in 1970, and Guild bought the rights to the design and took on Beigel, who stated working on the project with Aaron Newman, Guild's chief engineer.

However, before the synthesizer entered production Dronge was killed in an airplane accident in 1972, and the project was dropped. Beigel and Newman left Guild and started talking about Beigel's idea for an automatic wah-wah pedal, developed from some of the concepts in his original synthesizer.

Newman showed various leading music dealers Beigel's prototype pedal, and encouraged by their enthusiastic responses, they formed their own company called Musitronics.[525] They set up a factory in a converted chicken coop in rural Rosemont, New Jersey, which was to remain the home of Musitronics for the entire time they were in business.[526]

Herb Ross, a leading industrial designer with an automotive background, came up with the distinct casing, for which they were granted a patent along with one for the electronic circuit. "We designed them so you could drop them off tall buildings and they'd still work," says Beigel. "We made the products as good as we possibly could. . . . What we tried to put together, and I think we succeeded, was something that was both a novel product and a work of art."

The original working name for the pedal was the Auto-Wah. Mu-Tron was suggested as a good contraction of the company name; "III" was Beigel's idea—there never was a Mu-Tron I or II![527] The advanced circuit was a no-compromise design using optical isolators for their low-noise characteristics and a

The Mu-tron III — still the benchmark envelope follower
(Mike Beigel)

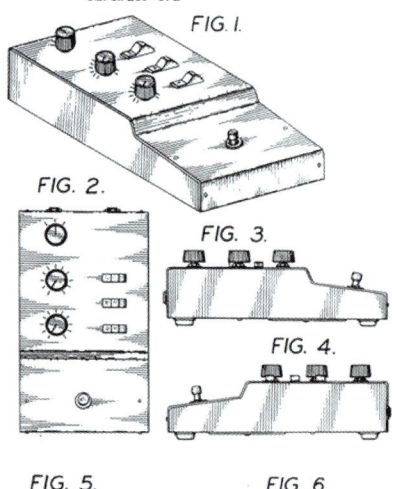

Mu-tron casing patent

twin-battery power supply to allow for a wide dynamic range. As Beigel put it, "That way, you could really smash on the guitar and not distort the whole effect."[528]

The Mu-Tron produces a similar effect to that of a mechanical wah-wah pedal; however, the modulation is controlled by the level of the input signal. The Mu-Tron had a simple but effective range of controls: Mode (selects high-pass, band-pass or low-pass filter operation), Peak (varies the volume of the cutoff frequency), and Gain (controls the sensitivity of the effect), and switches for Range (high or low frequency range) and Drive (sets the filter sweep direction down or up). The controls allowed everything from subtle wah-wah to extreme synthesizer-like effects to be produced; there was nothing else like it around at the time.

Musitronics soon found a name endorser in guitarist Larry Coryell, but things really took off when they sent a Mu-Tron III to Stevie Wonder, who used it with his Hohner Clavinet on the track "Higher Ground." Released in 1973, this track established the Mu-Tron III as a must-have pedal among professional musicians. It was the company's most popular product, and it remained in production throughout Musitronic's existence.

FZ described one example of how he used the Mu-Tron III in the "Non-Foods" series of articles he wrote for *Guitar Player* magazine in 1983: "And on 'Stink-Foot' there's an interesting sound where I'm using an acoustic guitar with a magnetic pickup on it and a Barcus Berry on the bridge. The Barcus Berry is going into one channel and the magnetic pickup is going to a Mu-Tron and the other channel, so you have a sharp attack and an envelope attack. It gives a lot of space."[529]

We found two cased Mu-Tron III circuits at Joe's Garage in 2012, as remnants of FZ's rack system. The one illustrated has a black face and engraved white control markings, and the second has a plain metal panel with handwritten labels attached. The whereabouts of the original casings are not known.

Mike Beigel told me of an early encounter he had with FZ: "I met Frank while still in college when Mothers gave a concert at MIT in about 1967 or so. We had a radio show on the MIT radio station and they all came down for an interview. It was a whole lot of fun, but unfortunately, almost nothing remains of all the taped shows from that time. At that time I had no idea that I would end up making products he used to such exquisite perfection! It's a long story."[530]

One of FZ's Mu-tron III modules
(Mick Ekers)

Hear it on:

Album: *Apostrophe (')*
Track: "Stink-Foot"

Track: As FZ says, the inclusion of the clean acoustic track really does add some space to the guitar sound, but the funky Mu-Tron III wah effect dominates on this tasty solo.

ZAPPA GEAR

Mu-Tron Bi-Phase

"On 'Pink Napkins' I'm using a Mu-Tron Bi-Phase and a harmonizer."
— FZ[531]

In 1973, Musitronics was employing over twenty people and riding high on the success of the Mu-Tron-III. They began thinking about what to make next. The first idea was for a very complicated bucket-brigade flanger called the Phase Synthesizer; a few prototypes were made, but it became apparent that it was too complicated to be commercially viable. So instead, Beigel and Newman decided to develop a phase-shifter pedal, which would be easier to make and more commercially viable; they called it the Phasor.[532]

Once again Musitronics did not compromise on quality, using relatively expensive op amps in the circuit at a time when most people were using FETs. Beigel observes: "The Mu-Tron Phasor . . . was better than anything else on the market in terms of audio performance, but we still weren't really pleased with the noise level because it was perceptible, which was not okay with us . . . . . We made a six-stage phase shifter, whereas other products, such as the MXR Phase 90, were four-stage phase shifters."[533]

Then in 1974, Newman had the inspired idea to produce the Bi-Phase, a massive pedal measuring 10"×14", containing two phase circuits that could be used in parallel or series and stereo and mono configurations. Each phaser had depth and feedback controls, and there were two Sweep Generators, variable speed low-frequency oscillators that controlled the effect. The LFO could be switched between a square and a sine wave shape, and an optional footpedal could be used to vary the sweep frequency, or control it directly.

The original design sounded too clean to be musically satisfying, so Beigel added a feedback control: "I decided to put a feedback control around the phase-shift loop so that instead of

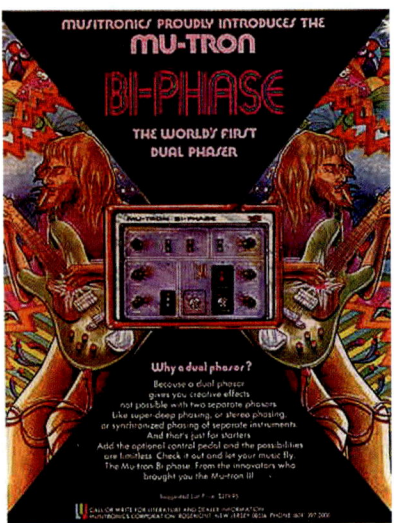

The original Bi-phase advert

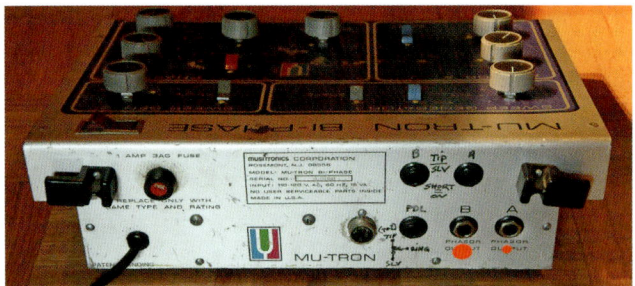

Rear panel of the UMRK Bi-phase
(Mick Ekers)

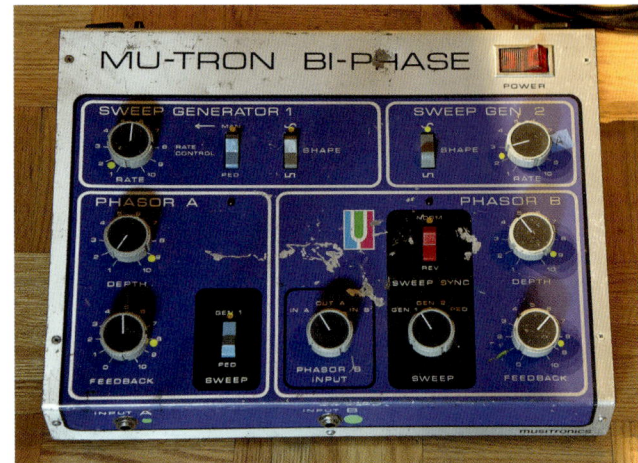

Mu-tron Bi-Phase at the UMRK in 2012, this unit also toured with DZ
(Mick Ekers)

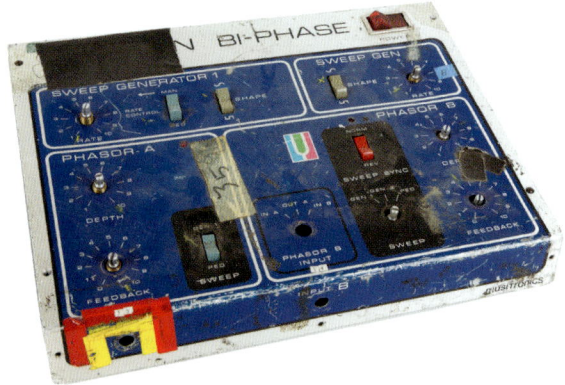

FZ's touring Bi-phase as sold in auction, well used!
(ZFT)

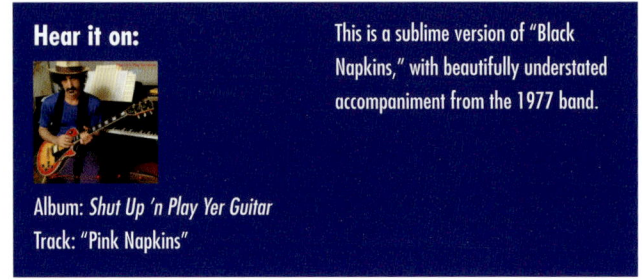

Hear it on:
This is a sublime version of "Black Napkins," with beautifully understated accompaniment from the 1977 band.

Album: *Shut Up 'n Play Yer Guitar*
Track: "Pink Napkins"

130

distorting the signal it emphasized the peaks where the phase shifter didn't cancel the signal. This made the sound more interesting without distorting . . . . I made sure the Bi-Phase had as many ways of being controlled with oscillators, pedals, or external inputs that I could possibly stick into one box."[534]

The unit came with cutout cards that fit over the case with marked settings for Stereo Phasing, Super Phasing, and Two-Speed Phasing settings. Once again, Musitronics had produced a winner, despite a price tag of $279.95—over $1500 in today's money! They also sold a single-phaser version, which was known as the Phasor II.

The Bi-Phase was generally considered the best phase pedal on the market and was used by many leading musicians including FZ keyboard player George Duke, and of course FZ himself. Beigel remembers meeting FZ around this time after a rehearsal: "He was interested in an effect sort of like an ultra-clean ultra-wide compressor for 'frailing' a lot of notes: fingering the notes on the frets with the left hand but not plucking with the right hand."[535]

I found one of FZ's Mu-Tron Bi-Phases on a shelf in the UMRK control room. It has been modified with additional pedal and footswitch connectors on the back panel. DZ took it on tour with his band ZPZ in his effects rig before he downsized to a Fractal Axe-FX–based system, and it is still in full working order as far as I know. A Bi-Phase that FZ used on tour was sold in the 2016 auction,[536] in far shabbier condition than the one I saw. With knobs, some controls, and connectors missing, it sold for $ 2,812.50.[537]

Mu-Tron Octave Divider

"I used a Mu-Tron Octave Divider for a minute"

—FZ[538]

In 1975, despite having built up a range of market-leading products, Musitronics was still not making much money, mainly because of the high manufacturing costs of their no-compromise designs. Seeking to diversify, they began to manufacture US versions of the Dan Armstrong range of mini effects units (see the Green Ringer section for more on this). Armstrong's engineer George Merriman worked together with Mike Beigel on some of these.

Merriman and Beigel joined forces to work on the next Mu-Tron product, the Octave Divider, paying special attention to getting the device to follow the input signal. As Beigel notes, "Tracking the fundamental frequency of a guitar accurately and quickly is a major topic in musical product design." Beigel continues, "It used a couple of new principles that Merriman actually got patented. The circuit stabilized the response of the guitar . . . the Octave Divider used the guitar signal as the source material for the octave, so the octave sounded like the guitar. In addition, we stuck the Green Ringer circuit in it so it would produce a fairly reliable octave above as well as an octave below."[539]

Incorporating the Ringer was an inspired decision, giving the pedal a unique dirty octave sound above the signal as well as some funky distortion. As already noted, FZ loved the Green Ringer and had it built into several of his guitars, so the tone must have been very appealing to him.

Launched in 1976, the Octave Divider was built to the usual Musitronics high standards, with a Mu Tron III–type case. It had rotary controls for Mix (varying the proportion of the dry and wet signals) and Tone, plus on/off switches for Ringer, Stabilize, and Bass-Only (which took out the input signal).

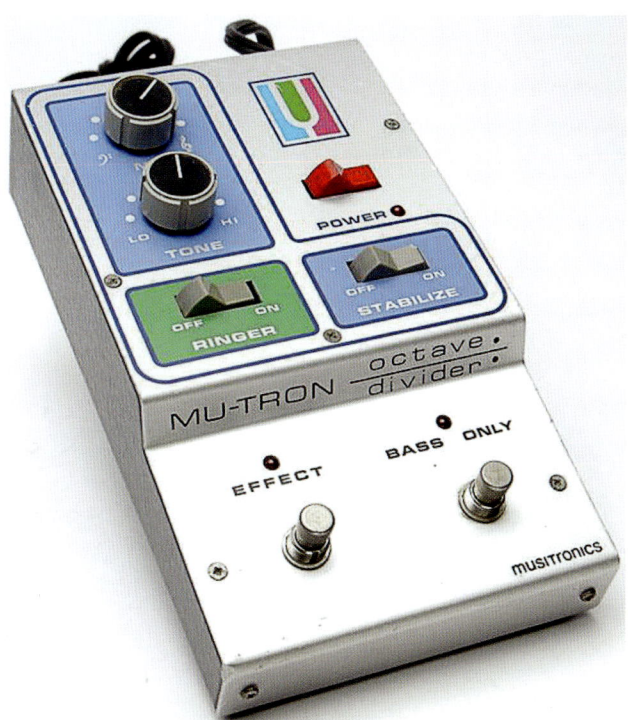

The Mu-tron Octave Divider
(Mike Beigel)

The complete Musitronics Range of effects units in the late 1970s
(Mike Beigel)

ZAPPA GEAR

Guitar Player magazine later asked FZ if he used an octave divider on *Return of The Son of Shut Up 'n Play Yer Guitar*:

FZ answered: "I used a Mu-Tron Octave Divider for a minute. It comes in and goes out . . . . It does [sound raspy], but you can change the tone of the octave divider. It doesn't have to be a blare. What I was using on some of the *Shut Up* tapes was a special cabinet that had a low-end section powered by a 200-watt Marshall into an 18" speaker, just to accommodate the octave divider."[540]

One of the special cabinets turned up in the Joe's Garage sale listed as a "Flag Systems custom three-way guitar cab (1×18", 2×15", 2×10") giant FZ speaker cab (needs new 10" speakers)," selling for the bargain price of $600. I wonder if anyone bought this monster! As far as I know, the rest of the giant cabinet was powered by Crown DC300 power amplifiers—it must have sounded earth-shattering!

In his 1978 system FZ had a pair Octave Dividers (along with his Mu-Tron IIIs) patched into the Dirty channels feeding his Boogie and Vox amps. I know that FZ also owned a Mu-Tron Vol-Wah pedal, as one was bought from a Joe's Garage sale in the 1990s by a friend, but I have unable to find any evidence that FZ used it himself.

Still looking to diversify, Musitronics next embarked on a disastrous venture to build the Gizmotron mechanical guitar sustaining device invented by Kevin Godley and Lol Creme of the band 10cc. Designed to be mounted on the bridge of the guitar, it had six buttons that triggered small motorized friction wheels that rotated against the guitar strings. The effect was similar to bowing the strings like a violin. Built into a light plastic casing, the Gizmotron proved impossible to manufacture consistently, and Musitronics wasted a small fortune on futile R&D on the product, from which they never recovered financially.

The last electrical products they introduced were the Vol-Wah pedal and the Flanger, but very few of these were made. Against Beigel's, wishes the board sold Musitronics to the ARP Instrument company at the end of 1978, but ARP had an albatross of their own around their necks, in the shape of the doomed Avatar guitar synth, and went out of business themselves soon afterwards (see the ARP 2600 section for more on ARP).[541]

Beigel went on to work for various electronic design projects, including a stint with former rival Electro-Harmonix where, among other things, he designed their successful QTron pedal, a version of the Mu-Tron III design. He is now energetically working on bringing his own range of effect units to the market under the Mu-FX brand, something for which many musicians have been eagerly waiting.

Oberheim VCF-200

". . . the Oberheim VCF. I've got an example of that on this new album."
—FZ [542]

One of the most unusual guitar effects FZ used is featured on the track "Ship Ahoy" from the *Shut Up 'n Play Yer Guitar* album. Recorded in Osaka, Japan, in 1976, it features a robotic random wah-wah type of effect, also heard briefly during "Black Napkins" from the *Zoot Allures* album, recorded at the same concert. He later told *Guitar Player* magazine how it was done: "It's an Oberheim voltage-controlled filter triggered by a sample/hold unit. It sets up a kind of rhythm that makes an accompaniment for you."[543]

Oberheim Electronics was formed by audio engineer and synthesizer pioneer Tom Oberheim in LA in 1969, and for several years their main commercial activity was making effects pedals for the Maestro company. In 1976, they introduced the Voltage Controlled Filter (VCF) pedal, model number VCF-200, under their own name. It is effectively the same as the Filter Sample/Hold pedal that Oberheim had previously been building for Maestro.

The VCF-200 cleverly combined a sample and hold circuit with VCF and envelope follower circuits, such as used in auto-wah devices like the Mu-Tron. Often found in synthesizers, a sample and hold circuit takes a periodic sample of an internal white noise source and holds the voltage at that level until the

A very clean example of a VCF-200
(Music Swop Shop)

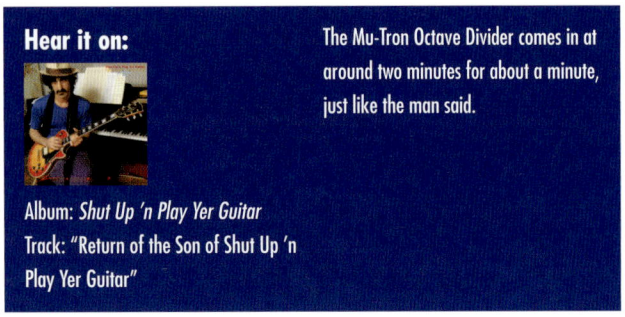

Hear it on: The Mu-Tron Octave Divider comes in at around two minutes for about a minute, just like the man said.

Album: *Shut Up 'n Play Yer Guitar*
Track: "Return of the Son of Shut Up 'n Play Yer Guitar"

next sample. The result is a series of random voltage steps, which in the VCF varies the filter wah effect. The VCF 200 had a Range control that varied the center frequency of the filter and a switch to select the envelope follower or the sample and hold. The envelope follower effect was similar to the Mu-Tron, but it was the random filter effect produced by the sample and hold that made the pedal unique. The Speed control set the rate at which the samples were taken. The unit was powered by two 18-volt batteries. The whole was encased in a sturdy 7"×3"×6» white metal case featuring Oberheim's famous Trucking Note logo.

When FZ took the VCF 200 on his spring 1976 tour, it would have been a brand new pedal, and he may have been given a prototype to test. He featured it on a new ending section of "Zoot Allures" (named "Ship Ahoy" on *Shut Up 'n Play Yer Guitar*), and kept it in his repertoire for the next couple of years. He had a couple of units built into his Blue Box rack system, but I found no trace among the remnants discovered at the UMRK (see the Effects Racks section). Oberheim did not make the pedal for long, focusing the business on the new range of synthesizers. Working examples of the VCF 200 (or the Maestro FSH) are comparatively rare these days and you might expect to pay around $500 if you find one, although there are DIY circuit boards available for those of you handy with a soldering iron.

Oberheim went on to make the acclaimed range of Oberheim polyphonic synthesizers and the legendary DMX drum machine, and he was a key figure in the development of the MIDI standard. Oberheim Electronics went out of business in the mid-1980s, but in 2009, Tom Oberheim launched a range of analogue synthesizer modules based on his 1970s designs. [544]

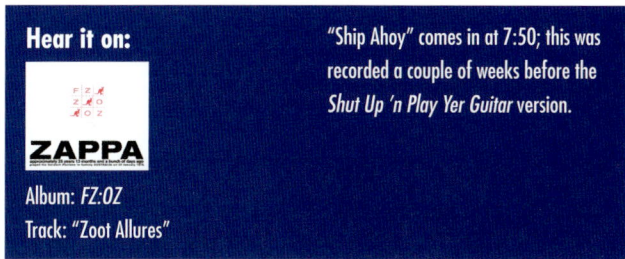

Hear it on:
"Ship Ahoy" comes in at 7:50; this was recorded a couple of weeks before the *Shut Up 'n Play Yer Guitar* version.
Album: *FZ:OZ*
Track: "Zoot Allures"

The GP-8, complete with handy block diagram. Unfortunately the diagram was not replicated in the manual, so you would have to make a copy before putting it in your rack!
(Taro Tsutsui, Dig the Rare)

Effects Units

Roland GP-8

"I was trying for a clean sound on the '88 tour. I used my custom-built Stratocaster and a Roland GP-8"

—FZ[545]

The GP-8 Guitar Effects Processor was one of the first units of its type; it was introduced by Roland in 1987, with the advertising slogan "This Display Marks the Dawn of a New Era in Total Effects Control." Supplied in a 19" rack-mounted case with various buttons and a bright red LED display panel, at first glance it could be taken for a purely digital studio effects unit. In fact it contains eight serially connected guitar effects circuits, presumably based on those found in Roland's BOSS pedal range of the time.

The included effects are named Dynamic Filter, Compressor, Turbo Over Drive, Distortion, Phaser, Equalizer, Digital Delay and Digital Chorus, connected in that order.[546] With the exception of the 12-bit digital Delay and Chorus modules, all the effects circuits are analogue.

The GP-8 could be controlled via a MIDI device or with the optional (non-MIDI) Roland FC-100 footpedal board. It could store 128 named patches, each holding a particular combination of effects and their particular settings, such as Tone, Drive, and Turbo On/Off for the Turbo Over Drive effect. Each patch could be programmed directly from the buttons on the front panel of the unit.

In 1987, Dweezil Zappa got hold of a Roland GP-8 multi-effects unit and demonstrated it to FZ; as he recalls: "my Dad liked the sound of many of my presets on the GP-8, so I went to *Guitar Center* and bought him one. I copied all of my presets into it."[547] FZ obviously did like it because on the 1988 tour he opted to use one to process his clean sound. Although specifically designed for live stage use, the GP-8 was known for briefly muting the signal when a patch was changed; not ideal if switching effects in the middle of a song. FZ's new guitar tech Merl Saunders was not especially happy with incorporating the unit; in his own words: "I was like 'Dude, you can't have this shit!'"[548]

However, Saunders soon found out that FZ "wanted to use what he wanted to use, so we had to make everything fit . . . and then I came up with the idea . . . on a lot of his stuff, there's a really clean sort of thin acoustic-electric sound. So there was a switch on his Strat so that it went straight from the pickups, just line in to the GP-8, which gave you that acoustic sound because there were no preamps. I remember the only way he could control it was the volume pedal on the board."[549]

For some reason I cannot imagine FZ spending a lot of time punching the buttons on the unit to select different patches; I'm guessing he found one of DZ's patches that he liked and then used that. The final programming was done by Saunders and

FZ's Synclavier assistant, Bob Rice. FZ described the setup: " . . . that clean sound was processed through a Roland GP-8, or whatever you call it. It's an effects box that has the whole assortment of effects—compression, flange, blahdy-blah. That was on a separate footswitch so I could either turn it on or off."[550]

Although long out of production, the GP-8 is still quite popular on the secondhand market; many studios keep it on their equipment lists, and it is still in use by more than a few pro musicians. It is certainly a very convenient package for eight classic BOSS circuits from the 1980s, and it is known for its warm analogue sound.

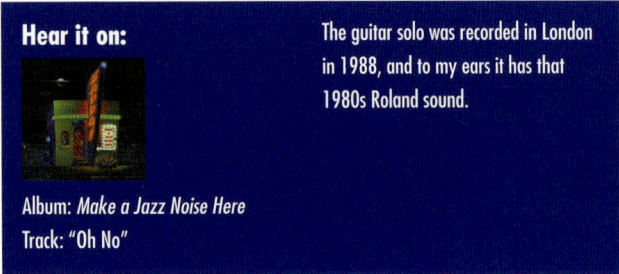

Hear it on: The guitar solo was recorded in London in 1988, and to my ears it has that 1980s Roland sound.

Album: *Make a Jazz Noise Here*
Track: "Oh No"

MicMix Dynaflangers

"I think the Dynaflangers were the most unique thing that he (FZ) used, and got the most unique sound from."

— Dweezil Zappa[551]

In his "Non-Foods" series of articles that appeared in *Guitar Player* magazine, FZ was asked how he got the doubling effect on his guitar: "I use a device called a MicMix Dynaflanger. There are actually two of them being used at the same time. You see, the Dynaflanger has an envelope follower built into it. So if you set one of them up to go sharp when the envelope is hit hard, and the other one to go flat when the envelope is hit hard, then you're going to get this doubling effect . . . and it really sounds like two instruments playing the same thing."[552]

The model 265 Dynaflanger was introduced in 1978, by Dallas, Texas–based MicMix Audio Products Inc. This single unit rack module was a mono device, and was designed to be used in a stereo pair. The unique feature of the Dynaflanger was that the flanging effect could be modulated by the input signal, varying the amount of phase by following the envelope of the amplitude or the frequency of the input in either a high-pass or low-pass filter mode, using either a normal or inverse relationship. It also had a pair of modulator controls to vary the rate and depth to which the signal is delayed and a continuously variable Flanger Phase Polarity control.

FZ soon found how he could use a pair to produce a doubling effect, as he described above, and he made this part of his signature sound, using it extensively on his albums in the 1980s. FZ went into some more specifics when talking about the *Ship Arriving Too Late to Save a Drowning Witch* album: "I used a MicMix Dynaflanger and Aphex compressors. The signal is compressed after the flanging. And the flanger is set to follow the envelope of the high-frequency decay, rather than the amplitude envelope . . . It gives a totally different sound. It makes a more pillowy effect from that particular device."[553]

Dweezil Zappa has some more insights: "Of all of Frank's great tonal experiments, the Dynaflanger tone is my favorite. It is the most difficult to duplicate as well. I'm not sure he ever actually used it live the way he did in the studio. He spoke of using the Dynaflanger envelope follower to dynamically alter the pitch with a short delay. That modulation mixed with a dry signal made a very realistic and natural doubling effect. Additional phase shifting from a Mu-Tron or Small Stone plus a wah pedal made for some amazingly rich harmonics and a beautiful stereo image."[554]

MicMix Audio are no longer in business, and working Dynaflangers are hard to find, although they do crop up for sale from time to time. DZ had a pair of FZ's units installed in his original ZPZ touring rack, but has now retired them as he is concerned that they might get damaged on the road. In 2012,

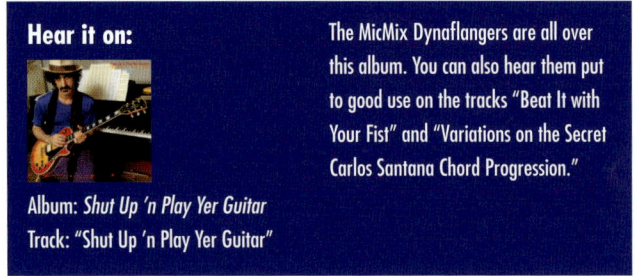

Hear it on: The MicMix Dynaflangers are all over this album. You can also hear them put to good use on the tracks "Beat It with Your Fist" and "Variations on the Secret Carlos Santana Chord Progression."

Album: *Shut Up 'n Play Yer Guitar*
Track: "Shut Up 'n Play Yer Guitar"

A pair of rack mounted Dynaflangers
(Tony Miln, Soundgas)

effects pedal manufacturer Pigtronix made a prototype pedal board for DZ that emulated the DynaFlanger, combining four of their production pedals with a custom control voltage convertor unit. They now market a pedal called the Quantum Time Modulator that emulates the Dynaflanger and other effects.[555]

ProCo Rat

"He used a Rat something, all that stuff"

—Merl Saunders[556]

ProCo Sound was founded in 1974 by Charlie Wicks in Kalamazoo, Michigan, and the company started out building audio interfaces and cables.[557] Then, as now, ProCo were primarily concerned with making low-noise professional audio components, yet, almost unintentionally, they also ended up producing one of the dirtiest-sounding fuzz/distortion boxes ever made.

Down in the factory basement in 1978, where he used to repair and modify other manufacturers' distortion units, engineering director Scott Burnham thought he could produce something better, and came up with the prototype Rat.

Based on a similar circuit to the refined MXR Distortion+, Burnham used silicon diodes (MXR used germanium), which gave a harder clipping effect and used a lower-value resistor in the output stage. This resulted in massive amounts of gain that would drive the op-amp into distortion at high settings. As well as distortion and volume controls, he added a much-needed tone control to manage the massive amounts of treble produced by the circuit.[558] The result was an astonishingly versatile stomp box, which at low settings could produce a relatively smooth fuzz tone, but when cranked up, generated massive over-the top heavy metal distortion, like nothing else around at the time.

FZ had been said to use a ProCo Rat on stage in the 1980s, and I'd read mentions on Internet forums that FZ kept a ProCo Rat floorside on the 1988 tour, but I had found no firm evidence. I was pleased when Merl Saunders confirmed that he used one; it is one of the classic distortion pedals, and well worthy of inclusion.

Originally the Rat was hand-built to special order in a hand-painted off-the-shelf project box, but after they made just twelve of these pedals, demand was such that ProCo started mass producing them in 1979. Notable Rat users include Jeff Beck and David Gilmour, as well as Dweezil Zappa's friend Warren de Martini, lead guitarist for the coincidentally named glam/heavy metal outfit Ratt, who may have introduced the Rat to the Zappa household.

During the 1980s, the Rat went through a couple of cosmetic changes: the tone control was renamed "filter" in 1981 and the action reversed so turning it clockwise reduced the treble, and the unit was rehoused in a smaller case in 1984. Apart from these alterations, the Rat was essentially unchanged from Burnham's 1978 prototype.[559]

FZ would have used one of these "small-box" Rats, as they are known; the next variant, the Rat 2 was introduced in 1988, sometime after he had already started the Broadway the Hard Way tour. Both RAT and ProCo brands were incorporated into the ACT lighting group in 2017, and various versions of the Rat are still being produced.[560]

A 1984 'Small Box' Pro co Rat
(Michael Marti, Yeahman's Vintage & Used Guitars)

CHAPTER FOUR
KEYBOARDS AND SYNTHESIZERS

"I've got a warehouse full of keyboards."

— FZ[561]

Farfisa Professional Organ
Fender Rhodes
RMI Electra Piano
Wurlitzer EP200A Electric Piano
Hohner Clavinet and Pianet/Clavinet Duo
Hammond B3 Organ
ARP 2600
Minimoog
Moog Taurus
Electrocomp 101
EML Poly-Box

EML SynKey 1500
Korg VC-10 Vocoder
E-mu Modular Synthesizer
Yamaha CS-80
Pollard Industries Syndrum
Synclavier
Roland PAD-8 Octapad
Roland Super Jupiter
LinnDrum
Bösendorfer 290 Imperial Grand Piano
Guitar Synthesizers

Note

From the earliest days of the Mothers of Invention, FZ provided nearly all the equipment for his bands, especially the keyboards, although in a few cases musicians brought their own, such as Don Preston's homemade synthesizer and George Duke's ARP Odyssey. He also bought a wide range of keyboards for his recording and rehearsal studios. For reasons of space, I have restricted myself here to those instruments of special interest; either those FZ had modified or used in an unusual manner, or ones that he specifically mentioned in some context.

I will just briefly mention some of the others; I hope that I will be able to cover all of these in more detail at some time. The keyboard next to Ian Underwood in the photograph inside the cover of the *Burnt Weeny Sandwich* album is a Gibson G-101 combo organ. FZ owned several Yamaha electric pianos, played by George Duke, Tommy Mars, and Peter Wolf, among others. I saw a CP-80 in its case wedged behind some shelves at Joe's Garage in April 2012; two CP-80s and a CP-70 were sold in the 2016 auction.[562] An ARP PE4 String Synth that Tommy Mars had in his rig for awhile and an Oberheim Eclipse digital piano were also included in the auction. Robert Martin and other keyboard players in the late 1980s bands used the Yamaha DX-5 and later DX-7 synthesizers and Roland digital pianos; between them these could replicate the sounds of almost any of the instruments previously taken on the road.

Farfisa Professional Organ

"I've never bought a Farfisa (laughs). That equipment was Frank's."
— George Duke[563]

When FZ hired young jazz musician George Duke to play with the new version of the Mothers of Invention in 1970, he gave him a Farfisa combo organ to play, along with a Fender Rhodes piano.

The Professional 222 was Farfisa's newest model, launched in 1968, and their most expensive single manual organ. At the time, it was one of the most feature-laden combo organs around. It boasted three basic voices (Flutes, Clarinets, and Sharps) in eight different footages.

In keyboard terminology, "footage" refers to the approximate length of the pipes required to produce a range of notes on a traditional pipe organ. The longer the pipe, the lower the note that is produced, doubling in length for each octave. Footages on portable organs normally range from 16-foot for the very lowest notes to one foot for the highest register. Large cathedral organs may have 32-foot pipes, and very rarely 64-foot.

The Professional also included percussion (again in eight footages) selectable for single or multiple-triggering, three percussive sustain voices (8' only), and vibrato selectable separately for each voice type (a rather unusual feature). Percussion is an organ effect that generates an additional transient when a note is played. The four voices could be mixed in any amounts by using the four sliders.[564]

The five-octave keyboard had grey natural keys and white accidental keys, and the unit was designed so that it could be tilted forward on its stand so that you could play it standing up if you were in a "rocking teenage combo."

Advertising in the 1960s: "Our new Farfisa is so out of sight we don't know how to begin describing it"

The list price in 1968 in the US was $1,095 (or 345 guineas in the UK)[565], which included a soft carrying case with a built-in hard keyboard cover, unlike the removable hard lid supplied with most organs of the type. Designed to be played through an amplifier, the Professional did not have any built-in speakers or amp, but still weighed in at a hefty 73 lbs. (33 kg). It did come with a simple passive volume pedal.[566]

The Farfisa company was formed in Italy in 1948 out of the merger of the accordion companies Settimio, Soprani, Scandalli, and Frontallini, and the name came from "FAbbriche Riunite de FISArmoniche," which translates to "United Factory of Accordions."

They produced their first transistor organ in 1962. No doubt inspired by the success of the Vox Continental portable organ, also introduced that year, Farfisa capitalized upon their experience of accordion technology and introduced the Combo Compact in 1964.

They went on to develop a highly successful range of console and combo organs, at their peak running three factories in Italy; their main plant in Aspio Terme was located on a street named Via Farfisa.

In 1972, Farfisa was bought by the American conglomerate Lear Siegler, which discontinued the Professional range in 1975, later selling the brand on to the Bontempi company, of Potenza, Italy, who still produce keyboards under the Farfisa name.

George Duke with the Mothers of Invention at Bath in 1970, showing the Fender Rhodes perched on top of a Marshall 4×12 cabinet and the Farfisa Professional to his right
(Odile Noel)

Duke told me that at the time he considered himself a serious contemporary jazz musician, and thought the Farfisa was somewhat beneath him. However, although popular with many unsophisticated pop groups, the Professional 222 was also used by such luminaries as Sun Ra, Sly and the Family Stone, and Tangerine Dream. Duke can be seen on stage at the Bath festival in the UK in 1970, with the Farfisa visible to his right. By the end of the year, Duke was playing a Hammond organ, and it is not known what happened to the Farfisa.

Fender Rhodes

"I'm having modifications done on all my keyboards to bring them up to studio quality sound. This includes rebuilding the preamps in all of them and having the Rhodes done in stereo."[567]

—FZ

FZ's Suitcase model amplifier (also showing the Korg Vocoder covered later)
(Mick Ekers)

The Fender Rhodes electric piano was the invention of Harold Burroughs Rhodes, who was born on 28th December, 1910, in the San Fernando Valley, California. Introduced to jazz by his brother, Rhodes started learning piano, but became unhappy with traditional teaching methods.

In 1929, his piano teacher moved away from the area, and he took over her roster of students, with a mission to teach the instrument in a new, modern way, suitable for both jazz and classical music.

Stressing the importance of self-study, improvisation, and knowledge of the mechanics of the instrument, he developed the highly successful Rhodes Method of study. By 1940, he was managing a nationwide chain of schools known as The Harold Rhodes School of Popular Piano.[568]

Rhodes joined the US Army Air Corps in WWII, and was asked to instigate a program of teaching piano to wounded soldiers, as an aid to rehabilitation. Faced with the need for a lightweight instrument that could be played in bed, Rhodes designed the Xylette, a 2 1/2–octave portable piano, using short metal tubes instead of strings (made from surplus aluminum pipes used in the construction of B-17 bombers). Around 125,000 were built between 1942 and 1945, and Rhodes was awarded the Medal of Honor.[569]

After the war, Rhodes went into business selling a three-octave amplified version of the Xylette called the Pre-Piano. He later refined the design using metal rods and bars instead of tubes, and produced a 72-key piano that aroused the interest of Leo Fender. They joined forces, and after various designs and prototypes had been rejected, the Fender Rhodes Piano Bass was launched in 1960. Essentially the bottom 32 notes of a piano, it could produce a fair approximation of a bass guitar and was notably used by Ray Manzarek, keyboard player with the Doors.[570]

Fender was not keen on the tone of the Rhodes' higher registers, and it was not until 1965, after CBS had taken over the Fender company, that the first full-range (73-note) Electric Piano was introduced. It had a silver metalflake-finished top, and was supplied complete with a combined stereo amplifier and speaker cabinet upon which the keyboard rested, containing two 12" and two 10" speakers.[571]

The tone source for each note was described as "tuning fork of unequal legs, one leg formed from a metal bar, and the other being a thin flexible rod or tine which is struck by a hammer when the key is depressed."[572] A small spring could be slid up and down the tine to adjust the pitch. The whole assembly could be moved relative to the electric pickup to adjust the volume produced. A piano-style sustain pedal caused a small felt pad to be applied to each tine to dampen the note.[573] When the Rhodes is played gently, a clear bell-like tone results; but when a note is played hard, the tine is deflected producing a more distorted tone, rich in overtones.

As rock music became louder, many bands left the Fender speaker unit at home and connected the keyboard to more powerful amplification; the Mothers of Invention used Marshall and Orange amplifiers. Fender responded by introducing the Stage model in 1970, which had four steel legs for support and passive electronics designed to be played through an external amplifier. The original design with the speaker cabinet was renamed the Suitcase Model, and both designs had a plain black top. Both 73-note and full-size 88-note versions were available, and in 1974, CBS changed the brand name to just Rhodes.[574]

The pre-1974 Fender Rhodes badge
(Mick Ekers)

ZAPPA GEAR

Ian Underwood played an original "silver-top" Fender Rhodes with the early Mothers of Invention and later FZ bands. When George Duke joined the band in 1970, he was provided with a black-top Stage Piano during the first tour. He later used his own instrument, often playing it through various effects units: "Yeah, well, I remember I used to play this little Oberheim ring modulator that I used to love, it was black with a little gold or yellow lightning strike across it, and I used to love it with the Fender Rhodes, and the Echoplex was a big thing back then, on the Rhodes and whatever else you used it on."[575] Duke is explicitly credited on the *Waka/Jawaka* album as playing "ring-modulated and echoplexed electric piano."[576]

In later years, FZ was less keen on his keyboard players using certain effects on stage: "If, say, you put a Rhodes through a Bi-Phase, you get this horrible clipping sound if the guy really wants to play it hard. If the guy is really banging on it, the voltage he's putting out is driving the box crazy. It makes distortion. Naturally, the keyboard player is enraptured with what he's doing; just wailing away, but the kids out in the audience are hearing this big crackle, this unmusical noise. It's irritating."[577]

During the 1970s, the Rhodes became widely used in jazz, soul, and rock music, featuring heavily in recordings by Miles Davis, Stevie Wonder, Ray Charles, the Beatles, and many more. It revolutionized the sound of popular music and became the biggest-selling professional electric piano of all time. George Duke was a major exponent of the instrument, known not just for his work with FZ, but also with jazz saxophonist Cannonball Adderley.

The original Suitcase model played by Ian Underwood was destroyed in the Montreux fire, but subsequent FZ bands usually featured at least one Rhodes in the keyboard department; Tommy Mars and Peter Wolf both played them at various times in the 1980s.

I did not see any Rhodes keyboards when I visited the UMRK, but there was an original amplifier unit in storage at Joe's Garage, which could have been the partner of the keyboard that Underwood played. FZ also owned a Fiesta Red 1960s Piano Bass; it was sold in the 2016 auction for $4,480.[578]

The last mechanical Rhodes was manufactured in 1984; the name was sold to the Roland Corporation, which produced some digital electronic designs that bore little resemblance to the original designs. In 1997, Rhodes bought the name back from Roland, and the Rhodes Music Corporation was formed. A brand-new mechanical model, based on the original design, was introduced at the NAMM show in 2007, and was demonstrated by George Duke.[579]

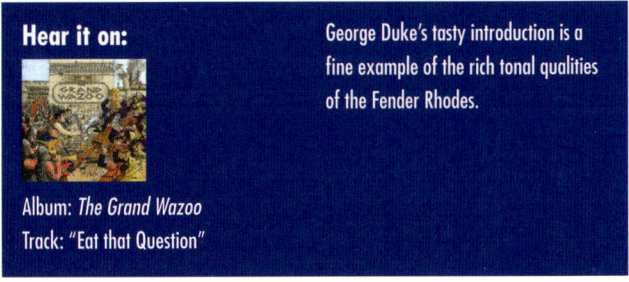

Hear it on:
Album: *The Grand Wazoo*
Track: "Eat that Question"

George Duke's tasty introduction is a fine example of the rich tonal qualities of the Fender Rhodes.

Ian Underwood's RMI and silvertop Rhodes at Bath, note the RMI switches in grey box. The other box is a Maestro effects unit for his electrified saxophone. Howard Kaylan is in the foreground
(Odile Noel)

FZ's Piano Bass — labelled 'Jesse Stone' for some reason
(ZFT)

RMI Electra Piano

"Don Preston played an RMI electric piano. It didn't sound very good but it was easier to carry than a Fender Rhodes"

—FZ [580]

The RMI Electra Piano was an integral piece of touring equipment played by several FZ keyboard players during the 1960s and early 1970s, notably Don Preston, Ian Underwood, and George Duke. It was in fact an electronic piano; unlike the Fender Rhodes or the Hohner Clavinet, which amplified the sounds produced by a vibrating rod or metal reed, all of its tones were generated electronically.

The Electra Piano and Harpsichord (to give it its full name) was introduced in 1967 by the North Carolina company Rocky Mount Instruments (to give them their full name), a subsidiary of the Allen Organ Company. It had a two-tone blue and black case, 61 keys, a volume pedal, and a sustain footswitch. Above the keyboard was a bank of seven switches that could be selected in any combination. There were five voices—piano (loud and soft), harpsichord (loud and soft) and lute, plus two effects: accenter and organ mode.[581]

Unlike many similar instruments of the time, which derived all of the different pitches from a single set of twelve oscillators, the Electra Piano had an individual tone generator for each note, which resulted in a significantly richer and more consistent tone. The keyboard was not pressure-sensitive, so it had to be played more like an organ than a piano. The organ mode effect gave the notes a longer sustain when switched on, but it did not sustain them indefinitely as one might expect; they gradually decayed, producing a unique effect. The accenter mode added a percussive effect to each note played, simulating the hammer of a piano.[582]

The 300A, with a retail price of $895, was a big hit commercially. Although it did not play or sound particularly like a piano, it had a useful range of sounds, particularly when the voices were combined. It was reliable and stayed in tune well, and as FZ noted was relatively easy to carry.

In 1969, it was upgraded to the all-black model 300B, which had an improved piano sound and a longer sustain when the organ mode was selected. It went on to become a staple item in many prog-rock keyboard players' rigs, including Jon Lord of Deep Purple and Rick Wakeman of Yes.

By 1970, FZ could obviously afford to pay enough roadies to carry two Fender Rhodes for the band, as George Duke and Ian Underwood were both playing them at the Bath festival. However, he may have revised his opinion of the unique tones of the RMI, as Ian Underwood also had an Electra Piano on stage.

The shaped top of the case had been removed and replaced with a flat cover to allow the Rhodes to rest on top of it, so it is not possible to tell if this is the original 300A used by Preston, or (as I think likely) the later 300B. The switch bank had been put into a small metal case attached to the RMI by a flying lead; this can be seen on top of Underwood's Rhodes in the Bath Festival photo. This would probably make the RMI the first keyboard that FZ had specially modified; there would be many more, of course.

RMI continued producing 300 series keyboards until 1980, when they launched their new digital DK-20 model. However, the DK-20 and similar models did not sell, and the company was closed down by its parent in 1982. I have found no evidence of FZ using an RMI after 1971; the instrument played by Underwood was almost certainly destroyed in the Montreux Casino fire.

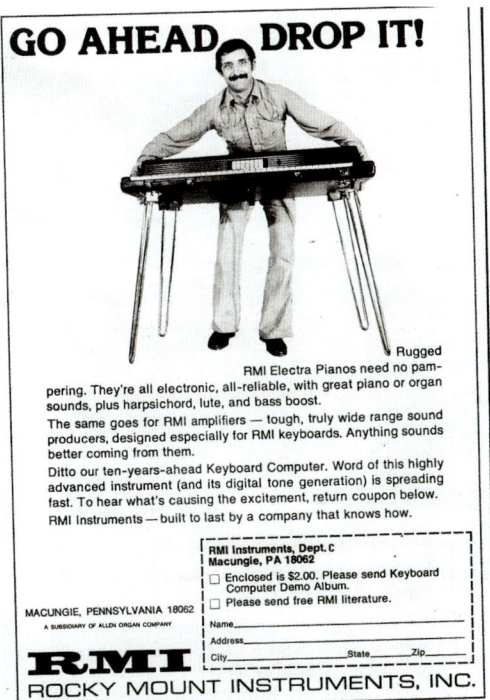

Note the original position of the switch bank above the keyboard in this optimistic advert

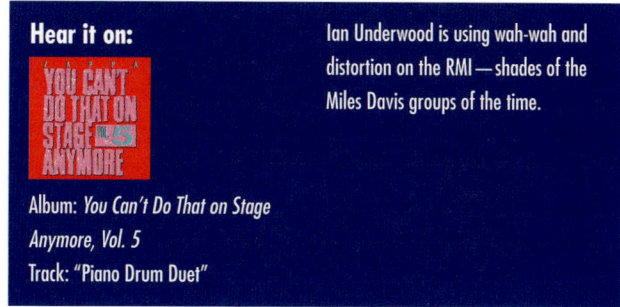

Hear it on:
Album: *You Can't Do That on Stage Anymore, Vol. 5*
Track: "Piano Drum Duet"

Ian Underwood is using wah-wah and distortion on the RMI—shades of the Miles Davis groups of the time.

Wurlitzer EP200A Electric Piano

"He'd also have a little Wurlitzer electric piano down there in front of the band."

—*Arthur Barrow*[583]

The Wurlitzer EP200A electric piano may not seem particularly significant among the various keyboards that FZ bought for studio and touring purposes, but bass player Arthur Barrow told me that he had a particular use for it. When rehearsing the band, particularly when working on new songs and arrangements, FZ liked to have the Wurlitzer set up at the front of the band so that he could conveniently use it to demonstrate parts of the song that might not be best suited for playing on guitar.

Barrow recalls: "He had no keyboard technique at all, so to speak; he'd kind of poke his finger at it, didn't play like a proper piano player at all! But you know sometimes it was easier for him to find the notes on the keyboard to show something to Tommy (Mars) . . . or he was singing, and he might not have his guitar on, and he could just walk over to it and play a note here or there."[584]

The Wurlitzer Company was founded in Cincinnati in 1853 by Franz Rudolph Wurlitzer (1831–1914), and is perhaps best known for the Mighty Wurlitzer pipe organs that it produced between 1914 and 1940, and the jukeboxes that were first produced in 1933.

However, they also produced a successful range of portable electric pianos between 1955 and 1982. Similar to the rival Fender Rhodes electric piano, the Wurlitzer used individual metal reeds (the Fender used thin metal rods) that were struck by a felt-covered hammer using a mechanism similar to a conventional piano. The sound produced by each reed was converted to an electric signal by an individual electrostatic pickup. At low volume it produced a mellow tone similar to its Fender rival, but when played more aggressively it had a brighter, slightly overdriven tone which was more popular with rock and pop musicians.

The 64-note portable model EP200 was introduced in 1968, and revised with an improved amplifier as the EP200A in 1972. It featured a built-in solid-state amplifier with two small front-mounted speakers, a variable tremolo circuit, and a mechanical sustain pedal attached by a cable.

It was housed in a lightweight plastic case (usually black) with detachable metal legs. Although the metal reeds were prone to fracture under heavy use, and tuning required filing away or adding to the lump of solder on the end of the reed,[585] it proved very popular with working bands in the 1970s.

Wurlitzer produced other models, aimed more at the home and educational markets, but the 200 series is the one most often seen on stage or in the studio. It remained in production until 1980, and is still used by many professional musicians, notably George Duke, who still occasionally records with his old 140B (an earlier model but still much the same inside as the 200). Duke took his 140B on tour with FZ during the 1970s, sometimes playing the same melody with his right hand on the Wurlitzer and his left on his Fender Rhodes, creating a beautifully rich and mellow tone.

In 1980, FZ told *Keyboard* magazine of the difficulties he had getting his synthesizer virtuosos Tommy Mars and Peter Wolf to play simple lines on the humble Wurlitzer during the recording of *Joe's Garage*. "We needed some tracks laid down on a Wurlitzer electric piano, without any jazz motifs or cadenzas. That's all I wanted. There are a lot of keyboard players in the world who cannot imagine that that would be fun to do. Tommy is one of 'em. Peter wasn't all that thrilled about it either."[586]

Bob Harris used one on stage along with a Yamaha CS-80 during his tenure with the band as a keyboard player (1980).[587]

One of FZ's Wurlitzer EP200A's at the UMRK
(Mick Ekers)

Although FZ never played the Wurlitzer himself on stage, he kept a couple of them in stock; one was still in evidence at the UMRK in January 2012.

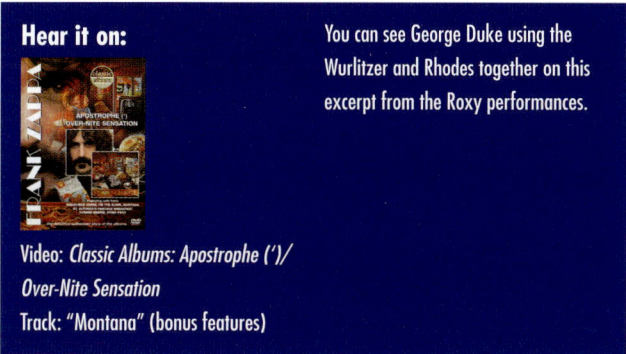

Hear it on: You can see George Duke using the Wurlitzer and Rhodes together on this excerpt from the Roxy performances.

Video: *Classic Albums: Apostrophe (')/Over-Nite Sensation*
Track: "Montana" (bonus features)

Hohner Clavinet and Pianet/Clavinet Duo

"I've got a Clavinet and a Pianet/Clavinet combination"

— FZ[588]

The Hohner Clavinet was another keyboard instrument that FZ used in many of his bands. It was used a lot by George Duke in the 1970s, and later keyboard players Eddie Jobson, Tommy Mars, and Peter Wolf also played Clavinets.

Hohner Musical Instruments was founded by Matthias Hohner in the small town of Trossingen in Germany in 1857, where he built the first mechanized harmonica factory. Before then the harmonica, originally a tool for piano tuners, had been traditionally handmade at home. The company became the world's leading maker of harmonicas, a position it still holds today, and diversified into accordions and other instruments.[589]

In the 1960s, designer and musician Ernst Zacharias took the company in a new direction when he became interested in making compact electric versions of traditional keyboard instruments. In 1962, the Hohner Pianet, one of the first electric pianos, went into production. The tone was produced by a metal accordion reed, which was placed in proximity to an electric pickup. As each key was depressed, a leather and foam adhesive pad lifted the reed up until it sprang free and started vibrating.

The design did not allow for any form of sustain pedal, and it made little difference how hard you played the keyboard. Although Zacharias had intended it for home use, it became a popular instrument among 1960s rock bands such as Manfred Mann, the Zombies, and the Blues Project.[590]

Zacharias turned his attention to producing an electric clavichord, and came up with the Clavinet, which was launched in 1964. The Clavinet has 60 keys, each of which causes a rubber hammer to press the string onto a metal anvil, similar to the guitar technique of pressing a string hard onto a fret known as "hammering on." After the note has been struck, extra pressure on the key (aftertouch) can be used to bend the note slightly.

The strings have to be tuned like a guitar, and are dampened by a weave of woolen yarn that passes over and under the strings at one end. Two electric pickups at either end of the string can be blended like those of a guitar to give different tones.

The Clavinet D6 model became a major success after Stevie Wonder used it on the track "Superstition," following which it seemed like everyone wanted to include its percussive funky sound in their records. Many keyboard players used the Clavinet in combination with the mellower-sounding Fender Rhodes, which inspired Hohner to produce the combined Clavinet/Pianet Duo in 1978, hoping to take some business back from Rhodes.[591]

The Duo allowed the player to blend the two sounds in together, or split the keyboard between the two instruments. Different combinations could be selected by a set of rocker switches and a rotary switch; other switches selected the Clavinet pickups and tone. The output sockets on the back allowed the two instruments to be combined or passed to separate effects or amplifiers if desired.[592]

Although taking up little more room than a regular Clavinet, the duo was notoriously heavy, due to the additional weight of the Pianet mechanism. It was only made for a few years; competition from synthesizers and Japanese instruments caused Hohner to stop manufacturing keyboards altogether in the early 1980s.

UK Advert for the Clavinet-Pianet Duo

ZAPPA GEAR

FZ had both Tommy Mars and Peter Wolf assigned to clavinet duties at various times—one of them would have had a plain Clavinet, the other the Duo. The whereabouts of FZ's Clavinet is unknown. When I visited Joe's Garage, I found the Duo wedged in a cupboard beside one of FZ's massive Sony digital tape recorders and it was not possible to take it out and photograph it. From what could be seen it looked in good condition and hopefully is still in reasonable working order.

FZ's Duo in 2012 in a closet at Joe's Garage
(Mick Ekers)

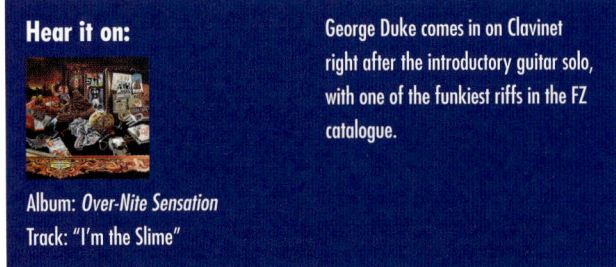

Hear it on:
Album: *Over-Nite Sensation*
Track: "I'm the Slime"

George Duke comes in on Clavinet right after the introductory guitar solo, with one of the funkiest riffs in the FZ catalogue.

Hammond B3 Organ

"I just spent about $8,000 on this special Hammond organ . . . ."
—FZ[593]

As you might expect, FZ's Hammond B3 organ was indeed special, as he described it to *Keyboard* magazine: "I had it transistorized and put in a road case, and I put a voltage follower on it . . . so that you can run the Minimoog or any other modern synthesizer with it. I also had a special set of Syndrums so that you could get a scale of 61 bongos or 61 tom-toms or 61 woodblocks or whatever . . . you can get any of the Syndrum sounds along with the sound of the organ."[594]

The Hammond organ was patented by the American inventor Laurens Hammond in 1934. Born in 1895 in Evanston, Illinois, he showed an early talent for engineering; designing an automatic transmission system for cars at the age of fourteen. He graduated from Cornell University in 1916 with an honors degree in mechanical engineering. By 1933, Hammond was proprietor of the Hammond Clock company, selling electric clocks, which used the patented synchronous electric motor that was to become a key part of the Hammond organ technology.[595]

To keep his company in business during the Great Depression, Hammond knew he had to diversify, and in 1933 turned his mind to the challenge of producing an electronic organ. Starting with the keyboard mechanism stripped from a piano, he tried various techniques until he came up with the tonewheel mechanism that is at the heart of the Hammond sound. The tonewheel is a small metal wheel with even spaced teeth or notches cut into its edge. When rotated in proximity to an electromagnet, it generates an electric signal that can be amplified and output through a loudspeaker. The pitch of the note produced depends on the speed of rotation and the number of teeth on the wheel.

Hammond and his engineers came up with a design consisting of 91 different wheels, each driven at various speeds via a gear train driven by his synchronous motor. This was enough to

The Hammond B3 at Joe's Garage in 2012
(Mick Ekers)

Keyboards and Synthesizers

Switch panel in front of lower manual
(Mick Ekers)

Note the gap where the 'one-foot' drawbar was
(Mick Ekers)

Non-functioning top 'B' key
(Mick Ekers)

generate all the pitches required for the fundamental notes on the keyboard and the harmonic overtones, which are multiples of the fundamental. Each key on the organ could produce up to eight harmonics, which could be blended in various proportions using a system of drawbars, producing an almost infinite variety of tones.[596]

This mechanism was used in various models of Hammond organs essentially unchanged for forty years. Although originally intended just for use in churches, the Hammond organ was adopted by an ever-increasing number of popular musicians, and by the 1970s had become the main keyboard instrument for many jazz, blues, and rock bands. The model B3 was produced from 1955 to 1974, and is the archetypical Hammond organ, with two manuals of 61 keys, chorus/vibrato and percussion, nine preset keys, and two sets of nine adjustable harmonic drawbars for each manual. It came in a walnut or cherry case and had a removable 25-note radiating detachable pedalboard. The whole thing, with the supplied wooden bench, weighed 425 pounds.[597]

In those days it was quite common for musicians to have their Hammonds modified for road use, removing the organ from its stock wooden cabinet and repackaging it in a smaller, lighter case, leaving the pedalboard behind and replacing the valve preamplifier with a solid-state unit.[598] Not so many went as far as FZ by adding outputs to control a synthesizer and a custom Syndrum unit! (See the Pollard Industries Syndrum section for more on this.)

Tommy Mars told me that when he first joined the band in 1977, the Hammond B3 was effectively still standard: the voltage follower modifications were probably carried out in 1979. Mars loved the results: "To have the Syndrums on the organ was incredible. I had the Syndrums connected to the bottom keyboard, and the Minimoog connected to the top keyboard; which was OK but you couldn't do any expressive stuff, you couldn't add vibrato, obviously."[599]

There was one drawback for Mars: "The problem was I had to lose the one-foot drawbar. If you are an organist, that drawbar puts the icing on the cake ... that one-foot is the highest drawbar, and it is the most sensitive. But that's the drawbar they needed to make it voltage controlled ... so I never had that and it was sort of a thorn in my side, being an organist."[600]

On my visit to FZ's old rehearsal studio, Joe's Garage, we were pleased to find the B3 still safely stashed away in a flight case; fortunately, the foam lining had not perished (see the Yamaha CS-80 section). Both of the black B keys in the upper manual were depressed (possibly intentionally non-functional); and as Mars noted both of the one-foot drawbars have been removed. There is a narrow aluminum shelf fitted to the front of the unit with two separate control panels built in.

The left-hand one has a red flick switch, eight rocker switches color coded to match the drawbars, and four rotary controls with three black and one yellow switch. The smaller right-hand panel has one black and two white rocker switches, and two

145

medium-size black toggle switches. None of these controls are labelled; presumably some are for the Syndrum and Minimoog interfaces.

The organ still looked in reasonably good condition; hopefully at some stage it will be put into the hands of someone who understands such things and be played again. It may not have had as much road use as originally intended; when *Keyboard* magazine asked FZ if he was still using it he replied: "No, we didn't take it on the last tour. It was too much of a temptation for Tommy to noodle on. It's got a lot of possibilities."[601]

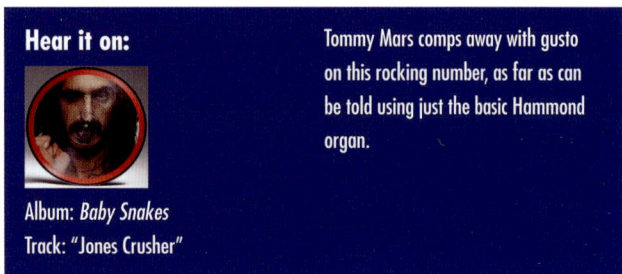

Hear it on: Tommy Mars comps away with gusto on this rocking number, as far as can be told using just the basic Hammond organ.

Album: *Baby Snakes*
Track: "Jones Crusher"

ARP 2600

"The way I learned was by buying an ARP 2600, getting the manual, and just sitting around and piddling with it."

—FZ[602]

ARP Instruments Inc. was founded in 1969 by electronics engineer and entrepreneur Alan R. Pearlman. They introduced the 2600 model in 1971, intending it primarily for the educational market. It consisted of a small selection of the most useful modules from the massive ARP 2500 (the synth seen in the film *Close Encounters of the Third Kind*), internally wired together in a useful default configuration.

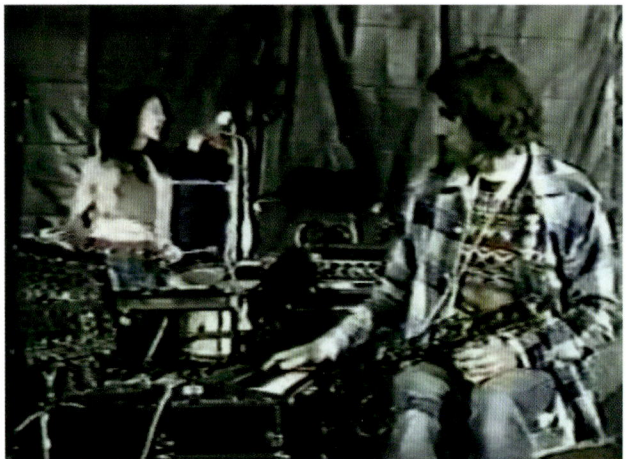

Ian Underwood playing FZ's ARP 2600 during the legendary Stockholm concert in 1973
(still from Oppåpoppa, 1973)

The classic ARP 2600 with built in case
(Vintagesynth)

Each module had a selection of sliders to control the various parameters, a helpful block diagram, and sockets enabling the user to override the internal connections with patch cables. (This type of system is known as a "Normalized Modular synthesiser.") It came with a separate four-octave keyboard, an internal amp and speakers, and a built-in reverb unit.[603]

It was a brilliant design, combining the ease of use of an integrated synth like the Minimoog with the flexibility and creative potential of larger modular units. Although the ARP marketing team insisted that early models were assembled in a modern-looking but impractical blue metal frame, Pearlman's wishes finally prevailed and it was built into a sturdy black case.[604] In this form, it proved reliable and rugged enough to stand up to touring use, and became very popular with working musicians, initially attracted by high profile endorsees such as Stevie Wonder, Herbie Hancock, and Pete Townshend.

When FZ bought his ARP 2600, the sale was likely made by Tom Oberheim, later of Oberheim synthesizer fame, who at the time was ARP's sales representative.

FZ certainly chose the perfect instrument to learn on; the 118-page illustrated manual was written as a training course for students and beginners, including a large introductory section on the basic principles of sound synthesis. It is still a recommended text for anyone interested in electronic music production.

FZ played it himself on several recordings, and explicitly credits himself on the *Man from Utopia* album as playing the ARP 2600. It was also put to good use by many of the keyboard players in various FZ bands, notably Ian Underwood in the 1970s and Peter Wolf in the 1980s. FZ tried to persuade George Duke to play one but he found it too complicated to use, eventually purchasing his own ARP Odyssey[605], a simpler integrated synth derived from the 2600.

The 2600 remained in production until ARP went out of business in 1981, and still has a reputation as one of the best analogue synthesizers ever produced. These days they command a high price on the secondhand market; however, there are some reasonably priced software versions available.

Hear it on:
Album: *Wazoo*
Track: "Approximate"

Ian Underwood "whips it out" six minutes into this astonishing piece of music.

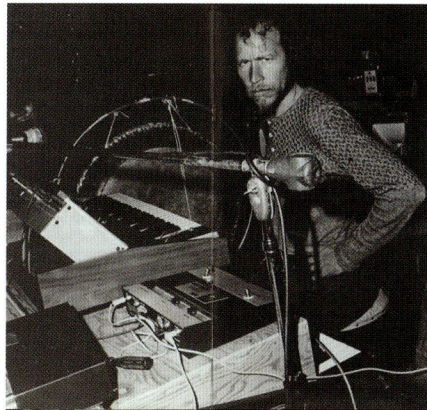

Don Preston and his Minimoog from the Mothers of Invention Tour Book 1971

Minimoog

"Then I got a Minimoog and a lot of other kinds of synthesizers . . . ."
— FZ[606]

When the first production Series 900 Moog synthesizers became generally available in 1967, there was considerable interest among the new breed of LA-based rock musicians. Moog's LA sales representative Paul Beaver, and his musical associate Bernie Krause, offered classes in the use of this exciting new instrument, as well as giving individual lessons at night for various luminaries including Beatles producer George Martin, the Beach Boys, and FZ.[607]

Krause remembers that FZ stood out from the other students: "While most of those musicians we taught came away with ways to reduce the synthesizer's potential to the creative limits of their respective imaginations, Frank Zappa was different. Paul and I always felt that here was a special individual; working with him energized us rather than leaving us feeling drained at the end of a session."[608]

They didn't manage to sell FZ a Moog, but their paths were to cross obliquely again, when Krause provided synthesizer programming for Judy Henske and Jerry Yester's album *Farewell Aldebaran*, released on FZ's Straight record label in 1969.

Robert Arthur "Bob" Moog (pronounced "mogue") was born in New York in 1934, and developed an early interest in electronic musical instruments, making his first theremin at the age of fourteen. He partly paid for his college and university studies by selling theremin kits via mail order, under the brand R.A. Moog Co. After gaining a Ph.D. in engineering physics from Cornell University in 1963, he turned his back on the academic world and moved into full-time theremin manufacturing, opening up his factory in the village of Trumansburg in New York State.[609]

Minimoog brochure cover 1972

In 1963, Moog met the young composer Herb Deutsch, and the two discussed the possibilities of making a new electronic instrument. In 1964, Moog, working with Deutsch, produced what were to become the basic building blocks of all analogue synthesizers: voltage-controlled amplifiers, filters, envelope generators, and oscillators producing various waveforms. Crucially, these circuits were all designed as discrete modules that could be combined and interconnected in various ways, and control each other with their output voltages.[610]

Moog's use of voltage control also meant that his circuits could be controlled with a suitably engineered piano-type keyboard; this was unlike many of the other people working in the field who were looking to use their devices to create a brand-new form of music, for which keyboards based on the traditional 12-note chromatic scale were inappropriate.

Moog gradually started selling custom synthesizers based on these and similar modules, and in 1967 they launched the 900 series, which received a huge sales boost in 1968 with the worldwide success of Wendy Carlos's *Switched on Bach* album,

The classic Model D Minimoog
(Mick Ekers)

realized entirely on a Moog synthesizer. For a couple of years Moog was selling all the 900 Series synthesizers he could make, but by 1970, sales had dropped dramatically. The studio and rock-star market had been saturated, and the large instruments were too expensive for the average working musician to afford, too complicated to use in a live performance, and too delicate to be taken on the road.

While Moog was fully occupied fending off the taxman and creditors, engineer Bill Hemsath embarked on a part-time R&D project during his lunch breaks. He decided to build a portable synthesizer using cast-off modules and components that he took from the graveyard area of the factory. He assembled a unit with two oscillators, an envelope generator, and a filter unit, which he put into a small wooden cabinet. The Min Moog, as he called it, had no patch cord sockets; all the modules were wired together internally in what was a popular standard configuration, and it had a built-in three-octave keyboard with modulation control slider on the left—the modern portable synthesizer had been born. Over the next couple of years three more prototypes were developed, culminating in the Model D, which now had three oscillators and an added noise generator, pitch and modulation wheels at the left of the 44-note monophonic keyboard, and the patented pop-up control panel.[611]

The Model D was deemed ready for production and was launched in 1970, with a recommended price of $1,495. For the first time, a synthesizer was available in music stores with an intuitive control layout, sturdy design, and a distinct and musical sound that made it a huge hit with rock and jazz musicians. It was a huge success, remaining in production for over ten years and selling over 12,000 units.[612] Hemsath noted that one factor in its popularity was the sound produced by Moog's ladder filter circuit: "Our instrument had punch to it, because we inadvertently overdrove the filter input like crazy . . . and nobody knew that until a month or so after we had started production, and everybody said, 'Leave it alone!'"[613]

By the time FZ bought his own Minimoog, it was an essential instrument in almost every rock band's arsenal. During the 1970s and 1980s, he had had pretty well all his keyboard players using a Minimoog at one time or another, including Don Preston, Tommy Mars, Peter Wolf, and George Duke. Percussionist Ed Mann and bass players Scott Thunes and Arthur Barrow also used one on occasion, and FZ possibly played a Minimoog himself on the *Zoot Allures* album.

In a live situation, FZ was sometimes less than enamored of the Minimoog, complaining about Peter Wolf's preference for using his Minimoog for soloing over the mighty E-mu synth: "The keyboard player who was using it (the E-mu) couldn't even fathom what to do with it because when it came time to play a solo the first thing the guy did was get his little Minimoog out and go 'eeeee,' you know? I mean, that's distressing to me."[614]

In 2002, Moog designed an updated version of the Minimoog—the Moog Voyager, which still used the same analogue circuits of the original but added patch memory, MIDI control, and other modern refinements. In 2001, Moog was awarded the Swedish Polar Music Prize, with the following citation: "Robert Moog is being awarded the Polar Music Prize

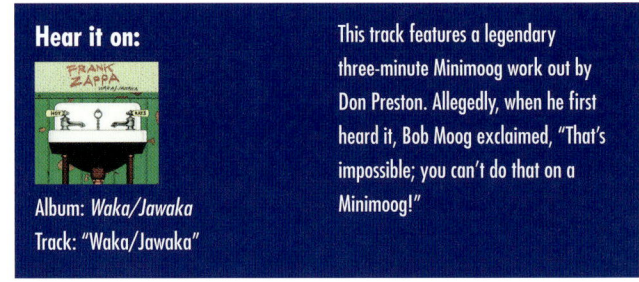

Hear it on:
Album: *Waka/Jawaka*
Track: "Waka/Jawaka"

This track features a legendary three-minute Minimoog work out by Don Preston. Allegedly, when he first heard it, Bob Moog exclaimed, "That's impossible; you can't do that on a Minimoog!"

for 2001 for his design of the Minimoog, the first compact, easy-to-use synthesizer, which paved the way to the realm of electronic sounds that has revolutionized all genres of music during the past half-century."[615] He died on 28th April, 2005, but his company Moog Music Inc. still sells analogue synthesizers and theremins, as well as modern digital products.[616] The original Minimoog is still a collectable and playable classic instrument, as venerated among keyboard players as early Fender Telecasters are among guitarists.

Moog Taurus

"Hey can we put the Taurus bass pedals under the organ?"
— Tommy Mars[617]

When Tommy Mars joined the band he bought along his own Moog Taurus bass pedal synthesizer, which he tended to keep on stage under the electric piano. FZ bought another unit and Tommy Mars made a suggestion: "I said 'Hey can we put the Taurus bass pedals under the organ, and then have the last octave of the organ also have the bass pedals on the manual.' They hooked it up that way so I had the bass pedals under the organ, and it also would be the last octave of the upper manual."[618]

Moog Music Inc. introduced the Taurus pedal synthesizer in November 1978. It had originally been intended to be part of a three-piece ensemble synthesizer called the Constellation; a prototype was developed for keyboard player Keith Emerson of ELP, but it was never put into production.

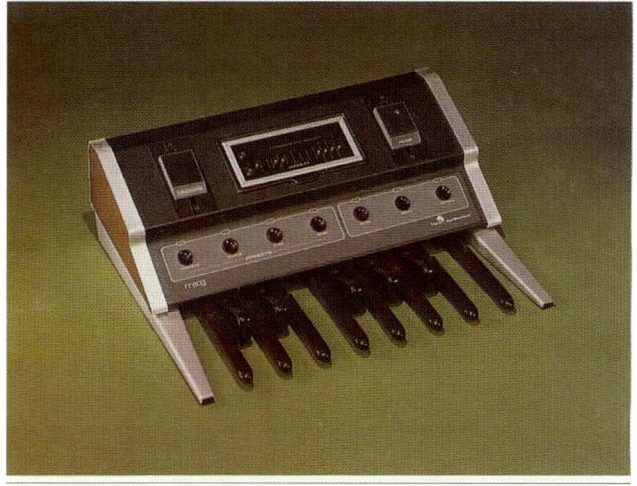

An early Taurus flier

The Taurus was a monophonic, analogue bass synthesizer designed to be played with the feet, modelled after organ pedalboards. It came with three preset sound patches, called Bass, Tuba, and Taurus, and one user-programmable Variable patch. Its simple controls consisted of two large sliders controlling the filter cutoff and loudness; four footswitches to select the patches, and three for portamento, decay, and pedalboard octave selection.

The synthesizer itself was a basic design with just two oscillators (producing sawtooth waveforms only), a filter, and an envelope shaper. The Variable patch was programmed via a small inset panel of slider controls. The 13-note pedal board had a "low note priority" circuit, so that if the player depressed two notes, the instrument would sound the lowest note.[619]

The Taurus was produced until 1981, and was a considerable success; apart from the Zappa band, it found use with Yes, Rush, Genesis, the Police, and many others. It was ruggedly built, easy to use, and had a killer bass sound, particularly the Taurus preset, which at volume could be felt as much as heard. In 1981, Moog Music replaced it with the Taurus II, with 18 pedals and a raised pedestal control unit, but it did not have the sonic depth of the original and was a relative failure, discontinued in 1983.

Mars gleefully recalls having two Tauruses at his feet: "Sometimes I used to play them both together, you know what I mean; the whole house would really rock when you play a low C down there with both of those Taurus bass pedals under the organ and the piano. Course it used to almost give me a hernia, from the angle you have to play it at . . . ."[620] Gail Zappa told me that FZ was not a fan of this overbearing effect for long![621]

Moog Music Inc. is currently producing the Taurus III pedal synthesizer, which is based entirely on the analogue Taurus I synthesizer circuit, but with many modern enhancements including MIDI control, more presets, and velocity-sensitive pedals.[622]

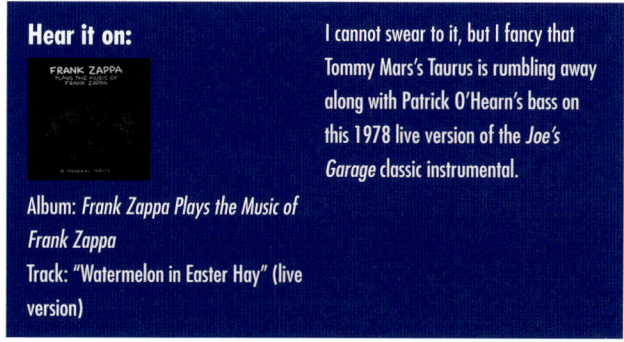

Hear it on: I cannot swear to it, but I fancy that Tommy Mars's Taurus is rumbling away along with Patrick O'Hearn's bass on this 1978 live version of the *Joe's Garage* classic instrumental.

Album: *Frank Zappa Plays the Music of Frank Zappa*
Track: "Watermelon in Easter Hay" (live version)

ZAPPA GEAR

ElectroComp 101 Synthesizer

"... and Frank said 'we've got to have more ElectroComps'"
— *Tommy Mars* [623]

Tommy Mars introduced the ElectroComp 101 synthesizer to FZ at his first audition in 1977. He turned up with various keyboards, including his 101 in its little wooden case. Mars recalls, "Frank said, 'What's this?' and I undid it and I played something, and of course my signature sound was sort of a French horn kind of brass sound that it did... his jaw dropped, because I don't think he'd ever heard a synth do that kind of sound with that kind of expression."[624]

FZ certainly liked that sound; and after getting his giant E-mu modular synth setup to emulate the horn sound (see the E-mu section), he told Mars that he needed to get some more. Mars directed him to Electronic Music Laboratories in his home state of Connecticut, where he had bought his, and FZ ordered three units. Mars recalls that EML were delighted to get what was quite a prestigious account for a relatively small company.[625]

EML was founded in 1968, in Vernon, Connecticut, by Dale Blake, Dennis Daugherty, Norman Millard, and Jeff Murray. The four engineers had worked together at Gerber Scientific, and formed the company when they were facing being laid off. They started producing synthesizers for the educational market, using circuits designed by fellow audio engineer Fred Locke.[626]

Their first model, the ElectroComp 100, was produced from 1970 to 1972, when it was superseded by an improved version, the ElectroComp 101. The 101 was a portable normalized modular synth, like the ARP 2600, with a pre-wired configuration that could be overridden via the 1/4" patch bay. It had four oscillators with continuously variable waveforms, and, uniquely for such a small machine, the 44-note keyboard was Duophonic, meaning you could play two notes at the same time.

It also included a voltage-controlled, 12 dB/octave, multi-mode resonant filter; two envelope generators; a continuously variable ring/amplitude modulator; a noise generator; and a sample-and-hold module. This was a pretty impressive arsenal of modules for a portable machine, and as the 101 allowed control voltages and audio signals to be interconnected in almost any order, made it the most flexible portable synth at the time.[627]

An ElectroComp advert from 1972

Tommy Mars with ElectroComp and Poly-Box in 1978
(still from Baby Snakes, 1979)

Detail of FZ's modified front panel
(Mick Ekers)

Tommy Mars used this flexibility to configure his signature French horn patch. He used two oscillators; one was fixed and the pitch of the other was modified by the envelope follower (usually used to control the volume of a signal). As he put it, "The attack would raise the pitch, the decay would decline the pitch, and the sustain would be where the pitch ended up," a concept that astounded the E-mu engineers, who had never thought of doing such a thing.[628]

Although EML started out mainly selling the 101 to universities, they soon started finding users in the music business. The 101 was easy to transport, as the keyboard and the electronics panel closed up into a sturdy wooden case, and it stayed in tune longer than the competition, as it used modern op-amps in its oscillators. Moog and ARP were still using transistors in their circuits, which were quite sensitive to changes in temperature.

The 101 came with a 70-page instruction manual, which include the following advice in the "Filter Operation" section: "Filter Maintenance – After every 100 hours of operation apply a sine wave to the output of the Filter to back flush the trapped overtones to unclog your filter." But then they rather spoilt things by immediately following this with the sentence "(Please note the previous paragraph is the one intentional joke in the manual)." If you don't get the joke, ask your local synthesizer geek to explain it to you.

Selling for $1,495, the 101 was very competitively priced; optional extras included a reverb unit ($100), various footpedals, an expression wheel for the keyboard ($50), and an EML 101 T-shirt ($5).

In 1972, the ElectroComp 101 probably was the best portable synthesizer in the world, as their advertising claimed; and EML manufactured about 1,000 units in total. However, they never achieved their aim of becoming the world's top-selling synthesizer manufacturer, and gradually fell behind in the face of increasing competition. They stopped manufacturing synthesizers in 1976, but remained in operation until 1984, servicing their synthesizers and designing and producing electronic circuits.

The 101 was used by various other band members in the late 1970s, including Arthur Barrow. When Barrow joined the band in 1978, he already owned an ElectroComp 101, which created an immediate bond between him and Mars. They still work together on various musical projects, and Barrow keeps Mars's original E101 at his studio.

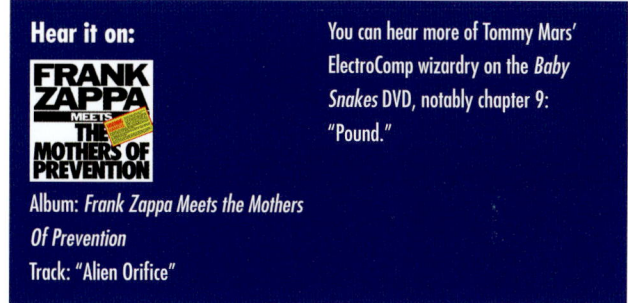

Hear it on:
Album: *Frank Zappa Meets the Mothers Of Prevention*
Track: "Alien Orifice"

You can hear more of Tommy Mars' ElectroComp wizardry on the *Baby Snakes* DVD, notably chapter 9: "Pound."

FZ's ElectroComp 101 at the UMRK
(Mick Ekers)

ZAPPA GEAR

EML Poly-Box

"I play an EML ElectroComp synthesizer with a Poly-Box hooked up that gives you instant chords; you can do some amazing things with that."
— Tommy Mars[629]

The Poly-Box is a unique piece of analogue synthesizer technology (similar in concept, if not execution, to the Electro Wagnerian Emancipator guitar synthesizer mentioned earlier), which provided a neat and clever way to add some polyphonic capability to a monophonic synthesizer. EML designed it to work with other brands such as Moog and ARP, as well as their own models.

EML described it as follows: "Poly-Box is a pitch following variable chord generator controlled by your synthesizer and Poly-Box's own keyboard with built-in memory. Poly-Box takes a single pitch from your synthesizer and creates two banks of pitch sources. Each pitch bank contains thirteen simultaneously available pitch sources at precise semitone intervals—covering an entire chromatic octave. The pitch banks may be in the same or different octaves, and can cover the range from one above to three octaves below the synthesizer oscillator."[630]

The Poly-Box took an input signal from a synthesizer and tracked the pitch, generating additional notes from its own oscillators. The one-octave keyboard allowed selection of any of the thirteen semitone intervals. It could be played either dynamically, or with chord shapes saved in its memory (such as a major seventh), whereupon it would track the input signal, generating chords from the input melody. The tracking circuit was fast and accurate, and could follow any pitch glides and vibrato effects that had been applied to the input signal.

The Poly-Box had two banks of oscillators, which could be set up to two octaves apart; voicing was limited to a pulse waveform. It had a simple low-pass filter to vary the tone between mellow and bright, and a Phasing control that allowed one bank of oscillators to be detuned by a varying amount. The output could be fed back into the synthesizer VCA with the envelope triggered by the Poly-Box keyboard.

It was built to the usual EML high quality standards with glass-epoxy circuit boards, Allen-Bradley potentiometers, and silver and gold switch contacts. A row of red LEDs above the keyboard indicated which notes the Poly-Box was producing. The sturdy aluminum panel was painted a bright orange color and the unit was finished off with cherry wood endplates; later some were produced in plain black cases.

Tommy Mars often used the Poly-Box in conjunction with his ElectroComp 101, using "a stack of the ElectroComp playing a French horn sound, and the Poly-Box playing chords that followed that by pitch with the same envelope."[631] When FZ was playing at the Palais des Sports in Paris on the 11th June, 1980, he invited the noted composer and conductor Pierre Boulez onstage and asked Mars to show him his keyboard set-up. The awe-struck Mars demonstrated the Poly-Box, and remembers that Boulez's eyes lit up and he said, "I've been writing stuff just like this!"

FZ developed particular types of music notation to accommodate the parallel chord tracking ability of the Poly-Box: "You can just add a little inscription at the head of the bar, kind of like a key signature. Next, you write a single line, and, if the guy sets his synthesizer up right, that single line will yield parallel chords tracking around. So it saves you a lot of writing on paper."[632]

The Poly-Box was introduced in 1977, with a list price of $475, and although it remained on the EML catalogue until the company closed in 1984, only 130 were produced.[633] Tommy Mars still has his.

Hear it on:
DVD: *Live in Paris 1980*
Track: "Waka/Jawaka"

You can see Mars using the Poly-Box on the DVD of this French TV broadcast.

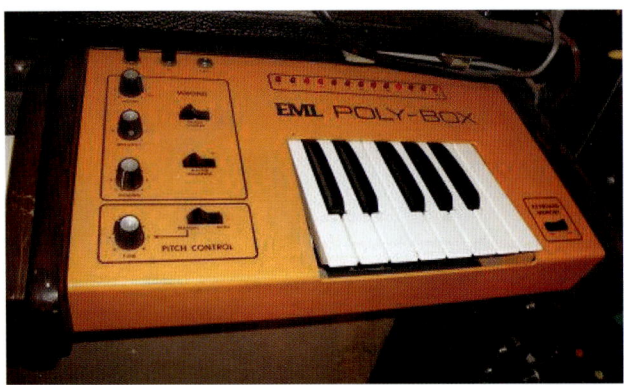

Tommy Mars's EML Poly-Box
(Arthur Barrow Studio)

FZ's SynKey 2000
(ZFT)

EML SynKey

"And the little SynKey, that little piccolo sound, was the hardest to tune because it was the most exposed."

— *Tommy Mars*[634]

SynKey 1500 front panel detail: custom switches, and markings made by Tommy Mars
(David Bagsby)

Electronic Music Laboratories came up with another unique product when they introduced the SynKey, one of the first programmable polyphonic synthesizers, in 1976. It was not truly polyphonic, as it would only detect one note played on the keyboard at a time, but contained thirteen oscillators, one for the primary tone and twelve more for semitones, any of which could be selected by pressing a switch. The semitones could be switched up or down an octave.

The oscillators produced a wave shape that could be varied from a pulse through several sawtooth variations through to a square wave. The SynKey also included a noise generator, voltage-controlled filter, voltage-controlled amplifier, and a low-frequency oscillator. The keyboard had an aftertouch feature, called Second Touch by EML, which produced variable amounts of filter sweeps, vibrato, and pitch bends by pressing harder on the key.[635]

The original model 2001 used small punched cards to save the program settings; they introduced the non-programmable 1500 version in 1978. The SynKey was used by various FZ keyboard players, including Tommy Mars, Peter Wolf, and Eddie Jobson.

Tommy Mars used his for a specific effect: "If you ever notice a picture of the band in that period, over my mixer you'll see a keyboard that I never play—it was used just as an interface.... When you're listening to a stack of the ElectroComp playing sort of a French horn sound ... you'll hear a very high little piccolo sound on the top of the whole stack; that's the SynKey. That's basically what its dedicated job was, to play piccolo parts."[636]

When remembering the difficulties of keeping all his analogue synthesizers in tune, Mars noted that his use of the SynKey made it particularly difficult. FZ had the 1500 SynKey modified with various additional outputs and switches, enabling them to

Modified SynKey 1500 rear panel showing connections for other synthesizers
(David Bagsby)

be driven by the ElectroComp or other sources, as can be seen in the photographs. Tommy Mars identified this model from the chalk marks as being the one used by Peter Wolf.

EML only made around seventy-five SynKeys, and FZ bought two of the last production run, according to Mark Vail's book *Vintage Synthesizers*.[637] The 1500 model pictured was purchased from the ZFT in the Joe's Garage sale, and the owner told me it was still in full working order.[638] The 2000 model shown has no obvious front panel modifications; it was sold in the 2016 auction for $4,062.50.[639]

FZ's SynKey 1500
(David Bagsby)

Hear it on:

You can hear it prominently (played by Eddie Jobson) at the end of the first phrase (30 seconds into the track).

Album: *Zappa in New York*
Track: "Pound for a Brown"

ZAPPA GEAR

Korg VC-10 Vocoder

"Mars, I've got the greatest instrument for you, you are absolutely going to have a heart attack . . . I've bought you a choir!"

—FZ[640]

Korg advert for the VC10

Keyboard player Tommy Mars was sick, and stayed in his hotel while FZ and the band went shopping at Manny's Music in New York, on 15th October, 1978. One of the items FZ purchased was a brand new Korg VC-10 vocoder. These had only recently become available. When he told Mars on his return (quoted above), he was referring to the days when Mars worked as an organist and choirmaster.

Mars had heard of vocoders, but had never seen or heard one before, and was somewhat nonplussed to find it set up for him at the sound check for the evening's concert at Stony Brook University. Although Mars had not had any time to learn how to play it, FZ said, "You're going to use it tonight, aren't you?" to which Mars replied, "Frank what are you talking about? I've just got it!" Nevertheless, FZ insisted, and it was used for the first time at the show that evening.[641]

The vocoder is a device used for modulating a musical sound source, which supplies the pitch, with the continuously varying tonal characteristics of a human voice. The vocoder analyzes and divides the voice signal into different frequency bands (the greater the number of bands, the more accurate the effect), and the continuously varying level of each of these bands is applied to the corresponding frequencies of the input signal (typically a synthesizer).

So for example, if you say some words into the microphone while playing a chord on a synthesizer, the frequency spectrum of the voice is applied to the input musical signal, and the synthesizer will appear to sing the words. The vocoder was by no means a new invention; it was originally developed in the 1930s as a means of encoding and decoding speech for secure radio transmission. It was not until the late 1960s that it was seriously used for musical purposes, and in 1970, synthesizer pioneer Robert Moog and musician Wendy Carlos developed an early 10-band prototype that was used on the soundtrack of the film *A Clockwork Orange*.[642] Commercial vocoders specifically aimed at performing musicians appeared in the late 1970s, notably the VSM201 from Sennheiser, the German microphone and headphone manufacturer, and the Vocoder 5000 from EMS, the pioneering British synthesizer manufacturer.

However, these were expensive, complicated to use, and required a separate microphone and input signal (such as a synthesizer). Even the "budget" EMS 2000 cost around £2,000 (in a previous existence, the author would have been found demonstrating one at the 1979 NAMM trade show in Atlanta).

FZ's Korg Vocoder at Joe's Garage in 2012
(Mick Ekers)

Keyboards and Synthesizers

The extra microphone socket
(Mick Ekers)

When the Japanese synthesizer manufacturer Korg introduced the VC-10 in 1978, it was the first to include everything that was needed in one package. Combining a 20-band vocoder with a polyphonic keyboard and optional microphone, it was ready to run out of the box, simple to use, and practical for live performance. The 32-note keyboard operated a simple synthesizer, with a single sawtooth waveform; it could be switched up or down an octave and had a pitchbend expression wheel. The simple black panel featured a single VU meter and a minimal set of controls, but included inputs for external sources, the ability to mix in the original voice signal to aid intelligibility, and vibrato and chorus effects.[643] Costing around $750, it was priced low enough to make it an affordable unit for working musicians (and an impulse buy for FZ).

Tommy Mars described the VC-10 as very expressive, with a beautiful women's choir sound, and he remembers that it also had a more robotic sound: "we called it the 'Ant' sound; it had no vibrato, it sounded very robotic, and it sounded like alien kind of voices, and Frank actually loved that."[644] It required some skill to use in a live situation, as external sounds picked up by the microphone could trigger the unit and cause ambient feedback, and Mars had to carefully position the microphone to avoid this.

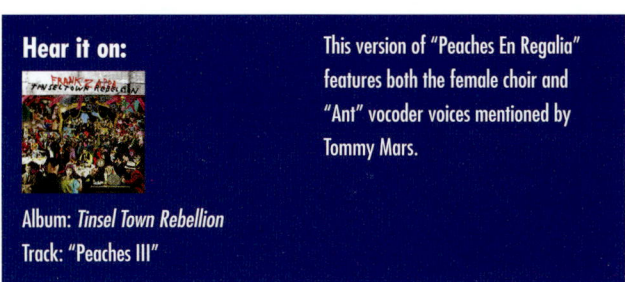

Hear it on:

This version of "Peaches En Regalia" features both the female choir and "Ant" vocoder voices mentioned by Tommy Mars.

Album: *Tinsel Town Rebellion*
Track: "Peaches III"

It was used extensively by the band during 1979 and 1980, and is featured on many tracks to be found on the *Sheik Yerbouti*, *Joe's Garage,* and *Tinsel Town Rebellion* albums. Tech Arthur Sloatman modified the VC-10 with an extra microphone input, so that it could be used by either Mars or FZ at various points in the show.

Mars remembers playing tricks on FZ with the VC-10 on the road: "sometimes he'd just give me a look like 'I want my voice on the vocoder' and I would know that, but then sometimes I would trigger it when . . . he didn't even ask for it, which used to freak him out; he didn't know where it was coming from (laughs)."[645] The VC-10 was manufactured from 1978 to 1982, and the circuitry was incorporated in later Korg synthesizers. Despite its budget status, it is still regarded with affection by many musicians of the time. Mars said: "I always liked the Korg vocoder versus any other one; there was something real sensitive about it."[646] I found FZ's Vocoder in storage at Joe's Garage in 2012. I was glad to see it is still around.

E-mu Modular Synthesizer

"I've invested thousands of dollars on very exotic, advanced synthesizer equipment. I have a humongous E-mu setup"

—FZ [647]

The earliest synthesizers, first developed in the 1960s, were nearly all modular systems, so called because they were made up from a variety of discrete specialized modules. The modules were built to a standard system of sizes (E-mu units were all 6" high and multiples of 3" wide), so they could be slotted together into a suitably designed enclosure. The circuitry was all analogue, and the parameters of one module could be controlled by variable voltages produced by another.

The control panel for each would include various input, output, and control connections, designed so that they could be interconnected in any way the user required, using patch cables. Buyers could design their own systems by choosing the specific modules that they wanted, mixing and matching oscillators, filters, envelope followers, etc.

E-mu Systems (the name was derived from the words "electronic music"), originated in the University of California, Santa Cruz in 1971, when Dave Rossum and some friends got together in the summer to try and build their own synthesizer. Rossum was a graduate microbiology student, but had a "road to Damascus" moment when he helped unpack the university's Moog 12 modular system: "As people there started playing it, I realized that I intuitively knew as much about it as anybody else in the room . . . it just seemed natural to me."[648] The friends built a couple of prototypes and then started on a production model known as the E-mu-25 (named after their favorite psychedelic drug—I make no judgement, this was 1971).

155

ZAPPA GEAR

FZ in front of the E-mu in 1990, from the *Peefeeyatko* documentary
(still from Frank Zappa: Peefeeyatko, 1991)

Later that year, Rossum's old friend Scott Wedge came to visit, and he also became fascinated with synthesizers. After building and selling a second 25, the pair agreed that making a no-compromise modular synthesizer was the way forward: "We decided to make the best we could possibly make; any time we found a component, a design, or anything that would make it better, we put it in unless it was just totally cost-prohibitive."[649]

In 1972, Rossum and Wedge formed a real company called E-mu Systems, and moved the organization to Santa Clara, where they started selling basic synthesizer modules. They sold their first complete modular synthesizer in 1973, and gradually built up a clientele of academic establishments and rich professional musicians. Originally the company name was spelled "Eμ" (the symbol "μ" is the Greek letter mu); this was changed to "E-mu" when the company was incorporated in 1979 ("foreign" characters are not allowed in the names of US corporations). The E-mu looked different; unlike the black-colored panels of almost every other synthesizer, the modules had brushed aluminum panels with a bright blue border. The clean look was reinforced by E-mu's policy of no calibration marks around the control knobs, "with the intent that the user could add them as he wishes."

With its sturdy construction, ultra-reliable components, and highly stable oscillators that would stay in tune much longer than the competing ARP and Moog designs, E-mu began to earn a reputation as the Rolls-Royce of synthesizers. The E-mu was designed from the outset to be suitable for live as well as studio use; standard firm-wire patches could be inserted at the rear of the unit so that the unit could be programmed for a specific set of sounds. The patches could be overridden by inserting cables on the front panel if required, but there was no need for the keyboard player to fiddle around with cables during a live performance—a major selling point.

FZ took delivery of his custom E-mu synth in 1976. It was one of the largest and most complicated systems that they ever built. It was built into two 4100 walnut system cabinets,

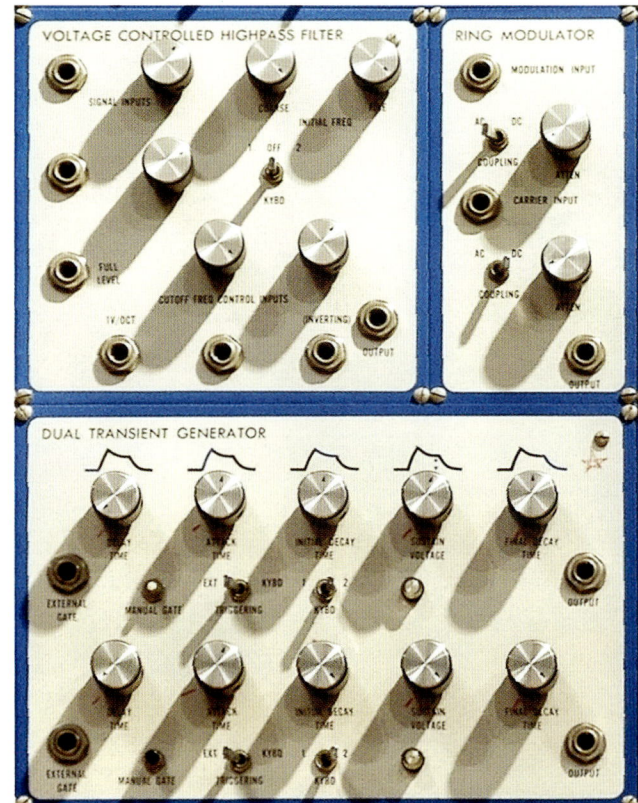

Three modules, with user-added calibration markings on the Dual Transient Generator
(Mick Ekers)

Cabinet one—the custom module at the middle of the bottom row is a guitar synthesizer interface
(Mick Ekers)

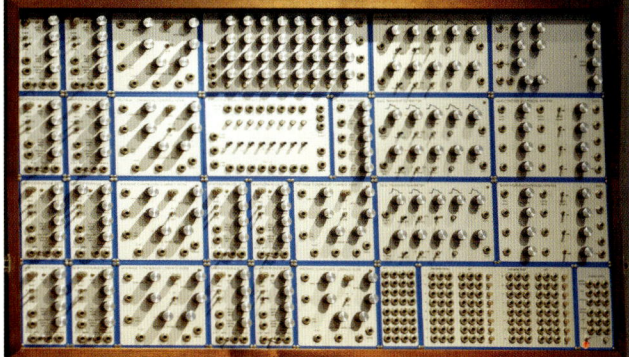

Cabinet two—with sequencer and polyphonic keyboard inputs
(Mick Ekers)

each approximately 45" wide by 26" high, containing a total of fifty-six modules. The system was designed so that the two cabinets could be operated independently; cabinet one as a traditional monophonic synthesizer with an extensive range of sounds and effects, and cabinet two as a fully polyphonic instrument with twelve oscillators and sequencer modules.

Also included were a pair of 4000 mono keyboards and the new 4060 polyphonic keyboard and sequencer. The 4060 keyboard could produce up to sixteen polyphonic channel outputs of control voltage and gate. The sequencer in the 4060 was capable of storing about sixty key depressions; each additional 4065 16K RAM board (maximum three) added 2,000 notes of storage capability.[650]

It was the world's first microprocessor-controlled polyphonic keyboard and sequencer (the outputs were analogue control voltages—MIDI was still several years away) and was one of E-mu's first patents.[651]

For several years, E-mu earned a steady stream of royalties from other synth manufacturers such as Oberheim and Sequential Circuits, who used this keyboard technology in their products.

The list price of the 4060 in the early 1970s was $3,000, and each 16K board would have cost several hundred dollars. (Yes, children, a basic 16GB memory stick has a million times as much memory!) Bearing in mind that each module was a handmade piece of audio equipment built with the highest quality components, it is small wonder that FZ estimated that the system finally cost around $50,000.

Unsurprisingly, FZ never had the time or inclination to become fully conversant with programming or playing it himself: "It requires a technician. It's fairly easy to set it up and put it all together. It's portable; it was designed to be taken on the road. But there's so many modules and stuff built into it that I prefer to have someone who is conversant with the electronic ins and outs of it set it up for me and tell the keyboard player what to do with it. I have enough to worry about with the console without having to worry about the synthesizer. It's got fourteen oscillators or something like that."[652]

Violinist and keyboard player Eddie Jobson fondly remembers programming this beast when he started working for FZ. Having owned one of the first EMS Putney synthesizers (an influential UK design), he was no stranger to the world of voltage-controlled oscillators and envelope followers. However, it was only used in rehearsals while Jobson was in the band, and he never had the chance to play it on the road.[653]

FZ eventually had the polyphonic E-mu cabinet programmed to sound like a five-piece brass section. This came about after keyboard player Tommy Mars brought his small ElectroComp synth along to his audition. According to Mars, FZ's jaw dropped when he played some of his signature French horn sounds on it, as he'd never heard that kind of sound from a synth.

The Musée de la Musique ledger entry for the E-Mu
(Mick Ekers)

Mars tells what followed: "And I said, 'This E-mu that you have?' and he was just like, you know, so proud of his E-mu, and the only sound that he had on it, which is the easiest sound in the world to make, was like a little pipe organ sound, like an eight foot and a four foot, no envelope, no nothing. I said, 'You mean with all this that's all you got (laughs), that's all you got?' and he says 'Yeah?' and I said, 'Well I don't think you noticed that the ElectroComp is very similar, I could set this sound up exactly for you on the E-mu, and then you'd have five voices, you'd have complete polyphony.' And in those days that was like the, you know, going to the emerald city, like follow the yellow brick road! Frank got so excited he says 'OK, do that.'"[654]

Mars passed the audition, and sure enough, when he turned up at rehearsal a couple of weeks later, Dave Rossum, Scott Wedge, and Marco Alpert (E-mu sales rep at the time) were there, and FZ got them to firm-wire it like his ElectroComp patch.[655] When FZ allowed Mars to take the E-mu home for a few weeks so that he could familiarize himself with it, one incident convinced him that it had a personality of its own.

Early one morning, after staying up all night experimenting with the instrument, he finally pressed the stop button on the sequencer, but the E-mu kept on playing: "It was like *Twilight Zone* or something. I had to pull the plug on it in the end, saying, 'Jesus I hope this thing stops playing!'"[656]

Nonetheless, Mars was very attached to the E-mu and its sequencer: "it was extremely expressive and it had tone qualities that I had never used before. The E-mu components are real top-notch, state-of-the-art equipment." He told me of happy times setting up a sequence on the E-mu and jamming with FZ: "one thing that was so great about the E-mu was the sequencer . . . I could set up really interesting vamps on it, and I can remember jamming on the chord changes to "Purple Lagoon" with Frank. And it was so great because you couldn't do that, no instrument could really do what that did in 1977 . . . it was something you dreamed about being able to do."[657]

But, like more than a few musicians, the E-mu found that touring can make you crazy. Subject to high temperatures from the stage lights, even the relatively stable E-mu oscillators required tuning several times in a set, and the strain of being repeatedly packed up, travelling to the next gig, and being set up again started to take its toll on this complicated piece of equipment.

In fact it was the partying that finally did it in; Marco Alpert told me: "at some point, the entire system found its way into the line of fire of a glitter cannon, resulting in many small bits

ZAPPA GEAR

The 4000 monophonic keyboard
(Ivan Schwarz)

The control panel of the 4000
(Ivan Schwarz)

The 4060 polyphonic keyboard
(Ivan Schwarz)

The digital keypad on the 4060 control-panel
(Ivan Schwarz)

of metallic glitter finding their way into the guts of the system, after which, despite meticulous attempts to find and extricate them all, it was never quite right again."[658]

Mars recalls, "the E-mu after a couple of years on the road started getting 'un-roadable'; it would start spitting out this digital diarrhea man, you wouldn't even know when . . . all of a sudden it would go (imitates broken synth) 'brr, kaarava brr brr mmu mmu,' you know, having a nervous breakdown on stage."[659]

FZ reluctantly agreed with Mars that the E-mu could not be relied on, and it was replaced by a Yamaha CS-80. Unfit for touring, it was installed in the UMRK studio, and for a time FZ experimented with using CS-80 keyboards to control it.

However it was eventually usurped in 1983 by FZ's new Synclavier and was rarely used after that. FZ recalled that Stevie Wonder asked to hire it in 1980, but whether he actually did is not known.

In 1980, Alpert gave FZ a private demonstration of the first E-mu Emulator sampling keyboard: "I spent a delightful evening with FZ at his home in LA . . . Frank introduced me to his entire family, we sampled Moon Unit into the Emulator, and he played me some of the tapes that would become *Shut Up 'n Play Yer Guitar*. He eventually decided not to buy an Emulator (not 'hi-fi' enough) and bought a Synclavier instead, but it remains one of my best E-mu memories."[660] E-mu built around 125 modular systems; the range was discontinued in 1981, by which time digital systems like the Synclavier and the Fairlight had taken over the large synthesizer market.

Towards the end of his life, in June 1992, FZ donated the E-mu to the Musée de Musique in Paris. The original keyboards had been put in storage, and could not be found when the synth cabinets were shipped to France. By the time they turned up, the museum had already built the exhibit, and said that they had no room for them! Eventually all three keyboards were sold in the Joe's Garage sale to synthesizer enthusiast Ivan Schwarz, who sent me photographs of the two that are still in his possession.

The two system cabinets are prominently featured on the wall of the twentieth-century music gallery in the Paris museum. It seems fitting that they are in the company of various percussion instruments and two sirens that belonged to FZ's inspiration, the composer Edgar Varèse. The E-mu brand is still in existence as part of the Creative Labs group, and is probably best known today for the ground breaking Emulator series of samplers, which largely drove the sampling revolution in the 1980s.

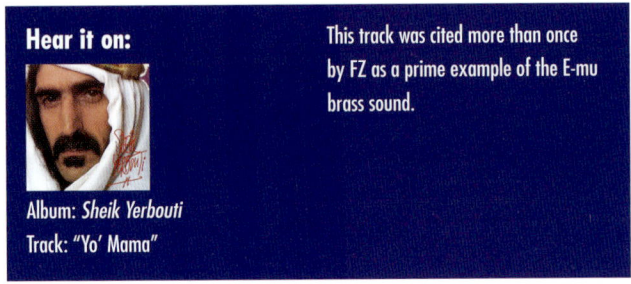

Hear it on:
Album: *Sheik Yerbouti*
Track: "Yo' Mama"

This track was cited more than once by FZ as a prime example of the E-mu brass sound.

YAMAHA CS-80

"I said 'Let me give the CS-80 a try, but it's not going to be like the E-mu,' and it wasn't, it absolutely wasn't. But what it was, was something tremendous"

— Tommy Mars[661]

In January 1979, the FZ band was rehearsing for an intensive two-month tour of Europe. Tommy Mars told FZ that they urgently needed a replacement for the ailing E-Mu synthesizer, and suggested that the Yamaha CS-80 might be suitable.

Yamaha released the CS-80 in 1977; it was in many ways a revolutionary instrument. It was the first polyphonic synthesizer that fit the requirements for professional touring musicians. It was reasonably reliable, transportable (although at 220 lbs. (100 kg) in weight, it needed two people to move it), and at $7,000 did not quite cost the earth (although it was certainly not in the reach of most semi-professional musicians).

The CS-80 was also truly polyphonic, with eight individual voices, each of which had two oscillators. At a time when other so-called polyphonic instruments, such as the ARP Omni, were little more than glorified electric organs, it was unique in this respect.[662]

The twin oscillators available for each note made for a very rich and distinctive sound, and the CS-80 also featured a wooden weighted keyboard with a unique polyphonic aftertouch feature, which allowed the player to modify individual notes by pressing harder on the key after the note had been played. It had twenty-six preset voices, which could be modified to a certain extent, and four programmable voices. These were set up by four miniature copies of the main control panel, normally hidden under a lift-up lid. It also featured a long ribbon controller for pitch bends and glides, a powerful ring modulator, and a comprehensive filter section.[663]

Mars only had three weeks to get to grips with the CS-80 before the tour, but he was soon a big fan of the instrument: "It brought me to a new level of expression, having that marriage of digital and analogue. There were certain things you could do that you could never even hope to do with the E-mu, and more than anything it was reliable."[664]

Mars particularly liked the aftertouch keyboard: "I can remember coming up with a string quartet sound, and it used to just melt Frank, the sensitivity of each finger being able to have a different level of vibrato and volume, and the ring modulation on it was incredible. I used to do so much with the portamento and the ring modulation that you would have needed three or four different instruments before."[665]

The CS-80 was also played by Bob Harris during his time with the band in the late 1980s: "The Yamaha was quite a machine, big and bulky, but state of the art at the time. Tommy Mars developed a horn patch for it that was great."[666]

By the time of FZ's 1984 touring band, more powerful (and considerably lighter) digital synthesizers such as the Yamaha DX series had rendered the CS-80 obsolete, and it was retired from use on the road. However, the responsiveness of the keyboard prompted FZ to experiment with using modified CS-80s as controllers for his E-Mu synthesizer:

"On a more massive scale, there's Frank's $50,000 E-mu modular system . . . He uses it in conjunction with two Yamaha CS-80 synthesizers, which have been modified with log-to-linear converters, enabling the pressure-sensitive CS-80 keyboard to drive the E-mu."[667] See the E-Mu Synthesizer section for more on this.

Yamaha discontinued the CS-80 in 1980; fully working examples are now rare, and expensive to buy and maintain. The French company Arturia produce a respectable software

FZ's touring CS80 serial number 1110
(ZFT)

emulation called the CS-80V,[668] but by all accounts no instrument since has ever sounded quite like the CS-80.

We found one of FZ's CS-80s in storage at Joe's Garage in 2012, still in a large flight case. When we started to remove the lid, we discovered that the foam in the case had perished, and as the resulting fine dust is hazardous, we closed the case immediately. The two CS-80s eventually showed up in the 2016 auction[669], the one illustrated (serial number 1110) showing significant signs of road use. The other model (serial number 1701) was in cleaner condition, looking more or less identical in design but without the control wheels next to the keyboard. They sold for $21,875 and $19,200, respectively.[670]

Tommy Mars in 1981 with (left to right) Yamaha CS-80, Korg VC-10 and ElectroComp 101. Below them is a Fender Rhodes; just in shot at left is the Hammond B3
(still from *The Dub Room Special!*, 1982)

Hear it on:
This track features a typical example of Tommy Mars' CS-80 horn sound.

Album: *You Can't Do That on Stage Anymore, Vol. 6*
Track: "Ms. Pinky"

Pollard Industries Syndrum

"We started doing something on the last tour that I think Pollard is going to be pretty thrilled about when he hears it."

— FZ[671]

Although not the very first drum synthesizer on the market, the Pollard Industries Syndrum was the one that made the instrument popular, and for a while it seemed that every pop record featured it patched to give the effect of bird-like tweets falling in pitch. It was available in various configurations; the most popular was the four-drum Quad unit, which was used by drummer Terry Bozzio and percussionist Ed Mann on various tours in the late 1970s.

The Syndrum was invented by session drummer Joe Pollard and engineer Mark Barton in 1976, who formed Pollard Industries. Joe had been trying to find a way to make his drums heard above loud electric guitars and met Barton, who had already designed and built some electronic drum prototypes.

They formed Pollard Industries and started building Syndrums in South El Monte in California, and soon picked up many celebrity users including Keith Moon and Queen's Roger Taylor.

The Syndrum Quad (also available in single Syndrum and double Syndrum Twin configurations) consisted of four small drums and a bright blue control unit. The set also included a pitchbend foot pedal and a foot-operated kill switch. Each drum consisted of a shallow metal shell with a single 8" diameter head.

Each drum included a trigger, which fired off one of the four sound modules in the control unit (commonly called the "brain"). The unit had two main sliders controlling the master output level and the headphone volume. Each sound module

Terry Bozzio's Quad Syndrum 'brain' in 1977
(still from *Baby Snakes*, 1979)

had sliders for Volume, Sustain, Sweep (pitch variation), Vibrato speed and intensity, and coarse and fine pitch controls. Switches enabled selection of two types of pink noise (snare sounds), sweep rise or fall, and sawtooth, triangle, or square wave.

FZ had Bozzio and Mann use their Syndrums as synthesizers as well as drums: "Terry Bozzio got to be very good with the Syndrum; he can control them fantastically well and still be playing his set. . . . if you put the sustain on the Syndrum up to a very long time, you can hit it and get like a constant pitch coming out. And if you move the little knob, you can play tunes on it. So I had chorales between the two keyboard players and the two Syndrums . . . all I did was conduct a downbeat, and anybody could hit any note they wanted on that downbeat. And every time I'd conduct a beat, they'd pick another note. The results were fantastic."[672]

Once again, FZ not only embraced a new technology but also persuaded the manufacturer to extend it to the limit. He had Pollard Industries build him a custom Syndrum module that could be triggered by the voltage control output that he had built into his Hammond organ. This enabled Tommy Mars to produce runs as if he had sixty-one tuned Syndrums: "To have the Syndrums on the organ was incredible, and a lot of times people didn't know that I was making that sound; they would think it would be the Syndrums, but it was actually coming from the organ."[673]

The Syndrum was expensive ($1700 for a quad set), and although it was used by a good number of name drummers, the company did not make much money. After a couple of years Pollard and Barton sold the business to Research Development Systems Inc., who produced a couple of improved versions and a budget Syndrum unit, called the CM, but within a few years they had gone out of business.[674]

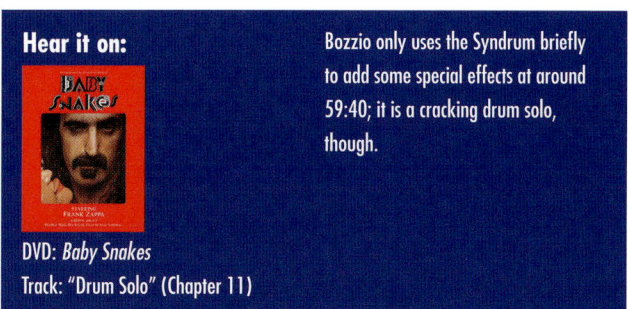

Hear it on:
DVD: *Baby Snakes*
Track: "Drum Solo" (Chapter 11)

Bozzio only uses the Syndrum briefly to add some special effects at around 59:40; it is a cracking drum solo, though.

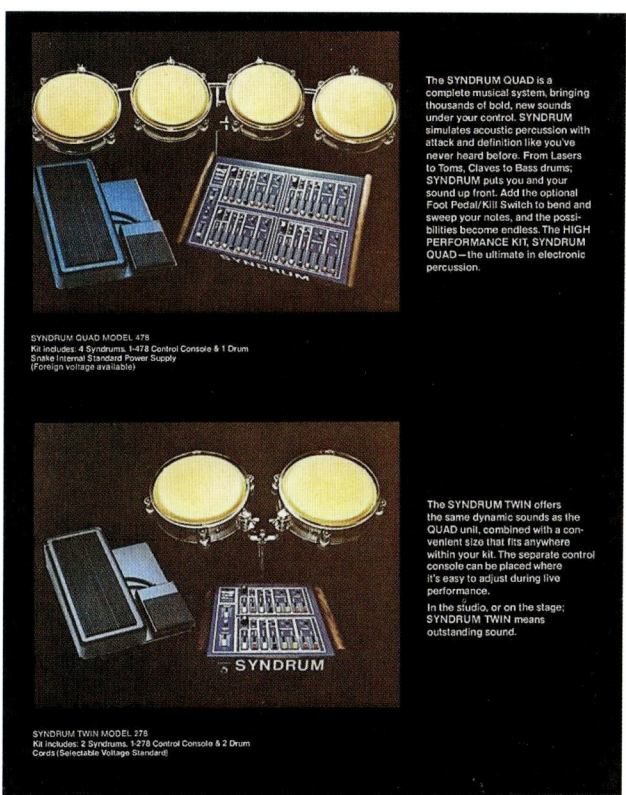

The Quad and Twin systems from the RDSI Syndrum catalogue

Terry Bozzio and Ed Mann were both endorsees

ZAPPA GEAR

Synclavier

"What I've been waiting for ever since I started writing music was a chance to hear what I wrote played back without mistakes and without a bad attitude. The Synclavier solves the problem for me."

—FZ[675]

In late 1983, FZ took delivery of a piece of musical equipment that profoundly revolutionized his methods of composing and realizing music. As he said, the New England Digital Synclavier was what he had been waiting for all his musical life; or putting it another way: "Forget about the orchestra. It's beyond the orchestra. Because what this enables me to do is the same thing a painter gets to do. You get to deal with the material in a real and instantaneous way. You go boop and it's there."[676]

The Synclavier was invented by Jon Appleton, a Dartmouth College music professor and experimental composer; Sydney Alonso, a digital electronics specialist at Dartmouth's engineering school; and Cameron Jones, a bass player and engineering student with a talent for writing software.

Originally trying to develop something to allow students to save and restore patches for the college's massive Moog synthesizer, the three ended up producing an early microcomputer with limited music synthesis abilities called ABLE. When Jones graduated in 1974, they formed New England Digital (NED) to market it, setting up in Norwich, Vermont.

After several years of research and development, they produced the original Synclavier in 1977, which was the first portable computer-based synthesizer that could be controlled from a keyboard. It also included a sixteen-track sequencer—the first to use multiple tracks, enabling a piece of music with multiple voices to be replayed at will.

The Synclavier was officially launched in 1978, with a price of $13,000. In the first year, they only sold a dozen or so, mostly to universities and research institutions. They were considering closing the company when they met with composer and analogue synthesizer fan Denny Jaeger. He persuaded them to let him take a Synclavier back to his base in California to see if he could improve it.

Jaeger worked on improving the sound synthesis capabilities of the instrument while the NED team worked on the software and hardware. By 1980, the instrument had been completely reborn as the Synclavier 2. It contained 256 preset sounds, including a very credible violin sound and other orchestral instruments, as well as totally unique voices. The sequencer could store fifty-four minutes of music, and it also included software to turn the notes played into printed standard notation. Jaeger was probably right when he called it "the most advanced digital machine in the world." The Synclavier was launched at the May 1980 Audio Engineering Society in Los Angeles. At the same show, the Linn LM1 drum machine and the Fairlight CMI synthesizer were unveiled—the digital music age had well and truly arrived![677]

NED had decided to go for the very high end of the electronic music market, intending to sell the product to film and recording studios, science and educational faculties, and very rich rock stars. The first Synclavier system that FZ bought cost around $250,000!

Hear it on:
As David Ocker says in the CD notes, "Listen along next time you feel the urge to wear a powdered wig."

Album: *Francesco Zappa*
Track: "Opus IV: No. 1 1st Movement: Andantino"

NED made no compromises when they built the Synclavier keyboard; the red illuminated buttons were famously the same as those used on the console of the B52 bomber. This may have seemed like a marketing ploy to help justify the phenomenal price of these units, but it was an inspired choice. As Synclavier consultant Steve Hills put it, "Musicians are notorious for bullying machinery. Cigarette ash, soft drinks, beer, sweaty fingers, and temper tantrums all add up to a tough life for a keyboard. NED, with a stroke of brilliance, went to the military for a button that was fast acting, sensitive, could be viewed from any angle in any ambient light, but didn't blind the user in the darkened smoke-filled late night studio session, and above all took punishment."[678]

The heart of the system was a computer called ABLE, built around the RCA 1802 microprocessor and designed by NED specifically for the purpose of music and sound production. For the time it was very efficient at moving around the large amounts of data required for digital sound manipulation, and had a very advanced mathematics coprocessor. It is commonly reported that a modified ABLE design was used by NASA on the Galileo space probe, resulting in it being treated as classified

FZ and his Synclavier work station at the UMRK
(still from At Home With Frank Zappa, 1989)

Keyboards and Synthesizers

FZ's Synclavier keyboard at the UMRK in 2012
(Mick Ekers)

The top of the Synclavier unit and the Sample to Disc recording unit
(Mick Ekers)

computer equipment, with restrictions on its sale outside the United States. This is apparently why you won't find any service manuals around.[679] I've been unable to confirm this, but certainly the Galileo computers were based on the RCA 1802.

One thing that users did get for their money was a continuously evolving system. NED built the Synclavier like a small mainframe computer (which in effect it was), using a modular design with each function on a separate card. This made it easy for memory, disk drives, and peripheral devices to be upgraded, and new features could readily be retrofitted to older Synclaviers. NED frequently produced new versions of the software programs; again, these were designed to be backward-compatible with older systems.

By the time FZ bought his, they had added a computer terminal with bespoke software programs: Script, Music Printing, and G Page (you could only program the original models with the piano keyboard and buttons.). "There are three different ways to type in. One is in a language called Script . . . but that's more like writing a computer program, so it has no charm for me. Another way is with their Music Printing program. You can enter or delete notes with the cursor while looking at real music on staves . . . . The third way to type is a facility called the G Page. The screen is split into three columns; the left-hand one tells you the start time of the note, the center column gives you the name of the pitch and a number which tells you the octave that the pitch lives in. And the right-hand column gives you the duration. All that is editable, so you can move the cursor around, add and delete notes, change start times, which changes the rhythm, and change the pitch and the octave and how long the note lasts. I divide my time between doing stuff on the G Page and doing stuff in the Music Printing."[680]

FZ's first recorded used of the Synclavier was on the *Thing Fish* album. In 1987 he told *Keyboard* magazine: "Listen to the 'Crabgrass Baby' track, which opens up Act II. The background vocals are a repeated vocal chant with this computer voice singing over it, and they were our first attempt at stereo sampling using the mono system."

The massive main Synclavier case
(Mick Ekers)

163

ZAPPA GEAR

The Synclavier keyboard flight case
(Mick Ekers)

FZ's first full Synclavier project was the *Francesco Zappa* album, a collection of baroque string trios written by his eighteenth-century namesake. His assistant David Ocker typed the music into the system and then FZ arranged it using the Synclavier's built in synthesizer tones. He later said: "it was written for two violins and an upright bass . . . even if I had suitable synthesizer replicas for those instruments, I'm not sure that would have made the most interesting album. So I just added a little Technicolor to it and let the music speak for itself."[681]

Over the next two years significantly more complicated pieces were produced for the *Perfect Stranger* and *Mothers of Prevention* albums, and by 1986, FZ and his team had started to get the measure of the instrument. FZ had upgraded his original system, which now had 56 voices, 24 MB of RAM, two 80 MB Winchesters and a 20 MB Winchester.[682] FZ spent eight months producing his next album, the Grammy award–winning *Jazz from Hell*.

By this time, he had started using sophisticated combinations of sampled and synthesized sounds, resulting in unique sonic effects. FZ explains how the lead voice was produced for the track "Night School": "It's a stereo sample, a combination of trumpet with pitchbend and grand piano. The piano notes are not short. They attack, and then as they ring off, you get to hear an unusual noise, which is the acoustic piano playing bends. That's a real easy thing to do on the Synclavier."[683]

In 1987, FZ decided to take a band out on the road again, for what turned out to be his last tour. He decided, with some trepidation, that the Synclavier was going to come along for the ride: "It's a massively complicated rehearsal problem, in order to make it work invariably night after night. That's the main thing that concerns me about taking it out; when you take things on the road, they do break. Guys do drop them, and that's a big worry. If you have a very technologically oriented show, you have to carry spares. And the problem about carrying a spare Synclavier is it's a quarter of a million dollars."[684]

I found the flight case for the keyboard at Joe's Garage, bearing a red sticker saying, "Delicate instruments, Don't Drop." FZ's fears about the instrument proved groundless.

Merl Saunders, Jr. told me that FZ brought along his own Synclavier tech and "It never went down; I mean that was one thing. Bob wasn't the keyboard tech, he just did the Synclavier. And basically, Frank would put shit together and he would sit and edit stuff in the afternoon and then it may have been in the show that night."[685]

Saunders used it as a very expensive tuning fork: "I had a Peterson Strobe (electronic instrument tuner) that I would tune from the Synclavier, and then I would calibrate all the other tuners to the Peterson. So basically, the horns and everybody else took their tuning from me!" The Synclavier was used both for special effects and musical loops that FZ could trigger from the keyboard: "there were always like orchestral parts within there and I think he had them set up as loops so they would play four-bar patterns." One tune was on the Synclavier in its entirety: "I think the only song that was on it was 'Yo Cats,' like the entire thing was on there. So whenever they played 'Yo Cats,' they played it to the Synclavier. I mean the whole thing except for the drums, because I remember Chad would play to a click track."[686]

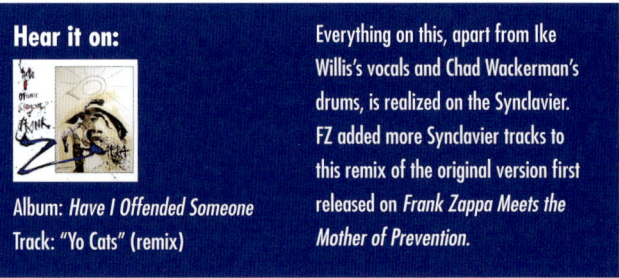

Hear it on:
Album: *Have I Offended Someone*
Track: "Yo Cats" (remix)

Everything on this, apart from Ike Willis's vocals and Chad Wackerman's drums, is realized on the Synclavier. FZ added more Synclavier tracks to this remix of the original version first released on *Frank Zappa Meets the Mother of Prevention*.

Of course, it turned out that it was not the instruments but the humans that were the problem on this tour, and as is well known, the band blew up and FZ cancelled the tour midway through. When he got back to LA he needed a new Synclavier programmer and assistant, and hired Todd Yvega, who NED had recommended.

Yvega owned his own Synclavier and had plenty of experience working on soundtracks for TV shows: "Actually his system was pretty archaic when I started here; I ended up lending him mine, because it had stereo voices in it and his didn't."[687] Yvega continues: "And, in fact even when the Ensemble Modern was in town, we were using my system and there was a lot of mixing up of the parts."

"And right about his fiftieth birthday, Gail made a rather substantial purchase of a completely upgraded system for him that was just everything but the kitchen sink. And at that point I think he had the largest Synclavier in the world in terms of total memory and voices and all that sort of thing. But some of it never worked; it was just too big. It couldn't get the power, or over-heated too easily, something like that."[688] The upgrade did indeed make it the world's largest integrated composition, sampling, and production system for digital recording. With the addition of six MegaRAM 64 MB sample memory cards and a custom expansion chassis for 32 additional voices, Zappa's

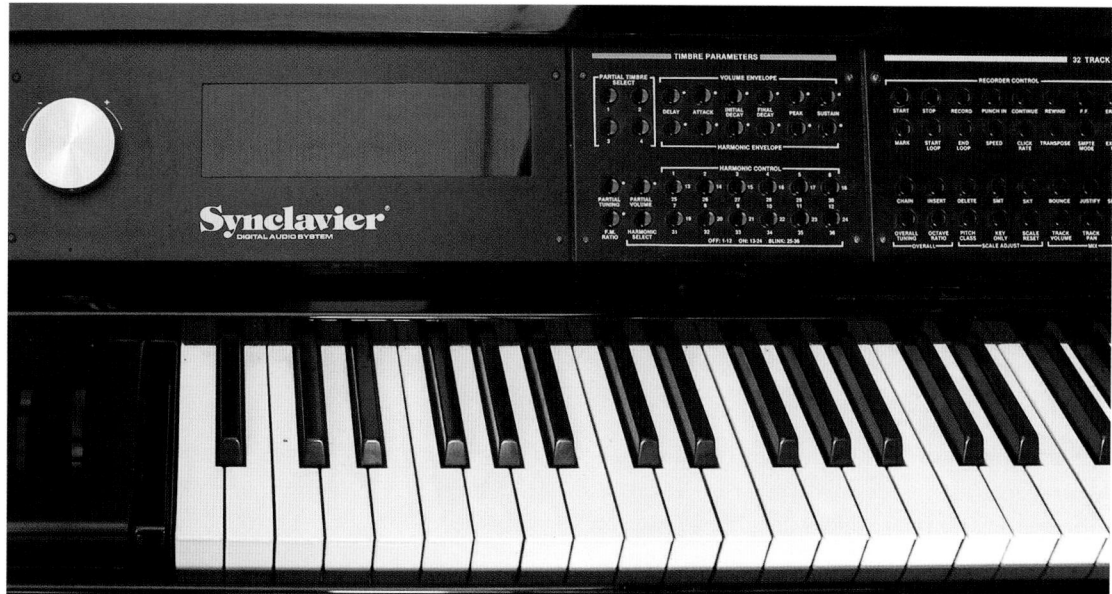

The big control knob and LED display of FZ's 'V/PK' Synclavier keyboard at the UMRK in 2012 (Mick Ekers)

Synclavier 9600 system boasted 128 voices and 384 MB of sampling RAM.[689]

FZ used the Synclavier almost exclusively in his final years, producing an enormous amount of material. Major projects were the albums *Yellow Shark*, *Civilization Phaze III*, and *Dance Me This*. Other Synclavier pieces were used as the soundtrack to the Cousteau Society documentary *Alaska: Outrage at Valdez*.

As well as giving him total control over the notes played and how they sounded, the Synclavier also changed the way FZ composed. Pieces could now continuously evolve thanks to the non-destructive editing facilities of the Synclavier (the original version of an edit was retained). A piece could be written, realized, and saved to tape, but later on it might be edited or extended, remixed, parts assigned to different samples, and so forth. As Todd Yvega points out in the sleeve notes to the *Feeding the Monkies at Ma Maison* CD, FZ rarely considered a piece complete; his tape recordings were often just an interim or draft version of a piece.

In 1992, NED went out of business. FZ had advised them some years earlier that they should widen their product range: "Well, I gave a suggestion to one of their guys that they ought to give some thought to the low end of the consumer spectrum. I have nothing but praise for the device, except for the fact that it's as expensive as *** . . . if you were to get a Michael Jackson–size unit, you could spend close to half a million dollars, and that limits the number of units worldwide that you can sell. That's why they ought to think about doing something less expensive, so that they can stay in business long enough that they can repair it when it goes down. I'm thinking ten or fifteen years down the road, because I expect to still have this thing and still be making music on it, and if there is no NED down the road, then what have you got?"[690]

Brandon Amison of Synclavier specialists Yaking Cat Studios gives his perspective on NED's pricing strategy and business overheads: "The prices on Synclaviers were based on two primary factors. Those who owned the machine or needed parts generally had money to burn, so to speak. NED took advantage of this. Second, there were about eleven guys at the top of the company pulling down six-figure incomes. Sting was paid to perform for the NED employees and their spouses at a big gala at the Roxy in New York. There were NED offices across the globe with marble desks. Spend, spend, spend. And make your customers pick up the tab."[691] Once NED started losing market share, they increasingly targeted the film studio market, dropping support for such features as music printing and guitar interfaces. However, it was not enough to save the company.

When I visited the UMRK, I found that the Synclavier was not currently in a working configuration. The keyboard was safely wrapped up on a shelf in the studio, and the two massive rack units containing the Synclavier itself were in a small closet at the back of the control room. I didn't have a wide enough angle lens on my camera to take a single picture of the Synclavier; the 9600 case was so tall that NED put massive lead weights in the bottom to keep it from tipping over. On top of the main case was the Sample to Disc recording unit.

The keyboard unit was the second-generation 76-note V/PK model. This stood for Velocity/Pressure Keyboard, which could be played expressively; the first version was not touch-sensitive. The first thing I noticed was the sheer weight and quality of the V/PK; it has a black lacquered finish to rival FZ's Bösendorfer piano, and a beautiful keyboard with heavy wooden keys, accented with a traditional red felt strip attached to the fall board.

To the left of the keys are pitch and modulation wheels, and immediately above is a ribbon controller. On the left of

ZAPPA GEAR

The back panel of the Synclavier keyboard
(Mick Ekers)

the control panel is a large silver control knob. This was used to vary whatever parameter had been selected. Next to this is a large 32-character LED display window, and then five panels, each with a bank of 32 buttons. The panels are logically grouped by function; panel one is used to create synthesized sounds or modify sampled sounds, panels two and three control the 32-track sequencer, panel four is used to store and recall sounds and sequences, and panel five controls keyboard effects and modifies synthesized and sampled sounds.[692]

Yvega told me how much he liked the feel of the instrument: "with the weighted keyboard and all that, I just always liked that tactile . . . y'know; the buttons were big, the knob was big, you weren't like on a computer with a mouse trying to get into some microscopic area and pull down a menu. It was all about (taps fingers frantically on the table) touching really fast with your fingers, it was muscle memory. It was like playing a guitar."[693]

I talked to Yvega about the Synclavier sounds having a distinct, almost analogue feel to them: "Yeah, it had a certain something. They did have a kind of brute-force approach; they actually would change the sample-rate playback to change the pitch, whereas the Fairlight just did some in-software resampling and kept a constant rate. And there was no dithering; they didn't have any jitter control. Sydney Alonso later said that 'I realize now, we did this wrong,' but that's what gave the Synclavier its character; it did have a certain sound to it that I personally liked. I thought it was just good and ballsy."[694]

Over the years various companies have provided servicing and repair facilities, and there are still several working Synclaviers around the world to this day.

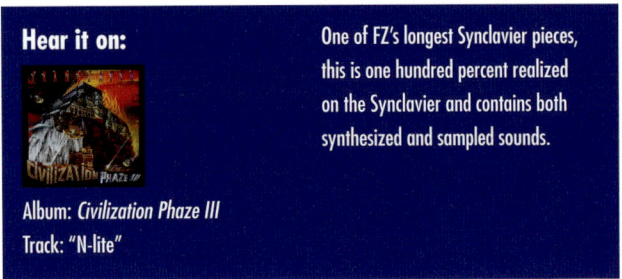

Hear it on:
Album: *Civilization Phaze III*
Track: "N-lite"

One of FZ's longest Synclavier pieces, this is one hundred percent realized on the Synclavier and contains both synthesized and sampled sounds.

ROLAND PAD-8 OCTAPAD

"You can do interesting things with this Roland device called an Octapad"
— FZ[695]

Introduced in 1985, the Roland Corporation's PAD-8 Octapad was the world's first MIDI-compatible percussion controller. It did not have any built-in sounds; it was designed purely to control an external synthesizer module. Roland got the size and configuration right the first time: the eight square touch-sensitive pads were large enough to be usable with either sticks or hands, but the unit was compact enough (520 mm by 330 mm) to fit in a briefcase.

Eight pads were enough to simulate a full drum kit, but could also control a useful array of ethnic percussion sounds, or an octave of tuned percussion. The Octapad could be mounted on a stand, so that drummers could easily add it to their conventional drum set, usually placing it to the left of the hi-hat cymbal.

As well as drum machines, the Octapad could control any MIDI sound source, including synthesizers like the Synclavier. The sensitivity and other parameters could be individually adjusted for each pad. Up to four different patches could be saved in the unit's memory, and the rear panel included six inputs for connecting additional Octapads or other external controllers, such as bass drum or hi-hat pedals.

Launched only two years after the MIDI specification came out, the Octapad was a groundbreaking development in the field of electronic percussion, and was very popular with drummers looking to tap into the digital musical revolution. FZ's drummer Chad Wackerman had an Octapad as part of his onstage kit on the 1988 tour.

Many synth-pop bands of the time would feature the unit on its own, with a wistful looking singer standing behind one, tapping out "post-modern" rhythmic patterns. The Octapad rapidly became a standard piece of equipment for any modern drummer.

FZ recalled Wackerman introducing him to the Octapad: "Chad, our drummer, brought one over the other day and I

Keyboards and Synthesizers

The Octapad in Chad Wackerman's kit in 1988
(*still from* En directo desde Barcelona, Frank Zappa, *1988*)

Early Roland advert for the Octapad
(Author's collection)

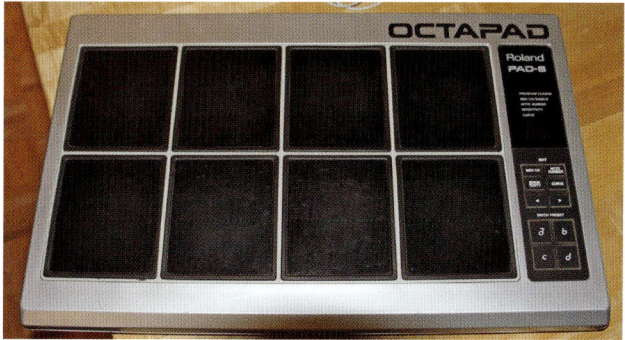

FZ's Octapad at the UMRK in 2012
(Mick Ekers)

plugged it into the Synclavier. I started out as a drummer, so I can fluke around on it, do little flams and stuff like that. With it, you can enter types of rhythms that are impossible to do on the keyboard."[696]

Immediately realizing the potential of the device, FZ didn't restrict its use to drum sounds. He told *Electronic Musician*, "... this Roland device called an Octapad, which is just this little set of plastic squares that you hit with a stick and it has a MIDI output on it. So if you have any percussion technique at all, you can do rolls on the pad, and roll a percussion sample in the machine; or if you have a mandolin sample, you can trill the mandolin. This (Synclavier) keyboard doesn't speak very well for fast repeated notes, but one buzz roll with sticks on an Octapad will let you enter that kind of data into the sequencer."[697]

He made good use of it on his Grammy award–winning *Jazz from Hell* album, on which all the Synclavier parts were either typed directly into the console, or performed on the Synclavier keyboard and Roland Octapads.[698] FZ also used an Octapad on stage—for some dates on the 1988 tour he had one set up next to the Synclavier and used it to play samples with drumsticks during the number "Pound for a Brown." Guitarist Mike Keneally noted: "That was a neat portion of the show which got people in the audience going 'hoo-wa, hoo-wa!'"[699]

While I was interviewing Todd Yvega about his time as FZ's Synclavier programmer, we were both equally delighted when he noticed an original Octapad, tucked away on its side on a shelf in the UMRK control room: "Holy cow! That's the Octapad! . . . We used this all the time." [700]

Yvega remembered; "He'd (FZ) call you to come up and just play these amazing things on the Octapad, and then he would apply tone-rows to them and turn them into melodies and things with the rhythm of Vinnie (Colaiuta)."[701] Yvega explained that once something was entered into the Synclavier in this way it could be reverse compiled to overcome the limitations of the Octapad's eight notes; "You could turn it into text, where you had the time the note starts, the pitch, the duration, velocity and whatever, and then you could use some word-processing tools that would superimpose other pitches on the ones that were there, so that you could take some very interesting thing that was done with a lot of nuance in it, and apply tone-rows."[702]

Roland later extended the Octapad to include built-in drum sounds, and introduced a new version, the SPD-30, which still follows the same basic physical design of the original.[703]

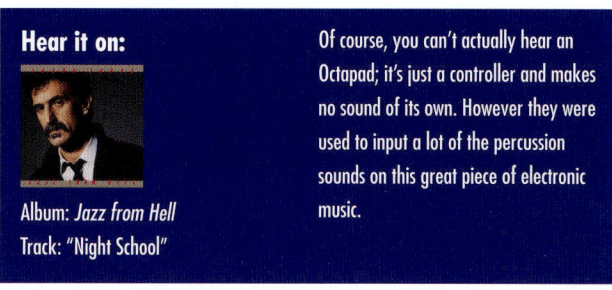

Hear it on:
Album: *Jazz from Hell*
Track: "Night School"

Of course, you can't actually hear an Octapad; it's just a controller and makes no sound of its own. However they were used to input a lot of the percussion sounds on this great piece of electronic music.

Roland Super Jupiter

"Hooked together, the MKS80 and MPG80 were exactly what the name 'Super Jupiter' suggested. They were the business."
—Sound on Sound Magazine[704]

Tucked into a corner in the UMRK, next to FZ's Bösendorfer piano, I spotted a wooden rack full of black Roland Synthesizer modules. Todd Yvega told me that FZ used this as an outboard device for his Synclavier, as an alternative to the native Synclavier samples.[705] The rack contained an MKS-80 Super Jupiter, an MPG-80 Super Jupiter Programmer, and an MKS-20 Digital Piano.

Launched in 1984, the MKS-80 was Roland's eagerly awaited follow-up to the popular Jupiter 8 synthesizer, and it caused some consternation when it turned out to be just a rack unit with no keyboard. Roland launched their ground-breaking Total Midi System that year, which consisted of two dedicated controller keyboards, the MKB-1000 and MKB-3000, and a set of separate rack units designed to go with them, including the MKS-80, MPG-80, and MKS-20.

The MKS-80 was an eight-voice polyphonic synthesizer module with 16 VCOs (Voltage controlled Oscillators). It had a memory capacity that could store 64 different patches, and the optional M-64C Memory Cartridge could hold an additional 192. It could be used as a standalone sound module, but the only way to program in sounds was to laboriously enter each parameter one-by one using the 16 buttons on the front panel.

Fortunately for musicians used to the sliders and knobs on their all-in-one synthesizers, Roland also made a dedicated programmer unit called the MPG-80, which had a reassuring array of sliders and knobs for adjusting the waveform, envelope, and all the other components of a synthesized sound. Put together,

FZ's rack of Roland Synth Modules at the UMRK in 2012. Not shown in the picture is a Korg 3-M immediately above the MPG-80. This was one of the later generation of digital sound modules, and was not introduced until 1989, possibly the date when the rack was built (Mick Ekers)

the two units made a very powerful combination, and formed one of the last great analogue synthesizers.

The MKS-20 Digital Piano was the world's first MIDI piano module, and had four sounds each for piano, clavichord, harpsichord, and electric piano, plus various onboard sound effects such as chorus and tremolo. This may seem a limited range, but bear in mind that the MKS-20, like the MKS-80, was a purely analogue device.[706]

FZ had no need for the Roland keyboards; with his Synclavier's new MIDI capabilities, he could just connect it directly to the MKS-80 and MKS-20. The possibilities of the new MIDI interface were truly revolutionary at the time, and FZ seized on the possibilities with glee, at one stage considering adding a Fairlight to his system: "Now that the Synclavier has MIDI, you can have it drive the Fairlight. You can breed 'em."[707]

Roland were the first company to separate sound-producing systems from performance devices, something that seems commonplace now, but was not feasible before the advent of MIDI.[708] Before long a whole host of ever-more powerful keyboards and sound modules would appear from every synthesizer manufacturer, and digital devices soon supplanted analogue modules. The MKS-80 was discontinued in 1987, which marked the end of the analogue era for Roland.

LinnDrum

"In fact, one of the things we did recently was to overdub a set of drums on some tapes which were originally done with the Linn rhythm box."
—FZ[709]

In the early 1980s, FZ often recorded tracks with just one or two musicians at a time playing along with a drum machine, finally getting the drums overdubbed by a real drummer. He described the process as follows: "I would program the drum box and I've got at least twenty hours of very complicated drum tracks on reels of tape. So I would make up the drum parts and bring in a bass player and have him play on top of that and add some chord changes to it, write a melody to that, write some words to that, and add the drums last. And then maybe redo the bass and we have a synthesizer which can take care of all keyboard and horn parts."[710]

FZ felt that this was the most efficient way to concentrate on getting the best sound and performance out of each musician. From 1982 onwards, it would be the LinnDrum that he used for this purpose; for the first time, he had a programmable device that sounded something like a real drum set.

Arthur Barrow remembered FZ using this process on "Tink Walks Amok" for *The Man from Utopia* album: "We started with a drum machine beat and started layering parts on top of that."[711]

Keyboards and Synthesizers

Linn Electronics were never afraid of bold advertising claims. At the time of this advertisement, they were probably right
(Author's collection)

fig04-20-02.jpg
(Mick Ekers)

Front and rear views of FZ's LinnDrum at the UMRK in 2012
(Mick Ekers)

The LinnDrum was the brainchild of American musician, inventor, and engineer Roger Linn. Linn started his career in musical technology in the early 1970s, when in high school he started modifying and selling fuzz boxes, and installing pickups and electronics in guitars as an after-school job.

An accomplished guitarist and songwriter, he started thinking about building a drum machine to help him record song demos: "I could play guitar and bass and fake it on keyboards, but drums were always the hardest part to both play and record. The only drum machines at the time were non-programmable and sounded like crickets. I wanted to create something that sounded real and was programmable."[712] He built his first prototype in 1976, and by 1979, he had set up Linn Electronics in Hollywood to sell the original LM-1 drum machine.

The LM-1 was genuinely revolutionary, the first programmable drum machine to use recorded samples of a real drummer rather than using synthesized drum sounds (the samples were mostly recorded by LA session drummer Art Wood).[713] It cost $5,000 and around 500 were made, selling mainly to the good and the great of the rock and pop business. Demand was such that after making the first batch, Linn engaged Bob Easton's 360 Sounds to manufacture the LM-1.

In 1982, the LinnDrum was introduced as the successor to the LM-1, selling for around $3,000. As well as being somewhat more affordable, the LinnDrum expanded upon the LM-1 by adding crash and ride cymbals (not available on the LM-1 because the cymbal samples would have taken up too much memory), greater sample lengths, and five live drum-trigger inputs. Different sets of drum samples were available, which could be switched by opening the lid and changing the sound chips in their sockets!

The programming system featured innovative functions such as Error Correction (now known as quantization) whereby manually input drum beats could be moved to the nearest correct fraction of a beat, and a variable Swing option allowing a shuffle feel to be introduced to a track. Drum tracks could be entered digitally as a sequence of numbers, or recorded in real time by tapping out beats on the unit's buttons.

Each of the 15 drums could be mixed and panned separately, and each had its own individual output, as well as feeding into the master stereo outputs. Five trigger inputs allowed selected drums to be controlled by external devices.

The LinnDrum came with 42 prerecorded drum patterns, and it could hold another 54 in memory; complete tracks could be recorded on audio cassette tapes (in the same way as computer programs were on some of the earliest microcomputers). About 5000 of the new units were sold, and it is fair to say that they set the tone of 1980s popular music, being used on countless popular records. In addition to FZ, other users of note were Prince, Madonna, Michael Jackson, Stevie Wonder, and many more.[714]

When FZ recorded the snappy instrumental track "We Are Not Alone" on *The Man from Utopia*, he laid down a

LinnDrum track that was not subsequently overdubbed, and credited himself on the album sleeve as playing LinnDrum. The track rattles along in a jolly and not noticeably mechanical way, and the drums sound good enough to fool most casual listeners. I can imagine FZ wondering if there was anything around that would let him program a whole band in a similar way . . . which of course there was: see the Synclavier section.

Linn Electronics closed down in 1986, due to competition from cheaper Japanese products, and Linn worked for Akai for many years designing various sequencers and similar devices including the legendary MPC, which was crucial to the development of hip-hop music. In 2002, Linn formed Roger Linn Design, "a small business engaged in the design, manufacture, and sales of high-tech products for musicians," based in Berkeley, California. They market the advanced Tempest drum machine, designed by Linn and Dave Smith, originally intended to be known as the LinnDrum II.[715]

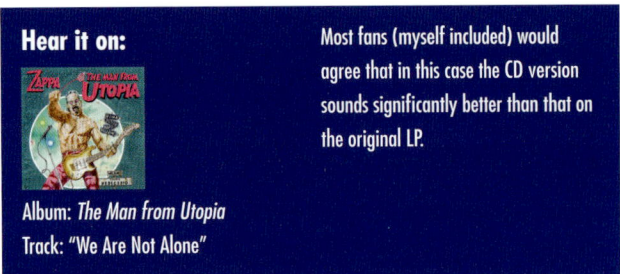

Hear it on:
Album: *The Man from Utopia*
Track: "We Are Not Alone"

Most fans (myself included) would agree that in this case the CD version sounds significantly better than that on the original LP.

Bösendorfer 290 Imperial Grand Piano

"I think of the piano as some sort of an elaborate percussion instrument"
— FZ[716]

FZ and Nicolas Slonimsky at the Bösendorfer
(still from A Touch Of Genius, 1994)

The Bösendorfer at the UMRK in 2012
(Mick Ekers)

FZ did a large part of his composing and arranging at the piano, and so always liked to keep one at home. Never a skilled keyboard player, he admitted: "I'm a plunker! I couldn't even imagine what it would be like to play the piano,"[717] and often he would engage keyboard players from his band, such as Ian Underwood, to play the parts he had written.

While he was living in his first house in LA, the famous Log Cabin, FZ just had a rented grand piano,[718] but when he started building the UMRK studio at his new house, he could afford to buy his own, and the studio gave him the space and justification to obtain a top-quality concert instrument.

Typically, this would not just be any grand piano; he went for the Bösendorfer 290 Imperial Grand piano, one of the best and most expensive production pianos in the world.

The Bösendorfer 290 was the only piano in production at the time that had nine extra notes at the low end of the keyboard, giving a full eight-octave range (the lowest note being C, while on a regular piano the lowest note is A). To avoid confusing players used to regular 88-key pianos, the top surfaces of the additional "white" notes are finished in black. This huge beast of an instrument is 9'6" long; the model number 290 is the length in centimeters.

The lowest note, technically known as Double Pedal C, has a frequency of just over 16 Hz (cycles per second); this is almost an octave below the lowest note on a 5-string bass guitar. This is just on the lower limit of the hearing range for humans, and will be felt as much as heard. For most of us, this is well beyond the capability of our hi-fi systems to reproduce.

The Bösendorfer piano company was established in Vienna by Ignaz Bösendorfer on the 25th of July, 1828, joining around 150 other piano builders in the city. Bösendorfer set about increasing the volume of the Viennese style of piano, which necessitated a more stable construction and stronger stringing. The company soon earned a reputation as the premier Viennese piano manufacturer, with a welcome endorsement by the composer Liszt who wrote, "The perfection of a Bösendorfer exceeds my

Keyboards and Synthesizers

FZ's Bösendorfer 290 Imperial Grand Piano
(7FT)

most ideal expectations . . . . " In 1839, Emperor Ferdinand I granted Bösendorfer the title of Imperial and Royal Fortepiano Purveyor to the Court.[719]

The company passed into the hands of Ignaz's son Ludwig in 1859, who saw the company adopt many key technological advances in piano design: the cast iron frame, cross stringing (the upper and lower ranges of strings are overlaid to save space and allow for wider strings to be used), and a special grand piano action. Around 1900, the composer Ferruccio Busoni commissioned a special concert grand, with a range extending to the low C that he required for his piano transcriptions of Bach's organ works. The Model 290 Imperial, as it was known, became the company's flagship piano, and can be found in many of the great concert halls of the world.[720]

In early 1981, FZ befriended the eighty-seven-year-old composer, conductor, and musician Nikolas Slonimsky after reading his *Thesaurus of Scales and Melodic Patterns*. FZ invited him to his studio and Slonimsky recalled, "Zappa led me to his studio, which housed a huge Bösendorfer piano. I asked how much he paid for this keyboard monster. 'Seventy,' he replied . . . . Zappa invited me to try out his Bösendorfer. I sat down at the keyboard and played the coronation scene from *Boris Gudunov*, which required deep bass sounds. Zappa was impressed by these Russian harmonies."[721] FZ later remembered the occasion: " . . . nobody has ever played that piano as loud as that man—and not jumping up and down like a madman, just from the strength of his arms and his spirit."[722]

Even when they are not being played, the extra low strings of the 290 add an extra deep reverberant quality to the instrument. FZ took advantage of these qualities in the summer of 1991, when he revisited a technique that he first used on the *Lumpy Gravy* album in 1967: "One day I decided to . . . cover it [the piano] with a heavy drape, put a sandbag on the sustain bottle and invite anybody in the vicinity to stick their head inside and ramble incoherently." He combined some of the 1967 material with the fresh dialogue recorded inside the Bösendorfer on his album *Civilization Phaze III*.[723]

FZ also sampled the Bösendorfer for his Synclavier: "Later, Zappa oversees and, with an acute ear, monitors two of his trusted studio workers, mix engineer Spencer Chrislu and Synclavier operator Todd Yvega, while they painstakingly sample all the notes on Zappa's 97-key Bösendorfer Grand Imperial piano"[724]—so it may be heard on some of his Synclavier pieces.

When we visited the UMRK in 2012 it was tucked away in one corner of the studio, spending most of its time safely covered in a padded dustsheet, but it was occasionally wheeled out in the middle of the live room for recording sessions. I am not a keyboard player, but when I saw it could not resist just playing the low C on its own. It sounded marvelous! FZ's bass player Scott Thunes was particularly enamored of this beautiful instrument: "I've asked Gail to give me the Bösendorfer, at least ten times, and she keeps on saying no!"[725] The Bösendorfer (serial number 32606) was sold in the 2016 auction for $115,200.

The Bösendorfer Company was purchased by the Yamaha Corporation in 2008, and is still making the 290 and other models in Austria, in much the same way that they were made over 100 years ago. Each piano takes about a year to produce.

Guitar Synthesizers

"The system really was six-channel stereo, and if you panned it out, you had a six-channel spectrum, you strummed a chord and it would all happen in glorious Technicolor."

—FZ[726]

There was a time in the mid-1970s when it seemed that the next revolution in music technology was going to be the guitar synthesizer. Never a keyboard player, FZ was, like many guitarists at the time, optimistic about the prospects of being able to drive a synthesizer with a guitar, and tried several of the systems that came along. In April 1975, he was asked if the guitar synthesizer would become popular: "I'm sure it will one day, but there's a lot of technical things wrong with it and it's not my idea of a good time."[727]

Hear it on:

Album: *Beat the Boots III – Disc Two*
Track: "Falling in Love Is a Stupid Habit"

This is the only known recording of FZ playing the Bösendorfer. It was recorded in 1981 for Jimmy Carl Black (you can hear his voice at the start saying "You ought to do it man . . . ") on Black's portable cassette recorder.

ZAPPA GEAR

360 Systems Polyphonic Guitar Synthesizer

One of the first systems that FZ seriously experimented with was the 360 Systems Polyphonic Guitar synthesizer. This would have been at some time in 1976, and it was built by his old friend Bob Easton, who had made him the Electro Wagnerian Emancipator some years before. The system was built around a set of six frequency follower circuits, one for each string, which converted the notes played to voltages that could drive a synthesizer like FZ's new E-mu system.

Special guitar pickups with a separate output for each string were required for this, and this work was given to Rex Bogue, who had already been experimenting with rebuilt Stratocaster pickups with six individual coils. Jim Williams remembers: "We made those six-coil pickups, and we put one of those in the bridge. We just popped it in where the lead pickup was and there you go, and we'd put some big honkin' multipin connector on the side and wired the outputs of that separately to the expander module. We created pretty much the first polyphonic guitar synthesizer that way. It drifted a lot, it was hard to stay in tune, but it was the first time it was ever done. Yeah, that was cool stuff!"[728]

The Polyphonic controller was usually connected to six Oberheim Synthesizer Expander Modules, which Easton modified and mounted in a single-panel unit with additional audio mixer controls. Easton told me that "Frank used the polyphonic synth, but he never bought one, and as far as I know it isn't on any album of his. The way he played is not very compatible with the 'clean note' expectation of anybody's converter—lots of percussive stuff."[729]

As FZ put it: "Before the frequency follower identifies the pitch, it has to hear the pitch, so your picking technique has to be exactly coordinated with the time your finger lands on the fret, otherwise . . . it doesn't do anything for a split second, so when I played this thing it always sounded like the synthesizer was talking late, because my technique relies a lot on the left hand."[730]

Easton told me that FZ experimented with hooking up the 360 systems unit to his new E-mu synthesizer. The E-mu has a couple of custom modules that FZ had built that look like specific guitar interfaces (these were not built by 360 Systems or E-mu). One unit was bought by John McLaughlin, who also used it with an E-mu synthesizer. 360 systems only sold a few Polyphonic Systems—at around $10,000! They later produced a single-voice unit built around an Oberheim synth module called the Spectre, and then a much simpler and cheaper unit called the SlaveDriver; but before long the advent of MIDI made all these devices obsolete.

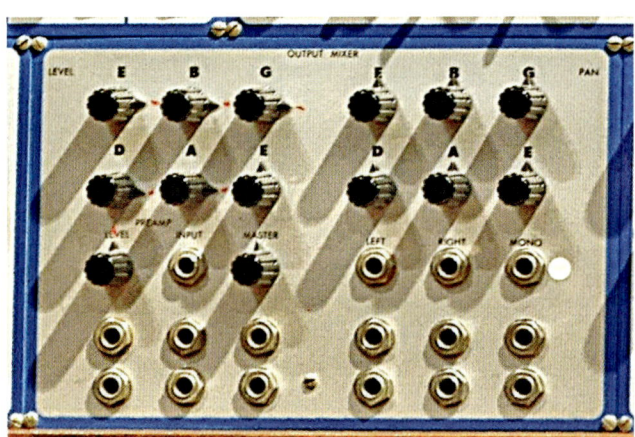

The custom guitar interface module from FZ's Emu synthesizer
(Mick Ekers)

Hear it on:
Album: Mahavishnu Orchestra, *Inner Worlds*
Track: "Inner Worlds Parts 1 & 2"

McLaughlin is to my knowledge the only person who recorded the 360 systems poly-synth with an E-mu modular synthesizer. This may give you some clues as to what FZ might have sounded like.

Bob Easton with the Polyphonic Synthesizer in *Synapse Magazine*, November 1976
(Author's collection)

Ampeg/Hagström Patch 2000 System

FZ tried a prototype of the Ampeg/Hagström Patch 2000 guitar synthesizer system while on tour in 1975, and used it in May 1975 at a show at the Armadillo World Headquarters in Austin, Texas.[731] Whatever numbers he used it on did not make it onto the *Bongo Fury* album; possibly, the recording is safely stored somewhere in the ZFT tape vault.

However, in February, 1977, after having given up on the 360 Systems synth, he talked about giving the Patch 2000 another try: "But there have been improvements in the guitar synthesizer line; there's one I'm getting when I return to the States that's made by Ampeg, and it's more suited to the way I play. It's a mono device . . . press down this fret and it gives you the voltage that gives you, say, F. But you can't play chords on it. I tried it, and because I do so much stuff with my left hand, it's a lot better for what I'm playing."[732]

The Patch 2000 project was a collaboration between the American Ampeg company, best known for its bass guitar amplifiers, and Hagström, the Swedish guitar manufacturer. The system consisted of a Hagström Swede guitar with the strings and frets wired to a small circuitboard built into the guitar, which scanned the strings and generated a voltage corresponding to the fingered notes. A special bridge and tailpiece electrically isolated each string, allowing the circuit to detect individual notes played, selecting the note from the highest fret and the lowest string fingered.

The circuitry onboard the Swede guitar connected to an Ampeg Patch 2000 pedalboard. The pitch pedal allowed you to raise the pitch in semitone steps up to a full octave above the note fingered, and the glide pedal controlled the portamento effect, varying the time it took for the synth to glide from one note to the next. Between the pedals was a fifth switch, which raised the synth note to a perfect fifth interval above the played note.[733]

The pedal only produced a control signal; it had to be connected to a separate voltage-controlled synthesizer to actually produce any sound. The guitar itself could be played and amplified like a normal instrument as it was also fitted with conventional pickups and controls, which were independent of the synthesizer circuit.

The Patch 2000 was launched at the NAMM show in 1976, and received a lot of attention, but it never achieved any significant sales volume. The system was relatively inexpensive at around $2000, and Ampeg noted in their promotional material that "You don't need to be a Zappa or McLaughlin to get your hands on a guitar synthesizer." About 500 were built, along with 275 bass guitar versions that were later produced, and it was discontinued in 1979. I have been unable to find any evidence of FZ actually using the system when he returned to the US in 1977, seeming to have abandoned his interest in guitar synthesizers for a while.

Synclavier II Digital Guitar

The NED Synclavier II Digital Guitar interface was one Synclavier accessory that FZ never ended up buying, although he trialled several versions. Introduced in 1983, it included a control unit styled and proportioned just like a section of the main Synclavier keyboard panel, right down to the 16 illuminated red buttons. The buttons replicated several of the major Synclavier control functions, including 16-track record and playback, as well as features specific to the instrument such as monophonic string and dynamic volume.

It required a suitable guitar with a Roland GR hex pickup, and was originally sold with an optional Roland G-303 guitar synthesizer. The control panel was designed to be attached to the guitar on a stalk. It cost $4,500 (without the guitar). In November 1983, FZ was looking forward to trying out the digital guitar interface, not as a means of making new guitar sounds, but as an input device for the Synclavier that he would be more proficient on than the keyboard: "They have a new guitar interface that's coming out where you can play your lines and it stores them in the computer . . . basically it allows a person who doesn't play keyboards to do all the compositional functions."[734]

In practice, it proved to be another disappointment, as FZ's guitar playing lacked the precision that was required: "The way in which I finger the instrument apparently is too slovenly for it to read. I don't mute every string after I play; there's no Berklee technique involved here. I grab it and whack it. You can adjust the sensitivity within certain parameters, but if you adjust the sensitivity higher, that means it's going to pick up fewer nuances, so where do you draw the line?"[735]

He investigated other guitar controllers that were around; one was made by Modulus Graphite which had a carbon fiber neck: "The neck is supposed to be more stable, and you're supposed to have better isolation, less false triggering, and so forth. There was less false triggering, but for the way I play, there was still too much."

On another occasion he tried Allan Holdsworth's SynthAxe, an unusual device that dispensed with strings entirely for pitch detection, having an angled touch-sensitive fingerboard and a set of small sensor strings that the player strummed. This still had problems for FZ: "The MIDI delay is something I can feel. Any time I can hear the sound of the pick and then after it the sound of whatever's supposed to come out, it bothers me. Even though it's just a few milliseconds apart, it makes me feel awkward."

Even if FZ had found a guitar controller he liked, he realized that on his current system the bandwidth required was going to be a problem: "on the guitar, you get to wiggle the intonation a little bit to make more subtle things happen. The trade-off, though, is that as you wiggle the strings and intonate it, all that nuance stuff, you generate masses and masses of numbers that fill your sequencer up very fast."[736]

ZAPPA GEAR

NED did sell a few Digital Guitar interfaces, notably to Pat Metheny and John McLaughlin, but the overall system costs put it out of the reach of most musicians. As far as I know, FZ had little further interest in the guitar synthesizer concept. Back in 1974, FZ had explained why guitar synthesizers were never likely to appeal to most guitarists: "If you've been playing guitar for a while, you hit a string and you know what it's supposed to sound like and what it's supposed to feel like . . . it's conducted through your hands back to your body when the string hits and you link up with the instrument. And suddenly you hit your string and a trumpet comes out, it feels really weird! (laughs)"[737]

The Digital Guitar controller mounted on a Roland G-303

CHAPTER FIVE
STUDIO AND RECORDING

"I see the whole studio as a musical instrument, something on the order of a pipe organ. In the way that a pipe organ gives an orchestral effect, it has a lot of tonal colors and a lot of power to it. The person who does the mixing is roughly the equivalent of a conductor in front of a symphony orchestra."

—FZ

The Utility Muffin Research Kitchen

JBL 4311B Studio Monitors

Allison/Valley People Kepex and Gainbrain

DBX Compressors

Ursa-Major Space Station SST-282

Lexicon 224-X

Eventide Harmonizers

Pal Studio 5-Track recording head

Apostolic Blurch Injector

Razor and Tape-Editing Block

Sony Digital Tape Recorder

Vintage Studio Microphones

Crown PZM Microphones

AKG Dummy Head Microphones

Yellow Shark Microphone Hoop

Note
When FZ built his Utility Muffin Research Kitchen studio, he installed racks full of the current state of the art in signal processors, a large collection of vintage and modern microphones, numerous tape recorders, a video recording suite, and a whole range of other studio equipment. To cover the full story of the UMRK and its gear would require a complete book of its own. In this section, I will again restrict myself to those items that I think are of specific interest, or that FZ deemed worthy of mention.

ZAPPA GEAR

The Utility Muffin Research Kitchen

"I have a studio at my house—it's a private studio, it's not for rent to anyone else, it has a lot of top secret equipment in it, and that's that."

—FZ[738]

FZ finally amassed enough capital to build his own recording studio at his house in LA in 1979. This was no small project studio, as they are known today, but a professional-quality facility, using the state-of-the-art equipment for the time. The large control room had a 48-channel Harrison mixer, a 5-channel surround-sound monitor system with huge JBL speaker systems built into the walls, and racks full of the latest and best in studio sound-processing equipment.

The studio had a drum booth, a vocal booth, a real echo chamber, and a decent-sized live room large enough to hold a dozen or so musicians, along with his huge Bösendorfer grand piano. One advanced feature that FZ had installed was a sophisticated headphone monitoring system, his engineer David Gray recalled: "We had a whole little thing called a 'self-mix matrix.' Basically, you could send any channel to this routing matrix and each individual out in the room could get four channels that they could mix themselves in headphones."[739]

FZ had it fully equipped with tape recorders: "It's got a 24-track Studer multitrack, the 24-track Sony digital, a 16-track PCM-1610 Sony, a 4-track, a 1/2" 2-track, and a 1/4" 2-track Studer. The analog multitrack also has 8- and 16-track headblocks, and the 2-track machine plays at any speed, from 3 3/4 to 30 i.p.s. (inches per second) and all points in between. I can put on tapes that I made back in 1955 and re-EQ them and stuff."[740]

Detail of the Harrison 4832 console in 2012, in storage at Joe's Garage since being replaced by a Neve console in the late 1980's
(Mick Ekers)

The Harrison 4832 mixing desk featured one of the first effective automation systems. Called Autoset, the system used a small micro-computer with a 4" CRT monitor screen, and could record up to four different passes (the various mixer

Video, headphone monitor and microphone panels in the UMRK live room. Note the 'Self-mix' mixer connectors
(Mick Ekers)

176

settings that applied during the course of a piece), which could all be saved on one track of a tape recorder. On playback, a fader and selector switches allowed you to crossfade between any two of the four passes. This was pretty amazing stuff for the early 1980s.

Gail Zappa told me that at one point the LA authorities had revoked the permit for the building of the UMRK (which had taken them years to obtain), claiming that it was too large for a home studio, and that building a professional studio in a residential area wasn't allowed. Gail Zappa found a clipping in the *LA Times* about their neighbor, the photographer Julius Schulman, whose house had a very large studio, and regularly took classes there. She took the clipping in to the planning authorities and pointed out that to make music, "you need a lot of air to push around, so it's like making an air sculpture," and persuaded them to restore the building permit.[741] This was likely the first time that the term "air sculpture" was applied to FZ's music.

JBL 4311B Studio Monitors

"This album has been engineered to sound correct on JBL 4311 speakers or an equivalent."

—FZ [742]

The loudspeaker manufacturer JBL takes its name from the initials of James Bullough Lansing, the founder of the original Lansing Manufacturing Company, which started out in 1927 making loudspeakers for home radio sets. The company went on to develop high-power, full-range components for cinema sound systems for the new "talking pictures." In 1937, Lansing created what was, arguably, the first studio monitor speaker in the form of the Iconic, which was very successful: Les Paul himself used them in his recording studio. In the 1940s, Lansing developed the famous "voice of the theatre" high-output speaker systems, which became a cinema standard, and later the legendary D-130 15" low-frequency speakers. In the 1950s, Fender started using JBL speakers in their guitar cabinets; FZ favored JBL speakers in his 4×12 stage cabinets.

By the mid-1960s, the JBL 4320 large monitor speaker was used in recording studios worldwide, but JBL perceived the need for a more compact full-range speaker system.[743] They developed the smaller 4310 monitor, inventing the concept of the

JBL 4311 high up on the wall of the UMRK live room
(Mick Ekers)

The other 4311 in the UMRK live room, next to a tiny Yamaha NS-10M, another classic small studio monitor
(Mick Ekers)

ZAPPA GEAR

A 4311 complete with its grill cloth, installed facing upwards on the floor of the UMRK reverb chamber
(Mick Ekers)

"near field monitor." The 4310 was a three-way speaker system consisting of a distinctive 12" bass speaker stiffened with a white clay compound called Aquaplas, a 5" midrange, and a 1" tweeter. It was designed from the outset to be listened to at a close distance, to minimize studio acoustic problems. For this reason, the three speaker components were grouped as close together as possible, and the cabinet was small enough to be placed on the recording console. This became a huge success in large and small studios, and a considerable number were also bought for home use by hi-fi enthusiasts.

To satisfy the hi-fi market, JBL launched a purely domestic version of the 4310 in 1970, called the Century L100, which had a distinctive sculpted foam grill. It became one of the best-selling hi-fi speakers of the time, particularly in the US; 125,000 pairs were sold worldwide in the 1970s. Later, they made a slightly smaller version with a 10" bass unit called the L36, which was also deservedly successful (I have owned a pair of L36s since 1975, and they still sound wonderful).

In 1974, JBL introduced an improved studio version: the 4311 Control Monitor, available in a textured grey or oiled walnut finish. These were a phenomenal success, and surveys in the 1970s showed that pretty much every major studio had a pair of 4311s in the control room, the UMRK being no exception. The advantage of the 4311 was that if listened to from a close distance, the acoustics of the studio would have less effect on the sound. In widely differing studios, a pair of 4311s provided a consistent standard that was familiar to engineers and musicians alike.

The JBL 4311 received many industry awards, and in 2004, the JBL 4311 was inducted into the TEC Foundation Technology Hall of Fame.[744] It remained in production until 1982.[745]

Like most professional studios of the time, the UMRK had a full complement of large, powerful monitor speakers built into the walls. They could produce very high sound pressure levels and much extended bass, but, like all such massive systems, care had to be taken; a mix that sounded good on them could sound very weak on a normal domestic hi-fi system.

FZ explained: "One of the problems when you make a record is that you don't know actually what they're going to be playing it on. You don't know what the anomalies of the person's speakers are going to be, or the cartridge, or the condition of the stylus, or whether they like to turn up the bass all the way . . . there's no way to make it perfect, unless the listener has some kind of scientifically flat reproduction system in their home. And that's just not going to happen."[746]

FZ's engineer Mark Pinske recalls that they talked a lot about this issue[747] and, in the end, they decided to mix the entire *Ship Arriving Too Late to Save a Drowning Witch* (*SATLTSADW*) album on the 4311s. FZ knew that many people owned L100s, L36s, and similar speakers, and thought he might be able to optimize the recording for what was actually in their homes.

When the original LP release of *SATLTSADW* was released, FZ added the following note to the lyric sheet: "This album has been engineered to sound correct on JBL 4311 speakers or an equivalent. Best results will be achieved if you set your preamp tone controls to the flat position with the loudness control in the off position. Before adding any treble or bass to the sound of the album, it would be advisable to check it out this way first. FZ."[748]

The 4311s remained in use in the control room for some time, and were still in evidence tucked away high up in the live room at the UMRK in 2012. They are the final 4311B model, which was introduced in 1979. FZ also installed a 4311 at one end of the echo chamber of the UMRK as the source for the reverb signal, which was also still in place.

FZ was asked if he purposely emphasized the bass guitar on the *SATLTSADW* album: "I think that's a result of mixing on the 4311s; it just gets accentuated. It's up in the mix, but not to a radical extreme for a comfortable listening level."[749] For whatever reason, this experiment in mixing was not repeated on any later albums.

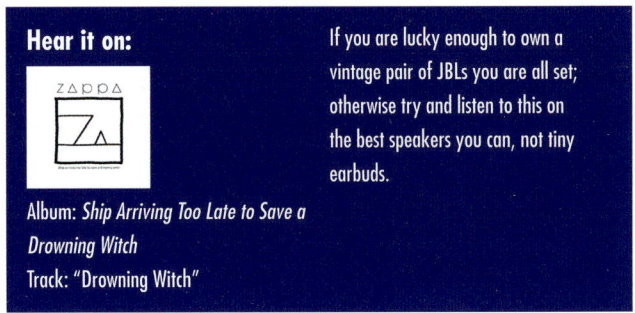

Hear it on:
Album: *Ship Arriving Too Late to Save a Drowning Witch*
Track: "Drowning Witch"

If you are lucky enough to own a vintage pair of JBLs you are all set; otherwise try and listen to this on the best speakers you can, not tiny earbuds.

Allison Kepex and GainBrain Units

"I think Paul [Buff] is definitely one of the pioneers of the modern multi-track recording industry. He's a genius."

— FZ[750]

After Paul Buff sold his studio to FZ (as told in the Pal Studio 5-Track Head section), he moved on to work for Art Laboe at Original Sound studios in Hollywood. While working at Original Sound, Buff formed Allison Research to market the studio equipment he had invented. The company was named after his wife, who he met while she was working as a waitress at the Cucamonga Maltshop, a piece of biographical trivia that FZ mentioned more than once and obviously found appealing.[751]

The two key products Allison produced were the Kepex and the Gain Brain. The Kepex (KEyed Programmable EXpander) was a device for removing extraneous noise from a sound source, such as noise from an amplifier that might be heard between the notes of a guitar solo.

The attractive company logo featured a cute portrait of Allison Buff; this was certainly a marketing plus but it also tempted studio visitors to steal the badges and they are missing from many units these days. It was the first high quality commercially produced noise gate (as such devices are known), and it could also be used for special effects by allowing a second sound source to control its action.

According to the brochure: "The Kepex is . . . a gain expander that can be adjusted to absorb the low-level noises that you decide are objectionable. . . . an exterior key input is provided which can control the gain with a second independent audio signal. This feature allows some far-out control for creating stereo effects and electronic music synthesis."[752]

The Gain Brain's main use was as a limiter, to control an audio signal and stop it from exceeding the level where it might cause distortion on a recording (I am oversimplifying here, but this book is not a manual in sound recording techniques, so bear with me). The units could be mounted in individual cases, but were more commonly sold in a compact rack unit that would hold up to sixteen Kepex or Gain Brain units. They became standard studio equipment in the 1970s, and were used particularly to provide some of the massive drum sounds popular in that era. Famously, Alan Parsons used a Kepexed drum sound to create the heartbeat heard on Pink Floyd's *The Dark Side of the Moon*.

In 1980, Buff merged Allison Research with his friend Bob Todrank's Valley Audio company and formed Valley People. Valley People sold a variety of modular studio rack units, including improved Mk II versions of the Kepex and Gainbrain units. Twice as wide as the original modules, they were a big improvement; the instruction manual for the Kepex II described it as "the logical extension to the original Kepex . . . a fully new design, providing many new features, as well as significant refinements in control functions and audio performance."[753]

FZ had a pair of Gain Brains and Kepexes in his touring rack and bought a set of five Kepex II and four Gainbrain II units for his UMRK studio.[754] When mentioning them, he

Hear it on:

Album: *The Buff Organization*
Track: The Kepex demonstration tape
Alison Buff extols the virtues of the Kepex and demonstrates its functionality on this charming and humorous recording. It is available as an individual digital download, and also as part of *Paul Buff Presents the Pal and Original Sound Studio Archives*.

FZ's Valley People series 800 modules, as originally installed in the UMRK
(Mick Ekers)

would often refer to Paul Buff as a genius, retaining this respect and admiration throughout his life. The units illustrated were sold in the 2016 auction (minus one of the Kepex II modules) for $1,280.

Buff later moved into the design and manufacture of hi-tech photo lighting equipment, but there are still many recording studios listing Kepex and Gain Brain units in their inventories, especially those offering an analogue recording facility.

DBX Compressors

"Some of the other really great clean sounds from the 70's were mostly direct and sweetly compressed with a DBX 160 compressor."

—DZ [755]

FZ kept a DBX 162 compressor limiter in his 1970s touring rack, and as DZ notes, he regularly used DBX compressors in the studio, particularly when recording guitar tracks.

DBX Inc. was founded by the American inventor and audio engineer David Blackmer (1927–2002) in 1971 to produce a range of high-quality audio noise-reduction products designed to improve the quality of tape-recorded sound. They used a technology called decibel expansion (hence "DBX"), and DBX equipment became widely used throughout the sound and film industries.

DBX introduced the DBX 160 compressor in 1976, and later a linked stereo version, the 162. Blackmer's goal was always to make recorded sound indistinguishable from the original: "My intention is to get all the products we can to have distortion under one part per million."[756] Supposedly, he was not keen at first on producing a device that reduced the dynamic range of a signal.[757]

Nonetheless they were hugely successful, their advanced "feed forward" technology making them sonically superior to other compressors on the market, particularly at high compression ratios, and they soon became a recording studio standard.

In the UMRK control room, I found a pair of vintage DBX 160s dating back to the original build of the studio, and a stereo 162 that came from FZ's touring rack. In storage at Joe's Garage there was a 1980s 900-series modular system case containing three compressors and a selection of other modules. DBX is still making professional audio equipment today, and the 160 series continues with the contemporary 160A and other models. The early units are still prized for their quality and natural-sounding characteristics.

FZ's DBX 900 system with a 902 de-esser, 3 × 903 compressors, 2 × 904 noise-gates and a 905 parametric equalizer
(Mick Ekers)

The Ursa Major Space Station SST-282

"We have an Ursa Major Space Station . . . we do quite a bit of ambience simulation here and have a lot of different aromas to choose from."

—FZ [758]

FZ was always interested by the acoustic properties of different rooms, to the extent of taking recordings of them. In April 2011, Gail Zappa told interviewer Kevin Ferguson: "One of Frank's favorite things to collect, as an audio collector, was room tone."[759] In the late 1970s, the Ursa Major SST-282 and other similar units offered, for the first time, the prospect of modelling a wide range of different environments from small rooms to very large spaces. Beyond that, they could emulate sound spaces that were physically impossible in the real world.

Ursa Major was founded in 1977 in Belmont, Massachusetts, by Chris Moore, who had resigned from his position as project engineer at Lexicon, frustrated at unadventurous management and unfulfilled promises of share options. Moore left with the ambition to build the first low-cost digital reverberator, and to form his own company, which he was determined would be run cooperatively.

Moore told me: "Everybody had one share and only one share, and that gave you one vote. The salary scales from the lowest to the highest paid were compressed to a maximum of three to one, and everybody got a share of the profits. The philosophy is that all work that is necessary to accomplish a goal is to be respected, and given equal respect. If what you do is put parts in circuit boards and solder them, it does not make you less of a citizen than if you plan a marketing strategy. So I wanted that, that was reflected in the compressed salaries."[760]

This philosophy produced results; Moore and his workers were able to turn his concept into a fully fledged prototype in

A DBX 162 and a pair of 160s at the UMRK in 2012
(Mick Ekers)

Studio and Recording

Inventor Chris Moore with the prototype Space Station at the AES convention in 1978

Early Ursa Major advertisement, with some similarity to the photo of Chris Moore overleaf

less than a year, which Moore exhibited at the AES Convention in LA in 1978. Astonishingly, the team designed the system without the aid of a computer, using punch cards to enter programs in the early memory chips. The result was the SST-282 Space Station.

Some further sense of the culture of this fledgling company can be drawn from Moore's comments on the company name and logo: "The sleeping bear logo tied the company name, Ursa Major (Great Bear constellation) with space, as suggested by the product name Space Station. The name Space Station itself is a play on words, as in a station from which you can manipulate acoustic space."[761]

At the heart of the SST-282 was enough digital memory to hold around 250 milliseconds of audio, and 24 delay line "taps." Each tap could take an output from the original signal at various delay times, and these signals could be processed in various ways and fed back into the signal path to produce simulations of different audio reflections. A sophisticated proprietary technique randomized the reverberation delay taps to avoid the delayed signal feeding back.[762] The front panel of this 3U-high rack unit contained a surprisingly easy to use combination of push buttons and rotary controls. The buttons selected from sixteen various programs to provide different effects and decay times. The main rotary controls were laid out in a logical left-to-right path with input volume, bass and treble controls, level controls for the different taps, and feedback and output level controls.

Although not cheap at around $2000, the SST-282 was the first high-quality digital delay unit within the reach of smaller independent studios. Competing directly with considerably more expensive units such as the classic EMT-250 introduced in 1976, it quickly became a classic, and was used widely on much of the music of the time, particularly as a guitar and vocal effect.[763] Originally produced in a blue case with silver knobs, the design soon changed to the user-friendly black panel with colored knobs design, like FZ's unit.

The SST-282 was not without its quirks and anomalies, and Moore was never totally happy with the design, with characteristic honesty pointing out in the original brochure, "In the reverb mode only, there is some noise that may be heard during very pure solos of voice flute or tone,"[764] even though this would be inaudible in most situations. However, the distinct character of the unit was an important factor in its remarkably long life, during a period that saw the development of ever more sophisticated and cheaper competing products.

FZ's Ursa Major Space Station in 2012
(Mick Ekers)

ZAPPA GEAR

In the booklet from the CD *Frank Zappa Plays the Music of Frank Zappa*, Dweezil Zappa notes that FZ used the Space Station on the *Joe's Garage* version of the track "Watermelon in Easter Hay." Known as one of FZ's signature guitar pieces, the recording features very rich and complex stereo reverb effects.

In the book *Academy Zappa*, T.H.F. Drenching singles this out for specific criticism in the article "'Watermelon in Easter Hay,' the Function of the Reverb Unit and the Poverty of The Individual Spirit."[765] Responding to such an article is well beyond my terms of reference in this context, but its very existence reinforces a major premise of this book; that in many cases FZ's use of equipment was a significant component in the overall construction of his music.

I found FZ's SST282 still in a rack in the control room of the UMRK; as far as I know, it is still in good working order. The SST282 remained on sale for the best part of a decade; around 1,900 units had been made when production ended in 1986, not long after AKG bought the company in a hostile takeover. In 1989, Ursa Major was closed down and Moore formed a consultancy firm, Seven Woods Audio. However, after more than ten years, he found himself still thinking about the Space Station: "I did want to see if I could make a digital Space Station . . . and it would be fun."[766] In 2003, he produced a small desktop version, containing all the original features and more, in a box around the size of a guitar effects pedal.[767] When I talked to Moore in 2012, he was still working on ideas for future hardware products.

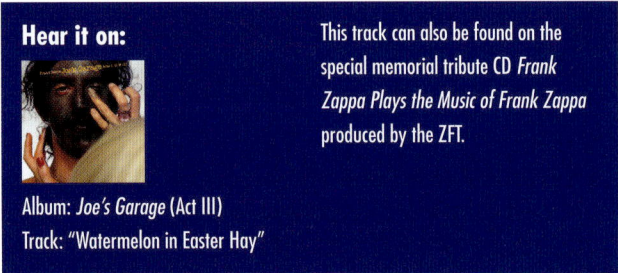

Hear it on:
This track can also be found on the special memorial tribute CD *Frank Zappa Plays the Music of Frank Zappa* produced by the ZFT.

Album: *Joe's Garage* (Act III)
Track: "Watermelon in Easter Hay"

FZ's 224X units –a lot of metal is involved in their construction!
(Mick Ekers)

Lexicon 224-X

"That device lets you specify your own acoustics; you can build a room and do what you want."

— FZ [768]

In January 1983, FZ was urgently looking for a location to record the *London Symphony Orchestra* album, as the original venue had turned out to be too small for the 105 musicians. The only place large enough that was not already booked was a big sound stage at Twickenham film studios, which among other things had been used for the Beatles films *A Hard Day's Night* and *Help*. In *The Real Frank Zappa Book*, FZ mistakenly stated that it had been used for the James Bond films, confusing it with Pinewood Studios, where *200 Motels* had been made.[769]

The large room was acoustically quite dead, with a fairly uneven frequency response, so to overcome this FZ decided that each segment of the recording would have its own different artificial acoustic environment, created using the Lexicon 224-X digital reverb processor.

He later mixed each section as if it had occurred in its own discrete acoustical space. In some cases, he would use dissimilar echo programs for parts of the orchestra at the same time, so

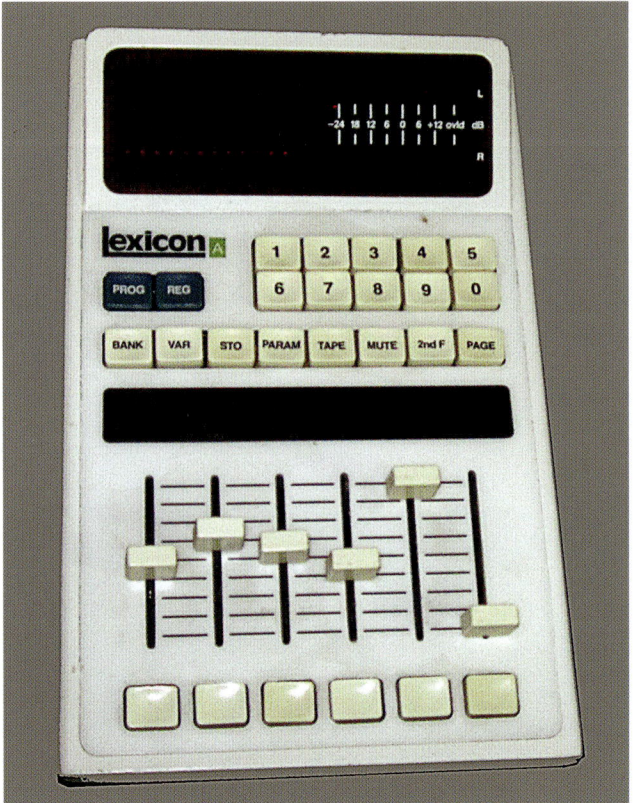

One of FZ's 'LARC' Lexicon Alphanumeric Remote Controls
(Mick Ekers)

Studio and Recording

that (for example) the strings might sound as if they were playing in a completely different room to the percussion section.[770]

As FZ explained in an interview in *Digital Audio* magazine: "That's one of the most interesting aspects of the *London Symphony Orchestra* album. Using a bunch of homemade room programs on the 224-X, I changed the size and shape of the imaginary rooms, according to the mood of each portion of the piece. Later, I edited the tapes so you go smoothly from one acoustic space to another, from a big room, to a vast space, and back. It changes the way you hear the music."[771]

The Lexicon company had its roots in 1969, when MIT lecturer Dr. Francis Lee developed a digital delay line for use in medical heart monitoring equipment. It soon became clear that it had potential audio applications, and in 1971, Lee's company Lexicon produced the world's first commercial digital audio processor in collaboration with New York–based Gotham Audio: the Delta T-101 digital delay.[772]

Lexicon soon started to gain a reputation for pioneering digital products, but it was the 224 series that was to establish their name in the audio industry. The 224 was invented by Dr. David Griesinger, who had started working on a digital reverb unit that incorporated a microcomputer into the design. He demonstrated his prototype to Lexicon, who bought the invention and offered Griesinger a job to help refine the product. One of Griesinger's key design concepts for the new reverb was that it should have a separate control unit for adjusting parameters and selecting programs.

The model 224 Digital Reverberator, as Lexicon called it, was launched at the AES convention in 1978.[773] The brain of the unit was encased in a large black 4U rack case, containing the Intel 8080 microprocessor board and six other large circuit boards containing 12-bit digital/analogue convertors and a large number of 74S/LS-series logic chips, all state-of-the art components for the 1970s. It had two inputs and four outputs, and came with interchangeable programs simulating echo chambers, plate reverbs, and rooms. The 224-X version was a major enhancement to the original model, doubling the audio bandwidth to 16 kHz, and the later 224-XL added a more sophisticated remote-control unit known as the LARC (Lexicon Alphanumeric Remote Control).[774]

The power and flexibility of the unit, combined with the convenience of the outboard control, which could be operated while seated at the mixing desk, quickly established the 224 series as the industry standard. Although more expensive than the previously mentioned Ursa Major Space Station, at $7500 it was half the price of the market leading EMT 250, and FZ could afford to keep several in stock: "We have two Lexicon 224-Xs and two of the older Lexicons in the truck."[775] The control units for the 224-Xs were mounted on FZ's satellite console in the UMRK, just below the remote control for the Sony tape decks. It is the author's opinion that FZ's fascination with these

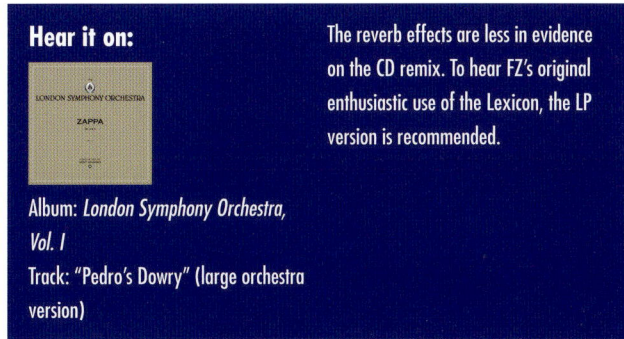

Hear it on:

Album: *London Symphony Orchestra, Vol. I*
Track: "Pedro's Dowry" (large orchestra version)

The reverb effects are less in evidence on the CD remix. To hear FZ's original enthusiastic use of the Lexicon, the LP version is recommended.

devices would cloud his judgement when he remixed his early albums for their first CD releases, as he added what are generally considered obtrusive amounts of digital reverb to many of them.

FZ considered his use of the 224-X a significant element of the *LSO* recordings, giving the device a credit on the album sleeve notes for "Imaginary Ambience Reconstruction."[776] As well as creating artificial sonic environments. he also made use of it for special effects: "And there's other places where there is a small rototom which he hits and the sound ricochets back and forth; that's part of the reverb program that I built into the Lexicon 224-X."[777]

Now part of the Harman group, Lexicon still produces professional audio products; many studios are still using original 224 units, and the 224-X is now available as a high-end software plug-in for computer music systems. I was pleased to find FZ's pair of massive 224-X units in storage at Joe's Garage, along with two control units, still looking in good condition. The two 224-Xs and the controllers were sold in the 2016 auction for $5,440, and a pair of the later LARC control panels were also sold for $896.[778]

FZ's original Lexicon remote controls, still joined together
(Mick Ekers)

ZAPPA GEAR

Eventide Harmonizers

"One thing that I've enjoyed using has been the Eventide Harmonizer that I have included on the board."

— FZ[779]

An Eventide H949 powered up
(Tony Miln, Soundgas)

Eventide Clockworks Inc. was founded in New York in 1970 by recording engineer Steve Katz, inventor Richard Factor, and businessman Orville Greene. They produced various specialized electronics products, including some early digital delay units, notably the 1745M, which had an optional pitch-change module—the first such product available with a frequency response suitable for music.

Working away on his own in the front room of his NYC railroad apartment, Eventide engineer Tony Agnello developed what became the famous H910 Harmonizer.[780] When Eventide introduced the H910 at the AES convention in 1974, it caused a small sensation. It was the first commercially available audio pitch shifter that could change the pitch of a sound in real time by any interval, and when it was released in 1975, was an almost immediate success.

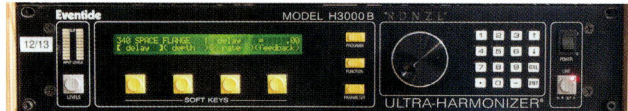

FZ's 'RDNZL' H3000B, powered-up at the UMRK
(Mick Ekers)

FZ's Harmonizer keyboard controller
(Mick Ekers)

Underlining the musical capabilities inherent in the name "Harmonizer," it had an optional keyboard controller, which allowed the pitch to be changed by specific musical intervals. One of the earliest people to get their hands on one was David Bowie's producer Tony Visconti, who famously described its effect to Bowie: "It fucks with the fabric of time."[781]

In 1977, the H949 model was added to the line, which added a finely controllable, very small pitch change capability, useful for "doubling" vocals or instruments. It also had a "deglitch" circuit, which allowed pitch-shifted recordings to be produced largely free of objectionable artefacts. FZ installed one in his rack system, and was particularly fond of the doubling effects available: "One day I decided to set the pitch control at 99, instead of some lower figure, so that means that the double note is a small percent flat from your original note, and it comes out about 30 milliseconds late. So I've got that split left and right.... When you strum chords through that it makes them sound really full."[782]

FZ did not just use the Harmonizer on his guitar; when asked about the effects used on the forthcoming *Läther* album,

An Eventide H910
(Tony Miln, Soundgas)

he said: "We used a Harmonizer on the bass. So where we have Harmonizer on bass, it was split left and right, which gave us a real nice sound on the bass."[783]

Eventide introduced the revolutionary model H3000 Ultra Harmonizer in 1987, which combined pitch shift and delay functions with a whole raft of additional special effects, which could be programmed and combined in numerous saved configurations. It featured the world's first intelligent diatonic pitch-shifting algorithm, and went on to become one of the most successful and highly used multieffects units ever produced. Various versions were produced; FZ had the H3000B Broadcast model installed at the UMRK, which had various additional patches and sound effects designed for radio use.

In 2012, I saw one of FZ's original model H949s in a rack in the control room, along with his Ultra Harmonizer H3000B, which had been engraved with the word "RDNZL" (after the FZ composition of course, but why!). Both units appeared to

Hear it on:

Album: *Zappa in New York*
Track: "The Purple Lagoon/Approximate"

You can hear the left/right split that FZ refers to on Patrick O'Hearn's tasty bass solo at 8:30. This track also appears on the *Läther* album.

be in full working order. We later discovered a rather dusty Eventide keyboard controller in storage at Joe's Garage, which appeared to have been little used.

Eventide is still producing advanced electronic equipment, including the latest generation hardware and software Harmonizers. After leaving the company in the 1980s, inventor Agnello recently returned to Eventide, and is now the president of the audio division: "I conceived the H910 as new kind of musical instrument. My goal was to give musicians and engineers a new way to create and sculpt music; to create an instrument that allowed them to change pitch, to add depth, and to layer harmonies. I was ecstatic that people like Frank Zappa and Tony Visconti embraced it and used it to explore new audio landscapes."[784]

Pal Studio 5-Track Recording Head

"But he didn't stop there because he needed a tape recorder, so he built one. He made the world's first 5-track recording machine"

—FZ[785]

Paul Buff, described by FZ as an "amazing gentleman,"[786] was someone who provided an immensely significant turning point in FZ's career. Buff had grown up in the small town of Cucamonga, California, and after learning military electronics in the Marines, he set up a small recording studio called Pal on Archibald Avenue in 1957.[787] Buff knew nothing about the music industry and had very limited funds, but undeterred, he built his own mixing desk in an old bathroom vanity unit. He then modified a Presto 1.4" tape recorder to handle 1/2" tape, and built his own 5-track recording head stack from some Norelco mono recording heads.[788] This was at a time when most major recording studios were recording in 3-track at most.

Buff taught himself to sing and play drums, bass, guitar, keyboards, and saxophone, and wrote and recorded his own material, using his ability to multitrack record. FZ started working with Buff at his Pal studio in 1960, making his own recordings and collaborating with Buff on various demos and novelty pop records, receiving an invaluable hands-on education on the basics of record production, engineering, and arranging. Pal only achieved limited commercial success, despite recording a couple of hit records including the Surfaris hit "Wipe Out," and in 1964 Buff sold the studio to FZ, including all the equipment. FZ renamed Pal Studio Z, but never made any money from it, and after falling behind in his rent, abandoned the studio in 1965. It was demolished for road-widening purposes in 1966. The Presto deck is long gone, but FZ kept the unique 5-track record/playback stack.

You can see the Presto tape recorder behind FZ in this local newspaper photograph of FZ in the Pal studio in 1964

FZ described it as follows: "... he bought a bunch of heads and machined this stack that was about six inches across. And the heads weren't stacked on top of each other, they were staggered, because at the time there was no material that could give you enough insulation between the heads if you stacked them one on top of another. So he has five heads in a row that were erase heads, and then five more in a row that were record and playback, so it wasn't like three distinct groups of heads, it was two distinct groups. Because of this unique arrangement with the heads stacked in a diagonal way, those 5-track masters can't be played on any head other than the original."[789] At the time of the interview, FZ was not sure exactly where the head stack was, assuming it was in a box of garbage somewhere down in the vault.

Fortunately, the head-stack was rediscovered, and Gail Zappa secured it in a small box packed in tissue paper and

Paul Buff's five-track recording head
(Mick Ekers)

ZAPPA GEAR

put it "somewhere safe." I could barely contain my excitement when she produced it for me to photograph; neither could ZFT vaultmeister Joe Travers, who had assumed it had been stolen! In 2004, Dweezil Zappa was still hopeful that they might find a way to get a machine to work with the head stack.[790] That hasn't happened yet, but thanks to FZ's foresight in keeping the heads, there is still a possibility that those early master tapes could be played again one day. You can read more about the astonishing Mr. Buff in the Alison Kepex and Gainbrain section of this book.

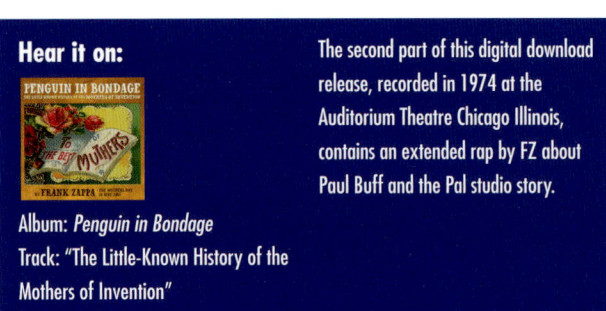

Hear it on:
Album: *Penguin in Bondage*
Track: "The Little-Known History of the Mothers of Invention"

The second part of this digital download release, recorded in 1974 at the Auditorium Theatre Chicago Illinois, contains an extended rap by FZ about Paul Buff and the Pal studio story.

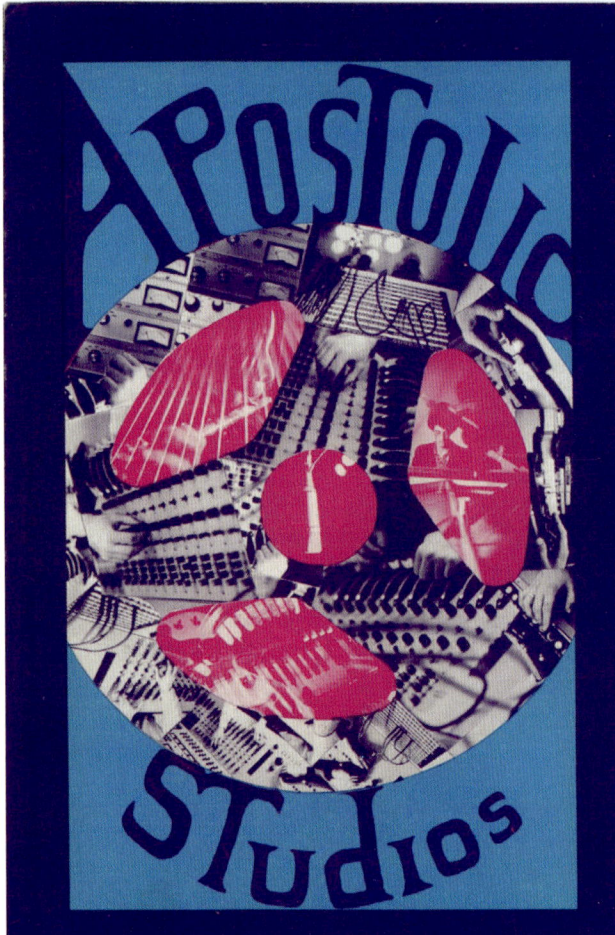

Cover of the Apostolic Studios brochure

THE APOSTOLIC BLURCH INJECTOR

"It was a little box this big . . . with three buttons on it."
— FZ[791]

FZ used Apostolic Studios in New York extensively during the late 1960s, recording sessions for *We're Only in It for the Money*, *Weasels Ripped My Flesh*, and other albums. Several tracks on these albums feature strange electronic effects that were produced with a device known as the Apostolic Blurch Injector.

Apostolic Studios was founded by John Townley in 1967, at 53 East 10th Street, New York. It was one of the first independent studios built specifically to cater for the new generation of rock bands, combining a laid-back atmosphere with state-of-the-art equipment, including one of the first 12-track recorders, a modern-style mixing desk with linear faders rather than rotary level controls, and various advanced items of outboard equipment.[792]

It also employed Dick Kunc, a talented and creative young engineer with whom FZ had an immediate rapport. He told *Mix* magazine, "During the time we were doing *Uncle Meat*, I was working with an engineer [Richard Kunc] who was real cooperative, just trying to do any kind of weird thing we asked him to do . . . he built a little box with three pushbuttons; we called it the Apostolic Blurch Injector. And we took various tracks of different types of material and cranked them up into the distortion range and then by poking the buttons you'd get these little rhythmic bursts of white noise, brown noise, pink noise . . . . But instead of being derived from a noise generator on a synthesizer, it was completely distorted voices, instruments, percussion, whatever. We cranked off reams and reams of tape of this kind of material."[793]

The sound sources were a mixture of industrial noises, horses, and some of the ethnic instruments available at Apostolic,

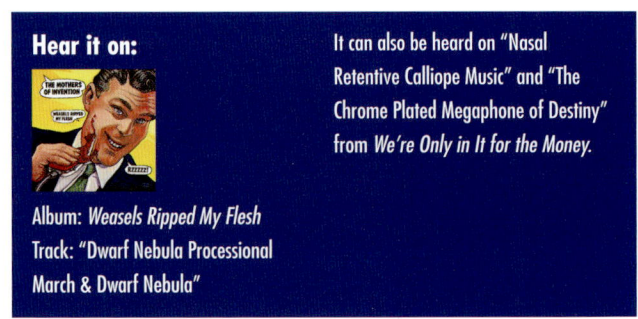

Hear it on:
Album: *Weasels Ripped My Flesh*
Track: "Dwarf Nebula Processional March & Dwarf Nebula"

It can also be heard on "Nasal Retentive Calliope Music" and "The Chrome Plated Megaphone of Destiny" from *We're Only in It for the Money*.

such as a tambora and koto. The recordings were then played backwards, slowed down, or speeded up, and the final results were assembled onto what FZ called "blurch tapes," which were played back on a two-track recorder. Short bursts of these blurch tracks were inserted into the main 12-track recording by pushing the buttons on the injector.

There is some confusion about the name of this device; some sources refer to the device as the Apostolic Vlorch Injector, and FZ guitarist Mike Keneally suggests that it should be "Blorch" on his website.[794] Gail Zappa told me that it is definitely "Blurch," a term she invented at the time when Moon Zappa was a baby, to describe the combined burp and small vomit event that small babies do.[795]

John Kilgore, who was an apprentice engineer at Apostolic Studios at the time, remembers it as a 12-button keyboard.[796] FZ is quite specific that the device had three buttons: "This particular console didn't have a stereo fader; it had three master faders: a separate fader for the left, the center, and the right, so you could fade out the center and leave the left and right, or whatever. So these three buttons on this box corresponded to inputs to the three master faders, and you could play it rhythmically."[797] Apostolic Studios closed in the early 1970s, as a result of "over-expansion, competition, and a business world which utterly coopted our concepts," according to Townley.[798] Whatever happened to the Blurch Injector is not known.

The Razor and the Tape-Editing Block

"It took me a long time to get used to handling a razor blade like that."
— FZ[799]

The tape-editing block was always a vital part of FZ's studio toolkit, used for precision cutting and joining together (or splicing) pieces of magnetic tape. Readers only familiar with contemporary computer-based digital recording would be astounded at how much music editing was done simply by cutting up pieces of magnetic tape with a razor blade and sticking them together again. In the days of tape recording, this was generally the only way to get a clean edit. Accurate editing directly on a tape recorder was usually impossible, because of the time taken to get the tape up to speed, and the delay caused by the gap between the record and playback heads. All you could really do on most machines was add a new piece of music several seconds after the previous one had finished.

The editing block was a finely engineered lump of metal with a shallow channel machined into it that was just wide enough to hold a piece of tape laid flat. Across it were cut narrow slots, used to guide the razor blade. The slots were angled

An editing block and razor on one of the UMRK tape machines in 2012
(Mick Ekers)

(usually) at 89, 60, and 45 degrees. Most professional tape machines had the block built in to the deck; but freestanding ones were also used.

The two pieces of tape to be joined are overlaid on the block with the edit point lined up over the required angled slot. The edit points are marked on each piece of tape with a chinograph (wax) pencil. The two tapes are cut precisely by guiding the razor through the slot—the topmost cut piece is removed and a piece of adhesive splicing tape is applied to make the join. The splicing tape is then trimmed at the edges of the tape. The 89- (or sometimes 90-) degree slot is used to butt-join pieces together; such joints require great precision, as unless there is silence across the join, an abrupt change of volume or a click or drop-out of some sort may be heard. The other angles produce a crossfade from one piece of music to the next.

FZ started learning this skill when he first began working at the Pal studio in 1962. As with most of the techniques that he needed for his work, he became an absolute master of the craft. He would break down and reassemble pieces of music, combining fragments of dialogue, sound effects, guitar solos, and other musical elements, even incorporating material from different recording sessions (sometimes years apart). FZ used the technique heavily on many of his early albums; *Lumpy Gravy* is a particularly complex example of this. Working in this way is a slow and laborious task; he took nine months to edit the two-track master tape of *Lumpy Gravy*, which was constructed from literally hundreds of pieces of tape.

In 1969, FZ had this to say about the process: "The editing technique is an extension of the composition . . . after I've got that onto a piece of quarter-inch tape I can examine it, chop it up, integrate it with non-musical material . . . to call that 'editing technique' sounds like someone sat there and cut out all the mistakes . . . . I just wanted to make that point about editing . . . because it took me a long time to get used to handling a razor blade like that. I just recently purchased my own machine that will enable me to do that work at home and now I spend sometimes ten or eleven hours in a row, just sitting in front of that machine chopping tape up—because I really like to do it."[800]

FZ bass-player Arthur Barrow was present at a recording session for the *Zoot Allures* album before he joined the band. FZ wanted to punch in drummer Terry Bozzio directly onto the 2" 24-track analogue master tape. Barrow recalls: "I was kind of amazed at his boldness . . . where he wanted to punch out he would just slice the tape, just cut it right there and put a piece of leader tape in to protect the next piece of music, punched in the drum part . . . then take out the leader tape, splice it back together, and it was a perfect punch!"[801] Barrow remembers that when he joined the band, FZ would happily cut and splice delicate digital tape, and kept a pair of white cotton gloves that he wore for this task. FZ's Synclavier engineer Bob Rice also remarked on this: " . . . and he was so good at doing razor blade edits on analogue tapes that he continued to use the technique on digital tapes, which was really dangerous, before Sony was able to provide a digital editing system that was affordable."[802]

FZ continued to use the editing block throughout his career, although on later albums the edits were less frequent and dramatic. Even when working with the Synclavier, he was still limited by the constraints of his hardware, and for making any major edits, only his razor blade and cutting block would do: " If you've got 16 tracks and you have a complicated orchestration in there and you suddenly want to make a drastic change from one section of the music to another, the only way to do it, unless you have more channels or more RAM, is to print the two sections onto the tape and cut them together."

The track "Inca Roads" on the *One Size Fits All* album features a substantially edited version of a guitar solo that can be heard in its entirety on *You Can't Do That on Stage Anymore, Vol. 2*. FZ talked to David Mead for *Guitarist* magazine about the editing techniques he used on this track:

> **DM (incredulously):** "Those were all razor edits—literally cutting up the tape?"
>
> **FZ:** "That's right."
>
> **DM:** "But everything's right on the beat. You'd never know that you're not hearing the complete story."
>
> **FZ:** "I'm a pretty good editor."[803]

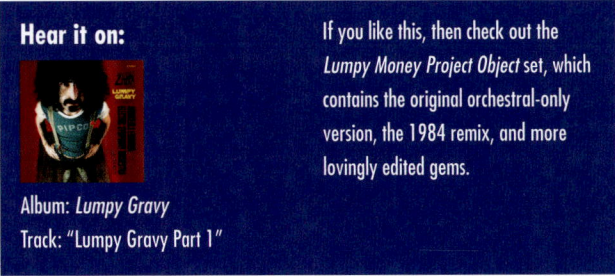

Hear it on:
Album: *Lumpy Gravy*
Track: "Lumpy Gravy Part 1"

If you like this, then check out the *Lumpy Money Project Object* set, which contains the original orchestral-only version, the 1984 remix, and more lovingly edited gems.

Sony Digital Tape Recorders

"You can do sounds on digital that you can't on analogue. The sound is clear, and the dynamic range is ridiculous. Little things like that make all the difference in the world."

— FZ[804]

As well as the previously mentioned Lexicon digital reverb units, FZ pioneered another piece of new technology when recording the LSO sessions: the Sony PCM-3324 24-track digital tape recorder. FZ had hired the Island record company mobile recording truck for the session, which had been recently equipped with the first two production PCM-3324s. Engineer Mark Pinske recalled that he was initially cautious about the brand-new machines, and as there were also two 3M 79 analogue recorders in the truck, he "had the crew put together an extra snake so we could run both machines, in a little room, simultaneously with the digital machines."[805]

They brought all the tapes back to the US and hired Sony's third production machine to evaluate the digital recordings. After a month or so of using it, FZ was so enamored of the Sony recorder that he bought one outright.[806] When talking about his use of digital reverb on the LSO recordings, FZ remarked, "That's fairly heretical from a normal classical engineering standpoint, but then so is 24-track digital recording."[807]

Up until the late 1970s, the only multitrack studio recorders were analogue, and although the best machines and tape were capable of very high-quality recording, they had some significant disadvantages. One big problem was tape hiss—the low-level background noise present to some degree on all analogue tape recordings means that every time a piece of music is copied from one tape recorder or track to another the hiss accumulates, until it can become quite noticeable in quiet passages of music. Another problem was that different types of magnetic tape have different audio characteristics, which need to be adjusted for on the recorder; if you edit together recordings made

Sony PCM-3324 Machine 'B' in a cupboard in Joe's Garage
(Mick Ekers)

on different tape formulations, this can make the edits very noticeable.

Digital recorders convert each audio track into a series of numerical digits (much like on a CD or MP3 recording) before recording them onto the tape. Once digitized, the tracks can be moved around and copied without any sonic degradation, and the quality is not affected by the brand of tape used. Only when the digital signal is decoded back to an audio analogue signal will there be any loss of quality.

Leading engineer Dr. Toshitada "Toshi" Doi (who had already played a key role in the development of the CD) and a team of thirty researchers were behind the design of the Sony PCM-3324, which went into production in 1983.[808] The original model weighed 440 pounds, had a maximum recording time of 65 minutes, and cost $150,000. It used Sony's DASH (Digital Audio Stationary Head) technology, which meant that the tape could be physically edited with a razor blade, just like an analogue tape.

This was not the case with the many competing standards, which used a moving recording head that wrote the signal onto the tape in a continuous spiral, making it impossible to edit by cutting and splicing the tape. Sony also incorporated extremely high-quality convertors to encode the audio signal to digital. Sony had spent millions of dollars developing this new generation of convertors, which had two hundred times the resolution of their previous units. Dr. Doi visited the UMRK during the early days of the machine; it was only the eighth unit that had been made, and Sony took a keen interest in how the machine was working out.[809] Once, Pinske happened to be watching television, and asked Doi how good the picture would be if it could be improved by the same amount as the convertors; he responded that you would be able to "see every blade of grass growing."[810]

FZ eventually bought a second PCM-3324, and soon found some unconventional uses for the pair of machines, explaining: "You do a digital dupe of all 24 tracks for one machine to another using SMPTE, except that you don't transfer the bass track. Then you get a SMPTE offset number that moves the bass forward in time and do a second pass, where the bass is relocated earlier than in the original mix. You can also . . . move the rear wall of a building closer to the stage to give you a tighter sound by relocating an audience track."[811] FZ took one of the PCM-3324s on the road to record the 1984 US tour.[812]

Pinske made a digital backup of all the tapes, and they razor-blade edited it. "Frank would go through the movements, and we might have twelve takes of one section . . . and when they performed it the best, we would edit out that piece, and then tape it together to the one previous to it." Pinske estimated that there were over 1,000 edits: "We were counting them at one point; we got up to like 900, and we decided that counting them was ridiculous."[813]

This was very precise work (as noted in the previous section). The digital tape was considerably thinner and more

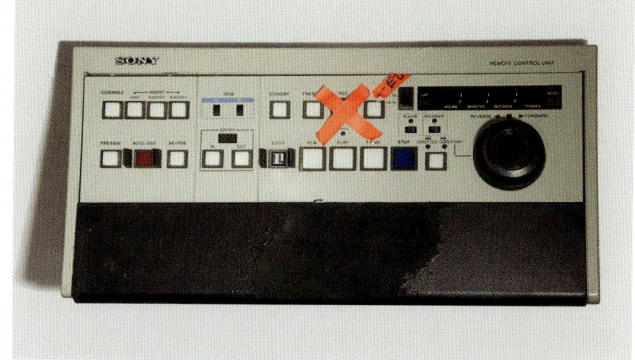

Sony remote control unit. Heavy use has worn away the covering on the wrist rest (Mick Ekers)

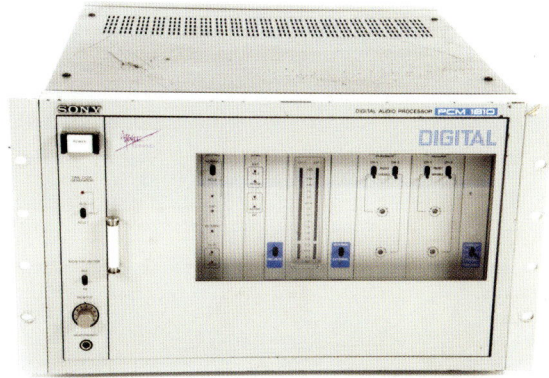

The PCM 1610 2 track mastering machine. The sticker shows that the unit has been enhanced by the Californian digital audio company Apogee Electronics (ZFT)

delicate than analogue tape, and despite the error-correction built into the Sony, the results were not always perfect, at least to FZ's ears: "If you want to change your mind, every time you un-make the splice and put it back together again you run the risk of getting a 'snat' or some little electric noise that happens . . . and there's some splices in this, I know where they are, where there are 'snats' and 'poots' and stuff, but most people wouldn't hear them."[814]

FZ also used a 2-track Sony PCM-1610 machine for mixing down to stereo, crediting both machines on the LSO album sleeve notes. Curtis Chan, the young Sony engineer who was assigned to babysit FZ's machines, was also given a "special thanks" credit. In the 1990s, Dr. Doi went on to head Sony's Digital Creatures Lab, producing Aibo, Sony's famous robot dog, and in 2003 the Qrio running humanoid robot.[815] Dweezil Zappa continued using the PCM-3324s for recording until the early 2000s, when he rebuilt the UMRK: "The digital format we were using at the time was Frank's original Sony reel-to-reel machines. By the time we were recording on them, they were at least ten years old, if not older . . . things just started dropping out, and we were hearing some digital distortion. It just disintegrated, imploded, nothing went into record. Somehow, it decided it was never going to play back again!" We found one

ZAPPA GEAR

of the 3324s squeezed into a cupboard in Joe's Garage. Both 3324s and the PCM 1610, along with a rackload of control units, interfaces, and remote-control units, were all sold in the 2016 auction.[816] The two mighty recording decks realized just $562 and $625.[817]

Digital tape recorders have all but disappeared from most recording studios, although when we visited the UMRK the PCM-3328 48-track machine was still being used by Joe Travers for restoring and archiving FZ's recordings. Thanks to Sony's clever design, the PCM-3328 can also play the 24-track tapes recorded on the earlier 3324.

Hear it on:
Album: *London Symphony Orchestra, Vol. 2*
Track: "Strictly Genteel"

Almost everything recorded by FZ from 1983 onwards was done on a Sony PCM-3324. This track is the one featuring the infamous allegedly inebriated trumpet section. FZ reckoned on making over fifty edits in this track — can you hear any of them?

Vintage Studio Microphones

"One day I decided to stuff a pair of U87s in the piano . . . and invite anyone in the vicinity to stick their head inside and ramble incoherently"[818]
— FZ

Over the years, FZ put together a collection of rare and valuable vintage recording studio microphones. Some readers may be astonished at their value; it is not unknown for them to sell for over $15,000. Like vintage musical instruments, these old microphones are prized by their owners for their special characteristics and individual tonal subtleties.

Like any serious recording engineer, FZ had his personal preferences for use in different applications: "As far as microphones go, I have different favorites for different instruments. I use U87s, Sony C-37s, AKG 414s. I like to use shotgun mics for the piano to get certain types of effects. For kick drum I like an RE20 or two U47s."[819]

It seems likely that FZ kept a pair of U87s with him on the road. He notes that on the track "Friendly Little Finger," "The solo and drone bass was recorded on a 2-track Nagra, 15 i.p.s., with a pair of Neumann U87 microphones in a rather wet-sounding dressing room, warming up before a concert at Hofstra University on Long Island."[820]

FZ famously mentioned the U47 on the *Joe's Garage* album, using the line "It looks just like a Telefunken U47," on the songs "Sy Borg" and "Crew Slut." The U87 crops up in *The Real Frank Zappa Book* when FZ is talking about watching a local TV evangelist in action: "I heard him announce (into a handheld Neumann U87), 'Jesus just told me that you have another thousand dollars in your pockets.'" I suspect that FZ was not just outraged by the preacher's money grubbing, but also by the casual misuse use of such an expensive microphone as the U87.

AKG stands for "Akustische und Kino-Geräte"—in English: "Acoustical and Cinema Equipment." The company

A Neumann U87 on duty in the UMRK
(Mick Ekers)

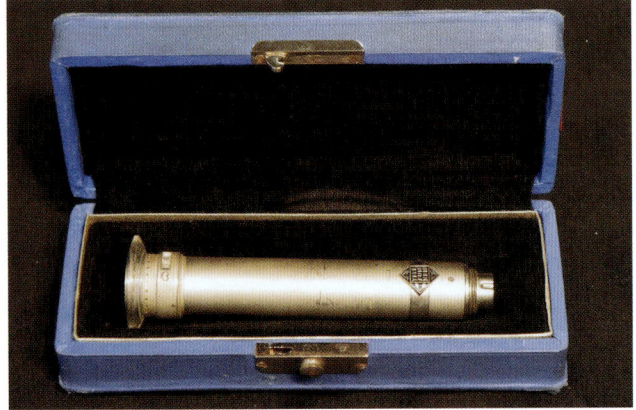

FZ's rare Telefunken M221A microphone
(Mick Ekers)

was founded in Vienna in 1947 by Dr. Rudolf Goerike and Ernst Pless. AKG soon started specializing in the microphones and headphones for which they are principally known, in 1953 introducing the legendary C12 large-diaphragm condenser microphone and the D12 dynamic microphone. They later introduced a stereo version built around two C12 capsules called the C24. In 1971, AKG launched the hugely successful C414, which used solid-state technology and included switches on the case to vary the directional characteristics, sensitivity, and low-end frequency response.[821]

Neumann is perhaps the most legendary name in microphone manufacturers. The company was founded in Berlin in 1928 by Georg Neumann and Erich Rickmann. The CMV 3 was the first ever mass-produced condenser microphone and stayed in production from 1928 until the end of WWII. 1947 was a landmark year; Georg Neumann invented the modern Ni-Cad rechargeable battery and the company launched the U47, the world's first switchable-pattern condenser microphone. Also distributed and badged by Telefunken, the U47 quickly became the standard vocal microphone in studios worldwide.[822] Famously, Frank Sinatra refused to record with any other microphone, and Beatles producer George Martin used it on almost everything (vocals, drums, guitars, and the tambourine) when recording *Rubber Soul*, later describing it as simply his favorite microphone.[823]

In 1949, the U49 followed, which had a remotely switchable pattern, followed the next year by the U50 omnidirectional microphone. In 1960, they introduced their last valve-driven microphone, naming it the U67 to give it continuity with U47 it was intended to replace. The U67 was another huge success and soon became the new studio standard, becoming so well-known that in 1965, Neumann were able to run an advertising campaign consisting of just a photo of a U67 and the words "ask anyone."[824]

In the 1960s, Neumann also produced the Kleine Microphone range of compact microphones such as the KM56 and KM64 illustrated, which contained the tiny Telefunken AC701k valve. In 1967, they introduced the solid-state version of the U67 called the U87; it turned out to sound pretty much the same as the U67 but was more reliable as it didn't require a valve. The U67 and U87 are still being made by Neumann over fifty years later, and they are still the benchmark studio microphones.[825]

Telefunken also distributed and branded microphones from the less well-known company Schoeps. Founded in 1948, in Karlsruhe, Germany, by Dr. Karl Schoeps, the company came to specialize in compact valve microphones and introduced the M221A in 1954. There was a wide range of capsules that could be fitted; FZ owned one with the M934B switchable Omni/Cardioid capsule, with a distinctive plastic baffle. The M221A was made in limited numbers for a few months before the capsule mounting design was reengineered and the M 221 B was introduced.[826]

'The Genius', Neumann M50B Nr.436
(Mick Ekers)

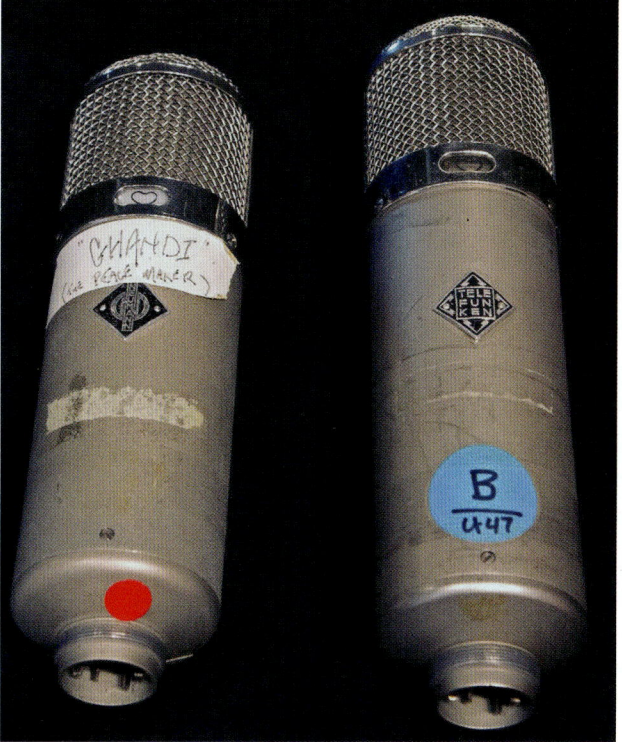

Two of FZ's U47s; a Neumann (Gandhi) and an un-named Telefunken
(Mick Ekers)

ZAPPA GEAR

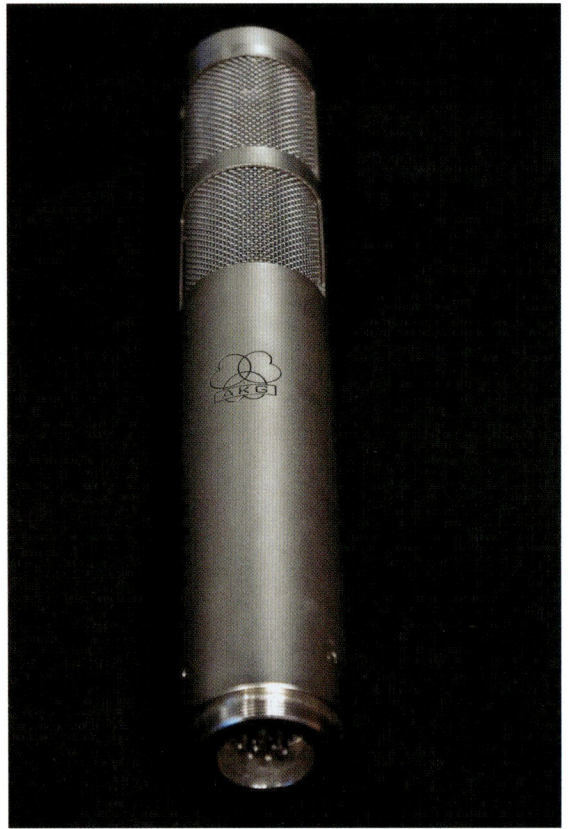

AKG C24 Mk 2 Nr. 1333
(Mick Ekers)

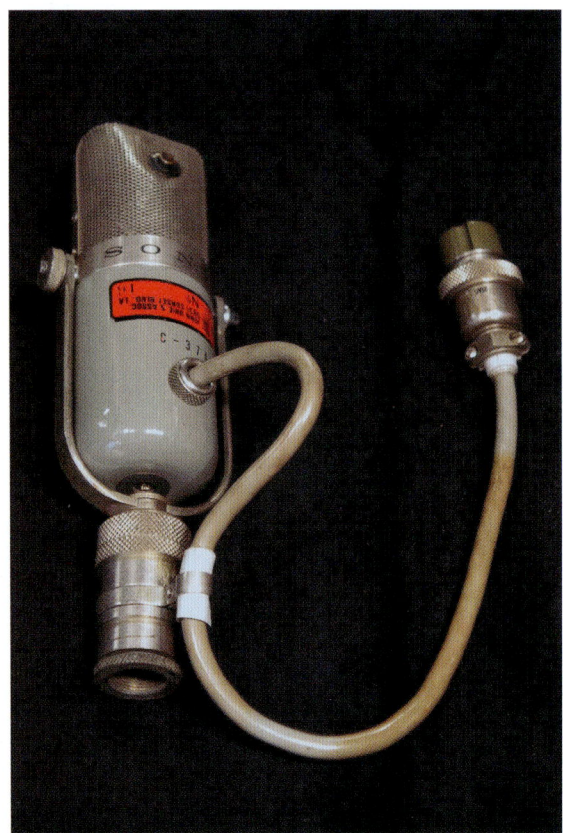

Sony C37A, another highly regarded valve microphone introduced in 1955
(Mick Ekers)

AKG D12; introduced in 1953, it became popular as a bass-drum microphone
(Mick Ekers)

A pair of AKG C414s
(Mick Ekers)

Neumann U67 internals showing the EF806S valve
(Mick Ekers)

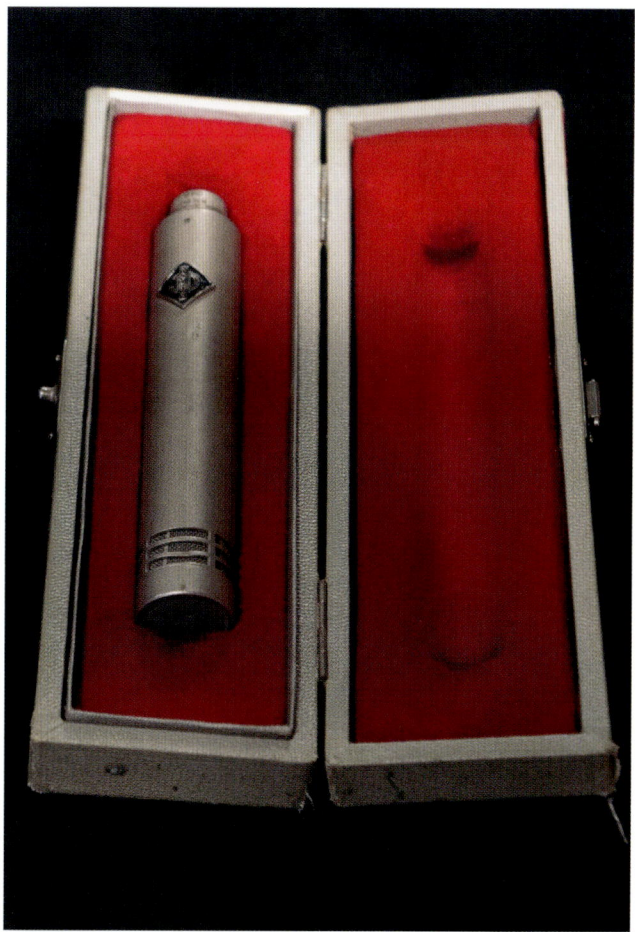

Neumann KM64, slightly battered
(Mick Ekers)

Neumann KM56
(Mick Ekers)

Another microphone of interest that FZ favored was the Sony C37A. This was designed by Sony engineer Kanane Nakatsuru in the mid-1950s. A slot in the back of the grill enabled selection of omnidirectional or cardioid characteristics, and it used a readily available 6AU6 valve, rather than the expensive AC701k found in its European competitors. It was the first Japanese-made condenser microphone, and was found to be particularly suitable for acoustic bass, guitar, banjo, and mandolin, as well as vocals. It still has its fans today, and many are still in use in studios.[827]

In 2005, the US Telefunken company started work on a project to restore FZ's collection: "We went through three Telefunken U47s; four Neumann M49s; a beautiful matched pair of Neumann M50s, circa 1950; and four AKG C24s, circa 1960. We also worked on an AKG C-12A that was missing a cable and power supply and rebuilt a custom Telefunken Ela M251 using the existing capsule. The work was completed in 2007. Other microphones included two U67s, nicknamed 'The Champ' and 'Schneider.'"[828] FZ gave names to many of his favorite microphones, including "Gandhi—the Peacemaker," "The Genius," and "El Pistolero." I think it is interesting that FZ gave names to microphones and other pieces of studio equipment such as drum machines, but never to his guitars, as far as I know.

During my visit to the UMRK in March 2012, I was shown some of the collection by engineer Richard Landers, who has worked on various projects for the ZFT. The microphones were all carefully stored in a securely locked and chained case, but were all in working order and ready for use in the studio.

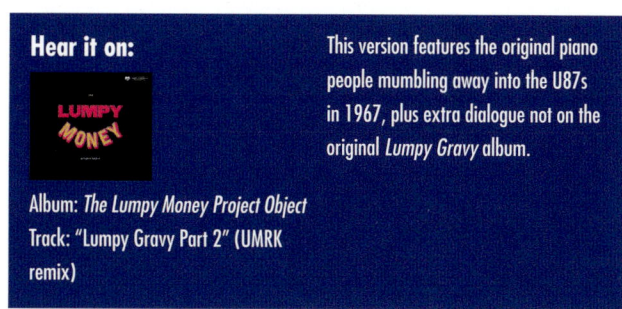

Hear it on:

This version features the original piano people mumbling away into the U87s in 1967, plus extra dialogue not on the original *Lumpy Gravy* album.

Album: *The Lumpy Money Project Object*
Track: "Lumpy Gravy Part 2" (UMRK remix)

ZAPPA GEAR

Crown PZM Microphones

"This is a PZM microphone, which is a really nice device, and it's one of the reasons why we're able to have a stereo dialogue track on this very cheaply produced show."

—FZ[829]

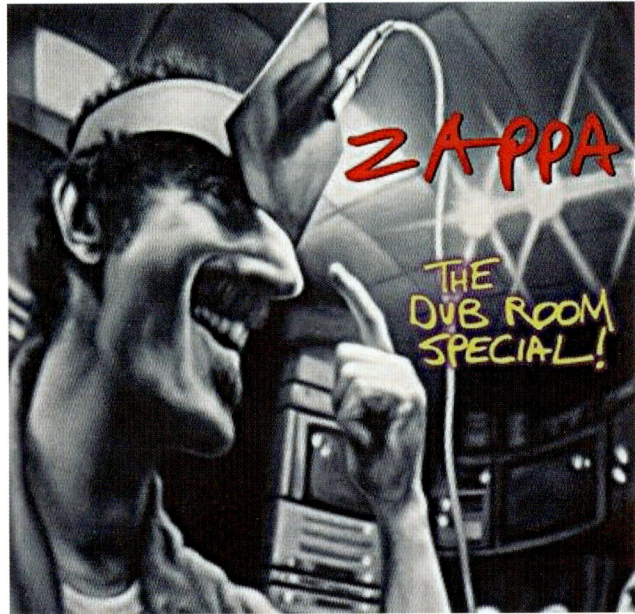

FZ with head mounted PZM on the *Dub Room Special* cover (ZFT)

Thus FZ explains the strange device he is wearing on his head in the introductory sequence of the *Dub Room Special* movie, adding, "This was hooked up so that Thomas Nordegg, the guy that's holding the camera, could actually wear it on his head, like this, so he could get very good stereo sound when he was taking these kinds of pictures."[830]

The Pressure Zone Microphone (PZM) was first marketed in 1980 by the Crown Corporation, more famous at the time for their massive power amplifiers, which were an essential part of most major bands' touring sound systems (FZ had some in his PA system and for a while used a pair as part of his clean onstage guitar rig).[831]

Crown was founded in 1947, in Elkhart, Indiana, by Clarence C. Moore (1904–1979), under the original name International Radio and Electronics Corporation (IREC). Moore, a longtime radio enthusiast who had returned to the US after working for several years in a missionary radio station in Quito, Ecuador, converted a former chicken coop into IREC's first production facility. Drawing on his experience, Moore started distributing open-reel tape recorders, specially modified to operate reliably under rugged conditions.

In 1949, he patented a design for the world's first tape recorder with a built-in power amplifier (15 watts), and IREC started manufacturing their own line of recorders. Over the years, the company diversified and started making stand-alone amplifiers, and in the 1960s changed its name to Crown International. In 1967, they launched the legendary DC300 150-watt-per-channel solid-state amplifier, which established Crown as world leader in the high-power amplifier field.[832]

Recording engineer Ron Wickersham and audio consultant Ed Long invented the Pressure Recording Process (PRP) in 1978. This process uses a pressure-response omnidirectional microphone facing down toward, and very close to, a sound-reflecting surface. By preventing phase interference between direct and reflected sounds, this resulted in a flatter frequency response than could be obtained with conventional microphones. Audio designer Ken Wahrenbrock developed a microphone based on this principle, which could be controlled and manufactured easily; coined the term PZM; and built some prototypes based around a hearing-aid type electret condenser capsule. In 1980, Wahrenbrock licensed Crown International to develop, manufacture, and market the PZMs, and ended up working for the company.[833]

A plastic dome PZM on a stand in the UMRK echo chamber (Mick Ekers)

194

Studio and Recording

In 1982, Wahrenbrock and his technician Vince Motel visited FZ and his sound engineer Mark Pinske at the UMRK to discuss his plans for using PZMs for the forthcoming LSO orchestral recording. After various tests and trials, FZ and Pinske proposed the PZM complement they wanted for the session, and Crown specially manufactured approximately forty various microphones, which FZ and Pinske took with them to London. Many of these were prototype designs, substituting round clear Plexiglas disks and larger rectangular sheets for the standard small black plate of the original design. The plan was to use the PZMs just for the strings and some percussion, and FZ had brought along a large number of conventional recording microphones for the rest of the orchestra. However, as the rehearsal started, Pinske discovered significant recording problems with many of the instruments, and at each break he was scrambling to replace as many other mikes as he could with PZMs.

One key characteristic of the PZM is that it doesn't look anything like a conventional microphone, consisting of a small black gadget attached to a plastic plate or dome. FZ noted that the musicians of the LSO looked on these unfamiliar devices with initial suspicion: "they're used to seeing those grey, heavy, serious-looking microphones . . . then somebody comes in and puts a plastic dome with a PZM in it over their heads and they go 'My tone, my precious tone, I'm going to sound plastic!'"[834]

However, Pinske said that when they understood it was a new type of microphone and that it had some very distinguishing characteristics, they kidded about it, but were cooperative and interested.[835]

The LSO recording was one of the very first times that an orchestra had been recorded in this way, with multiple close-miking of the instruments, digital recording, and the later addition of digital reverb and processing. Although FZ later voiced his dissatisfaction with some of the individual performances on the session, the instruments have a realism and presence that is rarely heard in a conventional orchestral recording.

FZ was very enthusiastic about the results he obtained with these new microphones, telling Wahrenbrock, "In a project this expensive, to put your entire trust in one specific kind of technology and have it pay off is extremely gratifying. We could have played it a lot safer and done it a different way, but I don't think that I could have gotten the same results. There is no way we could have gotten the sounds on these tapes without PZMs."[836] FZ specifically thanks Wahrenbrock in the album liner notes, and in the "Technical Information" section states, "Orchestral microphones: Crown PZMs (30 or 40 of them)."[837]

FZ never used PZMs in such a wholesale fashion again. But he later used a couple to record the ambient sound on *The Perfect Stranger*,[838] and installed several in the UMRK echo chamber, using regular PZM-30s on the floor and walls, and the plastic dome units in the middle of the space. They were still in place when I visited in 2012.

Crown is now part of the Harman group, and is still making high-quality amplifiers and microphones in its Elkhart factory. The PRP patent expired in 1999, although Crown still owns the PZM trademark and the technology is now widely used, with many similar devices available under the generic term "boundary microphones."

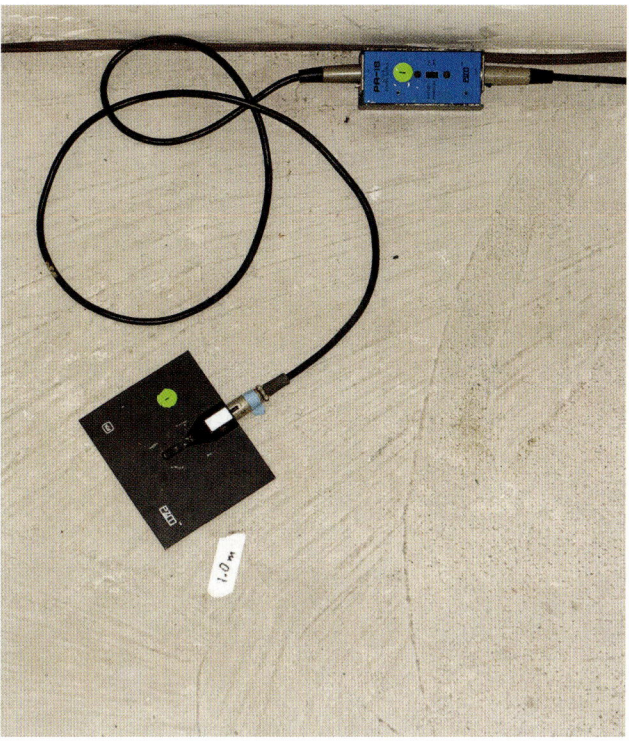

A PZM 30 on the floor of the UMRK echo chamber, the blue box is a PZM PA18 power supply unit
(Mick Ekers)

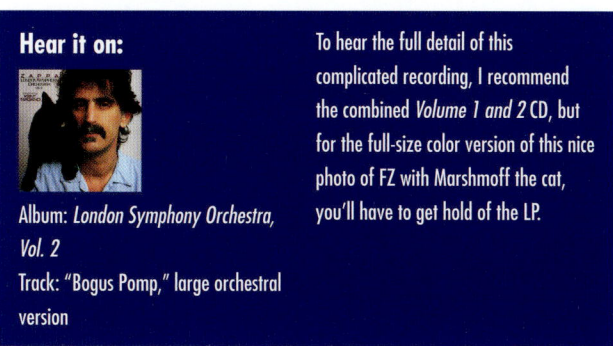

Hear it on:
Album: *London Symphony Orchestra, Vol. 2*
Track: "Bogus Pomp," large orchestral version

To hear the full detail of this complicated recording, I recommend the combined *Volume 1 and 2* CD, but for the full-size color version of this nice photo of FZ with Marshmoff the cat, you'll have to get hold of the LP.

AKG Dummy Head Microphones

"... it was recorded with one of those AKG Dummy Head microphones"
— FZ[839]

On a small shelf overlooking the main live room in the UMRK was a strange sculpted head, which looks like it has come from a stylized shop mannequin. It was in fact an AKG D-99 "dummy head" microphone, which contains a pair of microphones, each positioned behind a small opening in each "ear." One of the first commercial devices of its type, the D-99 was designed to record sounds in stereo just as they would be perceived by the human ear.

While this technique (known as binaural recording) can be implemented simply by using a pair of microphones in stereo placed close together, the purpose of the dummy head was to additionally reproduce the physical effects of a human head and ears, which affect and shape sound before it reaches our eardrums and give us a realistic impression of the position of a sound source within a three-dimensional space, rather than just in simple terms of stereo left and right.

With stereo headphones, the listener can get the effect of sounds emanating from all directions, including above and behind, in a way that is very difficult to recreate with stereo loudspeakers.[840]

The binaural technique is not new, and was first demonstrated in the transmission of an opera from the stage of the Paris Opera House in 1881. Inventor Clement Ader used pairs of carbon telephone transmitters across the stage, mixed down to two separate telephone lines per listener. The two receivers were placed against each ear, producing the binaural effect.[841] AKG made an early prototype head in 1949 for measuring purposes, which had two condenser microphones. The production D-99 was introduced in 1973, and was popularly nicknamed "the Harry," a name which AKG later officially adopted. It had two dynamic microphones mounted inside each "ear."[842]

In an interview in *Guitar* magazine in 1993, David Mead remarked that FZ had cited Terry Bozzio's "Hands with a Hammer" as a near-perfect drum sound: "That's true and you know it was recorded with just one of those AKG Dummy Head microphones and a C24; there's no close miking on the set at all. It's all just ambient miking. It's really a fat-sounding kit."[843]

As FZ said about "Hands with a Hammer," "With all the freeze-dried drum sounds heard on records today, this ambient 4-track recording of real drums, well-tuned, played with real skill, serves as a historic document. There is a whole generation of listeners out there who have never heard what real drums are supposed to sound like."[844] As well as the wonderful drum

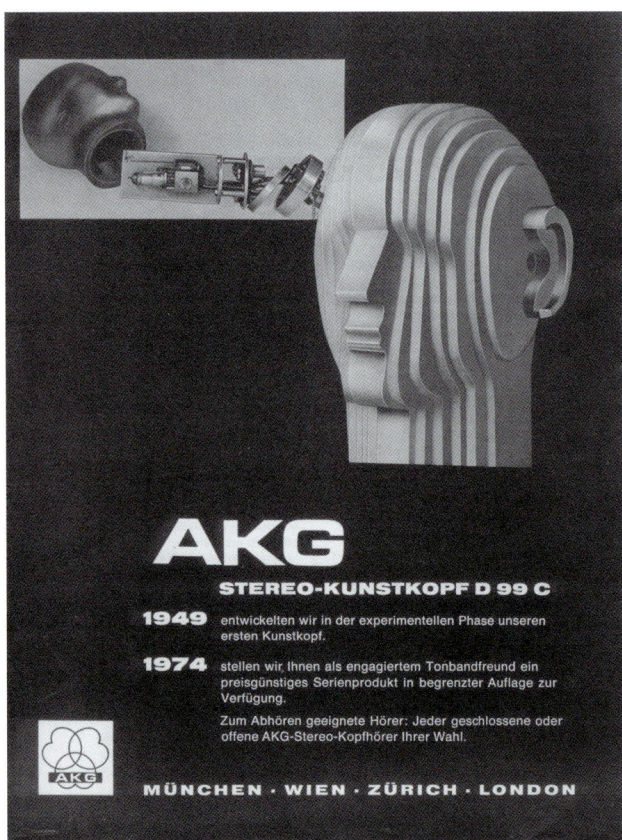

1974 AKG advert for the D99-C

FZ's 'Harry' at the UMRK in 2012
(Mick Ekers)

sound, the recording faithfully reproduces the ambience of the concert hall; on a good stereo system it really feels as if you are in the front row at the concert.

In the 1970s, Neumann also made a dummy-head microphone: the significantly more expensive model KU 80, which used phantom-powered condenser microphones, and, instead of mounting the microphones flush with the earhole like the AKG, had them inside the head at the end of a modelled ear canal.[845] There was also one of these mounted on a wall in the UMRK, but I have been unable to find out if FZ ever used it for a recording. Neither device would commonly have been used for studio recording, and it is not obvious to me what FZ had in mind when he had them placed in the UMRK; perhaps to capture the overall ambience of the studio, or maybe he just wanted a pair of ears in the live room.

After an initial flush of enthusiasm for binaural recording in the 1970s, shortcomings with the available technology became apparent. The positional effect varied significantly from one listener to another, and the need to use headphones was considered inconvenient. The technique fell out of favor, and the D-99 is no longer manufactured. However, with the increased advent of portable music players, where headphone listening is the norm, there has been a resurgence of interest in binaural recording. Neumann now manufactures a very sophisticated descendant of the KU 80, the KU 100, which at the time of writing retails at around 8,000 euros!

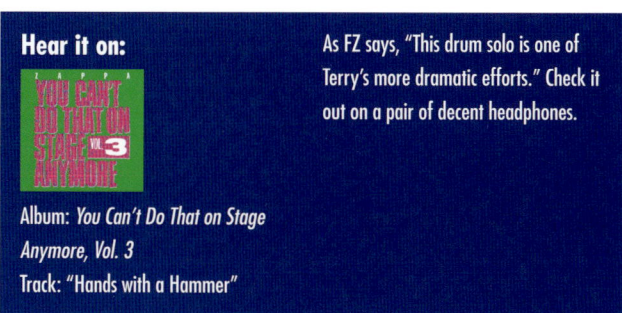

Hear it on:
As FZ says, "This drum solo is one of Terry's more dramatic efforts." Check it out on a pair of decent headphones.
Album: *You Can't Do That on Stage Anymore, Vol. 3*
Track: "Hands with a Hammer"

The microphone hoop at the UMRK in 2012
(Mick Ekers)

Yellow Shark Microphone Hoop

"He [FZ] asked me to carry it disguised as a bishop (in the concert). I didn't want to do that."

—Ali Askin[846]

Composer Ali Askin was largely responsible for transcribing, copying, and arranging the music for the various pieces that were played during *The Yellow Shark*, a program of FZ compositions performed at a series of concerts in Europe by the Ensemble Modern in September, 1992.

From the start, FZ conceived that the concerts should be experienced in surround sound, and a special six-channel sound system was designed by the UMRK team of audio specialists. David Dondorf (technical coordinator and stage monitor engineer) explained: "Frank envisioned something new . . . where the audience sat surrounded by six loudspeaker locations, the sound from each of these points being different mixes as determined by the score, each audience member hearing the show from a unique audio perspective."[847]

Further to this concept, FZ got his technicians to fit a metal hoop, approximately one meter in diameter, with cables and mountings for six equally spaced microphones. Each microphone could be fed, via the master mixing console, to one of the six speaker systems. The hoop was attached to a long handle and the idea was that during a concert an operator could place the hoop above a particular performer, such that the six microphones would place the individual musician's performance in the center of the sound image.

FZ called the device "the bishop," and tried to persuade Askin to dress up as a bishop and operate it on stage. This harked back to concerts where FZ had the original Mothers of Invention bass player Roy Estrada appear on stage in a bizarre chain-mail bishop's outfit; Askin refused. However, Askin told me that despite his refusal, "the bishop" did play a part in the proceedings: "The hoop was on stage and was used in two pieces ('Welcome,' 'Food Gathering'). A couple of musicians stood around or were 'hooped.'"[848]

I found the device in residence at the URMK in 2012, although the microphones had been removed. *The Yellow Shark* was the last orchestral project FZ was involved in before his death in 1993, too unwell to appear at all the concerts as he

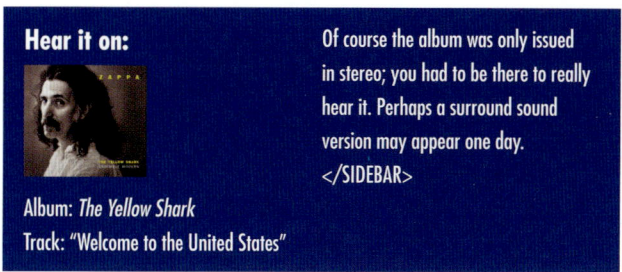

Hear it on:
Of course the album was only issued in stereo; you had to be there to really hear it. Perhaps a surround sound version may appear one day.
</SIDEBAR>
Album: *The Yellow Shark*
Track: "Welcome to the United States"

was suffering from the later stages of his illness. It is typical of FZ that, despite his failing health and among all the other complexities of putting such an ambitious project together, he was still experimenting with new techniques for recording and amplifying musical instruments.

The operator moves 'the bishop' into position during rehearsals for The Yellow Shark (*still from* AAAFNRAA, *1992*)

CHAPTER SIX
PERCUSSION AND OTHER GEAR

"Frank's drumming looked completely unnatural to me but it sounded absolutely great; he held his hands in the weirdest ways . . . it was just all wrong, there was no economy of motion with Frank it was just however he could get his body to do something, but the sound was fantastic; nobody played like that"
—*Ruth Underwood*[849]

Piccolo Snare

Cowbells and Concert Bass Drum

Deagan Commander Vibraphone

Bicycle

Kazoo

Haynes Mixer King

Ludwig Octa-Plus Drum Sets

Maestro Sound System for Woodwinds

La Peppina Coffee Machine

Pen, Paper, and Thesaurus

The Conductor's Baton

Note
If you have very specialized technical interests, you may still be hoping that this "other things" section may contain information about FZ's PA systems, lighting gear, filmmaking equipment, music stands, and who knows what else. If so, you will probably be disappointed, but rest assured that it is hoped that the *Zappa Gear* website may eventually include supplementary material that is of such minority appeal that it has no place even in such a book as this. Meanwhile, I hope you will find some interest in this arbitrary collection, which includes some of my favorite sections, and yes, I think the coffee machine *is* important.

ZAPPA GEAR

Piccolo Snare

"It's just a lousy little snare drum, but it's a start."

— FZ[850]

One of FZ's personal percussion instruments was a small vintage snare drum of the type know as a piccolo snare. A regular snare drum has a depth of about 6"; a piccolo is about half that depth and is tuned to a higher pitch. Early photos of the Mothers of Invention show drummer Billy Mundi using the snare in his setup in 1966. FZ included it in Ruth Underwood's percussion station in the 1970s, and most likely used it on "It Must Be a Camel" on *Hot Rats* and other albums where he added his own percussion effects.

Ruth told me how FZ would play it when he joined her on percussion on the track "Uncle Meat": "Frank would throw in all those extra little notes on these four drums: two bongos of mine, and then a piccolo snare drum, and a field drum . . . just those four little insignificant drums in my station, and Frank made the most use out of those, he just threw in the perfect notes."[851]

On the DVD *The Drummers of Frank Zappa*, Chad Wackerman remarks that it was part of the kit he was given to audition on: " . . . a funky little 20" Ludwig bass drum, and a couple of the concert toms from your [Ralph Humphrey's] kit, flat ride cymbal, a 13" piccolo snare, like—oddball."[852]

This prompted Ruth to tell how FZ was looking for the drum near the end of his life: "About six months before he died he called me up (in person) and he wanted to know if I had any idea where that piccolo drum was. I thought that was just the most poignant, heartbreaking thing, with everything he was dealing with, and the physical pain he was in, and the rush to try and get as much done as possible before he couldn't work anymore . . . he wanted that drum, for God knows what."[853]

Ruth was unable to help FZ at the time, and often wondered about the drum. After I finished my interview with Ruth at the UMRK in 2012, she went downstairs to talk to ZFT vaultmeister Joe Travers. While we were busying ourselves photographing FZ's Marshall amplifiers, we heard shrieks of excitement from the far end of the studio. We went over to find Joe showing Ruth the piccolo snare, which had been found! The smile on Ruth's face shows her delight that it had not been lost.

Inspecting the drum, I found a small badge on the side that identified it as being made by WFL Drums. WFL stands for "William F. Ludwig," and was the name of his company from 1937 to 1959 (see the Ludwig Octa-Plus Drum Sets section for more on Ludwig). The style of the badge identifies the year of manufacture as being between 1955 and 1959.[854]

The drum is still in very good condition for its age, with few signs of corrosion or damage to the fittings, although it has obviously been played a lot. It has been fitted with a modern Remo head, which looks hardly used. How and where FZ came by the drum is not known; he spoke of his parents getting him a small snare drum when he was fourteen. It would be nice to think this was the same drum, but he later said that it had been rented and was eventually returned to the store.[855]

Joe Travers, Ruth Underwood and FZ's piccolo snare
(Mick Ekers)

FZ's 'WFL Drums' piccolo snare at the UMRK in 2012
(Mick Ekers)

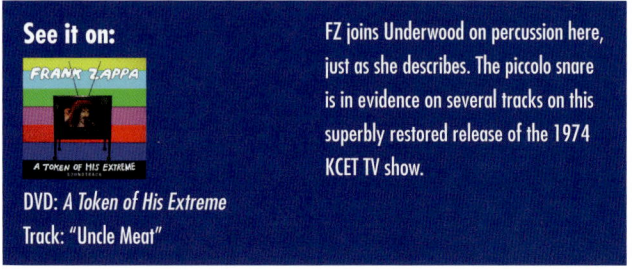

See it on:
DVD: *A Token of His Extreme*
Track: "Uncle Meat"

FZ joins Underwood on percussion here, just as she describes. The piccolo snare is in evidence on several tracks on this superbly restored release of the 1974 KCET TV show.

Cowbells and Concert Bass Drum

"I mean the main feature of the drum set was the cowbells!"
— *Ralph Humphrey*[856]

Aside from the piccolo snare already mentioned, Joe Travers had another piece of percussion equipment to show Ruth Underwood during our visit to the UMRK. This was a steel bar with four miscellaneous cowbells attached. Ruth was delighted to see these again, remembering them from her time with the Roxy band, and could not resist straightening the smallest one while we were photographing them!

It looks like they were a remnant of either Ralph Humphrey's or Chester Thompson's kit. Thompson and Humphrey mention the cowbells on the *Drummers of Frank Zappa* DVD:

> **RH:** I had a set of cowbells. You had a set of cowbells too?
>
> **CT:** I had a set of cowbells; a little cluster of them.
>
> **RH:** I mean the main feature of the drum set was the cowbells![857]

FZ was photographed at the UMRK in 1982 with some of these cowbells, along with his collection of woodblocks and the bongos that he used to play, but I only got to see the cowbells. One striking piece that I found in the UMRK was this huge 40" Ludwig concert bass drum, suspended from a heavy-duty

Ruth straightens out the cowbells
(Mick Ekers)

movable stand. At first glance I thought that this might be the same instrument that Ruth Underwood played in the Roxy performances, but that one had a plain shell finish and black hardware. When and where this one was obtained is not certain; it was probably purchased at the time the UMRK was built. FZ certainly liked the look of this instrument, and more than once posed with it for photographers. It was sold in the 2016 auction (complete with a touring flight case) for $10,000.

The giant concert bass drum at rest in the UMRK
(Mick Ekers)

FZ and his percussion toys at the UMRK in 1982
(Chris Walters—Getty Images)

ZAPPA GEAR

Deagan Commander Vibraphone

"And he told me to show up the next day, with my gear or just come with sticks; he had his vibraphone set up at the Garrick"

— Ruth Underwood[858]

Ruth Underwood in full flight on the Deagan during the legendary shows at the Roxy in December 1973
(still from Roxy, the Movie, 2015)

The vibraphone is a relatively modern tuned percussion instrument. The instrument evolved from the basic steel marimba during the 1920s, as a result of parallel developments by Herman Winterhoff of the Leedy Manufacturing Company in Indianapolis, and Henry J. Schluter of the Deagan company in Chicago. Leedy trademarked their instrument the "vibraphone," and Deagan called theirs the "vibraharp," but vibraphone or simply "vibes" became the most popular name.[859] The instrument became very popular, not only in the worlds of jazz and popular music, but was also written for in the classical music world. Deagan became the leading manufacturer of tuned percussion instruments in the US, along with Musser (also of Chicago and founded by an ex-employee). In 1978 the Deagan company was sold to the Slingerland Drum Company, and the Deagan trademark and patents were subsequently purchased by the Yamaha corporation in 1986.[860] Original Deagan vibraphones are still much sought-after by musicians.

With a range of three octaves ascending from F, the vibraphone is essentially a set of tuned metal bars (steel or aluminum) arranged like a piano keyboard. The bars are suspended above individual metal tube resonators, which amplify the fundamental pitch. Each of these has a rotating disc vane just inside the top, which causes a repeated opening and closing of the resonator. The vanes are powered by a variable speed electric motor and when moving, give rise to the distinctive tremolo effect of the instrument. The vibraphone is usually played with rubber- or wound yarn–tipped mallets and has a sustain foot pedal similar to that of a piano.[861]

FZ owned a vibraphone in the early 1960s, and it seems likely that he doubled on vibraphone as well as guitar with Joe Perrino and the Mellotones (see the Fender Jazzmaster section). FZ played vibraphone on "Memories of El Monte" by the Penguins, released in 1963, and also on the *World's Greatest Sinner* soundtrack. According to Barry Miles, he sold his vibraphone to Paul Buff along with his drums and Jazzmaster guitar when he purchased Pal studios in 1964.[862]

By the time the Mothers were playing their legendary residency at the Garrick theatre in New York in 1967, FZ had a vibraphone on stage again. Ruth Underwood told me how she and her brother saw FZ heading towards the Garrick while they were in queue to see a Tony Williams Lifetime concert at the Village Gate, also on Bleecker Street. As Ruth tells it, her

FZ's Deagan Commander Vibraphone (or Vibraharp as Deagan called it)
(ZFT)

The flight case for the Deagan, note the 'Mothers' sticker as mentioned in the text.
(ZFT)

Hear it on:

Video: *Roxy the Movie*
Track: "Echidna's Arf (Of You)"

Ruth Underwood is in action on the Deagan in the first section of this fiendishly complicated piece before switching to marimba. Hardcore fans may like to hear an earlier and slightly slower arrangement recorded at Helsinki in August 1973, on the *Road Tapes Venue #2* CD.

brother "did everything but trip Frank up as he was walking to work . . . and said 'Frank, Frank, you gotta hear my sister play! She's the world's greatest marimbaist!' And Frank actually stopped and was intrigued by that idea. And he told me to show up the next day with my gear or just come with sticks, he had his vibraphone set up at the Garrick and we would do an audition."[863]

Ruth distinctly remembers that the instrument that FZ had at the Garrick was a Deagan Commander, as he lent it to Ruth for a while. She told me that as she "harbored the hope and fantasy of playing Frank's music with him . . . and some of these other musicians, I immediately went out and bought a Deagan Commander Vibraphone . . . and I thought if I just get the spatial sense of Frank's vibraphone, when my shot comes up, I can just say 'You mean like this?' and just dash it off on his vibraphone, as if I'd been playing it for years." Ruth heard nothing after the audition for several months, but eventually got a call to play a warm-up event for the band that December. She was then invited to play on the *Uncle Meat* recording sessions the following February, leading to an association with FZ that was to last many years.[864]

Ruth regularly played FZ's Deagan as part of her percussion setup when she worked with him in the early 1970s bands, notably in the Roxy performances. When we met at the UMRK she asked what had become of it, but Gail Zappa was not sure of its whereabouts and we did not get to see it. However, it was found and listed in the 2016 auction, complete with a flight case bearing the label "Zappa and the Mothers Est. 1960 Cucamonga CA." The lot was sold for $56,250.[865]

The Bicycle

"How long have you been playing bike, Frank?"
"About two weeks."

Another "instrument" without which this book would not be complete is the bicycle. In March 1963, a youthful, clean-shaven and suited FZ appeared in a novelty item on the popular *Steve Allen* US TV show on Channel 5. FZ recalled that he "Just called them up, and said I play the bicycle and you know, they were booking all kinds of goofy things on there."[866]

Two bicycles had been set up onstage, and in a very amusing interview with the affable Allen, FZ demonstrated the various sounds that could be obtained from a bicycle. With characteristic attention to technical detail, FZ told Allen that he was using a pair of "Louie Bellson–style drumsticks," and a bow that he had borrowed from the bass player in the studio band.

After FZ briefed Allen and the band, they performed what he called an "Improvised concerto for two bicycles, a pre-recorded tape, and the musicians in the back." The bicycle spokes

FZ with Steve Allen and bikes
(*stills from* The Steve Allen Show, *1963*)

were alternately bowed and plucked by Allen, while FZ variously blew into the handlebars, conducted the band, and played the bicycle with the drumsticks. The band accompanied with atonal noises, having been asked to "refrain from musical tones."

FZ apparently borrowed one of the bikes from his sister Candy,[867] but we have no further technical information on them. The spot is well worth watching, combining humor, musique concrète, and elements of Varèse; FZ finishes with a plug for his new single "How's Your Bird?", named after a Steve Allen catchphrase.

> **See it on:**
> Recordings of this can usually be found on YouTube and other video sources on the Internet—look for the complete sixteen-minute segment.

ZAPPA GEAR

The Kazoo

"... after the last line in the song the kazoo comes in and then the whole thing sort of deteriorates before your very eyes."

—FZ[868]

Many of the tracks on the album *Freak Out!* feature a kazoo, usually doubling the guitar part, but sometimes as a solo instrument. The budget for the album was relatively high, and there were plenty of horn players on the session who could have played the parts on a more conventional wind instrument; nonetheless FZ opted to use a kazoo on several tracks, including "Motherly Love," "Hungry Freaks Daddy," and "Who Are the Brain Police?" (as he describes above).

The kazoo is a small wind instrument, usually consisting of a tapered tube about 12 cm (5") long with the wider end flattened to form a mouthpiece. A hole in the tube leads to a chamber, which holds a membrane that vibrates and adds a buzzing quality to your voice when you hum into it. This type of instrument, known as a mirliton, has been used in Africa as far back as tribal history can trace, to disguise the sound of somebody's voice or to imitate animals, often for various ceremonial purposes.

Made from various materials such as bone, gourds, or bamboo, with an animal skin membrane, similar instruments have likely been used since prehistoric times for hunting purposes and as a means of communication.[869]

The modern kazoo was invented in the 1840s by the American Alabama Vest, and first manufactured in Macon, Georgia. It was launched at the Georgia State Fair in 1852 as the "Down-South Submarine." In 1912, travelling salesman Emil Sorg developed the idea of making metal kazoos with Michael McIntyre, a Buffalo tool and die maker. McIntyre moved to Eden, New York, where he went into partnership with Harry Richardson, the owner of a metal-forming plant. They began producing metal kazoos in 1914, and founded the Original American Kazoo Company in 1916. McIntyre received a patent for the kazoo in 1923.[870] The Eden factory is still producing metal kazoos today, using the original equipment, although when I last looked their website reported that the factory was down to a three-day work week, Tuesday to Thursday, due to declining orders.

We don't know what brand of kazoo FZ favored, but it is as likely as not to have been an Original American model. It's easy to see why the inherent silliness of the kazoo appealed to FZ, and he used it from time to time throughout his recording career. It remains the only instrument on which almost anyone, with a minimal amount of practice, can sound just like FZ. Just remember to hum into it, not blow!

A typical metal body kazoo
(Mick Ekers)

For comparison, FZ and his Midas touring desk in 1980

> **Hear it on:**
> Album: *The Lost Episodes*
> Track: "The Big Squeeze"
>
> This novelty (recorded for a Luden's cough-drop commercial in 1967) is the only track I can find where FZ is specifically credited with playing the kazoo. Although FZ made great use of the kazoo on many tracks on the *Freak Out!* album, it is not recorded who is playing.

Percussion and Other Gear

Haynes Mixer King

"Do you have any idea what this thing is?"

— FZ[871]

During the *Video from Hell* movie, FZ pulls out an aged piece of musical equipment from a shelf and remarks with amusement: "Do you have any idea what this thing is? This is the brains of our PA system from the Garrick Theatre, where we used to work in New York in '67. The whole band ran through this box, and a couple of speaker columns. I didn't know we still had this thing!"[872]

"This thing" was a Haynes Mixer King Model 800-6A solid-state six-channel PA mixer from the early 1960s. When *Video from Hell* was shot twenty years later it looked astonishingly primitive and quaint; compare it with the 36-channel Midas mixing desk that FZ was using for concerts in the 1980s.

The Haynes range was manufactured by the grandly named Amplifier Corporation of America. The earliest mention I could find of the company was in the 1940 Broadcasting Yearbook directory of manufacturers, listing their address as 17 West 20th Street, New York, and the manager as N.M. Haynes. At some time the company moved out to Westbury, New York, and they were purchased by Unicord in 1964, as a factory for the Univox line. Unicord in turn was purchased by Korg in 1985.[873]

Each of the input channels had a single high-impedance microphone input; volume, bass, and treble controls; and an echo/reverb switch. The output was routed via the Reverb/Echo loop to a large rotary Master Volume control and mono output to the amplifier. The original illuminated on-off push button had been removed, and a toggle switch mounted next to the hole in the casing.

If the speaker columns FZ referred to were the companion Haynes units, they would have been a pair of full-range units, each containing four 12" speakers in a vertical array, with a 100-watt amplifier built into the cabinet.

Although this may seem a very crude setup for a name group like the Mothers of Invention, this was the way PA systems were back then. In 1967, this was an acceptable piece of PA equipment, that would have been used by many professional and semi-professional bands. In their early days, I saw Pink Floyd and Led Zeppelin playing concerts using similar gear—mind you, they didn't sound very good!

I found this historical artefact on a shelf in a storage room at Joe's Garage, looking more or less as FZ left it; I would not be surprised if the simple 1960s circuits were still working. N.M. Haynes (I assume it was the same person) produced a few small technical audio books in the 1950s and 1960s. One was titled *Tape Editing and Splicing for the Professional and Amateur Tape Recordist*. I'm sure FZ would have approved.

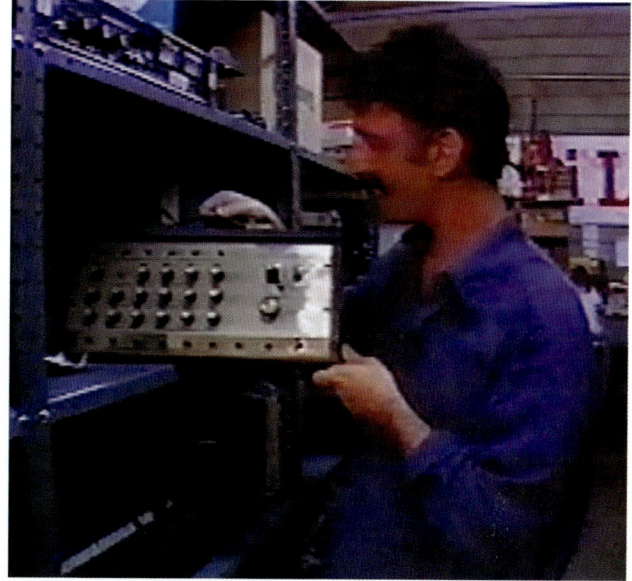

FZ and his 1967 'Mixer King'
(still from Video From Hell, *1987)*

The back of the Mixer King, just in case you were expecting some additional inputs and outputs!
(Mick Ekers)

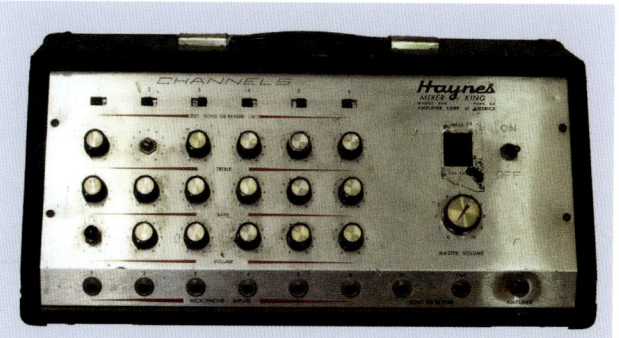

The control panel of the Haynes Mixer King
(Mick Ekers)

ZAPPA GEAR

Ludwig Octa-Plus Drum Sets

"My Pearl drum set went away and Frank got us two Octa-Plus Ludwig drum sets."

— *Ralph Humphrey*[874]

The Mahavishnu Orchestra were the support band on many dates during the Mothers of Invention's spring tour of 1973. Percussionist Ruth Underwoood was with FZ watching them play at one show; the Mahavishnu band were incredibly loud and fast, and virtuoso drummer Billy Cobham was all over his massive see-through Fibes drum set.

Underwood remembers; "His face changed . . . and I knew something was going to happen."[875] FZ wanted his band to be just as powerful, and one ingredient that he decided to add was more drums—so second drummer Chester Thompson was added to the lineup in October 1973.

FZ had fitted Ralph Humphrey's Pearl drum set with Barcus Berry transducers at one stage, but the results were not particularly satisfactory,[876] and sometime in early 1974 he bought a matching pair of maple Ludwig Octa-Plus drum sets for the band. These were the newest, largest, and loudest drum sets in the Ludwig range at the time.

The Ludwig drum company was founded in Chicago in 1910 by the German-born brothers William F. and Theobald Ludwig. Initially they were just producing bass drum pedals, but soon expanded into timpani and then other types of drums. By the 1920s, Ludwig was an established and successful company, but the demise of silent movies and the crash of 1929 hit sales of percussion instruments and the company was sold to C.G. Conn.

In 1937, William F. Ludwig formed his own company, called The WFL Drum Company. Ludwig bought back the rights to the brand name in the late 1950s, and the rejuvenated company started to reestablish itself. They received a massive boost in 1964, when Beatles drummer Ringo Starr appeared on television with a Ludwig-branded kit.[877]

By the 1970s, Ludwig had a reputation as one of the leading rock drum producers, keeping up with the demand for louder and larger kits. The 1973 Ludwig catalogue introduced concert toms, normal drums with the bottom resonant head removed to give the drums more attack and volume. The first sets to use these were the double bass drum Quadra-Plus and Octa-Plus sets.

The stock Octa-Plus configuration had eight melodic toms designed to be tuned to a true pitch, enabling melodic lines to be played.[878] Humphrey recalls that he and Thompson decided to tune their sets differently, with Thompson's set about a third higher, to help them tell "who was playing what and when."[879] Humphrey left in 1974, and for a time some of the toms found their way into Ruth Underwood's percussion section. When Thompson left the band in 1975 he bought one of the kits from FZ, who kept the other one.

Terry Bozzio auditioned for FZ in 1975, on one of the Octa-Plus sets, and played it on his first tour with the Mothers (the *Bongo Fury* band with Captain Beefheart on vocals), before he started using his own black Gretsch kit.[880] There were still some pieces of the kit in evidence when Chad Wackerman took his audition in 1981, as he recalled having to play on a put-together set of assorted drums including a couple of Octa-Plus toms.[881]

Seven drums were sold as a lot in the 2016 auction, and sold for $4,687.50.[882] What happened to the three missing toms

Chester Thompson and the Octa-Plus kit in 1974
(still from The Dub Room Special! ,1982)

Ludwig advert from 1980

and the other kit is not known. Ludwig stopped listing the Octa-Plus set in 1982. The company is still in business but fashions have changed, and there are no large sets of single-headed drums in their catalogue.

The incomplete Octa-Plus kit sold at auction in 2016
(ZFT)

Hear it on:
Listen out for the signature tom fills from Ralph and Chester on this track, an inspiration for drummer Phil Collins, who openly reused them when Chester joined his band.

Video: *A Token of His Extreme*
Track: "More Trouble Every Day"

Bunk Gardner with Maestro from the *Burnt Weeny Sandwich* album cover
(ZFT)

Maestro Sound System for Woodwinds

"The alto and tenor saxes were individually amplified by means of a contact pickup through a pair of Maestro woodwind effects units."
— FZ [883]

During 1968, Mothers of Invention horn players Bunk Gardner and Ian Underwood would often be seen on stage with a black box on a stand in front of them. The black boxes were part of the new Sound System for Woodwinds (SSFW), manufactured by the Gibson subsidiary Maestro.

Both clarinets and saxophones fitted with the special Maestro pickups could be plugged in to these units, and their sounds could be modified by various combinations of effects circuits. They could then be amplified like an electric guitar or keyboard. As the Mothers of Invention began to perform in larger venues, this was just what FZ needed to allow his horn players to keep up in volume.

In the late 1960s, there had been a small explosion in the availability of systems for amplifying woodwind instruments, after the development of various types of contact microphones designed specifically for the purpose. Maestro realized that with the possibility of amplification, many musicians would also want to use special effects like their guitar- and keyboard-playing colleagues. The pickups were built into a saxophone mouthpiece and a clarinet barrel, which could be fitted to existing instruments without drilling or modifying them, unlike some other devices.

The first SSFW model (the W1) was exhibited by Chicago Musical Instruments (Gibson's parent company) at the summer NAMM show in 1967. Their press release stated: "In addition to a number of instrumental 'voices' the Maestro gives the performer a fuzz tone and a jazz tone. Completely transistorized, the unit will perform through any good amplifier."[884]

The top panel had output sockets for optional stereo or mono use, a pair of Volume and Tone controls for the Bass and Treble voices, and between them Speed and Intensity controls for the Tremolo unit. Below these were a large black rectangular Cancel button and an illuminated on-off switch.

Next came another control panel with inputs for clarinet and saxophone, and a set of seven blue (bass voice) and four yellow (treble voice) switches labelled Jazz Tone, Fuzz Tone, Cello, Tuba, Bass Sax, Clarinet, Bassoon, English Horn, Oboe D'Amore, Muted Horn, and Natural Amp. The individual voices were produced by various permutations of the octave divider, fuzz, filter, and tremolo effects, and could be combined together if desired.

With his usual delight in technical minutiae, FZ states in the *Uncle Meat* sleeve notes that "Things that sound like a trumpet

ZAPPA GEAR

are actually clarinets played through an electronic device made by Maestro with a setting labelled Oboe D'Amore and sped up a minor third with a V.S.O. (variable speed oscillator)."[885] Gardner and Underwood would often use the octave effects in performance, and would sometimes run the signal from their SSFWs through a wah-wah pedal. After FZ disbanded the original Mothers of Invention in 1969, the SSFW was not used on stage by any of his later bands, although Underwood used his to good effect on the *Hot Rats* album.

Maestro later brought out an improved model, the W2, which added a set of footswitches, and later the W3 with separate controls for the octave divider. They were used by many progressive bands, such as Traffic and Van der Graaf Generator, and also by jazz musicians like Eddie Harris and Wayne Shorter. However, they fell out of fashion after a few years and were rarely seen in the 1970s; Gibson's new owners abandoned manufacture of all Maestro units in 1979. They still have their fans today, and working units sell for well over $1000.

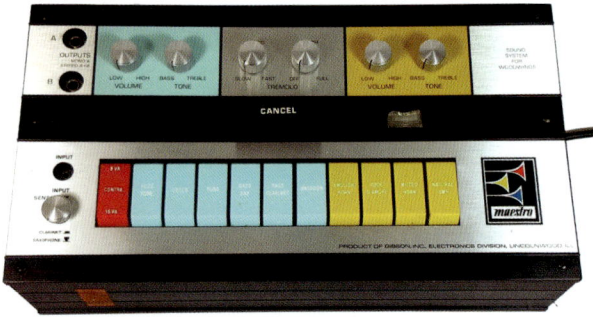

The Maestro Sound System for Woodwinds control panel
(Tony Miln, Soundgas)

Ian Underwood with Maestro on the Hot Rats cover
(ZFT)

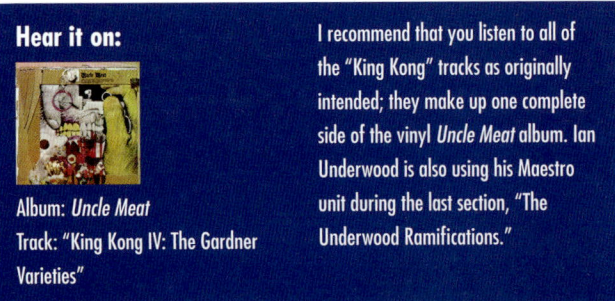

Hear it on:
Album: *Uncle Meat*
Track: "King Kong IV: The Gardner Varieties"

I recommend that you listen to all of the "King Kong" tracks as originally intended; they make up one complete side of the vinyl *Uncle Meat* album. Ian Underwood is also using his Maestro unit during the last section, "The Underwood Ramifications."

La Peppina Coffee Machine

"I like pepper, tobacco, and coffee; that's my metabolism."
—FZ[886]

On many occasions FZ spoke about his love for coffee and cigarettes, and he was renowned for copious and continuous consumption of both throughout his life, although he eschewed alcohol and mind-altering drugs of any kind. In an interview in the Finnish magazine *Suosikki*, he was asked if he had a drug problem and responded, "Yes, with coffee," continuing, "I'm an absolutely sober person. I don't consume alcohol. I don't smoke weed. But I drink gallons of coffee."[887]

During FZ's last tour in 1988, his newly recruited guitar tech Merl Saunders Jr. was given some other duties in addition to looking after the guitars and amps: "I actually had to make his coffee every day . . . I had a little road case with an espresso machine in it."[888]

During my second visit to the UMRK, Gail Zappa remarked that they still had the flight case and the coffee machine, and I jumped at the chance to see it. A small purple flight case was brought up from the basement, and sure enough it contained a small red coffee maker, with a separate compartment to hold the power lead and various small parts. This also contained a tin of Medaglia D'Oro Caffe Espresso. This was not an original and had been added by Diva Zappa; however, it is likely that this would have been a brand that FZ favored.

Subsequent research has identified the machine as a La Peppina espresso machine manufactured by the Italian company FE-AR. FE-AR was founded in Milan by Felice Arosio, and from the late 1950s to the mid-1980s produced, almost unchanged, a lightweight (3.5 kg) portable single-lever machine, originally named La Piccolina and marketed by Carimali, and later renamed La Peppina.

From the straight handle and the metal drainage grill this appears to be a late version of the 1000-watt Mk 2 design, manufactured around 1979.[889] It was distributed in California by A.B.C. Inc. of 9653 San Fernando Road, Sun Valley.[890]

I'm not making this up, by the way; I was delighted to find that there are people who care about vintage coffee machines just as seriously as some of us do about guitars, and have

Percussion and Other Gear

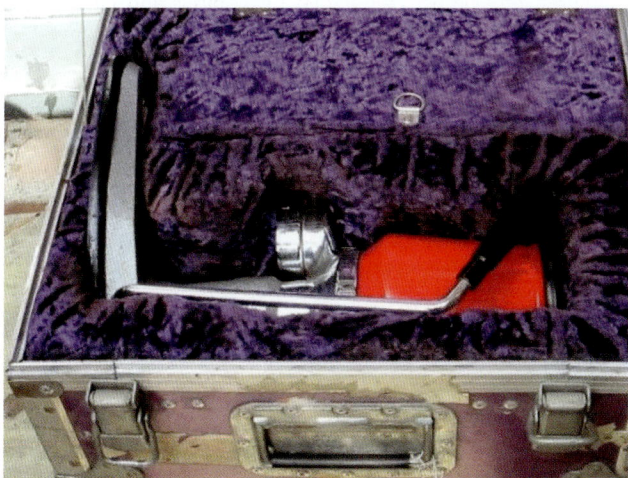

The flight case, Peppina coffee machine and replica coffee supplied by Diva Zappa (Mick Ekers)

websites dedicated to their history, literature, and maintenance. Hooray for geeks, coffee addicts, and the Internet!

Saunders also had to assist with FZ's smoking habit, and although they shared a preference for Winstons, he wasn't totally happy with this duty: "and he had this ashtray that he used the entire frickin' tour and on the last day, after the last show, I threw it out and broke it (laughs), I threw that and the coffee mug out."[891]

The coffee maker and flight case were offered as a special reward in the Kickstarter campaign to fund Alex Winter's Frank Zappa documentary film—working title *Who the F*@% is Frank Zappa?* [892]

Pen, Paper, and Thesaurus

"He brought out three scores, in manuscript and each measuring 13×20 inches, beautifully copied and handsomely bound."
— Nicholas Slonimsky[893]

Frank Zappa was (among other things) a virtuoso guitarist, bandleader, record producer, filmmaker, satirist, and political campaigner; but from the beginning to the end of his musical life he was above all else a composer. In his entry in the notes to the John Cage tribute album *A Chance Operation*, he describes himself simply as "American Composer." He put it another way in 1979, describing himself as "a person who gets up in the morning and spends his day sitting at the piano writing ballpoint pen notes on little pieces of paper."[894]

For most of his life pen (or pencil) and paper were the tools of his trade: "I would carry manuscript paper around with me in my briefcase and write music on the road, in a hotel or on an airplane. It was a very manual procedure, very time-consuming, and at the end you really didn't know what you were going to get till you heard it played."[895]

FZ's sound mixer in the early 1970s, Steve Desper, recollected: "Towards the end of my last tour with him, he was writing his symphonic work. Every available moment he would work on it. If we had a twenty-minute wait for a bus or something, he would break out his big folder, and spread out the score sheets. You would see him over in a corner, madly marking down notes and erasing others in refinement. This was a score for a symphony orchestra, so the score sheets were quite large."[896]

Most writers consult dictionaries and thesauruses at times, and FZ was a big fan of Nicholas Slonimsky's *Thesaurus of Scales and Melodic Patterns*, which he called "the bible of improvisation."[897] This astonishing book, which contains 240 pages crammed with almost every conceivable musical scale and melody, achieved popularity with many musicians; other notable users included Jaco Pastorius, John Coltrane, Henry Cowell, and John Adams."[898]

209

ZAPPA GEAR

FZ also built up his own dictionary of chords, or "Chord Bible," as he called it. Kurt Morgan, the ZFT's scoremeister (curator of written music) at the time, told me: "There are maybe fifty to sixty chords that are FZ's favorite chords, and he organized them by the interval from the top note down to the next note, so he'll start with minor seconds . . . and then work his way down to the largest interval, the major seventh."[899]

Although there are many fully orchestrated pieces written in FZ's hand, Morgan has found evidence that FZ used references to his Chord Bible as a form of musical shorthand: "I found pages that have just a melody with numbers above them, the numbers one through fifty something, being shuffled around on different pitches. It occurred to me that the chords of the Chord Bible were numbered and this was a shorthand, a way of writing really quickly."[900]

This fits with David Ocker's recollection of the time when he was orchestrating some of the pieces for the LSO sessions: "It was, as I remember, a kind of shorthand, it was my job to make it look good and make marks."[901]

When the Synclavier came along, Todd Yvega told Morgan: "These chords were entered into the Synclavier, to be able to be spit out at you at alarming rate, randomized, shuffled, stretched, whatever he wanted at the time."[902]

For FZ, one of the great features of the Synclavier was its Music Printing program, which allowed him to enter notes onto staves on the computer screen and print out parts: "After all those years of scoring with pen and pencil, it's a blessing to be able to write your own composition, push a button, and have all the parts printed out."[903]

Around about the time of the *Yellow Shark* project, the Finale computer program became available. Finale version 1.0 was written by Phil Farrand for the Coda Music Technology Company, and when it was launched in 1988 it was the first serious desktop publishing software package for music notation.[904]

FZ never used Finale himself, but had it set up so he could work remotely with arranger Ali Askin: "We're using [Coda]

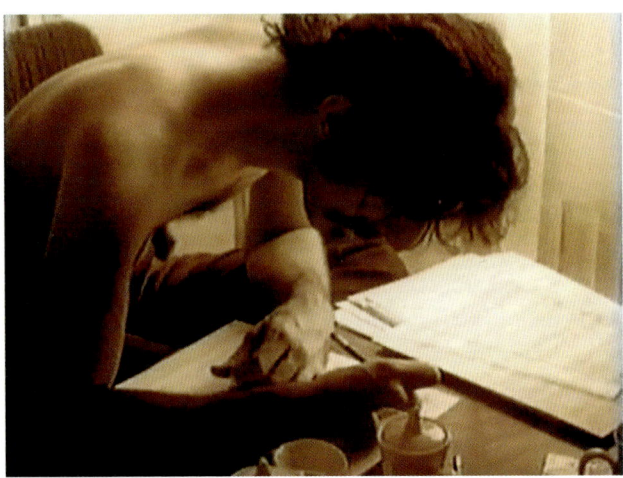

FZ composing in a hotel room
(*still from Frank Zappa: Peefeeyatko, 1991*)

The cover of Slonimsky's masterwork
(Mick Ekers)

Finale software. It runs on a Mac, is MIDI-interfaceable, and graphically it mops the floor with the Synclavier's music printing. It is probably the most complicated piece of musical software I've ever seen. I can take my sequences, transfer them via the MIDI port into Finale, and then send him floppies of the Synclavier stuff so he can manipulate the pictorial data in Germany."[905]

Finale remains one of the leading music-notation software packages, and is now sold by MakeMusic Inc. It is still a very complicated piece of software, but then composing and writing music is a very complicated activity. Slonimsky became good friends with FZ in his later years (see the Bösendorfer Piano section), and his thesaurus is still readily available.

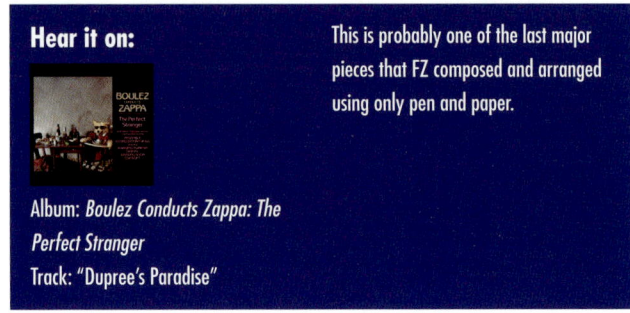

Hear it on:

Album: *Boulez Conducts Zappa: The Perfect Stranger*
Track: "Dupree's Paradise"

This is probably one of the last major pieces that FZ composed and arranged using only pen and paper.

The Conductor's Baton

"Frank gave it the full Toscanini and conducted their asses off."
— Tom Wilson [906]

FZ credited himself with "guitar and white stick with a cork handle" in his news release about the 1972 *Grand Wazoo* tour, reproduced in the booklet accompanying the *Zappa/Wazoo* CD. The significance of said white stick is underlined by its use as a graphic motif, in the album title and inside sleeve artwork.[907] The conductor's baton was a very important part of FZ's toolkit, and he used one right from the early days of his career.

Several of LA's top session musicians were called in for the *Freak Out!* sessions in 1966. Most of them were expecting a typical rock/pop recording session, where they would be expected to create the parts and generally carry the inexperienced band members; who would often end up not playing at all.

They were doubtless surprised when FZ turned up in a conductor's long tailcoat, and handed out the charts that they were to play. "Hey, we're really going to have to play," said one of the cello players. "This beatnik has written some music here!"

FZ stepped onto the podium that he had set up, pulled out a baton, and as Tom Wilson put it "conducted their asses off."[908]

FZ had a similar experience when he conducted the orchestral parts of *Lumpy Gravy* in 1967; where the initially skeptical, seasoned classical and jazz musicians were again won over by charisma, challenging and well-written scores, and the small white stick.

The 2016 auction had a lot titled "FZ's Conductor's Baton and Metronome."[909] The baton was a wooden-handled Hamel baton, made by the Hamel Baton Factory in Vesper, Wisconsin, who are still very much in business today.[910] The metronome was made by the German Wittner company. Gustav Wittner founded a precision mechanical factory specifically for the production of metronomes in 1895, and the company continues to make metronomes and other musical accessories.[911] The pair sold for $10,240.[912]

On many orchestral recordings he left the conducting to professional conductors Elgar Howarth (*200 Motels*), Kent Nagano (*London Symphony Orchestra*), Michael Zearott (*Orchestral Favorites*), and Pierre Boulez (*The Perfect Stranger*). The end results did not always meet with his complete satisfaction—one wonders if the untrained FZ could have produced better results. However, for the big band of the *Grand Wazoo*

FZ with his white stick with a cork handle in 1978
(Lynn Goldsmith — Corbis)

FZ with fly swatters on the 1988 tour, a nod to the Man From Utopia album cover
(Deepinder Cheema)

ZAPPA GEAR

(and the subsequent Wazoo and Petit Wazoo ensembles), FZ was wielding the baton in earnest, to great effect.

From the earliest days of the Mothers of Invention, FZ had used a series of ever-more-complex hand signals that he used to cue his band, indicating tempo and rhythm changes, special effects, and so on. As his touring bands got larger in the 1980s, FZ did not play guitar all the time, and would conduct some numbers from start to finish. This developed over the years, and he would more frequently augment his hand signals with the conductor's baton, or sometimes a drumstick, or a cigarette, or even a pair of fly swatters. Deepinder Cheemah (who also crops up in the Wah pedals section) threw two on stage in Milan in June 1988, and FZ used them as batons on the remaining dates of the tour! [913]

When things were going well and the musicians were responsive, few things in life made FZ happier than conducting a large band. He said this of conducting, "The orchestra is the ultimate instrument, and conducting one is an unbelievable sensation. Nothing else is like it, except maybe singing doo-wop harmony and hearing the chords come out right."[914] FZ's last public performances were as a conductor: guest conducting during the first and third *Yellow Shark* concerts at the Frankfurt Alte Oper on the 17th and 19th September, 1992. Despite the debilitating pain he was in from his illness, the smile on his face in the photo in the *Yellow Shark* booklet says it all.

FZ was as unique a conductor as he was a guitarist. I'll give composer/arranger Ali Askin (who arranged much of the *Yellow Shark*) the last word on this: "In the video (of the *Yellow Shark* broadcast) you can see what Frank's face was like. You see how he was laughing and conducting and making little gestures to the musicians. I have never seen somebody conduct like that. He says of himself, he's not a real conductor—which he isn't. But nobody is able to lead a group of musicians like he does. It's unbelievable. His little finger talks more than any big conducting movements of Karajan, I think. Just look at him when he's smoking. That tells a story."[915]

The baton and metronome from the auction. Note that this baton has a wooden handle and not a cork handle as FZ used in 1972
(ZFT)

Hear it on:
DVD: *The Torture Never Stops*
Track: "Strictly Genteel"

To listen to some of FZ's earlier conducting, check out the original orchestral edit of "Lumpy Gravy" in the *Lumpy Money* collection.

ACKNOWLEDGMENTS

This book would not have been possible without the help and support of so many lovely people. In particular I want to thank:

Gail Zappa, for trusting me, for allowing me into her house, and for her tireless efforts in keeping FZ's musical legacy alive, without which this project would never have started.

Dweezil Zappa, for your support, invaluable information, generosity with your time, and your attention to detail and dedication to bringing live FZ music to new generations of fans.

Ahmet Zappa, for your energy, enthusiasm, creative vision, and insights, and of course for making this finally happen.

Melanie Starks, for being there since the first meeting with Gail in London in 2010 and for all your help, not forgetting the rest of the team at the ZFT.

John Cerullo, Clare Cerullo, and the good people of Backbeat Books for turning the book into a reality.

My three sons Richard, Chris, and Steve, who have all played a major part in the inception and production of this book, and who are of course three of the finest young gentlemen on the planet.

Thomas Nordegg, for help and support over and beyond the call of duty during our visit to LA. I still owe you that dinner, Thomas!

Special thanks go to my good friends and fellow Zappa writers Andrew Greenaway and Scott Parker, for their unstinting help and encouragement over the years that this project has been running.

And finally, to everyone listed below (and to anyone I have inadvertently left out—forgive me), who have granted me interviews; provided advice, information, and photographs; and generally helped this project in so many ways. I am eternally grateful to all of you.

Ali N. Askin
André Cholmondely
Antal Adriaanse
Anthony Macari
Arthur Barrow
Arthur Tripp
Avo Raup
Bart Nagel
Bill Gubbins
Bob Bradshaw
Bob Easton
Bob Harris
Bob Lilly
Bobby Zappa
Carol Kaye
Cary Barnhard
Daniel Escauriza
Dave Weiderman
David Bagsby
David Ocker
Deepinder Cheema
Diva Zappa
Doug "Little Blues" Jones
Ed Seeman
Eddie Jobson
Eddie Persson
Elwood Francis
Eric Peterson
Erick Bianchi
Gaz de Vere
George Duke
Greg Heet
Greg Russo
Halden and Torsten
Holland Greco
Staff at Hollywood Orchid Suites
Howard Chatt
Ike Willis
Ivan Schwarz
Jacques Charbit
Jake K. at pedalarea.com
Jan Atze De Vries
Jasun Martz
Javier Marcote
Jas Tamburro
Jim Gardner
Jim Williams
Joe Travers
John Carruthers
John Townley
Jon Larsen
Jörn Eisenhauer
Josh Gannett
Josh Hall
Kelvin Phoon
Kim Ekers
Kit Rae
Kuoni "Kenny" Sugoni
Kurt Morgan
Staff at Leigh-on-Sea Public Library
Luisa Haddad at UCSC Special Collections and Archives

Acknowledgments

Marc Sabatier
Marco Alpert
Mark Linett
Mark Riseborough
Mark Schnoor
Merl Saunders Jr.
Mica Wickersham Thomas
Michael Krampe
Mick Zeuner (for the apostrophe!)
Mike Beigel
Mirco Wessels
Muffin Men
Napoleon Murphy Brock
Odile Noel
Patrick Gaumond
Pauline Butcher
Peder Andersson
Pete Cornish
Peter den Hoed
Peter Jay
Ralph Humphrey
Ray White
Richard Hemmings
Richard Landers
Robert Martin
Román García Albertos
Ruth Underwood
Sandro Oliva
Steve Buckbeck
Stuart Penny
Todd Yvega
Tom Oberheim
Tommy Mars
Tony Miln
Zappateers
  . . . and all my long-suffering friends, family, and colleagues.

NOTES

Introduction

1. TEC Les Paul Award acceptance speech, NAMM show 2012

Chapter One

2. *The Real Frank Zappa Book*
3. *Guitarist* magazine (UK), June 1993
4. Bobby Zappa, email to author, June 2011
5. *Guitarist* magazine (UK), June 1993
6. *Guitar Player* magazine, January 1977
7. Doug Jones, littlebrotherblues.com
8. *Guitar Player* website, guitarplayer.com
9. *Down Beat* magazine, February 1983
10. *Talking Guitars*, David Mead
11. *The Fender Book*, Tony Bacon and Paul Day
12. *The Electric Guitar*, Paul Trynka (Ed.)
13. *Ten Years On The Road with Frank Zappa and the Mothers Of Invention*, press kit booklet, 1974
14. *The Real Frank Zappa Book*
15. Fender Jazzmaster advertisement, 1958
16. *Fender: The Golden Age 1946–1970*, Martin Kelly, Terry Foster, Paul Kelly
17. *The Real Frank Zappa Book*
18. *Down Beat* magazine, February 1983
19. Paul Buff, conversation with Patrick Neve, 1998 unitedmutations.com
20. *Down Beat* magazine, February 1983
21. *Gibson Guitars: 100 Years of an American Icon*, Walter Carter
22. Gibson catalogue, 1955
23. Gibson website, gibson.com
24. *Gibson Electrics: The Classic Years*, A.R. Duchossoir
25. *Guitar Player* magazine, January 1977
26. Del Casher, *Vintage Guitar* magazine, January 1997
27. *Record Review* magazine, June 1982
28. *Down Beat* magazine, February 1983
29. Jim Williams, interview with author, February 2012
30. Ibid.
31. John Carruthers, interview with author, January 2012
32. Ibid.
33. *Musicians Only* magazine, January 1980
34. DZ, interview with author, January 2012
35. Ibid.
36. Ibid.
37. Hagström Guitars radio commercial, WOR New York, 1967
38. Albin Hagström website, albinhagstrom.se
39. Hagström Guitars radio commercial, WOR New York, 1967
40. Hagström catalogue, 1966
41. Ibid.
42. Unofficial Hagström website, hagstrom.org.uk
43. Scotty Moore website, scottymoore.net
44. *Record Review* magazine, June 1982
45. *Electric Guitars: the Illustrated Encyclopaedia*, Tony Bacon
46. Vintage Guitars Info website
47. *Zappa in France*, Christain Rose and Phillipe Thieyre
48. Bigsby Guitars and Vibratos website, bigsbyguitars.com
49. Cooper Owen website
50. Ted Owen website
51. Conversation with author, January 2012
52. Note to author, October 2014
53. Email to author, December 2011
54. Email to author, March 2011
55. *International Musician* magazine, June 1985
56. *Electric Guitars: The Illustrated Encyclopaedia*, Tony Bacon
57. vintage-guitars.blogspot.com/2006/04/gibson-sg-special.html
58. Vintage Guitar and Bass website, vintageguitarandbass.com/Gibson/SG_Special.php
59. *Gibson Guitars: Ted McCarty's Golden Era*, Hembree
60. Gibson ES thinlines website, es-335.net
61. Gibson thinline catalogue, 1970
62. Gibson specification sheet, 1978
63. *The Ultimate Guitar Book*, Tony Bacon
64. *Electric Guitars: The Illustrated Encyclopaedia*, Tony Bacon
65. *Vintage Guitars Info* website
66. *Vintage Guitar and Bass* website, vintageguitarandbass.com
67. *You Can't Do That on Stage Anymore, Vol.3*, liner notes
68. Mark Volman, email to author, October 2011
69. *You Can't Do That on Stage Anymore, Vol.3*, liner notes
70. Mark Volman, email to author, October 2011
71. Vintage Guitars Info website
72. *Guitares Jacobacci*, Lory, Sabitier, and Touché
73. *Rock* magazine, November 1972
74. *Ten Years on the Road with Frank Zappa* etc., press kit 1974
75. *Wazoo* CD booklet
76. *Guitares Jacobacci,* Lory, Sabitier and Touché
77. *Guitar Player* magazine, May–June 1979
78. *Fender: The Golden Age 1946–1970*, Martin Kelly, Terry Foster, Paul Kelly

Notes

79. *Amps!: The Other Half of Rock 'n' Roll*, Fliegler
80. *The Fender Book,* Bacon and Day
81. *Record Review* magazine, June 1982
82. Ibid.
83. Vintage Guitars Info website
84. *International Musician* magazine, March 1977
85. Napoleon Murphy Brock, email to author, February 2011
86. DZ, interview with author, January 2012
87. *Guitar Player* magazine, January 1977
88. J. De Cola (Gibson Guitars), *Premier Guitar* video 2013
89. *International Musician* magazine, March 1977
90. DZ, interview with author, January 2012
91. *International Musician* magazine, March 1977
92. *Guitar Player* magazine, January 1977
93. *The History of Rickenbacker Guitars*, Smith
94. Bartell Guitar and Basses website
95. The Acoustic Black Widow fan *pages* website
96. *Guitar Player* magazine, January 1977
97. *M.I.* Magazine, November 1979
98. DZ, interview with author, January 2012
99. Ibid.
100. Harvey and Alex Gerst article, tapeop.com website
101. *The Guitar World According to Frank Zappa* sleeve notes
102. Bartell Guitars website
103. Unfretted website
104. *Guitar Player* magazine, January 1977
105. Univibes website
106. *Jimi Hendrix Gear,* Heatley
107. *Guitarist* magazine, June 1993
108. Univibes website
109. Jim Williams, interview with author, February 2012
110. Ibid.
111. Ibid.
112. Ibid.
113. Eddie Jobson, conversation with author, August 2011
114. *Record Review* magazine, June 1978
115. *Guitar Player* magazine, February 1983
116. DZ, interview with author, January 2012
117. Merl Saunders Jr- interview with author, November 2011
118. DZ, interview with author, January 2012
119. Gail Zappa, zappa.com/messageboards
120. DZ, interview with author, January 2012
121. "The Jimi Hendrix/Frank Zappa Strat," *Dweezil Zappa World* website
122. DZ, interview with author, January 2012
123. Interview with author, February 2011
124. *Guitar Player (UK)* magazine, May 1979
125. Ibid.
126. *Guitar Player* magazine, May 1974
127. *International Musician* magazine, March 1977
128. Michael Gnapp, theguitarcolumn.com/2010/03/xylonix-guitars-by-michael-gnapp.html
129. Jim Williams, interview with author, February 2012
130. Ibid.
131. *International Musician* magazine, March 1977
132. Jim Williams, interview with author, February 2012
133. Kunio Sugai, interview with author, January 2012
134. Gail Zappa, interview with author, February 2012
135. *Guitar World* magazine, March 1982
136. *M.I.* magazine, November 1979
137. Ike Willis, conversation with author, August 2011
138. Anthony Macari, email to author, November 2010
139. *Electric Guitars: The Illustrated Encyclopaedia*, Bacon
140. Dave Lambert, strawbsweb.co.uk
141. "Celebrating 50 Years of Vox," guitarplayer.com
142. *Beat Instrumental* magazine, December 1971
143. *Guitar Player* magazine, February 1985
144. *Guitar World* magazine, March 1982
145. Bart Nagel, interview with author, February 2010
146. Ibid.
147. *Guitar World* magazine, March 1982
148. Bart Nagel website
149. Bart Nagel, interview with author, February 2010
150. *Guitar Player* magazine, January 1977
151. *Record Review* magazine, June 1982
152. DZ, interview with author, January 2012
153. FZ, TV interview with PA State Trooper Chuck Ash, November 1981
154. *Guitar Player* magazine, February 1983
155. Guitar Dater Project website
156. Gibson website, gibson.com
157. *Electric Guitars: The Illustrated Encyclopaedia*, Bacon
158. *The Ultimate Guitar Book*, Bacon
159. Ibid.
160. *Guitar Player* magazine, March 1982
161. Interview with author, January 2012
162. *Down Beat* magazine, February 1983
163. *Guitar Player* magazine, March 1982
164. DZ, interview with author, January 2012
165. *Beetle* magazine, July 1973
166. Ibid.
167. *Britannica Concise Encyclopaedia*, 2006
168. *Guitar Player* magazine, January 1977
169. *Linda McCartney: Life in Photographs*, Linda McCartney
170. *Guitar Player* magazine, February 1983
171. *Guitar Player* magazine, July 1982
172. *Guitar Player* magazine, February 1983
173. Carol Kaye, email interview with author, November 2010
174. *You Can't Do That on Stage Anymore, Vol. 3,* sleeve notes
175. Julien's Auctions website
176. *Guitar Player* magazine, May–June 1979
177. *Billboard* magazine, 13th May 1967
178. *Neptune Bound*, Tulloch
179. Danelectro Guitars website
180. Ibid.
181. *Jupiter Bound*, Tulloch

182. *Guitar Player* magazine, July 1982
183. *M.I.* magazine, November 1979
184. Elwood Francis, email to author, January 2012
185. Jerry Jones Guitars website
186. *International Musician* magazine, March 1977
187. *Guitar Player* magazine, January 1987
188. Gail Zappa, conversation with author, December 2013
189. *The Complete History of Rickenbacker Guitars*, Smith
190. DZ, interview with author, January 2012
191. Julien's Auctions catalogue, November 2016
192. Julien's Auctions website
193. *M.I.* magazine, November 1979
194. *The Fender Book*, Bacon and Day
195. Fender website
196. DZ, interview with author, January 2012
197. Ibid.
198. *Frank Talk: The Inside Stories of Zappa's Other People*, Greenaway
199. Julien's Auctions website
200. *Record Review* magazine, June 1982
201. *Guitar World* magazine, March 1982
202. Interview with Alan di Perna in 1988, reprinted in *Guitar World*, December 2003
203. *Guitar World* magazine, October 1995
204. Merl Saunders Jr., interview with author, November 2011
205. *Guitar World* magazine, December 2003
206. Ibid.
207. Kunio Sagai, interview with author, January 2012
208. Merl Saunders Jr., interview with author, November 2011
209. Julien's Auctions website
210. FZ in rehearsal, 1982
211. Merl Saunders Jr., interview with author, November 2011
212. *Guitar Player* magazine, May–June 1979
213. Merl Saunders Jr., interview with author, November 2011
214. DZ, interview with author, January 2012
215. *International Musician* magazine, June 1985
216. DZ, interview with author, January 2012
217. Jim Williams, interview with author, February 2012
218. *Guitar Player* magazine, February 1983
219. Ibid.
220. DZ, interview with author, January 2012
221. Ibid.
222. Julien's Auctions website
223. DZ, interview with author, January 2012
224. Kunio Sagai, interview with author, January 2012
225. *Society Pages* (US) magazine, September 1990
226. Gail Zappa, *FZ-OZ* CD liner notes
227. "The Ovation Guitar," Bob's Guitar Practice Tips website
228. Ovation Guitars website
229. *The History of the Ovation Guitar*, Walter Carter
230. DZ, interview with author, January 2012
231. *Guitar World* magazine, February 1999
232. *T'Mershi Duween* magazine, July-September 1991
233. *Society Pages* (US) magazine, September 1990
234. Julien's Auctions catalogue, November 2016
235. Julien's Auctions website
236. *Guitar Player* magazine, October 1968
237. *The Ultimate Guitar Book*, Bacon
238. Gibson guitars and amplifiers catalogue, 1966
239. Vintage Guitars info website
240. *Frank Zappa*, Dutch TV documentary (VPRO-TV February 1971)
241. DZ, conversation with author, December 2011
242. *International Musician* magazine, March 1977
243. Guild website, support section
244. Julien's Auctions catalogue, November 2016
245. *The Guild Guitar Book*, Moust
246. Guild Flat-top and Classic Guitars catalogue, 1976
247. *The Guild Guitar Book*, Moust
248. Ibid.
249. Guild Guitars website
250. Julien's Auctions website
251. *Guitar Player* magazine (UK), May 1977
252. Ibid.
253. C.F. Martin & Co website
254. *The World of Guitars*, Seguret
255. Richard Bamman, "The Martin Dreadnought Story," *Frets* magazine, May 1988
256. *The Guitar World According to Frank Zappa* sleeve notes
257. Mark Volman, email to author, October 2011
258. *Guitar Player* magazine, January 1977
259. Gibson full-range catalogue, 1964
260. *Premier Guitar* magazine, January 2012
261. Gibson full-range catalogue, 1964
262. Vintage guitars info website
263. *Guitar Player* magazine, January 1977
264. DZ, interview with author, February 2012
265. Tomas Delgado, email to author, June 2012
266. Candelas Guitars website
267. Julien's Auctions catalogue, November 2016
268. Bill Gubbins, *The Hot Rats Book*, Backbeat Books, 2019
269. Julien's Auctions website
270. DZ, interview with author, January 2012
271. Höfner website
272. Höfner catalogue 1971
273. Vintage Höfner website
274. Ibid.
275. Julien's Auctions website
276. Höfner website
277. "The Jazz Bass Guitar: A History and Appreciation," Fender website
278. Fender website
279. *Fender: The Golden Years 1946–1970*, Kelly, Foster and Kelly
280. *American Basses*, Jim Roberts
281. Arthur Sloatman, Facebook post, August 2012

Notes

282. Scott Thunes, conversation with author, November 2012
283. Julien's Auctions website
284. *Guitar Player* magazine, January 1977
285. *Down Beat* magazine, February 1983
286. DZ, interview with author, January 2012
287. Ibid.
288. Phased Systems advertisement, 1981
289. DZ, Interview with author, January 2012
290. *International Musician* magazine, August 1985
291. Merl Saunders Jr., interview with author, November 2011
292. Lecture & Q&A at Syracuse University, April 1975
293. Ernie Ball website
294. *Guitar Player* magazine, January 1977
295. *Guitar (UK)* magazine, June 1979
296. *Guitar World* magazine, March 1982
297. Ibid.
298. *International Musician* magazine, June 1985
299. Ernie Ball website
300. *Zappa The Hard Way*, Andrew Greenaway
301. Email to author, December 2011
302. Merl Saunders Jr., interview with author, November 2011
303. FZ, rehearsal recording at the UMRK, April 1982
304. *Down Beat* magazine, February 1983
305. Floyd Rose, "NAMM oral history" video on *Guitar* magazine website
306. *Vintage Guitar* magazine, December 2008
307. *Musician* magazine, September 1988
308. *Guitar Player* magazine, February 1983
309. Merl Saunders Jr., interview with author, November 2011

Chapter Two

310. FZ, *Guitar Player* magazine, July 1983
311. *Joe's Garage* song lyric
312. Ampwares website
313. *Fender: The Golden Age 1946–1970*, Martin Kelly, Terry Foster, Paul Kelly
314. *Frank Zappa, a Visual Documentary*, Barry Miles
315. FZ, radio interview KPFT-FM, October 1980
316. Standel Musical Instrument Amplifiers website
317. KSAN-FM San Francisco CA interview by Tom Donaghue, November 1968
318. Bill Gubbins, *The Hot Rats Book*, Backbeat Books, 2019
319. *Guitar Player* magazine, January 1977
320. *Fender: The Golden Age 1946–1970*, Martin Kelly, Terry Foster, Paul Kelly
321. Ibid.
322. *International Musician* magazine, June 1985
323. *Fender: The Golden Age 1946–1970*, Martin Kelly, Terry Foster, Paul Kelly
324. Julien's Auctions catalogue, November 2016
325. Fenderguru website
326. Julien's Auctions website
327. Acoustic Corporation advertisement, 1968
328. FZ interview with David Whalley, August 1970
329. *The Music Trades* magazine, April 1973
330. FZ, *Ahead of Their Time* liner notes
331. *Beefheart Through the Eyes of Magic*, John French
332. Acoustic Control Corporation unofficial homepage website
333. Julien's Auctions catalogue, November 2016
334. Julien's Auctions website
335. Acoustic Control Corporation unofficial homepage website
336. *Guitar Player* magazine, January 1977
337. Acoustic Control Corporation Price List, 1973
338. Acoustic Control Corporation catalogue, 1972
339. *Guitar Player* magazine, January 1977
340. Frank Marino, Mahogany Rush website
341. Vintage Guitar Geek website
342. Interview with Howard Smith, *The Smith Tapes*, 1970
343. *Guitarist* magazine, June 1973
344. *Down Beat* magazine, February 1983
345. Arthur Barrow, interview with author, September 2011
346. *Guitar Player* magazine, October 1995
347. DZ, interview with author, January 2012
348. Ibid.
349. *Frank Zappa et les Mothers of Invention*, Dister
350. Interview with Alan di Perna in 1988
351. Merl Saunders Jr., interview with author, November 2011
352. DZ, interview with author, January 2012
353. Julien's Auctions catalogue, November 2016
354. Julien's Auctions website
355. Ibid.
356. Ibid.
357. Ibid.
358. DZ, interview with author, January 2012
359. FZ, *Guitar Player* magazine, July 1983
360. Deserving much more than a basic reference is Rich Maloof's excellent book *Jim Marshall, the Father of Loud*, which proved invaluable in putting this section together.
361. *Modern Recording* magazine, March 1978
362. Pignose website
363. *Modern Recording* magazine, March 1978
364. *Mix* online magazine, January 2003
365. *Guitar Player* magazine, January 1977
366. *Guitarist* magazine, June 1993
367. Napoleon Murphy Brock, interview with author, November 2010
368. Eddie Jobson, conversation with author, August 2011
369. John Firth, *Matamp at 60*, Martin Celmins
370. Orange Amplifiers website, orangeamps.com
371. Orange Amp Field Guide website (now defunct), users.telenet.be/orangefg

372. FZ interview, Ina.fr TV station, December 1971
373. DZ, interview with author, January 2012
374. Oberheim advertisement, 1975
375. *Guitar Player* magazine, January 1981
376. Tom Oberheim, email to author, June 2012
377. Rory Gallagher website
378. *Record Review* magazine, June 1982
379. Mesa/Boogie website
380. Ibid.
381. *Bluebox for Bimbos*, 1978 notebook for FZ's tech crew, David Gray
382. *The Boogie Files* website, now defunct
383. Ibid.
384. DZ, interview with author, February 2012
385. *International Musician* magazine, June 1985
386. Acoustic Control Corporation catalogue, 1980
387. Acoustic Control Corporation price list, February 1980
388. Acoustic Control Corporation price list, April 1980
389. *Guitar Player* magazine, July 1983
390. Merl Saunders Jr., interview with author, November 2011
391. Four fifteen-ohm speakers linked together in parallel produce a combined impedance of approximately four ohms.
392. Merl Saunders Jr., interview with author, November 2011
393. *Guitar Player* magazine, 1988
394. Merl Saunders Jr., interview with author, November 2011
395. Carvin website (now closed)
396. Carvin Museum website
397. Moshe Albarez, conversation with author, January 2012
398. *SoundCheck* magazine, Germany 1988
399. *Guitar Player* magazine, October 1995
400. ICA letter of authenticity signed by Dweezil Zappa
401. Carvin website
402. *The Beat* magazine, August–September 1988
403. DZ, interview with author, January 2012
404. Seymour Duncan Convertible advert, 1986
405. Seymour Duncan Convertible user manual
406. Merl Saunders Jr., interview with author, November 2011
407. DZ, interview with author January 2012
408. "Joe Bonamassa Talks About the Seymour Duncan Convertible Amp," Youtube.com
409. DZ, interview with author, January 2012
410. Ibid.
411. Vox Showroom website, voxshowroom.com/us/amp/beat.html
412. *Bluebox for Bimbos*, 1978 notebook for FZ's tech crew, David Gray
413. Julien's Auctions catalogue, November 2016
414. Julien's Auctions website
415. Vox Showroom website
416. Thomas Organs website
417. Cision PR website
418. *Guitar Player* magazine, January 1977
419. Vox AC100 website
420. Ibid.
421. *Guitar Player* magazine, January 1977
422. Julien's Auctions website

Chapter Three

423. *Guitar* (UK) magazine, May 1979
424. FZ, *Down Beat* magazine, February 1983
425. *Cry Baby: The Pedal That Rocks the World* video, Jim Dunlop
426. *The Technology of Wah Pedals* website, R.G. Keen
427. *Vintage Guitar Magazine*, June 2002
428. *No More Mr Nice Guy*, Michael Bruce
429. *Guitar Player* magazine, May–June 1979
430. Napoleon Murphy Brock, email to author, February 2011
431. Boomerang instruction manual
432. "Maestro Boomerang Wah Pedal: Technical Data," DIY Guitarist website
433. AnalogMan website
434. *Guitar Player* magazine, May–June 1979
435. Deepinder Cheema, email to author, December 2010
436. Ibid.
437. Dallas Arbiter Sound City catalogue, 1968
438. Ivor Arbiter biography, Allmusic website
439. Sound City website
440. *Guitar* (UK) magazine, May 1979
441. *International Musician* magazine, March 1973
442. Ibid.
443. *Blue Box for Bimbos* notebook, David Gray
444. *Guitar* (UK) magazine, May 1979
445. DZ, interview with author, January 2012
446. Merl Saunders Jr., interview with author, November 2011
447. DZ, interview with author, January 2012
448. Kit Rae, email to author, 2012
449. *Premier Guitar* magazine, November 2010
450. The Big Muff Pi home page, kitrae.net/music/music_big_muff.html
451. *Guitar* (UK) magazine, May 1979
452. "Stones, Clones, and Muffs: The Electro-Harmonix Story," Electro-Harmonix Extravaganza website
453. Electro Harmonix website
454. *Guitar Effects Pedals: The Practical Handbook*, Dave Hunter
455. Pedal Area website
456. *Music Trades* magazine, October 2003
457. EHX website
458. Dan Armstrong, DanArmstrong.Org website
459. Ibid.
460. Dan Armstrong Effects website, danarmstrongeffects.com
461. DZ, interview with author, January 2012
462. *Guitar Player* magazine, October 1975

Notes

463. Ibanez, *FL-303 Instruction Manual*
464. Ibanez catalogue archive, ibanez.co.jp/anniversary/
465. Maxon website
466. *International Musician* magazine, March 1977
467. Gail Zappa, conversation with author, March 2013
468. *Summer of Love: The Making of Sgt. Pepper*, George Martin
469. Pro-Audio Company Names, AES website
470. *Guitar Effects Pedals: The Practical Handbook*, Dave Hunter
471. Ibid.
472. Music Emporium catalogue, 1980
473. In memoriam Keith Barr, *Mix* online website
474. Terry Sherwood obituary, Rector-hicks funeral home website
475. *Analogman's Guide to Vintage Effects,* Tom Hughes
476. Pedal Area website
477. *Guitar Effects Pedals: The Practical Handbook*, Dave Hunter
478. Pedal Area website
479. Analog Man website
480. *Guitar Player* magazine, February, 1983
481. Radio interview 1975/10/11, KPFT-FM Houston
482. *Guitar Player* magazine, July 1983
483. Merl Saunders Jr., *Guitar Player* magazine, October 1995
484. *Guitar* (UK) magazine, May 1979
485. Julien's Auctions catalogue, November 2016
486. Julien's Auctions website
487. Vintage DBX website
488. DBX website
489. DZ, interview with author, January 2012
490. Mica Wickersham, email to author, May 2012
491. Alembic website
492. *Grateful Dead Gear*, Blair Jackson
493. "Alembic F-2B Preamp," Gilmourish website
494. DZ, interview with author, January 2012
495. Mica Wickersham, email to author, May 2012
496. *Guitar Player* magazine, January 1977
497. Bob Easton, email to author, September 2011
498. *Guitar Player* magazine, January 1977
499. Bob Easton, email to author, October 2011
500. Ibid.
501. *Waka/Jawaka*, album sleeve notes
502. Bob Easton, Email to author, October 2011
503. Ibid.
504. *Hot Flash* magazine, May 1974
505. Tel-Ray Morley web page
506. *Hot Flash* magazine, May 1974
507. *International Musician* magazine, February 1979
508. Tel-Ray Oil can addicts forum
509. Morley Pedals website
510. Greg Heet, email interview with author, January 2012
511. EBow website
512. *Synapse* magazine, May–June 1977
513. *Guitar Player* magazine, May 1988
514. Greg Heet, email interview with author, January 2012
515. Ibid.
516. EBow website
517. "Imagine Twenty Harps on a Stage," Arpaviva Recordings website
518. *Guitar Player* magazine, July 1983
519. Ibid.
520. West Michigan Music Hysterical Society website
521. Effects freak website
522. Ibid.
523. Godlyke website
524. *Hot Flash* magazine, May 1974
525. *Vintage Guitar* magazine, September 1997
526. *The Stompbox: A History of Guitar Fuzzes, Flangers, Phasers, Echoes & Wahs*, Art Thompson
527. Effects Database website
528. *The Stompbox: A History of Guitar Fuzzes, Flangers, Phasers, Echoes & Wahs,* Art Thompson
529. *Guitar Player* magazine, July 1983
530. Mike Beigel, email to author, February 2012
531. *Record Review* magazine, June 1982
532. *Vintage Guitar* magazine, September 1997
533. Ibid.
534. *The Stompbox: A History of Guitar Fuzzes, Flangers, Phasers, Echoes & Wahs*, Art Thompson
535. Mike Beigel, email to author, February 2012
536. Julien's Auctions catalogue, November 2016
537. Julien's Auctions website
538. *Guitar Player* magazine, July 1983
539. *Vintage Guitar* magazine, September 1997
540. *Guitar Player* magazine, July 1983
541. *Vintage Guitar* magazine, September 1997
542. *Guitar Player* magazine, January 1977
543. *Guitar Player* magazine, July 1983
544. Tom Oberheim website
545. *Down Beat* magazine, July 1991
546. Roland GP-8 instruction manual
547. Dweezil Zappa world website
548. Merl Saunders Jr., interview with author, November 2011
549. Ibid.
550. *Guitar World*, December 2003
551. DZ, interview with author, January 2012
552. *Guitar Player* magazine, July 1983
553. Ibid.
554. DZ, interview with author, January 2012
555. Pigtronix website
556. Merl Saunders Jr., interview with author, November 2011
557. ProCo sound website
558. *Guitar Effects Pedals: The Practical Handbook*, Dave Hunter
559. Rat Distortion website
560. ACT Lighting website

Chapter Four

561. *Keyboard Magazine*, June 1980
562. Julien's Auctions catalogue, November 2016
563. George Duke, interview with author, January 2012
564. Combo Organ Heaven website
565. Farfisa Compact Organs price list, 1968
566. Farfisa advertisement
567. *Keyboard* magazine, June 1980
568. "The Rhodes Electric Piano: Against All Odds," Frederik Adlers, FenderRhodes website
569. FenderRhodes website
570. *Vintage Synthesizers*, Mark Vail
571. Ibid.
572. Rhodes Keyboard Instruments service manual 1979
573. Ibid.
574. FenderRhodes.com
575. George Duke, interview with author, January 2012
576. *Waka/Jawaka* album sleeve notes
577. *Keyboard* Magazine, June 1980
578. Julien's Auctions website
579. Rhodes Music Corporation website
580. *Ahead of Their Time* album sleeve notes
581. Synth Museum website
582. *Vintage Synthesizers*, Mark Vail
583. Arthur barrow, interview with author, February 2011
584. Ibid.
585. Wurlitzer Electric Pianos service manual
586. *Keyboard* magazine, June 1980
587. Bob Harris, email to author, October 2011
588. *Keyboard* magazine, June 1980
589. Hohner website
590. Barry Carson in *Vintage Synthesizers*, Mark Vail
591. *The Synthesizer and Electronic Keyboards Handbook*, David, Crombie
592. Hohner Clavinet/Pianet Duo user manual
593. *Synapse* magazine, January–February 1979
594. *Keyboard* magazine, June 1980
595. Hammond Zone website
596. *Fifty Years of Musical Excellence*, Hammond Co. pamphlet, 1984
597. Hammond-Leslie FAQ website
598. Ibid.
599. Tommy Mars, interview with author, September 2011
600. Ibid.
601. *Keyboard* magazine, June 1980
602. *Down Beat* magazine, May 1978
603. Vintage Synth explorer website
604. *Vintage Synthesizers*, Mark Vail
605. George Duke website, georgeduke.com
606. *Down Beat* magazine, May 1978
607. *Analog Days*, Pinch and Trocco
608. Bernie Krause, interviewed by James Gardner, 30 March 2010
609. Moog Archives website
610. *Analog Days*, Pinch and Trocco
611. "A Brief History of the Minimoog," Moogmusic website moogmusic.com/legacy
612. *Vintage Synthesizers*, Mark Vail
613. "A Brief History of the Minimoog," Moogmusic website moogmusic.com/legacy
614. *Synapse*, January–February 1979
615. Polar Music Prize website
616. Moog Music website
617. Tommy Mars, interview with author, September 2011
618. Ibid.
619. *Taurus Pedal Synthesizer Owner's Manual*, 1978
620. Tommy Mars, interview with author, September 2011
621. Gail Zappa, comments on original manuscript, November 2014
622. Moog Music website
623. Tommy Mars, interview with author, September 2011
624. Ibid.
625. Ibid.
626. Preservation Sound website
627. Vintage Synth website
628. Tommy Mars, interview with author, September 2011
629. Ibid.
630. EML Poly-Box user manual
631. Tommy Mars, interview with author, September 2011
632. *Down Beat* magazine, May 1978
633. *Vintage Synthesizers*, Mark Vail
634. Tommy Mars, interview with author, September 2011
635. Vintage Synth Explorer website
636. Interview with author, September 2011
637. *Vintage Synthesizers*, Mark Vail
638. David Bagsby, email to author, June 2012
639. Julien's Auction website
640. As told by Tommy Mars, interview with author, September 2011
641. Tommy Mars, interview with author, September 2011
642. Wendy Carlos, wendycarlos.com/vocoders.html
643. "Vocoders Part 4: Korg VC-10," by Phil Jones, *Melody Maker* magazine
644. Tommy Mars, interview with author, September 2011
645. Tommy Mars, interview with author, September 2011
646. Ibid.
647. *Keyboard* magazine, June 1980
648. *Polyphony* magazine, November–December 1981
649. Ibid.
650. E-mu Systems technical catalogue, 1978
651. E-mu Systems website
652. *Down Beat* magazine, May 1978
653. Eddie Jobson, conversation with author, August 2011
654. Tommy Mars, interview with author, September 2011
655. Marco Alpert, email to author, October 2011
656. Tommy Mars, interview with author, September 2011

Notes

657. Ibid.
658. Marco Alpert, email to author, October 2011
659. Tommy Mars, interview with author, September 2011
660. Marco Alpert, email to author, October 2011
661. Tommy Mars, interview with author, September 2011
662. Hollow Sun website
663. *Sound on Sound* magazine, July 1995
664. Tommy Mars, interview with author, September 2011
665. Ibid.
666. Bob Harris, email to author, October 2011
667. Alan di Perna, *Keyboards, Computers & Software* magazine, April 1986
668. Arturia website
669. Julien's Auctions catalogue, November 2016
670. Julien's Auctions website
671. *Down Beat* magazine, May 1978
672. Ibid.
673. Tommy Mars, interview with author, September 2011
674. Bob Henrit, "Vintage View: Syndrum," Mike Dolbear website
675. *Keyboards, Computers & Software* magazine, April 1986
676. *Electronic Musician* magazine, September 1986
677. *Perfecting Sound Forever*, Greg Milner
678. Steve Hills, The unique Synclavier website
679. Ibid.
680. *Keyboard* magazine, February 1987
681. Ibid.
682. *Sound Engineer and Producer* magazine, April 1987
683. *Keyboard* magazine, February 1987
684. *Keyboard* magazine, February 1987
685. Merl Saunders Jr., interview with author, November 2011
686. Ibid.
687. Todd Yvega, interview with author, January 2012
688. Ibid.
689. *EQ* magazine, March 1994
690. *Keyboard* magazine, February 1987
691. Brandon Amison, Yaking Cat Studios website
692. Synclavier Manual II, "Music Production and Sound Design"
693. Todd Yvega, interview with author, January 2012
694. Ibid.
695. *Electronic Musician* magazine, September 1986
696. *Keyboards, Computers & Software* magazine, April, 1986
697. *Electronic Musician* magazine, September 1986
698. *Keyboard* magazine, February 1987
699. Mike Keneally website, 1988 tour diaries
700. Todd Yvega, interview with author, January 2012
701. Ibid.
702. Ibid.
703. Roland website
704. Gordon Reid, *Sound on Sound* magazine, February 1998
705. Todd Yvega, interview with author, January 2012
706. "The History of Roland," *Sound on Sound* magazine, February 2004
707. *Keyboards, Computers & Software* magazine, April 1986
708. "The History of Roland," *Sound on Sound* magazine, February 2004
709. *Record Review* magazine, June 1982
710. Ibid.
711. Arthur Barrow, ARF website
712. Roger Linn, Industry Interview 2003, Sonic State website
713. Roger Linn Design website
714. Ibid.
715. Ibid.
716. *Keyboard* magazine, June 1980
717. Ibid.
718. Pauline Butcher, email to author, October 2011
719. Bösendorfer website
720. Ibid.
721. *Perfect Pitch*, Nicolas Slonimsky, 1988
722. *New Yorker* magazine, January 1996
723. *Civilization Phaze III*, CD booklet
724. *Pulse!* magazine, August 1993
725. Scott Thunes, interview with Andrew Greenaway, April 2012
726. *International Musician* magazine, March 1977
727. FZ lecture & Q&A at Syracuse University, April 1975
728. Jim Williams, interview with author, February 2012
729. Bob Easton, email to author, October 2011
730. *International Musician* magazine, March, 1977
731. Hagstrom.org UK unofficial website, http://www.hagstrom.org.uk/hagstrom_fans.htm
732. *International Musician* magazine, March, 1977
733. Ampeg advertising brochure, 1976
734. *Guitar Player* magazine, November 1983
735. *Guitar Player* magazine, June 1986
736. Ibid.
737. FZ, lecture & Q&A at Syracuse University, April 1975

Chapter Five

738. *Music Technology* magazine, February 1987
739. *Mix* magazine, January 2003
740. *International Musician* magazine, June 1985
741. Gail Zappa, conversation with author, January 2012
742. *Ship Arriving Too Late to Save a Drowning Witch* LP, lyric sheet
743. Lansing Heritage website, audioheritage.org
744. TEC foundation website, tecfoundation.com
745. JBL Studio Monitor System reference chart
746. *Guitar Player* magazine, February 1983
747. *Mix on-line*, January 2003
748. *Ship Arriving Too Late to Save a Drowning Witch* LP, lyric sheet
749. *Guitar Player* magazine, February 1983

750. *Modern Recording* magazine, March 1978
751. CHUM-FM Canada radio interview, 23rd November 1973
752. Kepex Model 500 brochure
753. Kepex II Operating Instructions
754. *Guitar* (UK) magazine, June 1979
755. dweezilzappaworld.com
756. David Blackmer, interview at AES convention, September 1999
757. "TECnology-Hall-of Fame: 1976 DBX 160VU Complimiter," Mix website
758. *Digital Audio* magazine, October–November 1984
759. KPCC Southern California Public Radio, April 2011
760. Chris Moore, interview with author, February 2012
761. Seven Woods Audio website
762. Space Station user manual
763. Ursa Major article, *Sound on Sound* website, May 2005
764. Seven Woods Audio website
765. *Academy Zappa*, Ben Watson and Esther Leslie (ed.)
766. Chris Moore, interview with author, February 2012
767. Seven Woods Audio website
768. Radio interview, KPFA-FM Berkeley Morning Concert, 2nd May 1983
769. *The Real Frank Zappa Book*, FZ with Peter Occhiogrosso
770. *Sound Engineer and Producer* magazine, April 1987
771. *Digital Audio* magazine, October/November 1984
772. TECnology Hall-of-Fame, Mix website
773. *Digital Audio* magazine, October–November 1984
774. Benden Sound technology website
775. *Digital Audio* magazine, October–November 1984
776. *London Symphony Orchestra, Vol. 1*, sleeve notes.
777. Radio Interview, KPFA-FM Berkeley Morning Concert, 2nd May 1983
778. Julien's Auctions website
779. *International Musician* magazine, March 1977
780. Sonic Scoop website
781. *Tony Visconti: The Autobiography*, Tony Visconti
782. *International Musician* magazine, March 1977
783. *Modern Recording* magazine, March 1978
784. Sonic Scoop website
785. *The Little-Known History of the Mothers of Invention*, ZFT digital download
786. *The Real Frank Zappa Book*, FZ with Peter Occhiogrosso
787. *Cosmik Debris*, Greg Russo
788. *The Little-Known History of the Mothers of Invention*, ZFT digital download
789. *EQ* magazine, March 1984
790. DZ, *Sound on Sound* magazine, September 2004
791. *Music Technology* magazine, February 1987
792. John Townley's Astrocktail website, astrocktail.com/Apostolic.html
793. *Mix* magazine, June 1983
794. "The Poodle Bites!", Mike Keneally website, keneally.com
795. Gail Zappa, conversation with author, March 2012
796. John Kilgore, The International Electroacoustic Community, August 1996
797. *Music Technology* magazine, February 1987
798. John Townley website
799. *International Times*, August 1969
800. Ibid.
801. Arthur Barrow, interview with author, September 2011
802. Bob Rice, sonalksis.com website
803. *Talking Guitars*, David Mead
804. *Digital Audio* magazine, October–November 1984
805. "The Complete Mark Pinske Interview," mixonline website
806. Ibid.
807. *Sound Engineer and Producer* magazine, April 1987
808. "Studio Recorders Go Digital," Sony website
809. FZ Interview, KPFA-FM Berkeley Morning Concert, 1983/05/20
810. "The Complete Mark Pinske Interview," mixonline website
811. *Sound Engineer and Producer* magazine, April 1987
812. Julien's Auctions catalogue, November 2016
813. "The Complete Mark Pinske Interview," mixonline website
814. FZ Interview, KPFA-FM Berkeley Morning Concert, 20th May, 1983
815. "The Sony AIBO Story," Sony Aibo website
816. Julien's Auctions catalogue, November 2016
817. Julien's Auctions website
818. *Civilization Phaze III* liner notes, 1994
819. *Modern Recording* magazine, March 1978
820. *The Guitar World According to Frank Zappa* sleeve notes
821. AKG website
822. Neumann website
823. Steven Paul, "1989 Vintage Microphones," *Mix* magazine
824. Coutant website
825. Neumann website
826. Elvo mikrofonbau website
827. Mix Guides, Vintage products, Sony c37a
828. "Telefunken USA Completes Restoration of Zappa Microphone Collection," Telefunken website
829. *The Dub-Room Special* movie
830. Ibid.
831. "The Complete Mark Pinske Interview," mixonline.com
832. Crown Audio website
833. "Exploring the Boundaries," Ken Hamberg, BHPPhotoVideo website
834. *The Real Frank Zappa Book*, FZ with Peter Occhiogrosso
835. PZM Memo (Crown Audio publication), October 1983
836. Ibid.

Notes

837. *London Symphony Orchestra, Vol. 1 & 2,* liner notes
838. *Digital Audio* magazine, October–November 1984
839. *Talking Guitars*, David Mead
840. "The Wonderful World of Binaural Recording," Head-fi website
841. *Radio drama: Theory and Practice*, Tim Crooke
842. *All the World's a Stage . . .* , AKG promotional leaflet, 1997
843. *Talking Guitars*, David Mead
844. *You Can't Do That on Stage Anymore, Vol. 3*, liner notes
845. Neumann KU-80 brochure
846. Ali Askin, message to author, June 2012
847. David Dondorf, *Yellow Shark* CD booklet
848. Ali Askin, message to author, June 2012

Chapter Six

849. Ruth Underwood, interview with author, January 2012
850. *GQ Scene* magazine, Fall 1967
851. Ruth Underwood, interview with author, January 2012
852. *The Drummers of Frank Zappa*, Drum Channel DVD, 2007
853. Ibid.
854. Vintage Drum Guide website, vintagedrumguide.com
855. *The Real Frank Zappa Book*, FZ with Peter Occhiogrosso
856. *The Drummers of Frank Zappa* DVD, 2009
857. Ibid.
858. Ruth Underwood, interview with author, January 2012
859. Deagan Resource website
860. *The Slingerland Book*, Rob Cook
861. *The Vibraphone*, Clifford Bevan and Barry Kernfeld, Grove Music Online
862. *Frank Zappa*, Barry Miles
863. Ruth Underwood, interview with author, January 2012
864. Ibid.
865. Julien's Auctions website
866. "*Guitar Player* Presents: Zappa!", 1992
867. *Cosmik Debris*, Greg Russo
868. Radio interview, WFMT-FM Chicago, 1968
869. Captain Kazoo website
870. Eden kazoo factory website
871. *Video from Hell*, Honker Home Video
872. *Video from Hell*, Honker Home Video
873. *Official Vintage Guitar Magazine Price Guide*
874. *The Drummers of Frank Zappa*, Drum Channel DVD, 2007
875. Ibid.
876. Ralph Humphrey, interview with author, February 2012
877. Vintage Ludwig Drums website, vintageludwigdrums.com
878. Ludwig Catalogue, 1973
879. *The Drummers of Frank Zappa*, Drum Channel DVD, 2007
880. Ibid.
881. Ibid.
882. Julien's Auctions website
883. *Ahead of Their Time,* sleeve notes
884. *Billboard* magazine, 8th July, 1967
885. *Uncle Meat,* sleeve notes
886. *The Real Frank Zappa Book*, FZ with Peter Occhiogrosso
887. *Suosikki* magazine, August 1976
888. Merl Saunders Jr., interview with author, November 2011
889. Lever Espresso Machines website
890. Orphan Espresso website, orphanespresso.com
891. Merl Saunders Jr., interview with author, November 2011
892. *Who the F*@% is Frank Zappa?,* Kickstarter campaign
893. *Perfect Pitch*, Nicolas Slonimsky
894. *Musician* magazine, August 1979
895. *Sound on Sound* magazine, February 1987
896. Steve Desper, Smiley Smile message board
897. Wiki Jawaka website
898. *Counterpoint and Polyphony in Recent Instrumental Works of John Adams,* Alexander Sanchez-Behar
899. Kurt Morgan, interview with author, March 2012
900. Ibid.
901. David Ocker, interview with author, February 2012
902. Kurt Morgan, interview with author, March 2012
903. *International Musician* magazine, June 1985
904. Phil Farrand website
905. FZ, *Guitar Player Presents: Zappa!*, 1992
906. *Frank Zappa*, Barry Miles
907. *Zappa/Wazoo*, CD booklet/cover
908. *Frank Zappa*, Barry Miles
909. Julien's Auctions catalogue, November 2016
910. Hamel Batons website
911. Wittner website
912. Julien's Auctions website
913. *Zappa the Hard Way*, Andrew Greenaway
914. *The Real Frank Zappa Book*, FZ with Peter Occhiogrosso
915. *The Yellow Shark*, CD booklet

GLOSSARY

4×12: A speaker cabinet containing four 12" speakers (also 2×12, 8x10, etc.).

6L6: A medium-sized thermionic valve, or vacuum tube, introduced by RCA in 1936. Commonly used in the power amplifier stages of guitar amplifiers.

12AX7: A miniature dual triode thermionic valve, or vacuum tube, with high voltage gain introduced by RCA in 1946. Commonly used in preamplifier and tone-control stages in guitar amplifiers. Also known as the ECC83.

Accidental Keys: The black keys on a conventional piano keyboard, which play notes identified by a sharp (♯) or flat (♭) sign, sometimes referred to as "sharps." See *Natural keys*.

Action: The height of the guitar strings above the fingerboard. Low action tends to make playing easier, but can degrade the tone of the instrument due to the strings buzzing against the fingerboard.

Active Electronics: As fitted to electric guitars, these are tone and volume control circuits, powered by one or more 9-volt batteries. They can actively boost as well as cut selected frequencies and the overall signal level. They are less commonly found as standard equipment on electric guitars, and are more popular on bass guitars.

AES: Audio Engineering Society, founded in 1948. The only worldwide professional society devoted exclusively to audio technology. It holds two conventions a year, one in the US and one in Europe.

Alnico: Magnetic alloy of iron combined with aluminum, nickel, and cobalt that is commonly used to make the magnets in guitar pickups and loudspeakers.

Archtop: A type of hollowbody guitar where the top of the body is carved or bent into an arched shape.

Binding: A protective and decorative strip of wood or plastic fitted to the edges of a guitar body, and sometimes the neck, soundholes, and headstock.

Bookmatched: Technique where two adjoining wooden surfaces, usually veneered, are cut from the same piece of wood in such a way that they can be opened like two pages from a book, with the grain forming mirror images.

Bout: The wider sections of a guitar body on either side of the narrower waist. The upper bout is the one nearest the neck, and the other is the lower.

Bridge: The bridge supports the guitar strings, transmitting the vibrations of the strings to the guitar body. It often features adjustable saddles—small metal parts on which the strings rest, allowing the vibrating length of the string and the guitar action to be adjusted.

Bridge Pickup: The pickup nearest the bridge of a guitar, which produces a bright sharp sound.

Bucket Brigade: An analogue device for delaying an audio signal. The stored signal is passed along a series of capacitors, like a line of people pouring water from one bucket to the next.

Cardioid Microphone: A unidirectional microphone, more sensitive to sound from the front than the rear, with a cardioid-shaped sensitivity pattern.

Coil Tap: A switch connected to a humbucking pickup that can remove one of the coils from a circuit, so as to produce a sharper single-coil tone.

Combo Organ: A portable, electronic organ of a type built during the 1960s and 1970s, and used primarily by rock bands (or "combos") of that era. Usually transistorized, they had a thin, electronic sound, detachable or fold-up legs, and brightly colored tops and switches.

Compression Driver: A high-efficiency type of loudspeaker driver commonly used in conjunction with an acoustical horn. Mostly used for high-frequency signal reproduction in high-power speaker systems.

Compressor: A hardware device used to compress the dynamic range of an audio signal, making quiet sounds louder and loud sounds quieter. Used for enhancing sound quality. Often combined with a limiter.

Condenser Microphone: One in which the sensor element forms part of a capacitor or condenser. Relatively delicate and often

Glossary

requiring a power supply, they are sensitive and accurate and more suited for studio work.

Cutaway: On a guitar, a curved indentation "cut away" from the body at the neck joint to facilitate the player's access to the higher frets. Some guitars have a cutaway on both sides of the neck, known as a "double cutaway."

Digital Delay (also Digital Delay Line or DDL): An audio device that uses digital random-access memory to produce a time-delayed signal. The input signal is converted to digital form, stored in the memory circuitry, and removed at some designated later time. It is then converted back to analogue form and fed to the output.

Dynamic Microphone: One in which the sensor element generates a signal electromagnetically. Robust and resistant to feedback, they are mostly used in live performance situations and for recording guitar amps.

Echoplex: The Maestro Echoplex, a tape-delay echo unit designed in 1959 by Mike Battle. The vacuum tube-based units produced in the late 1960s and early 1970s are generally recognized as some of the finest-sounding echo devices ever made.

EL34: A thermionic valve or vacuum tube for audio amplification introduced in 1953 by Mullard and its parent company Philips. A pair of these typically produces around 50 watts. Used in guitar amplifiers where distortion at relatively low output levels is desirable.

F-Hole: A soundhole in a hollowbody guitar like those found on violins, shaped approximately like an "f".

Fairlight: The Fairlight CMI (Computer Musical Instrument) digital sampling synthesizer designed in 1979, which competed in the market with the New England Digital Synclavier.

Fingerboard: The playing surface of the guitar that holds the frets. Usually a separate piece of hard wood, such as rosewood, attached to the neck. Also known as a fretboard.

Flat-Top: Literally a guitar body that has a flat rather than curved top; usually refers to a traditional steel-strung acoustic guitar.

Floyd: Popular term for the Floyd Rose vibrato system. See the section in the body of the book.

Florentine Cutaway: A cutaway with a sharp pointed bout. The term was probably coined by Gibson, who also referred to cutaways with a rounded bout as "Venetian."

Frets: The (usually) metal strips on the fingerboard of a guitar, against which the string is pressed (or fretted) to produce a note.

Fretboard: See *Fingerboard*

FX Loop (Effects Loop): The pair of connectors in an amplifier (or mixer) that can be used to route the signal through an external signal path or loop containing effects units (such as an echo unit) and then back into the amplifier.

Gauge (of a Guitar String): The gauge of a guitar string is its thickness, stated either as a decimal fraction of an inch, such as .009, or in thousandths of an inch, as in "24 gauge."

Harmonica Bridge: An adjustable bridge made by Schaller that was fitted to many Gibson and other guitars in the 1970s. So called because the rectangular shape of the casing and the slots in which the saddles moved was reminiscent of a harmonica.

Headstock: The part of the guitar at the end of the neck to which one end of the string is anchored. Usually it is fitted with tuners (or "machine heads"), which are used to adjust the pitch of the guitar strings.

Humbucking Pickup: An electric guitar pickup made with two opposed coils of wire surrounding two sets of opposite polarity magnetic pole pieces. This arrangement cancels out most external magnetic interference but at the expense of the higher frequencies. Humbuckers tend to have a fatter or thicker sound than single-coil pickups for this reason, and usually a higher output.

Intonation: The degree to which a guitar is in tune when played at different positions along the neck. Accurate intonation requires the length of each string to be slightly different, to compensate for their different thicknesses. A fully adjustable bridge is usually required to achieve this.

Joe's Garage: FZ's rehearsal studio in Los Angeles, now a storage facility. Also a great album!

KT88: A thermionic valve or vacuum tube for audio amplification introduced by GEC in 1956. A pair of these typically produces around 100 watts of output. Used in guitar amplifiers where a high output with low distortion is desirable.

Ladder Filter: A patented low-pass filter design by Bob Moog, so called because it used a ladder-like array of transistors. It was a key factor behind the unique sonic character of Moog synthesizers.

Limiter: A hardware device used to limit the dynamic range of an audio signal, keeping loud sounds below a threshold. Used to avoid distortion and also to enhance sound qualities. Often combined with a compressor.

Masonite: A type of hardboard made of steam-cooked and pressure-molded wood fibers in a process invented by William H. Mason. Notably used in construction of Danelectro guitars.

Middle Pickup: On guitars with three pickups, the pickup between the bridge and neck pickups, with a sound somewhere between the two.

MIDI: An industry-standard protocol that enables electronic musical instruments and equipment to communicate and synchronize with each other. First published in 1983, the original MIDI (Musical Instrument Digital Interface) spec is still the de facto standard for electronic music hardware.

NAMM: The National Association of Music Merchants, hosts of the world's largest musical equipment trade show: the NAMM show, held annually in Anaheim, California.

Nagra: Make of professional high quality portable reel-to reel tape recorders, often used on the road by FZ for recording his guitar solos.

Natural Keys: The white keys on a conventional piano keyboard, which play the notes of the C Major scale. See *Accidental Keys*.

Neck Pickup: The pickup nearest the neck of a guitar. This position tends to produce a warm, mellow tone.

Nut: A small slotted piece of (usually) plastic or bone that supports the strings of a guitar at the headstock end of the neck. The slots hold the strings in position, and usually set the height of each string above the fingerboard.

Omnidirectional (or Omni) Microphone: A microphone equally sensitive to sound from all directions.

P90: A Gibson single-coil guitar pickup first produced in 1946.

PAF Humbuckers: The original Gibson humbucker pickup, with a "Patent Applied For" sticker on the base, first produced in 1956.

Parametric EQ: An equalizer or tone control circuit in which all of the parameters of equalization can be adjusted: a) center frequency; b) the amount of boost or cut in gain; and c) the bandwidth, or Q. Semi-parametric EQ circuits only vary the center frequency and boost/cut.

Partridge Transformers: A range of high-quality, high-power audio transformers, manufactured by Transformers & Rectifiers Ltd, Surrey, UK, who acquired the Partridge business in 1968. Used in many UK-made guitar amplifiers.

Passive Electronics: As used in electric guitars, these are unpowered tone and volume control circuits. They can reduce the high or low frequencies, or overall volume, but cannot boost or amplify the signal. For many years the only type available, they are still standard on the vast majority of electric guitars.

Patch: A stored sound setting for a synthesizer or signal processing unit. Early synthesizers used cables ("patch cords") to connect different sound modules together. Musicians wrote down the locations of the patch cables and knob positions on a "patch sheet." Ever since, an overall sound setting for any type of synthesizer has been known as a patch.

Piezo Pickup: A type of pickup pioneered by the Barcus Berry company in the 1970s, which produces an electric signal from the physical vibration of the surface on which it is fixed. Also known as a transducer or contact pickup.

Pickguard: A protective panel (usually plastic) fitted to a guitar to protect the body from damage by the player's pick. Also known as a scratchplate.

Plain String: A guitar string that is just a "plain" piece of wire. See *Wound String*.

Plate Reverb: A reverb system that uses a transducer, similar to the driver in a loudspeaker, to produce vibrations in a large plate of sheet metal. A pickup captures the vibrations as they bounce across the plate, and the result is output as an audio signal.

Polepieces: In electric guitars, the small metal cylinders that concentrate the magnetic field of the pickup around the strings. Usually one per string, often as adjustable-height screws for varying the response of individual strings.

Polyphonic: Able to produce more than one note simultaneously. Usually refers to a synthesizer or keyboard; the first synthesizers were monophonic.

Q: A parameter describing the "quality" characteristic of a parametric EQ. The amount of Q refers to the steepness of the response curve (or bandwidth), so a high Q value will result in the equalizer affecting a narrow range of frequencies, and a low Q a wide range.

Rototoms: Low-profile, shell-less drums consisting of just a head mounted in a cast metal frame. They have a definite pitch which can be quickly adjusted in performance by rotating the head. Invented by the Remo company, they were usually added

Glossary

to regular drum kits in sets of three and were popular in the 1970s and 1980s.

Set Neck: Method of construction where the guitar neck is permanently set into the body and fixed with glue. This was the standard method used on most Gibson guitars.

Single-Coil Pickup: An electric guitar pickup made with a single coil of wire surrounding the magnetic pole pieces. They tend to have a brighter or clearer sound than double-coil humbucker pickups, but are prone to external magnetic interference, which can result in an audible buzzing or hum from the amplifier.

SMPTE: Commonly refers to the time code standard defined by the Society of Motion Picture and Television Engineers, used to synchronize audio and video material.

Soapbar Pickup: A (usually single-coil) pickup with a flat rectangular plastic cover approximating to the shape of a bar of soap.

Soundhole: An aperture in the body of a hollowbody guitar, designed to project the sound of an acoustic instrument. Usually refers to the round hole in traditional Spanish-style or flat-top guitars.

Sunburst: A style of finish on a guitar where a lighter color at the center of the body blends in to darker color(s) at the edges.

Tailpiece: A separate unit from the bridge used to anchor the ends of the guitar strings.

Theremin: An early electronic instrument invented by the Russian Léon Theremin in 1919. It is played without being touched by moving the hands near two metal antennas, which affect the pitch and volume of the output signal, respectively. It produces an eerie haunting sound, and was used in many early science fiction movies.

Through-Body Stringing: The arrangement where the guitar strings are anchored at the back of the guitar and pass through holes in the body before passing over the bridge. This tends to produce a very solid connection between the bridge and the body, and results in more sustain. The original Fender Telecaster used this design.

Tolex: The trade name of a flexible vinyl material introduced in 1945 by the General Tire company, used for covering guitar amplifier and speaker cases. The term is often used to describe any similar plastic-based covering.

Trapeze Tailpiece: A simple floating tailpiece design with an open trapezoidal shape, where one end is fitted to the end of the guitar.

Truss Rod: A metal rod built into a guitar neck, which can usually be adjusted to vary the curve of the neck and change the guitar's action.

Tune-o-matic Bridge: Gibson's name for their adjustable bridge design introduced in 1954. Each saddle could be moved forwards and backwards to correct intonation; the bridge is fitted to the body by adjustable height posts.

U: A rack unit, or RU, describes the height of a piece of rack-mounted equipment. One rack unit is 1.75 inches high; equipment is usually referred to as 2U, 4U, etc.

Utility Muffin Research Kitchen (UMRK): FZ's home studio that he built at his home in the Hollywood hills.

Vibrato Unit: Device fitted to a guitar, often combined with the bridge, which allows the player to change the pitch of the strings by moving an attached bar. Popularly known among guitarists as a "whammy bar." Often incorrectly called a "tremolo" unit—tremolo is the musical effect where the volume of a note is varied, not the pitch.

Vynide: A PVC-coated fabric originally designed and manufactured by ICI (Hyde) Ltd. in 1958. Used for covering guitar amplifier and speaker cases.

Winchester: Generic term for computer hard drives in common use in the 1970s–1980s. Named after the IBM 3340 Winchester system introduced in 1973, which featured the world's first self-contained, sealed disk drives.

Wound String: A guitar string made from a solid wire core with a continuous length of wire wound around it.

XLR Connector: An industry standard type of electrical connector used in professional audio, with circular locking connectors with three to seven pins.

Zero Fret: A fret placed on a guitar neck immediately next to the nut, at the "zero" position, claimed to produce more consistency of tone between the open and fretted strings.

ZFT: The Zappa Family Trust organization, set up by Gail Zappa to manage the legacy of Frank Zappa.

SELECTIVE BIBLIOGRAPHY

Tony Bacon, *The Ultimate Guitar Book* (Dorling Kindersley, 1991)

Tony Bacon, *Electric Guitars: The Illustrated Encyclopaedia* (Merchant Book Company, 2000)

Tony Bacon and Paul Day, *The Fender Book* (Backbeat UK, 1992)

Michael Bruce and Billy James, *No More Mr. Nice Guy* (SAF, 2000)

Pauline Butcher, *Freak Out! My Life with Frank Zappa* (Plexus Publishing, 2011)

Walter Carter, *Gibson Guitars: 100 Years of an American Icon* (Gibson Publishing, 2003)

Walter Carter, *The History of the Ovation Guitar* (Music Sales, 1966)

Martin Celmins, *Matamp at 60* (Ashridge Press, 2006)

David Crombie, *The Synthesizer and Electronic Keyboard Handbook* (Pan, 1985)

Tim Crooke, *Radio Drama: Theory and Practice* (Routledge, 1999)

Alain Dister, *Frank Zappa et les Mothers of Invention* (Albin Michel, 1975)

Michael Doyle, *The History of Marshall: The Illustrated Story of the Sound of Rock* (Hal Leonard, 1993)

A.R. Duchossoir, *Gibson Electrics: The Classic Years* (Hal Leonard, 2003)

Ritchie Fliegler, *Amps! The Other Half of Rock 'n' Roll* (Hal Leonard, 1993)

John French, *Beefheart Through the Eyes of Magic* (Proper Music Publishing, 2011)

Andrew Greenaway, *Zappa the Hard Way* (Wymer Publishing, 2010)

Bill Gubbins, *The Hot Rats Book*, Backbeat Books, 2019

Michael Heatley, *Jimi Hendrix Gear* (Voyageur Press, 2009)

Gil Hembree, *Gibson Guitars: Ted McCarty's Golden Era* (Hal Leonard, 2007)

Dave Hunter, *Guitar Effects Pedals: The Practical Handbook* (Backbeat Books, 2004)

Blair Jackson, *Grateful Dead Gear* (Backbeat Books, 2006)

Martin Kelly, Terry Foster, and Paul Kelly, *Fender: The Golden Age 1946–1970* (Cassell Illustrated, 2010)

Marie-Claire Lory, Marc Sabatier, and Marc Touché, *Guitares Jacobacci* (Somogy Editions, 2006)

Rich Malouf, *Jim Marshall: The Father of Loud* (Backbeat Books, 2004)

George Martin, *Summer of Love: The Making of Sgt. Pepper* (Pan Books, 1995)

David Mead, *Talking Guitars* (Sanctuary Publishing Ltd., 2004)

Barry Miles, *Frank Zappa* (Atlantic Books, 2005)

Barry Miles, *Frank Zappa: A Visual Documentary* (Omnibus Press, 1993)

Greg Milner, *Perfecting Sound Forever* (Granta, 2009)

Hans Moust, *The Guild Guitar Book* (Hal Leonard, 1995)

Trevor Pinch and Frank Trocco, *Analog Days: The Invention and Impact of the Moog Synthesizer* (Harvard University, 2002)

Jim Roberts, *American Basses* (Backbeat, 2003)

Christian Rose and Phillipe Thieyre, *Zappa in France* (Editions Parallèles, 2003)

Greg Russo, *Cosmik Debris: The Collected History and Improvisations of Frank Zappa (3rd edition, revised)* (Crossfire Publications, 2006)

Christian Seguret, *The World of Guitars* (Book Sales, 1999)

Nicholas Slonimsky, *Perfect Pitch* (Oxford University Press, 1988)

Richard R. Smith, *The History of Rickenbacker Guitars* (Centerstream, 1987)

Art Thompson, *The Stompbox: A History of Guitar Fuzzes, Flangers, Phasers, Echoes, and Wahs* (Miller Freeman Books, 1997)

Paul Trynka (Ed.), *The Electric Guitar* (Virgin Books, 2002)

Doug Tulloch, *Neptune Bound: The Ultimate Danelectro Guide* (Centrestream, 2008)

Mark Vail, *Vintage Synthesizers* (Backbeat Books, 2000)

Tony Visconti, *Tony Visconti: The Autobiography* (Harper, 2007)

Ben Watson, *Frank Zappa: The Negative Dialectics of Poodle Play* (St. Martin's Press, 1994)

Ben Watson and Esther Leslie (ed.) *Academy Zappa: Proceedings of the First International Conference of Esemplastic Zappology* (SAF Publishing, 2005)

Frank Zappa with Peter Occhiogrosso, *The Real Frank Zappa Book* (Picador, 1990)

SELECTIVE VIDEOGRAPHY

A Touch Of Genius—The Life And Times Of Nicolas Slonimsky/The First 100 Years. (1994). FilmAmerica, Inc.
AAAFNRAA. (1992). PPV, Germany
At Home With Frank Zappa—CBS This Morning. (1989). CBS
Baby Snakes. (1979). ZFT.
Does Humor Belong in Music. (1985). ZFT
En directo desde Barcelona, Frank Zappa. (1988). Television Espanola
Frank Zappa And The Original Mothers Of Invention. (1968). Ed Seeman.
Frank Zappa, Chorus. (1980). Antenne 2, France
Frank Zappa. (1971). VPRO, Netherlands.
Frank Zappa: Peefeeyatko. (1991). Henning Lohner.
Ivo Niehe—Profile. (1991). TROS, Netherlands
Late Night Line Up. (1969). BBC.
Norman Gunston Show. (1975). ABC, Australia.
Oppåpoppa. 1973. Swedish TV
Rehearsal at Hordern Pavilion, Sydney, Australia. (1973). GTK EPISODE 689.
Roxy—The Movie. (2015). ZFT.
The Dub Room Special! (1982). ZFT.
The Mike Douglas Show. (1976). NBC TV.
The Steve Allen Show. (1963). ABC: Channel 5.
Video From Hell. (1987). ZFT, Honker Home Video
We Don't Mess Around. (1980). Bayerischer Rundfunkt (BR).

ABOUT THE AUTHOR

Born in England in 1952, Mick Ekers is a lifelong Frank Zappa enthusiast, first seeing the original Mothers of Invention at the Royal Festival Hall in London in 1968. The archetypal teenage Zappa fan, he bought *all* the albums, playing truant from school one morning to take a twenty-mile train journey to a record shop that had an early imported copy of *Lumpy Gravy*, worried someone else might buy it before he got there! He learned to play bass guitar, making his first instrument from a hacked-about junk-shop electric guitar and an amplifier from the innards of an old tube record player. Fascinated by the new technology starting to appear, he made his own wah-wah pedal from a mail-order kit. All of this gear sounded dreadful, by the way!

In the 1970s he played in local bands, and toured Europe as roadie for the Moodies, a performance art/cabaret group. In the late 1970s, he found himself selling and hiring PA systems and synthesizers, and exhibiting at the NAMM show in the US, where several of the devices mentioned in this book first appeared.

Mick eventually moved out of the financial uncertainties of the music industry, but never lost his fascination with music technology. He took up a career in computing, married, and raised three sons (all musicians, as it turned out), who ended up playing a major part in this book's inception and production. Now retired, Mick is currently studying for a degree in Modern History and Politics at Essex University. Above music, writing, and photography, Mick likes nothing better than just hanging out with his family and grandchildren.

He lives in Leigh-on-Sea, a small fishing village thirty miles east of London on the Thames Estuary, with too many bass guitars, a fine vintage hi-fi system, more than enough CDs and vinyl records, and not quite enough old 35mm film cameras. *Zappa's Gear* is Mick's first book.